The Theory and Practice of Identifying Students
for Gifted and Talented Education Services

# Identification

Edited by
Scott L. Hunsaker, Ph.D.

Routledge
Taylor & Francis Group

NEW YORK AND LONDON

First published in 2012 by Prufrock Press Inc.

Published 2021 by Routledge
605 Third Avenue, New York, NY 10017
2 Park Square, Milton Park, Abingdon, Oxon OX14 4RN

*Routledge is an imprint of the Taylor & Francis Group, an informa business*

ISBN 13: 978-1-0321-4478-8 (hbk)
ISBN 13: 978-1-9312-8017-4 (pbk)

# Table of Contents

# PREFACE

I have experienced the paroxysms of gifted identification from multiple angles: public school teacher, district coordinator, parent, university professor, researcher, and professional consultant. I've experienced both confidence and discomfort within each role as I've realized the import of decisions made about the lives of individual children.

As a teacher, I've completed rating forms on individual students and struggled with the difference between ratings of "almost always" and "most of the time" on descriptors such as "sees relationships among concepts." I have felt the pressure to inflate my students' ratings to make them, supposedly, more competitive in a system that uses rigid identification criteria so that their failure to get into the gifted program wouldn't be my fault; yet, in the end, I've always chosen integrity over plausible deniability.

As a district coordinator, I've developed identification procedures for full-time programs and wondered what to do about teachers who give all their students high ratings on teacher rating scales. I've wrestled with the rationale for gifted programs in the face of limited spaces within a program (e.g., "Should gifted students who struggle with school be given precedence over gifted students who achieve well?") and modified protocols back and forth as teachers have complained that "we're not getting the students in the program that we should." I've listened to parents' stern rebukes, "You mean to tell me my son, with all his scores above the 90th percentile and all straight As, doesn't qualify for your program?"

As a parent, I've been acutely aware of the day the achievement test was being given to my first grader who had been nominated for the gifted program (a day his allergies gave him a headache, and he accidentally left his glasses at home). My wife and I have received the letter that regrets to inform us that our child didn't qualify. I've wondered why the letter told me only what the district was not going to do rather than what, given all the assessment that was done, they would be doing for my son.

As a university professor, researcher, and professional consultant, I've taught best practices in graduate courses, all the while discovering how often these practices are ignored in schools. I've been distressed, as I've walked into gifted classrooms in various parts of the country, at the absence of students who reflect the diversity of populations who live within a community. I've attempted to assist school leaders who understand that a theory-practice gap exists and who want to do the best by their students, but who also are constrained by the philosophical, political, and budgetary realities that exist in their states or districts. And I've tried to explain to others that no fail-safe system or ideal test exists.

Given these experiences, I've always been perplexed that no single text in the field of gifted education has ever been produced that introduces and explores in depth the research on and practice of identification of gifted and talented students. This is quite surprising, given that most university-based teacher preparation programs in gifted education require a course in the identification of gifted learners. Further, the one component of gifted education that is seemingly most likely to be in flux in most school districts is identification (Abeel, Callahan, & Hunsaker, 1994; Callahan, Hunsaker, Adams, Moore, & Bland, 1995).

Certainly there has been coverage of procedures, instruments, and issues in the leading survey texts used in introductory courses (e.g., Clark, 2008; Davis & Rimm, 2003; VanTassel-Baska, 1998) and in encyclopedic treatments (e.g., Plucker & Callahan, 2008; Robinson, Shore, & Enersen, 2007; Colangelo & Davis, 2002; Heller, Mönks, Sternberg, & Subotnik, 2000), and there have been smaller format books that focus on research (e.g., Renzulli, 2004), issues (e.g., VanTassel-Baska, 2008), or on practice (e.g., Johnsen, 2011). However, a comprehensive treatment of identification that brings together theory, research, and practice could serve the needs of both university instruction and school program development. This edited volume attempts to fill that void.

This text is divided into four sections.

- **Section I** focuses on the theoretical foundations for gifted identification. It consists of chapters that describe a theoretical basis for decision making, an approach to identification specific to one theory of giftedness, a call for pursuing identification from the theoretical basis of multiculturalism, and an application of a theory of absolute characteristics of gifted learners.

- **Section II** provides chapters on the professional foundations for gifted identification. Chapters in this section include presentations of legal and policy perspectives, as well as implications from professional standards in measurement, staff development, and program development.

- **Section III** offers guidance on identification practice. Chapters in this section describe basic stages of identification, decision-making strategies, and idealistic perspectives on identification.

- **Section IV** presents critiques and counsel relative to the most popular types of instruments used in gifted identification. These include ability testing, creativity assessment, teacher rating scales, and performance assessment.

Each chapter is authored by leading scholars or practitioners in gifted education whose years and varieties of experience provide them with an authoritative voice on the issues they address. Taken as a whole, it is my hope that this text will present the reader with multiple points of view that address the issues that seem to most trouble the field of gifted education in regard to identification including, but not limited to the following: (a) the gap between theory, evidence, and practice; (b) the inequitable representation of diverse populations in gifted programs, (c) the use of identification to bestow status rather than as an assessment process to inform instructional decisions, (d) the rigidity with which processes and instruments are used, despite instructions to the contrary in professional standards and testing manuals; and (e) the search for some *magic bullet* process or test that will make the identification process quick and easy.

The study guides included with each chapter are intended to help readers process and respond to ideas in the chapter. The guides take a slightly different approach from the exercises often found at the end of textbook chapters. The prompts for each chapter in this text are based on an adaptation of suggestions by Kellough (1997) for response journal entries intended to "assess for meaningful learning" (p. 207). Thus, rather than merely review information, the prompts assist the student in the central learning task of meaning making. Kellough's response categories are shown in Table 1.

As adapted in this book, journaling prompts give the reader an opportunity to (1) articulate key ideas in his or her own terms, (2) express opinions about important ideas, (3) integrate cognitive and affective reactions to chapter material, (4) connect chapter concepts with personal or professional experience, and (5) address preconceptions or potential misconceptions. Experience with these prompts has shown that, as students thoroughly and thoughtfully respond, they can experience meaningful learning through personal reflection, small group oral discussion, on-line threaded discussions, and whole class discussion.

I wish to acknowledge Sally Reis and Joe Renzulli for their initial and continued encouragement and trust throughout this project, beginning with a great conversation I had with Sally as I drove her around beautiful Cache Valley, Utah, in my van; the chapter authors for their diligence in responding in a timely fashion to my requests, for their flexibility as timelines necessarily changed, and for the insights they have shared throughout their professional work, but especially for this book; and Rachel Knox, editor from Creative Learning Press, for her positive attitude in encouraging and challenging my thinking and her persistence in making this book become a reality. Finally, I must acknowledge my Utah colleagues who've joined with me on so many levels as we have worked on behalf of gifted children in our state and endeavored to share what we have learned with others across the nation. Three deserve special mention: Debbie May, who began as a gifted coordinator in a neighboring school district the same year I began in mine and has been a willing collaborator and contributor ever since; Sue Sakashita, who welcomed me so enthusiastically when I first returned to Utah and immediately found multiple ways for me to use my current expertise and to develop new areas of expertise; and Becky Odoardi, whose expertise, drive, panache, and friendship have impacted not only me personally but ultimately have made a difference for the students she is so passionate about.

**Table 1.** Response Journal Prompts to Assess for Meaningful Learning (Kellough, 1997, p. 207)

| Category | Description |
| --- | --- |
| "I never knew that." | Responses are factual information; responses to new knowledge, to bits and pieces of raw information, often expected to be memorized. |
| "I never thought of that." | Responses are additional ways of perceiving; higher-level thinking as a result of reflection on knowledge. |
| "I never felt that." | Responses are connected to the affective, eliciting more of an emotional response than a cognitive one. |
| "I never appreciated that." | Responses reflect a sense of recognition that one's own life can be enriched by what others have created or done, or that something already known can be appreciated from an additional perspective. |
| "I never realized that." | Responses indicate an awareness of overall patterns and dynamic ways in which behavior is holistic, establishing meaningful and potentially useful connections among knowledge, values, and purposes. |

## REFERENCES

Abeel, L. B., Callahan, C. M., & Hunsaker, S. L. (1994). *The use of published instruments in the identification of gifted students.* Washington, DC: National Association for Gifted Children.

Callahan, C. M., Hunsaker, S. L., Adams, C. M., Moore, S. D., & Bland, L. C. (1995). *Instruments used in the identification of gifted and talented students.* Storrs, CT: University of Connecticut, National Research Center on the Gifted and Talented.

Clark, B. (2008). *Growing up gifted: Developing the potential of children at home and at school* (7th ed.). Upper Saddle River, NJ: Prentice-Hall.

Colangelo, N., & Davis, G. A. (Eds.). (2003). *Handbook of gifted education* (3rd ed.). Boston: Allyn & Bacon.

Davis, G. A., & Rimm, S. B. (2003). *Education of the gifted and talented* (5th ed.). Boston: Allyn & Bacon.

Heller, K. A., Mönks, F. J., Sternberge, R. J., & Subotnik, R. F. (Eds.). *International handbook of giftedness and talent* (2nd ed.). Oxford, UK: Elsevier.

Johnsen, S. K. (Ed.). (2011). *Identifying gifted students: A practical guide.* Waco, TX: Prufrock.

Kellough, R. D. (1997). *A resource guide for teaching: K–12* (2nd ed.). Upper Saddle River, NJ: Merrill.

Plucker, J. A., & Callahan, C. M. (Eds.). (2008). *Critical issues and practices in gifted education.* Waco, TX: Prufrock.

Renzulli, J. S. (Ed.). (2008). *Identification of students for gifted and talented programs.* Thousand Oaks, CA: Corwin.

Robinson, A., Shore, B. M., & Enersen, D. L. (2007). *Best practices in gifted education: An evidence-based guide.* Waco, TX: Prufrock.

VanTassel-Baska, J. L. (Ed.). (2008). *Alternative assessment with gifted and talented students.* Waco, TX: Prufrock.

# Section I.

# Theoretical Foundations

# INFORMATION THEORY AS A GUIDE TO DECISION MAKING

Scott L. Hunsaker, Utah State University

Educators make many decisions every day. Fogarty (2007) claims that the number of daily decisions is 1500. Whether the number is accurate or used as hyperbole is inconsequential. The point is well taken that innumerable decisions must be made each day that affect the lives of children. Fogarty differentiates these decisions as "on your feet" (p.9) decisions, which are made in the "heat of action" (p. 9), or "on your seat" (p. 9) decisions, which are made when an educator has time to be thoughtful and planful.

A more complete picture of educational decisions is given by Moss and Piety (2007), who have indicated that

> the types of decisions made range from moment-to-moment decisions classroom teachers face about "what to do next" and how to plan and enact lessons, revise curricular routines, solve particular pedagogical problems, or inform parents and guardians about students' learning; to decisions school and district leaders face about allocating resources, planning professional development, selecting and refining curricula,

developing local policies, and evaluating the impact of these choices; to decisions state and federal education professionals face about the design of indicator systems and other social structures to support district and local education agencies, research and development priorities, or the design and impact of fiscal policies. (p. 4)

Regardless of the level and extent of reach of any educational decision, stakeholders—be they students, parents, teachers, administrators, or the general public—want to have confidence that decisions are founded upon the best information available. Yet, as Moss and Piety have pointed out, because of varying contexts, professional educators have "different sources of evidence, different resources for interpreting the available evidence, and different constraints on practice" (p. 2). This means that to understand professional decision making, we must understand the nature of information—including the processes through which it is "attended to, interpreted, and used to frame problems and to inform and evaluate decisions and actions" (Moss & Piety, p. 3)

The purpose of this chapter is explore facets of the relationships among information, decisions, and actions, specifically as they relate to the professional decision making employed within gifted identification processes. First, I'll discuss the Information Cycle that contributes to the decision-making process and then present how it fits into decisions about gifted identification.

## THE INFORMATION CYCLE

The relationships among information, decisions, and actions are complex and often difficult to depict. Yet this has not stopped scholars from attempting the task. Phillips (2007) has pointed out that "even the most crass decision makers, unless they are completely dysfunctional, will engage in chains of reasoning that involve evidence that is judged to be pertinent to the decision context at hand" (p. 380). Phillips own conception of these chains of reasoning is as follows:

> An inquiry starts from a *problem* that we become aware of in the course of our professional or everyday experience. . . . Then, if our attention is captured by this problem, we think about it, analyze and probe it; eventually, if we are lucky, and inventive or smart enough, we might formulate . . . an answer—this is a creative activity, one that logic cannot elucidate. We then assess whether this hypothesis or theory or potential course of action solves the initial problem, via criticism and empirical testing and/or directed observation—that is, via amassing of data and the formulation of evidence. (p. 385, emphasis in the original)

This process sounds like what we've come to know as the *scientific method*, but Phillips is keen to observe that "scientists generally have an epistemic purpose—to determine what theories, laws, or hypotheses are true or probably true; whereas policy makers are focused on different matters—such as what politically palatable and economically feasible course of action is likely to remediate a social problem that has become important to the polity" (p. 377). While acknowledging the complex context of decision making from a policy perspective, Phillips leaves us with little guidance on how solutions are found; he seems to think it a rather mysterious process. Further, Phillips presents the process quite linearly, even though, in its complexity, the process is likely much more cyclic.

Phillips (2007) faults the narrowness of thinking of those who tend toward oversimplification of decision-making processes, particularly as it relates to views of the scientific method, though he himself "crudely" (p. 377) proffered the views on decision making given in the previous paragraph. Humans cannot resist the temptation to reduce the world to simple terms, as such simplification seems to make the complexity more understandable, approachable, parsimonious, and perhaps even more elegant. So, for example, Danielson (2008), in her work on reflection in teaching, refers to Donald Schön's terms of *reflection-for-action*, *reflection-in-action*, and *reflection-on-action*, which focus on the *when* of reflection. Van Manen (1991) suggested similar concepts but used different terms: *anticipatory reflection*, *active/interactive reflection*, and *recollective reflection*. These terms create a sense of clarity regarding reflection that is seemingly comprehensive and compelling to the mind. Spillane

4

and Miele (2007) refer to our preference for such concepts as *selective attention* and insist that reductive sense making helps us "maintain a certain level of cognitive efficiency" (pp. 49-50).

What such terms do not do, of course, is reveal the content of reflection, nor the relationships among the different types of reflection. Yet Van Manen (1991) reminds us, "Reflection in the field of education carries the connotation of deliberation, of making choices, of coming to decisions about alternative courses of action" (p. 98).

At the risk of being overly simplistic, yet being understood, Figure 1, the information cycle, illustrates the relationships among information, reflection, decision, and action. Information is at the core because it serves as both input and outcome of the other three activities. In other words, we become aware of opportunities as we cognitively and affectively filter information; our interpretation of this information as an opportunity is then returned to the system. Further, information is the content of reflection, yet as we reflect, we generate new information through insights gained from deliberation or serendipity. In like manner, we use information to make decisions, but once decisions are made, information about those decisions is put back into the system, usually in the form of a rationale or defense for the decision (Phillips, 2007). Finally, information, often in the form of a plan, is used to implement actions. As actions are carried forward, information comes back to the system about impacts of those actions. More will be said later about the various aspects of information, but first we must consider the remaining four elements of the information cycle (see Figure 1).

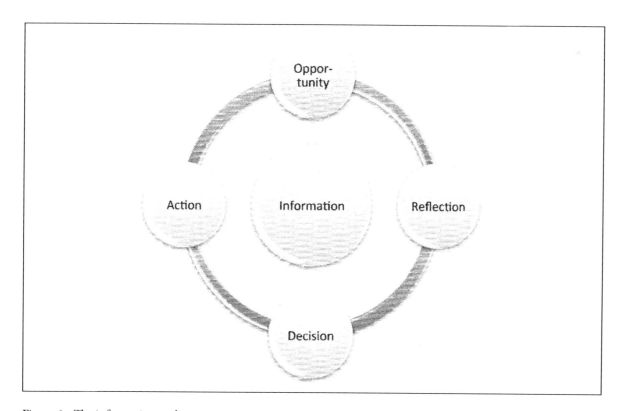

**Figure 1.** The information cycle.

## OPPORTUNITY

Opportunity is not just some Pollyannaesque version of the word *problem*. The word *opportunity* refers to much more than problems to be solved. It also includes phenomena to understand, potentialities to realize, purposes to fulfill, and priorities to set. Indeed, recent versions of the creative problem-solving model have employed the phrase *constructing opportunities* rather than *problem finding*. This language implies not only the broader application already referred to, but also a proactive role for the actor rather than a reactive role (Treffinger, Isaksen, & Stead-Dorval, 2006). Parnes (1988) has elucidated on this role by discussing how people achieve their visions, dreams, or desires. He explains:

> [We proceed] from examining "what *is*" to exploring "what *migh*t be," to judging "what *ought to* be," to assessing "what *can presently* be," to deciding "what *I will commit to do now*" . . . :

- "What is" refers to your awareness of the facts or data about a situation.
- "What might be" implies the generation of multiple-viewpoint, forward-thrusting definitions, approaches, and ideas toward the realization of objectives.
- "What ought to be" involves considered judgments about approaches and ideas.
- "What can presently be" refers to your choices and adaptations of approaches and ideas into what seems to be a manageable solution for now.

- "What I will commit to do now" becomes your best plan for gaining acceptance and implementing.

(p. 3, emphasis in the original)

Only as we become aware of or sense the opportunities around us can we begin to focus our energies on the information that will be most meaningful or beneficial in our reflections.

## REFLECTION

The word *reflection* implies a looking back, which seems to focus on the past; but, based on concepts such as those proposed by Van Manen (1991), we have come to use the term to refer to any enlightenment-seeking activity, whether it be for the past, present, or future. In addition to the timeframe of reflection, scholars have proposed modes of reflection. For example, Danielson (2008) proposed four such modes:

1. technological thinking, which accepts routine practices based on criteria of efficiency and effectiveness, as understood through appeals to outside authority (e.g., as long as a procedure works, it is unnecessary to reflect on how it might be changed);

2. situational thinking, which considers problems only within the confines of observable behaviors in a specific context (e.g., while a procedure works for most children, there is no need to reflect upon how it might be done differently; but if it doesn't work for a specific child in a specific classroom, then reflection is required either to figure how to bend the child to

6

Table 1. Reflective Questions to be Posed According to Period and Mode

| | | Reflection Times | | |
| --- | --- | --- | --- | --- |
| | | Anticipatory | Active/Interactive | Recollective |
| Reflection Modes | Technical | What is the procedure? | Am I following the procedure? | Did I follow the procedure? |
| | Situational | Should I use the procedure in this case? | Is the procedure working in this case? | Why did the procedure work or not? |
| | Deliberate | What data support is there for this procedure? | Are we doing this procedure in a way that makes sense, given the data? | What other data might we have used to better implement the procedure? |
| | Dialectical | Is this procedure the right procedure to use? | In what ways might I feel more comfortable with what I'm doing right now? | What other procedures are available that we might use in future in such a circumstance? |

the procedure or to adapt the procedure so it works for the child);

3. deliberate thinking, which seeks additional information from multiple sources to take the educator beyond the current situation (e.g., while recognizing the success of a certain procedure thus far, determining if the procedure has a sufficient research base behind it, in which case the procedure will either be affirmed [indicating no need for change] or contradicted [indicating the need for adjustment]);

4. dialectical thinking, which requires flexible thinking to reconstruct meaning, leading to transformations of practices (e.g., while a procedure may be working for the teachers, being willing to consider how it works from the students' point-of-view).

Combining Van Manen's reflection periods with Danielson's reflective modes provides a variety of questions we might ask about any particular opportunity. These are displayed in Table 1. As can

be seen from the questions in the table, reflection can lead to maintenance of the status quo or to radical changes, depending on the questions one asks oneself and the responses one is willing to attend to.

## DECISION

Eventually the decision-making process should lead one to making a choice, either through the exercise of one's agency or the force of one's will. The term *agency* implies that choices are made freely as one rationally considers multiple options. The term *will* connotes more emotional involvement in choices, as one is driven by desires and motivations.

This dichotomy, however, overly simplifies the decision-making process. Most human beings generally operate within both rational and emotional realms that contain both freedom and constraint. Stone (2002) argues that a purely rational basis for decision making is impossible and probably undesirable, given the complex, paradoxical nature of issues that are fraught with ambiguity. According to Stone, "The ideal of a perfect rationality would require a person to consider all possible alternatives (an infinite number), and evaluate all possible consequences of each" (p. 233). Airasian and Jones (1993) also suggested the impossibility of purely rational decision making when they stated:

> Problems experienced in real-world settings . . . rarely present themselves in neat, well-formed, universally-applicable ways. Instead they tend to be rather messy, confronting the practitioner with conflicted, indeterminate situations in which the appropriate solution is rarely clear and typically boils down to a choice among a number of reasonable alternatives. (pp. 242-243).

So, as Spillane and Miele (2007) declared, "Inundated with stimuli from our environment, we tend to notice things that are relevant to our goals and expectations . . . and ignore things that are not" (p. 49). However, Stone (2002) again reminds us, "Information is always incomplete, interpretive, and deliberately controlled. People can never have full information about all the alternatives available for satisfying a goal" (p. 76).

While Stone (2002) admits that there are "objective facts underlying all situations" (p. 379), she posits that "interpretations are more powerful than facts" (p. 28). It is the meanings we attach to facts that matter most in decision making, and, as Stone states, "Science cannot settle questions of meaning" (p. 379). The best we may claim is that choices are made within the context of community standards, norms, and customs as interpreted through an individual's "existing beliefs, values, and norms" (Spillane and Miele, 2007, p. 48), based on incomplete information, which as Spillane and Miele

state, "is always understood in light of what is already known" (p. 50).

Thus, decision making is "beset with by problems of uncertainty" (Stone, 2002, p. 236), which, however, is not necessarily a bad thing. Helsing (2007a, 2007b) has suggested that the educational enterprise is inherently uncertain, being centered on human relationships, but that uncertainty may be regarded as a decision-making style. She avers, "Teachers who recognize that the certainty of clear-cut answers is an impossible goal may also spare themselves from . . . frustration and feelings of incompetence" (2007b, p. 34). She further elucidates an advantage of uncertainty when she contends, "One must be willing to sustain that state of doubt or uncertainty in order to investigate [a] problem thoroughly without drawing premature conclusions" (2007b, p. 38). The role of uncertainty in inquiry is underscored by Peshkin (1993) when he lists the four sources of systematic study as that which is (1) unknown, (2) known thinly, (3) known uncertainly, or (4) known wrongly.

Helsing (2007b) cautions that an acceptance of uncertainty "does not preclude [one] from believing that there are better or worse ways of coming to and justifying . . . decisions" (p. 45). Airasian and Jones (1993) insist that teachers want to be seen as rational problem solvers who seek out the best technical methods, and Helsing would agree. It is, indeed, the uncertainty that leads an educator to apply methods for making a choice. He or she must make a choice, though, before discovering and interpreting all possible information, before establishing and applying all possible criteria, and before generating and analyzing all possible alternatives. The meta-decisions about which information, criteria, and alternatives to attend to are made within the "reciprocal influence of individual agency and social structure" (Spillane & Miele, 2007, p. 58) in which "human agency is . . . determined by the structure of the situation, [and] . . . the situation is itself constructed from the beliefs, intentions, and actions of individuals" (Spillane & Miele, pp. 57-58). Ultimately, decision making comes down to the development of an argument to justify a certain course of action (Phillips, 2007).

## ACTION

Action should be the natural result of the decision-making process. It is clearly apparent in Schön's conception of reflection-for-action, reflection-in-action, and reflection-on action (Danielson, 2008). It is in the implementation of an action that much of the unknown relative to a decision is revealed. That is, based on the outcomes or consequences of the action, we learn if a particular decision to act in a certain way was rational or not. "Actions are to be evaluated by their consequences," states Stone (2002, p. 241). This concept is critical in education because educational decisions have a direct effect on expectations of students, student outcomes, and long-term opportunities (Begeny, Eckert, Motarello, & Storie, 2008; Helsing 2007a). Again, a certain amount of uncertainty is present as one cannot know all the possible short-range or long-range effects of an action, consisting of both intended and unintended consequences, which include opportunity costs (Stone, 2002; Helsing, 2007a). Opportunity costs notwithstanding, what we should most likely strive for are those actions that continue to keep other action options open. It is usually best the choice we make not back us into a corner where we have no options, or even only one option, left.

## INFORMATION

Information can be defined as a unit of understanding. The word *understanding* here refers to something beyond mere comprehension of knowledge. Rather, it implies a foundational (hence the *under* part of understanding) grasp of a concept that includes, at a minimum, detailed description, appreciative explanation, and considered implications—in other words, a functional intrinsic theory about the concept. This view of information is illustrated in Figure 2.

This representation is built on the view from cognitive psychology that "the mind/brain [is] an information processing system, which, of course presumes that the world is made up of information ready to be processed" (Hruby, 2009, p. 193). Information is processed as an individual interacts with the universe. In Figure 2 the multidirectional arrows surrounding the black dot in the middle represent an individual's interactions. The black dot represents the individual, causing this graphic to seem fairly egocentric. Certainly an individual's interactions with the universe are centered on self, but these interactions pull an individual outside oneself, creating a need for the individual to negotiate through and with the universe. The dual sense of the word negotiate is important here. Negotiation can refer to an individual's attempts to navigate a course through the variety of demands placed on the individual. This navigation is well represented by the poem *Invictus* by William Ernest Henley, shown in Table 2. The other sense

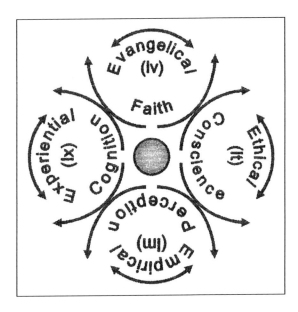

Figure 2. Information theory.

of negotiation—a give-and-take communication between parties to determine equivalent values within an exchange of goods or services—is well represented by the poem *Barter* by Sara Teasdale, also shown in Table 2.

The arrows in Figure 2 also represent the knowledge paradox. This paradox is often not realized until after one's primary education. As children begin school, they're often under the impression that knowledge is finite and learning is additive—the more they learn, the less they have to learn, until they eventually learn it all. As students move through secondary education, they begin to realize that knowledge is potentially infinite while learning in multiplicative—the more they learn, the more they're able to combine their learning in multiple ways with what they already know, but then they become aware that knowledge is expanding exponentially, so the proportion of total learning appears to diminish the more one learns. The desire for finite certainty as one negotiates

through and with the universe is represented by the curvilinear arrows on the outside of the figure. The potential for infinite uncertainty is represented by the curvilinear arrows that break through the boundaries set by the outside arrows, showing the possibility for uncertainty to take us "beyond what we think we know" (Helsing, 2007b).

In addition, Figure 2 represents the variety of formal and informal information sources used in decision making (Spillane & Miele, 2007). Through interactions with the universe, each individual develops four kinds of information that are used as one moves around the information cycle: evangelical information ($I_v$), ethical information ($I_t$), empirical information ($I_m$), and experiential information ($I_x$). In the material that follows, each information type will be defined and discussed. Specifics in the discussion will include the notion of provability within the information type, the screen through which the information type is negotiated, problems inherent with a collapse onto any one type of information, and problems inherent with totally ignoring any one type of information. Interestingly, the Council for Exceptional Children—The Association for Gifted Division recognizes all four types of information in the approval process for their professional standards that requires articulation of a knowledge base to support the standards ($I_t$) that consist of literature or theory-based knowledge ($I_v$), research-based knowledge ($I_m$), and practice-based knowledge ($I_x$) (Johnsen, VanTassel-Baska, & Robinson, 2008).

As individuals create information through negotiation when they interact with the universe, there is a danger that information will draw inevitably toward the individual in all his or her idiosyncracity

**Table 2.** Poetry Illustrating the Senses of the Word *Negotiate*

| Sense of the Word: Navigation | Sense of the Word: Exchange |
|---|---|
| *Invictus* | *Barter* |
| William Ernest Henley (1849-1903) | Sara Teasdale (1884-1933) |
| Out of the night that covers me, | Life has loveliness to sell, |
|     Black as the Pit from pole to pole, |     All beautiful and splendid things, |
|     I thank whatever gods may be |     Blue waves whitened on a cliff, |
|     For my unconquerable soul. |     Soaring fire that sways and sings, |
| |     And children's faces looking up, |
| In the fell clutch of circumstance |     Holding wonder like a cup. |
|     I have not winced nor cried aloud. | |
|     Under the bludgeonings of chance | Life has loveliness to sell, |
|     My head is bloody, but unbowed. |     Music like a curve of gold, |
| |     Scent of pine trees in the rain, |
| Beyond this place of wrath and tears |     Eyes that love you, arms that hold, |
|     Looms but the horror of the shade, |     And for your spirit's still delight, |
|     And yet the menace of the years |     Holy thoughts that star the night. |
|     Finds, and shall find me, unafraid. | |
| | Spend all you have for loveliness, |
| It matters not how strait the gate, |     Buy it and never count the cost; |
|     How charged with punishments the scroll, |     For one white singing hour of peace |
|     I am the master of my fate; |     Count many a year of strife well lost, |
|     I am the captain of my soul. |     And for a breath of ecstacy |
| |     Give all you have been, or could be. |

and self-centeredness (as represented by the outer curvilinear arrows). Thus, individuals are capable of making the error, with regard to information, of always focusing on one specific type of information. As a result, the model collapses in upon itself (or contracts) with rather distressing results. To borrow metaphorically from the field of physics, a singularity is created. Obviously in the four-dimensional space-time universe, a one-dimensional singularity is undesirable because all the rules become void and predictability breaks down (Hawking, 1996). For each type of information that the model can contract into, there is a specific type of singularity that occurs.

Another type of error occurs when one specific type of information is always ignored. While there is enough information in the system to prevent a collapse, one's negotiation with the universe will either slide or hook, to borrow metaphorically from the game of golf, diverting one away from whatever goal is to be accomplished.

15

## EVANGELICAL INFORMATION.

Evangelical information ($I_v$) refers to our spiritual, metaphysical, or intuitive ways of knowing. Through these means we develop the belief systems, operating theories, or world views that define what must be. The receptacle of this type of truth could, of course, be a being with omniscience, omnipresence, and omnipotence—in short, a divine being. Miller (2008), who claims to be evangelical about teaching biological evolution, cautions against thinking of the word evangelical only in terms of "religious fundamentalism" (p. 166), an association he claims most modern Americans would make. Rather, he suggests, "The word [evangelical] actually means nothing more than speaking the truth and bringing that 'good message' of truth to others" (p. 166). Of course, proving or disproving the truth of information taken on faith, the screen through which we negotiate evangelical information, would be seen by most as virtually impossible. However, as Ford (1975) has insisted for what she calls $T_1$, being unprovable does not make this type of information inconsequential. Many things of consequence, both for good and for ill, occur because of people's beliefs. Efforts to establish the truth of this type of information are generally based on appeals to the positive consequences believers experience, harking to the Apostle Paul's definition of faith as "the substance of things hoped for, the evidence of things not seen" (KJV, Heb. 11:1). The drive to convince others of the truth of one's own $I_v$, though not necessarily to convert others to it, is what gives this type of information its name. It would seem that the screen of faith through which evangelical information is obtained would lead one to an orientation toward certainty, as described by Helsing (2007a, b). However, carried to extreme, the collapse to a singularity of $I_v$ as a person's sole source of information would lead to the caricature of the religious zealot. The nature of this singularity is reflected in Helsing's (2007b) description of teachers who believe knowledge is certain. They become a concern because "such beliefs could lead them to oversimplify information, overemphasize any data that support their own positions, and be more resistant to changing their initial views" (p. 59). Such individuals begin to rely heavily on routines (i.e., rituals, rites) (Helsing, 2007a). In contrast, Ford (1975) has argued, somewhat tongue-in-cheek, "that *some* belief is basic to any paradigm of thought—even if it is a belief that beliefs should be banished from thought" (p. 17, emphasis in original). Such a belief and its accompanying failure to attend to evangelical information at all would lead one to become a cynic.

## ETHICAL INFORMATION.

Ethical information ($I_t$) refers to our social and emotional ways of knowing. Through these means we develop the laws, standards, rules, and mores that define *what should be*. The provability or falsifiability of this type of information occurs through reference to written and unwritten codes in place at various levels of our society and the degree to which these codes demonstrate that they are able to ensure the survival and propagation of our species. Paradoxically, these codes both maintain the status quo and provide for its alteration—and, in some cases, even its overthrow—at the same time. The screen through which this type of information is negotiated by the individual is conscience. Haidt and Graham (2007) have proposed that human beings in all cultures have five psychological foundations upon which moral intuition is based. These are

1. harm/care—a penchant to relieve suffering and to show compassion where care is needed;

2. fairness/reciprocity—a concern for reciprocal altruism, the establishment of individual rights, and fair treatment;

3. ingroup/loyalty—a preference for group solidarity promoted through heroism (i.e., a willingness to sacrifice for the group) and patriotism (i.e., performance of rituals that strengthen group solidarity);

4. authority/respect—a recognition of respect, duty and obedience toward legitimate authority, coupled with a responsibility of those in authority to lead with magnanimity and wisdom; and

5. purity/sanctity—a regard for a set of virtues through which the body is guarded and protected from contamination and disease.

Generally those who promote the maintenance of the status quo will found their interactions with their universe on all five intuitions. Those who promote change tend to focus only on harm/care and fairness/reciprocity, downplaying the importance of the other three intuitions. The caricature of the collapse to singularity of $I_t$ is found in the *prima donna*. Such a person would take personally and at face value the central axiom of the moral psychology movement in its infancy, as characterized by Haidt and Graham, "*Morality is about protecting individuals*" (p. 100, emphasis in the original). The prima donna, then, believes that laws, standards,

rules, and morés were made for her or his personal benefit, regardless of who is hurt along the way. The flip-side of this condition, the person who operates in life without reference to any $I_t$ is, of course, the sociopath. Stone (2002) taught that "all individual actions have side effects on others" (p. 78). Those who are concerned about $I_t$ are concerned with their side effects on others. Those who collapse onto $I_t$ only are concerned with others' side effects on them. Those who ignore $I_t$ intentionally induce negative side effects on others.

**EMPIRICAL INFORMATION.**

Moving clock-wise around Figure 2, we come to empirical information ($I_m$), which refers to the information we gain from observing the universe, as screened through our sensory-based perceptions. Clearly, this is a physical way of knowing and is provable through references to nature and, thus, defines *what appears to be*. The screen through which we negotiate this information is perception. Phillips (2007), building on the work of John Dewey, described this negotiation in this manner:

> Human inquiry . . . typically proceeds through five logically, but not necessarily temporally distinct steps: (1) a felt difficulty or nascent problem ( . . . called . . . the "irritation of doubt"); (2) its "location and definition"—in other words, making the problem explicit and deciding where its boundaries are located; (3) "suggestion of possible solution"—the creative act of hypothesis framing; (4) "development by reasoning of the bearings" of the hypothesized solution—in other words, the elucidation of testable consequences; and

(5) further observation and experiment to obtain evidence to facilitate confirmation or rejection of the hypothesis. (p. 386)

The collapse to a singularity on $I_m$ only is represented by the stereotypical view of the mad scientist; for example, Simon bar Sinister of the *Underdog* cartoon series of my childhood comes to mind. However, totally ignoring $I_m$ creates a sycophant—the obsequious individual, totally devoid of any skepticism, who agrees with whatever any authoritative person has to say. In the model, shown in Figure 2, $I_v$ and $I_m$ are drawn opposite one another. This placement shows a necessary tension in the model so that neither aspect of information can be ignored. Stone (2002) expressed this tension when she quipped that "policy obeys the laws of poetry rather than the laws of matter" (p. 161). Certainly she is not suggesting that good research cannot inform policy, but is asserting that other types of information, what has been called $I_v$ here, cannot be ignored. For teachers, the requirement to look at different types of information, in this case $I_t$ in conjunction with $I_m$, is further elucidated by Van Manen (1991), who stated, "Knowing how to act pedagogically in a specific situation involves empirical knowledge and a sense of values, norms, and moral principles. Broadly speaking, teachers must have factual information . . . as well as normative standards" (p. 42). Spillane and Miele (2007) echoed this idea, cautioning,

> It is sometimes assumed that judgments about the most appropriate course of action in a given education context can be inferred from relevant research findings. However, research findings merely inform practitioners about what the *general*

outcomes are of different kinds of decisions. They *do not* answer questions about what the social value of these outcomes is or should be . . . Nor do such research findings address what the *specific* will be when these decisions are made within a particular context. (p. 46, emphasis in the original).

**EXPERIENTIAL INFORMATION.**

Experiential information ($I_x$) is related to our cognitive, intellectual, or mental ways of knowing. It grows through the meanings we attach to the experiences we have and defines *what can be*. It is provable through reference to individual knowledge construction. Encounters with cognitively dissonant experiences will either maintain or alter our knowledge constructions through assimilation or accommodation, respectively, thus making cognition the screen through which we negotiate this type of information. A clear tension exists between $I_x$ and $I_t$, as explained by Stone (2002):

> There is no society on earth in which people are allowed to [pursue their self-interests] blatantly and exclusively, so that even if we only want to understand how people pursue their self-interests, we need to understand how conceptions of public interest shape and constrain people's strategies for pursuing their own interests. (p. 22)

A singularity collapse onto $I_x$ only would result in the despotic ruler who uses the agency through which he or she chooses experiences for self and others to control knowledge creation, dissemination, and application so it fits his or her construction of the world and society. The absence of $I_x$ would produce pedanticism—the view of life without experience of which professors in the *ivory tower* are often accused.

## THE CYCLE APPLIED TO GIFTED IDENTIFICATION

This cycle has implications for gifted identification on at least at two levels. The first is at the institutional level; the second is at the personal level.

### INSTITUTIONAL LEVEL IMPLICATIONS

Clearly the opportunity is before states, districts, and individual schools to optimize the potential of children as they develop into confident, contributing adults. However, this opportunity is constrained by limitations of resources, concepts, and, quite frankly, will. School budgets, of course, have been severely limited over the years. Tight budgets not only curtail the efforts that can be put into identification itself, but in the offerings that follow that identification, as well as in the professional development needed to prepare teachers to be responsive to what is learned about students through the identification process.

These constraints also limit the amount of reflection institutional personnel may be willing to do, as they are often caught up in the technical elements (see Table 1) of their identification processes, failing to move to higher levels of reflection. However, the higher levels of reflection shown in Table 1, when combined with the opportunities view expounded in the creative problem solving model (Treffinger, Isaksen, & Stead-Dorval, 2006), can lead us to finding better ways. Schools are wont to modify their identification procedures frequently (Callahan, Hunsaker, Adams, Moore, & Bland,

1995). Such frequent modifications invite careful institutional reflection leading to more and more defensible identification procedures each time. As suggested in the preceding material, there are several types of information that should be considered in decisions about identification procedures. Each of these will be considered in turn as it applies directly to gifted identification.

### EVANGELICAL INFORMATION ($I_v$)

Sternberg and Zhang (1995) proposed a pentagonal implicit theory of giftedness. An implicit theory is an "intellectual construction that resides in the minds of individual" (p. 88). Individuals use these theories as they interact or make judgments with other individuals they encounter. The implicit theory, then, becomes a personal operating theory or theory-in-use, as opposed to a formal theory (Putnam, 1991). According to Sternberg and Zhang's theory, people's intuition about what constitutes giftedness can be summed up in five criteria; (a) excellence, (b) rarity, (c) productivity, (d) demonstrability, and (e) value. They point out that an implicit theory is necessarily relativistic to time and place. Thus the content of the five criteria in the minds of educators and school patrons would have an impact on the processes and instruments that they would likely use in identifying students as gifted.

Another set of ideas about giftedness that could be classified as $I_v$ are often listed as myths (see, for example, Gallagher, 2006; Webb, Gore, Amend, & DeVries, 2007; Winner, 1996), though misconceptions would be a more accurate label. These misconceptions are beliefs people hold about giftedness, gifted individuals, gifted identification, and gifted education in general that are challenged by evidence from other types of information. Webb and his colleagues have provided a fairly comprehensive list of misconceptions that would very clearly have an impact on gifted identification procedures (see Table 3). An investigation of such misconceptions is imperative because, as has been pointed out by Maker (2005), educators' beliefs are one of the greatest impediments to gifted identification, particularly of students who come from populations traditionally not well served by gifted programs.

Within this context, it is imperative that professional educators articulate the theories that influence the decisions they are making about gifted identification procedures. Rather than relying solely on implicit or unsubstantiated beliefs, educators may wish to investigate the formal theories that have been propounded elsewhere. A useful volume for such an investigation may be the *Handbook of Gifted Education* edited by Colangelo and Davis (2003), which includes several theoretical perspectives on giftedness. In this volume, Chapter 2 elucidates how one specific theory can help inform the development of a gifted and talented identification procedure. In addition, Chapters 3 and 4 present other theoretical perspectives on the core attributes of giftedness and multicultural education. Deeper understandings of these points-of-view can also positively influence the development of identification procedures.

## ETHICAL INFORMATION ($I_t$)

In a study of ancient and traditional societies, Hunsaker (1995) discovered five themes that cut across cultures in their responses to gifted individuals: (1) that what is considered as gifted

**Table 3**. Misconceptions about Giftedness that Influence Identification Practices (drawn from Webb, et al., 2007, pp. xvii-xviii.)

- Gifted children are usually gifted in all academic areas.
- Giftedness is wholly inborn.
- Giftedness is entirely a matter of hard work.
- All children are gifted.
- Children become gifted because their parents push them.
- Gifted children seldom have learning handicaps.
- If you tell gifted children they have advanced abilities, they will become egotistical.
- Gifted children will show their abilities and talents in their school achievement.
- Gifted children are usually well organized and have good study skills.
- Gifted children's emotional maturity is as advanced as their intellect.
- Gifted children seldom have emotional or interpersonal issues.
- Gifted children enjoy demonstrating their talents and abilities for others.
- Parents cannot identify giftedness in their own children.
- Educators will know exactly how to work with gifted children.

behavior is culturally imbedded and relates to what a society sees as necessary for its survival; (2) that the source of giftedness is generally external to the individual, either through divine or genetic endowment; (3) that early training is needed for the development of gifts; (4) that gifts are distributed with rarity and that social status and gender have an influence on this distribution; and (5) that ambivalent feelings toward any individuals with gifts and talents were the norm. These themes, especially the final one, underscore the love-hate relationship our nation has had with the gifted for decades. This relationship was articulated by Gallagher in a 1986 article and has been well illustrated by a graphic representation of federal support for gifted education in Clark's (2008) widely used textbook on gifted education. In addition to the larger social values about giftedness, more formalized values could also influence decisions about the identification of gifted students. These include legal and policy perspectives as discussed in Chapters 5 and 6 respectively. There are also professional standards that need to be addressed both from the fields of measurement and gifted education itself. These are discussed in Chapters 7 and 8 respectively.

## Empirical information ($I_m$).

In a survey of beliefs about gifted identification, Schroth and Helfer (2008) claim that "issues regarding identification of the gifted have perplexed the field almost since its inception" (p. 155). Research on identification has investigated various procedures and instruments all in an effort to be as accurate as possible. Schroth and Helfer found that educators had most confidence in standardized tests, student work portfolios, and teacher nominations. They lacked confidence in parent and peer nominations. (In this text, the reader will encounter reviews of the research on intelligence tests, creativity tests, and teacher rating scales in Chapters 12, 13, and 14, respectively. Research on alternative assessments, such as portfolios, is also reviewed in Chapter 15.)

## Experiential information ($I_x$).

Important early research investigating teachers' experience in gifted identification (e.g., Jacobs, 1971; Pegnato & Birch, 1959) suggested that teachers were often not a good source for recognizing potentially gifted students. However, Renzulli and Delcourt (1986) countered with the argument that these early studies were tantamount to requiring teachers to guess their students' IQ scores and that perhaps, through education and experience, the teachers had other ideas of what constituted giftedness in mind. Hunsaker (1994) discovered that some teachers did experience a discrepancy between a school's official definition of giftedness and their personal conception. Teachers who held a discrepant view, however, usually did not employ their personal conception to improve the identification procedures in their schools. This inaction was rooted in three rationalizations: (1) school officials were already instigating change, and the teachers had learned through experience to be patient with such efforts; (2) the hierarchical structure in the school precluded teachers from advocating for change as they had learned, through experience, that they lacked the power to effectuate change; and (3) advocating for students who fit the personal conception rather than the school conception usually resulted in a rejection from the gifted program, and teachers had learned through experience to avoid harm to the student by withholding such advocacy. Other research has documented that teachers will often espouse one conception in their role as teachers when speaking in professional circles, but will implement another when actually teaching in the classroom (Spillane & Miele, 2007). For gifted identification to work most effectively, teachers are trained to teach in a way that will elicit the behaviors they are seeking in order to recognize potentially gifted children (Borland, 2004; Maker, 2005), yet research has documented that relatively few teachers implement any differentiation strategies that would permit them to see the true capabilities of their most advanced students (Archambault, Westberg, Brown, Hallmark, & Zhang, 1993). (Further discussion of the formal procedures recommended for and experienced by teachers in identifying gifted students is provided in Chapters 9 through 11.)

## PERSONAL LEVEL IMPLICATIONS

Finally, the information cycle has implications for gifted identification at a personal level. Educators can carefully review their beliefs ($I_y$) by asking what they personally believe about gifted children or what their personal conception of giftedness is. Beliefs about testing and assessment could also be queried. As educators begin to implement or critique an identification process, they can clarify how familiar they are with the research ($I_m$) on identification, assessment, and evaluation of gifted children and gifted programs, in addition to asking how skilled they are at interpreting that research. Educators should also seek to understand how gifted identification procedures fit within cultural attitudes ($I_t$) about gifted education. Finally, educators should assess their personal experiences ($I_x$) with gifted and talented learners, identification, and programs, and how these experiences can influence their work within a gifted identification system.

The personal level can also be understood outside the educational system and can be considered in terms of its impact on parents. This can best be illustrated through personal experience ($I_x$): My oldest son, Adam, was nominated for both Title I reading assistance and the gifted and talented program by his kindergarten teacher. I thought this showed a good awareness of the literature on twice exceptional students ($I_m$) on her part. Adam showed an extensive knowledge base and was sensitive to nuances of language, as evidenced through his advanced sense of humor, but he had not yet mastered sound-symbol association. My wife, Becky, and I were invited to complete a parent nomination form. I was impressed that this form included both positive and negative indicators of giftedness ($I_m$). Testing for this nomination would be conducted in fall of the first grade year.

Fall arrived, and Adam entered first grade. Because I was a graduate student at the time, it was my responsibility to get Adam out of bed and get him on the bus. This morning duty allowed me to spend a few minutes with him before I went to school, where I spent the remainder of the day, well into the night. One particular morning, I was late in getting Adam up. When I finally did, he complained of a headache. I moved him through the morning preparations anyway, after giving him some medicine. We weren't fast enough, so he missed the bus. I drove him to school and signed him in late at the office as required by school policy ($I_t$). After getting the appropriate pass, I escorted him to his first grade classroom. When we entered the classroom, the teacher exclaimed that Adam should be down in the gifted pull-out room taking the achievement test that was part of the identification process. I rushed Adam down to the appropriate room. The proctor had already begun reading the directions aloud as the students followed silently. Obtaining a test booklet, I perused the instructions and found where the proctor was reading, initially scanning them with my finger so Adam could see where to follow along. When I returned home, Becky met me at the door with Adam's glasses in hand, indicating that I'd forgotten to put them on him that morning. I drove back to the school with Adam's glasses and once again entered the testing room to give them to him. I left the room knowing full well that Adam's performance would be less than adequate to meet program standards ($I_t$).

Sure enough, a few weeks later we received a letter that informed us that Adam had not qualified for the gifted program. The letter also invited us to visit with an administrator at the school if we had questions or concerns. Needless to say, we had questions and concerns. Becky and I made an appointment with the administrator. Becky wanted to make sure the program leaders knew that the test results could not be considered valid by any stretch of the imagination given the conditions under which Adam took the test ($I_t$). I had one

question for the administrator. It went like this, "Your letter told me what you're not going to do for Adam. I want to know, given all the assessment you've done, what you are going to do for him." This query was based on my knowledge of national measurement standards that prohibit the use of one piece of information to make a negative decision about a child and that assessments should be used primarily to determine action rather that inaction ($I_t$).

The administrator's response was excellent. He acknowledge the difficulties of the testing situation, then he stated something like, "At our school, we believe [($I_v$)] that if a child is nominated for the gifted program, we need to respond to whatever it was that brought about the nomination, even if the child doesn't qualify for the gifted program per se. So, in Adam's case, we've decide that a partial placement makes sense. Clearly, Adam is not yet an independent learner, so he won't be taking part in those aspects of the program. However, Adam evidently does well in group discussions, so when the identified first-grade students meet for group discussions, Adam will be included in those."

During first grade, Adam was assisted by both the remedial reading assistance and the partial placement in the gifted program. It is my belief ($I_v$) that the purpose of any gifted identification process is to gather information to help educators and parents make the best decisions possible regarding the educational experiences of children. I trust you will find this message consistently throughout this book.

## REFERENCES

Airasian, P. W., & Jones, A. M. (1993). The teacher as applied measurer: Realities of classroom measurement and assessment. *Applied Measurement in Education, 6,* 241–254.

Archambault, F. X., Jr., Westberg, K. L., Brown, S. W., Hallmark, B. W., Zhang, W., & Emmons, C. L. (1993). Classroom practices used with gifted third and fourth grade students. *Journal for the Education of the Gifted, 16,* 103–119.

Begeny, J. C., Eckert, T. L., Montarello, S. A., & Storie, M. S. (2008). Teachers' perceptions of students' reading abilities: An examination of the relationship between teachers' judgments and students' performance across a continuum of rating methods. *School Psychology Quarterly, 23,* 43–55.

Borland, J. H. (2004). Issues and practices in the identification and education of gifted students from under-represented groups. Storrs, CT: University of Connecticut, National Research Center on the Gifted and Talented. [RM 04186]

Callahan, C. M., Hunsaker, S. L., Adams, C. M., Moore, S. D., & Bland, L. C. (1995). Instruments used in identification of gifted and talented students. Charlottesville, VA: University of Virginia, National Research Center on the Gifted and Talented. (RM 95130)

Clark, B. (2008). *Growing up gifted: Developing the potential of children at home and at school* (7th ed.). Columbus, OH: Merrill

Collangelo, N., & Davis, G. A. (2003). *Handbook of gifted education* (3rd ed.). Boston: Allyn & Bacon.

Danielson, L. (2008). Making reflective practice more concrete through reflective decision making. *Educational Forum, 72,* 129-137.

Fogarty, R. (2007). *10 things new teachers need to succeed.* Thousand Oaks, CA: Corwin.

Ford, J. (1975). *Paradigms and fairy tales.* London: Routledge & Kegan Paul.

Gallagher, J. J. (1986). Our love-hate affair with gifted children. *G/C/T, 9*(1), 47–49.

Gallagher, J. J. (2006). *Driving change in special education.* Baltimore, MD: Paul H. Brookes.

Johnsen, S. K., VanTassel-Baska, J., & Robinson, A. (2008). *Using the national gifted education standards for university preparation programs.* Thousand Oaks, CA: Corwin.

Haidt, J. & Graham, J. (2007). When morality opposes justice: Conservatives have moral intuitions that liberals may not recognize. *Social Justice Journal, 20,* 98–116.

Hawking, S. W. (1996). *The illustrated a brief history of time* (Updated and expanded ed.). New York: Bantam.

Helsing, D. (2007a). Regarding uncertainty in teachers and teaching. *Teaching and Teacher Education, 23,* 1317–1333.

Helsing, D. (2007b). Style of knowing regarding uncertainties. *Curriculum Inquiry, 37,* 33–70.

Hruby, G. G. (2009). Grounding reading comprehension theory in the neuroscience literatures. In S. Israel & G. Duffy (Eds.), *Handbook of research on reading comprehension* (pp. 189–223). New York: Routledge Taylor and Francis Group.

Hunsaker, S. L. (1994). Creativity as a characteristic of giftedness: Teachers see it, then they don't. *Roeper Review, 17,* 11–15.

Hunsaker, S. L. (1995). The gifted metaphor from the perspective of traditional cultures. *Journal for the Education of the Gifted, 18,* 255–268.

Jacobs, J. C. (1971). Effectiveness of teacher and parent identification of gifted children as a function of school level. *Psychology in the Schools, 8,* 140–142.

Maker, C. J. (2005). The DISCOVER Project: Improving assessment and curriculum for diverse gifted learners. Storrs, CT: University of Connecticut, National Research Center on the Gifted and Talented. [RM 05206].

Miller, K. R. (2008). *Only a theory: Evolution and the battle for America's soul.* New York: Viking.

Moss, P. A., & Piety, P. J. (2007). Introduction: Evidence and decision-making. In P. A. Moss (Ed.), *Evidence and decision making: 106th yearbook of the National Society for the Study of Education,* pt. 1 (pp. 1–14). Chicago, IL: National Society for the Study of Education.

Parnes, S. J. (1988). *Visionizing: State-of-the-art processes for encouraging innovative excellence.* East Aurora, NY: D.O.K.

Pegnato, C. W., & Birch, J. W. (1959). Locating gifted children in junior high schools: Comparison of methods. *Exceptional Children, 25,* 300–304.

Peshkin, A. (1993). The goodness of qualitative research. *Educational Researcher, 22*(2), 23–29.

Phillips, D. C. (2007). Adding complexity: Philisophical perspectives on the relationship between evidence and policy. In P. A. Moss (Ed.), *Evidence and decision making: 106th yearbook of the National Society for the Study of Education,* pt. 1 (pp. 376–402). Chicago, IL: National Society for the Study of Education.

Putnam, R. W. (1991). Recipes and reflective learning: "What would prevent you from saying it that way?" In Schön, D. A. (Ed.), *The reflective turn: Case studies in and out of reflective practice,* (pp. 145-163). New York: Teachers College Press.

Renzulli, J. S., & Delcourt, M. A. B. (1986). The legacy and logic of research on the identification of gifted persons. *Gifted Child Quarterly, 30,* 20–23.

Schroth, S. T., & Helfer, J. A. (2008). Identifying gifted students: Educator beliefs regarding various policies, processes, procedures. *Journal for the Education of the Gifted, 32,* 155–179.

Spillane, J. P., & Miele, D. B. (2007). Evidence in practice: A framing of the terrain. In P. A. Moss (Ed.), *Evidence and decision making: 106th yearbook of the National Society for the Study of Education,* pt. 1 (pp. 46–73). Chicago, IL: National Society for the Study of Education.

Sternberg, R. J., & Zhang, L. (1995). What do we mean by giftedness? A pentagonal implicit theory. *Gifted Child Quarterly, 39,* 88–94.

Stone, D. A. (2002). *Policy paradox: The art of political decision making.* New York: W. W. Norton.

Treffinger, D. J., Isaksen, S. G., & Stead-Dorval, K. B. (2006). *Creative problem solving: An introduction* (4$^{th}$ ed.). Waco, TX: Prufrock.

Van Menen, M. (1991). *The tact of teaching: The meaning of pedagogical thoughtfulness.* Albany, NY: State University of New York Press.

Webb, J. T., Gore, J. L., Amend, E. R., DeVries, A. R. (2007). *A parent's guide to gifted children.* Scottsdale, AZ: Great Potential Press.

Winner, E. (1996). *Gifted children: Myths and realities.* New York: BasicBooks.

## Chapter 1 Study Guide

**Prompt 1** *Knowledge*

Explain each type of information (i.e., evangelical information, ethical information, empirical information, experiential information) in your own terms and in a way that clearly distinguishes the four.

**Prompt 2** *Opinion*

Looking at *problems* as *opportunities* is considered hackneyed or trite by some. Do you agree? Why or why not?

**Prompt 3** *Affect*

Describe the feelings you experience when a lot of discussion is held and a lot of information is shared among professionals about a particular student but no action is taken? If you've not had such an experience, discuss this with a colleague and describe the feelings they have had. Why do these feelings occur?

**Prompt 4** *Experience*

Discuss how you or a colleague has used each of the types of information in making curricular and instructional decisions about students in your classes. How might your experience help you in using the different types of information in identifying students for gifted and talented education services?

**Prompt 5** *Preconception/Misconception*

Educators are strongly encouraged to use *evidence-based* instruction. Often, the evidence educators restrict themselves to is research (i.e., empirical information). Explain why this is potentially an error when evaluating ideas of instruction of students as individuals or groups.

# DEFENSIBLE AND DOABLE: A PRACTICAL, MULTIPLE-CRITERIA GIFTED PROGRAM IDENTIFICATION SYSTEM

JOSEPH S. RENZULLI & SALLY M. REIS, UNIVERSITY OF CONNECTICUT

## INTRODUCTION

In his classic work, *Diffusion of Innovations*, Everett Rogers (1962) detailed how new ideas and technologies come to be adopted within an organization or social system. In the first two stages, a decision maker gains initial awareness of an innovation and then is persuaded to actively seek more information about the innovation. In the third stage, the decision maker chooses to accept or reject the innovation. If the decision maker accepts the innovation, she proceeds to the fourth stage—implementation. Once the innovation has been implemented, the decision maker can observe the outcomes and determine whether she will continue or discontinue using the innovation (see Figure 1).

This chapter provides decision makers with knowledge that will facilitate the implementation of a multiple-criteria identification system for gifted programs and poses two key questions:

1. Why is a multiple-criteria identification system preferable to a traditional test-score based identification system?

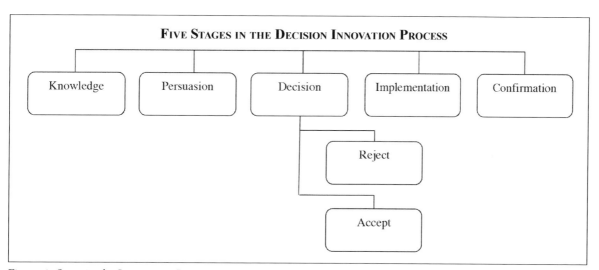

Figure 1. Steps in the Innovation Process.

2. How can my school system implement a multiple-criteria identification system in an practical, efficient, and feasible manner?

Answers to the first question endeavor to persuade decision makers that the current state of research on human potential requires a transition in the systems we use to identify children and adolescents for special programming in schools. After choosing to accept this innovation, decision makers can use the answers to the second question as a roadmap for both a practical and efficient implementation of multiple-criteria identification systems.

This chapter presents an identification system that addresses issues of excellence, equity, and economy in gifted education programs. It is supported by decades of thorough research concerning its underlying theories (Renzulli & Reis, 1994; Reis & Renzulli, 2004). It is designed to be economical in terms of the time and paperwork required for identification, to provide access to special services for both traditionally high-scoring students and those students whose potential may only be recognized through the use of a more flexible range of identification criteria. It is versatile enough to accommodate talent potentials in different domains, and it respects regulations made by district policy makers and state departments of education (especially important since these entities often provide much needed financial assistance).

The first order of business for any particular school or school system wishing to identify and serve high-potential youngsters is to decide on a conception or definition of giftedness. The identification system described in this chapter is based on the Three-ring Conception of Giftedness, a definition developed from research that identifies

three interlocking clusters of ability that characterize highly creative and productive people, as seen in Figure 2. These three clusters are (1) well-above average (not necessarily superior) ability, (2) task commitment, and (3) creativity. These clusters of ability are brought to bear on specific performance areas. The Three-ring Conception additionally posits that there are two kinds of giftedness: academic giftedness and creative-productive giftedness. Both of these types of giftedness are important and often interact, and both should be encouraged in special programs.

Further, this identification system is firmly based on the assumption that there should be congruence between the criteria used in the identification process and the program goals and types of services that constitute the day-to-day gifted program's activities in which students will be involved. It is therefore also linked to a broad range of services and teaching practices that are specifically designed to develop a variety of talents in young people.

Another critical consideration that went into developing this identification system is our firm

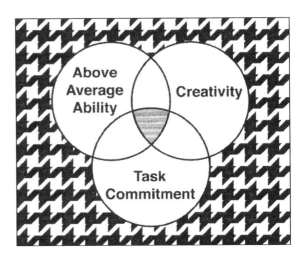

**Figure 2.** The three-ring conception of giftedness.

26

belief that we should label the services rather than the student. Instead of labeling a student as "gifted" or "not gifted," this identification system enables teachers to document specific strengths and use this information to make decisions about the types of activities and the levels of challenge that should be made available to the student. This system identifies students who would benefit from services that recognize both academic as well as creative-productive giftedness and provides opportunities to develop talents through an integrated continuum of special services.

A key feature of this identification system is the formation of a Talent Pool that includes students who have been identified by both test and non-test criteria. The system includes students who earn high scores on traditional measures, but also leaves room for students who show their potentials in other ways or who have high academic potential, but underachieve in school.

In districts where this system has been implemented, students, parents, teachers, and administrators have expressed high degrees of satisfaction with this approach. By eliminating many of the problems usually associated with identifying gifted students, we gain support from teachers and administrators, and by expanding services to students below the top few percentile levels usually admitted into special programs, we eliminate the sometimes justifiable criticism that we are denying entrance to students who are in need of special opportunities, resources, and encouragement. This identification system is not as tidy as using cut-off scores, but it is a more flexible approach to identifying and serving young people with great potential, and one

that can be completed in much less time than more traditional approaches.

## PERSUASION: WHY MULTIPLE CRITERIA?

As scientific study advances our understanding of how human potential develops over the course of a lifetime, the systems created to enhance that potential (i.e., the education system) should also change to reflect contemporary theories. In the field of gifted education during the past three decades, research has supported a broadened, expanded conception of giftedness (Renzulli, 1978; Gardner, 1983; Sternberg, 1985). A thorough review of this research is beyond the scope of this chapter (see, for example, Sternberg & Davidson, 2005; Dai, 2010), but to simplify a complex and active debate, very few researchers and theorists continue to accept an isolated IQ or achievement test score as a valid measure of a child's capacity for producing notable accomplishments over the course of the lifetime. It does not mean that IQ or achievement scores should not be included as *one of a number of criteria*, only that they should not form the entire basis for decision making in identification for gifted and enrichment programs. Despite these developments, the administrative tidiness of using a single IQ or achievement score in the identification process has persisted in America's schools.

## CONSIDERATIONS IN DEVELOPING IDENTIFICATION SYSTEMS

Districts just starting to develop gifted and talented programs and those with programs already in place both benefit from considering (or reconsidering) how to analyze the appropriateness of identification systems designed to select students for participation in those programs. The following questions constitute a starting point for reflection on the practical, political, and psychometric complexities of the issue:

1. Will this identification system be applicable to diverse school populations and groups of students that have been traditionally underrepresented in programs for the gifted?

2. How will we "label" students identified for these programs?

3. How much individual testing by school psychology staff will be required?

4. Will the system be economical in terms of the personnel time, group and individual testing costs, and other resources necessary to identify students?

5. Will the system be flexible enough to accommodate talent potentials across different domains such as music, art, drama, technology, and other non-verbal or mathematical talent areas?

6. Will it be flexible enough to make changes if student performance warrants a reexamination of selection or rejection decisions?

7. How will the system fit in with regulations of state departments of education (especially in those cases where some level of financial reimbursement is provided by state agencies for each identified gifted student)?

8. How will the system help avoid parental dissatisfaction or legal challenges?

In any plan to identify gifted and talented students, the following six important considerations should be kept in mind. Any number of identification approaches exists in the field, including some based on theories and research about the development of human potential and others based on beliefs and school district traditions and policies about the types of educational services that develop high levels of performance. An examination of these considerations can guide how decision makers respond to the aforementioned recurring and problematic questions.

**CONSIDERATION 1: THERE IS NO SUCH THING AS A PERFECT IDENTIFICATION SYSTEM.**

There is no perfect way to identify who is or is not gifted, just as there is no single best way to develop giftedness and/or talent potentials in special program candidates. Every identification system is a trade-off between the instruments and criteria selected, the ways we make decisions about any and all types of information we collect, and how much weight we give each type of information in the decision-making process. Because so many different conceptions of giftedness can be found in the theoretical and research literature, the first and most important decision we should make regarding practical procedures for identification is about the conception or definition of giftedness adopted by the school or school system. In some cases where state reimbursement is provided, state regulations mandate the definitions that guide identification and the number or proportion of students that can be served. There are programs, however, where additional students with high potential may be served if supported by local funds;

and in such cases, this group may be designated by a label that is different from the state-certified group designated as "the gifted" (e.g., Talent Pool, Advanced Learners, High Potential). Local circumstances notwithstanding, the conception or definition issue should be consistent with the types of services for which students are being identified, as discussed in Consideration 6.

A number of excellent resources exist to help decision makers reach agreement on a conception/definition decision. Appendix A (at the end of the chapter) presents a selected bibliography of the best resources to guide this decision-making process, and we recommend that decision makers examine and discuss these references to reach consensus before selecting or designing an identification system.

## CONSIDERATION 2: THE OBJECTIVE VS. SUBJECTIVE TRADE-OFF.

Tests of cognitive ability and/or academic achievement are the most frequently used type of identification information. These types of tests are considered objective because they rely on student performance rather than the judgment of others. Some people question the objectivity of these tests because the decision to use them is, in and of itself, a subjective act (e.g., imagine, for example, using an IQ test to select students for an advanced music or drama program). Another concern focuses on whether or not a one-hour "glimpse" into a young person's overall potential can be considered an objective appraisal of a student's total capacity for high-level performance.

Almost all other criteria (e.g., teacher, parent, peer, or self ratings; portfolio or writing-sample assessments; or grades earned in school subjects) are considered to be subjective as their use implies personal judgments that may be open to personal bias, an idiosyncratic view of giftedness, or inconsistent grading standards. Many argue that these types of criteria enable us to see other signs of potential such as motivation, creativity, leadership and executive functions (initiation, execution, and completion of tasks), and intense interest in a topic that is not reflected in more objective cognitive ability tests. If we view some of these non-cognitive skills as important, then we need to examine the degree to which we are willing to make trade-offs between objective and subjective information.

## CONSIDERATION 3: PEOPLE, NOT INSTRUMENTS, MAKE DECISIONS.

Regardless of the number or types of instruments used in a multi-criteria identification system, instruments only provide selected sources of information; they do not make decisions! Therefore, it is important to specify reasons for selecting the members (e.g. teachers, program coordinators, school psychologists, district liaisons) who will be involved in the information-processing and decision-making team. In addition, we must provide these team members with the level of orientation and training they need to become well-informed evaluators. Members from different areas of the school community may need different levels of training. Protocols for resolving the differences of opinion that will invariably emerge should be structured in advance, reducing the need for ad hoc solutions to team member disagreements.

How much "weight" will be given to the various instruments or decision-making criteria should also be determined before implementing the identification system. For example, if a decision is made to use two or three cognitive ability measures (e.g., aptitude test, achievement test, and course grades[1]) and only one measure of creativity (e.g., a creativity test or a teacher rating), there will be triple weighting of cognitive ability and single weighting of the creativity criterion. The relative emphasis on different sources of information should be aligned with the overall intent of the program. This consideration is important in both the design of the identification system and the interpretation of the information provided to the committee who will review students' records and subsequently make decisions.

## CONSIDERATION 4: AVOID THE MULTIPLE-CRITERIA SMOKESCREEN.

Most identification systems use a traditional nomination/screening/selection approach, and at least part of a multiple-criteria screening process is usually based on non-test information (e.g., teacher nominations and/or ratings). A problem arises, however, if the nomination or screening process only determines which students will be eligible to take an individual IQ test or a more advanced cognitive ability test. In such cases, the test still remains the ultimate "gatekeeper" for which students enter or do not enter the program. Unselected students are often those who were nominated for screening on the basis of one or more non-test criteria, but who did not make the cut after taking a cognitive ability test. In other words, a teacher

---

1. Course grades are not as precise as test scores, but they are reflections of cognitive ability so far as school performance is concerned. One should, however, be cautious of varying grading standards displayed by different teachers.

nomination or high ratings is only used as a "ticket" to take an individual or a group ability test, but in most cases, the test score is the deciding factor. Any highly positive attributes that might have been the basis for a teacher nomination, or favorable information discovered in the screening process, are ignored when it comes to the final selection decision. The danger here is, of course, that we may be systematically excluding high-potential students from culturally diverse backgrounds or students who have shown signs of high potential in other than the high verbal, mathematical, or analytic skills measured by standardized tests. What appears to be a multiple-criteria approach ends up being a smoke screen for a more traditional cut-off score approach.

The multiple-criteria smokescreen has other unintended side effects. Often, attempts to give the *impression* of a more flexible approach result in so much paperwork that it becomes inordinately time consuming, expensive, and unwieldy. In other cases, the smokescreen could be used to give the *appearance* of concerns for equity when such concerns don't really exist.

## CONSIDERATION 5: WHAT WILL WE CALL SELECTED STUDENTS?

A fifth consideration emerges from the discussion above and relates to the degree of specificity we are attempting to achieve in the identification process. The tradition has been to label all selected students as "the gifted," thereby relegating all others to a non-gifted category. In recent years, however, a large body of research has argued very forcefully against such a broad stroke labeling process (Frasier & Passow, 1995; Gardner, 1983;

Renzulli & Reis, 1997; Winner 1996; Sternberg, 1985), and in some cases recommendations have been made to do away with any labeling altogether (Borland, 2004). A more current trend is to document specific student strengths by preparing an electronic multiple-criteria profile (Renzulli & Reis, 1997; Field, 2009). We can use this strength-based profile to make more personalized decisions about the types of resources and activities recommended for talent development.

It would be nice to think that we can do away with any kind of labeling, but the reality is that we can't make accommodations for students if we don't recognize individual strength areas. Experience has shown that far too many teachers claiming to differentiate for all students have, in reality, provided minimal or no advanced level opportunities for high-potential students. Behavioral definitions (i.e., those targeting specific strengths) are important because, if we know and can document particular strengths, there is a greater likelihood that schools will attempt to cultivate these strengths in targeted students. This approach also helps to introduce an element of accountability into programming, and it gives direction to efforts that schools should take in evaluating their programs (Delcourt, Dewey, & Goldberg, 2007)

In recent years an approach that has gained in popularity is *to label the service rather than the student* (Renzulli & Reis, 1994; Renzulli & Reis, 1997). For example, in a school using the School-wide Enrichment Model, a special service offered to all students called an "enrichment cluster" enabled any interested students to participate in a class, "Statistical Techniques for Young Researchers." This class was specifically designed for upper

elementary students with strong aptitudes and interests in mathematics. Without needing to be labeled, students benefited from material that was much more advanced than the math being covered in their sixth-, seventh-, and eighth-grade math classes.

Another example of a labeled service is Curriculum Compacting (Reis, Westberg, Kulikowich, & Purcell, 1998; Reis & Purcell, 1993; Reis & Renzulli, 2005). Teachers use Curriculum Compacting in the regular classroom with students who have already mastered the concepts and skills in a given unit of instruction and/or who are capable of covering the regular material at a faster pace and higher level of comprehension than their classmates. The process involves specific procedures for identifying particular strength areas, documenting these competencies in a systematic fashion, and providing advanced-level enrichment and/or acceleration opportunities with the time gained from eliminating already mastered material. Students are identified for the service, but there is no need to label them.

## CONSIDERATION 6: THE RELATIONSHIP BETWEEN IDENTIFICATION AND PROGRAMMING.

Our final consideration addresses the congruence between the criteria used in the identification process and the goals and types of services that constitute the daily activities of students in a special program. Congruence between identification and programming is so important that it might be viewed as "the golden rule" of gifted education! For example, identification for advanced courses in a content area such as math is best accomplished through *math* testing, examination of previous *math* grades, teacher recommendations or ratings on *mathematical* skills, and perhaps even estimates of a student's motivation to work hard *in math*.

A problem arises, however, when we expect an "all purpose" gifted program to develop strengths that are unique to each child. If a general gifted program has a curriculum, or if individual teachers in the program choose most of the activities (e.g., the teacher's favorite Rain Forest Unit or play production), then little room exists for variations in students' interests, learning styles, or preferred modes of expression. In other words, the materials covered in the general gifted program may be different from the regular curriculum, but the prescriptive nature of what is to be learned uses essentially the same approach to teaching used in regular classrooms. Therefore, a related decision in developing an identification system is the selection of a *pedagogical* programming model that will be used to guide direct and indirect services to students regardless of how they are grouped or organized for special program services. In this case, we are not discussing organizational models, but rather what the teaching/learning process looks like within any predetermined organizational arrangement.

Again, there are numerous programming models recommended for serving this population, and these programming models can be divided into two categories. Organizational or administrative models address how we group students and move them from one activity to another (e.g., full-time classes, pull-out programs, centers where students go for a given period of time each week, regular class inclusion approaches). Theoretical or pedagogical models focus on the kind and quality of learning experiences that are offered within any grouping or organizational

arrangement. The Enrichment Triad Model (Renzulli, 1977), the Autonomous Learner Model (Betts & Kercher, 2009), and a variety of acceleration, problem-based learning, and Socratic-reasoning approaches are examples of theoretical or pedagogical models. The importance of this consideration in guiding the identification process suggests that program planners review the continuum of learning theories from which all pedagogy is derived, as seen in Figure 3. (An excellent resource for examining the range of programming options can be found in *Systems and Models for Developing Programs for the Gifted and Talented* (Renzulli, Gubbins, McMillen, Eckhart, & Little, 2009).)

By way of summary, the six considerations discussed above point out the "landscape" surrounding the always complicated and frequently controversial topic of identifying gifted and talented students for services in special programs. This discussion of the issues will not provide ready-made answers to the many challenges of identification system design, but it does provide an understanding of some historically encountered problems and may be helpful in avoiding the pitfalls encountered by so many persons who have set out on the journey of creating an efficient, effective, and equitable plan for identification.

## IMPLEMENTATION: THE NUTS AND BOLTS OF THE RENZULLI IDENTIFICATION SYSTEM FOR GIFTED PROGRAM SERVICES (RIS/GPS)

Now that we have reviewed the research, presented the evidence, and introduced the key considerations, we hope that you agree that a multiple-criteria identification system is preferable to a

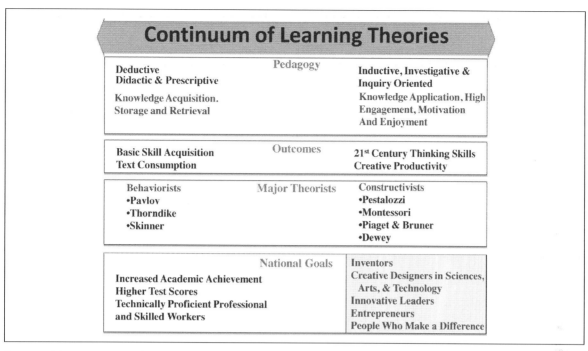

**Figure 3.** The continuum of learning theories.

traditional system. What next? The following section outlines a pragmatic approach to implementing such an identification system. The diagram in Figure 4 forms the basis for the step-by-step process to selecting students for services based on multiple sources. After following the steps in the Renzulli Identification System, identification team members can assemble a "Talent Pool" comprised of the students who have been identified through multiple ability/achievement scores, teacher ratings, parent ratings, peer ratings, and self-nominations.

### DECISIONS ABOUT TALENT POOL SIZE

The size of the talent pool is a function of two major decisions. The first is the number of special program personnel assigned to the program and the number of students that these personnel can provide adequate services to each week in such a manner that it makes a difference in the accomplishment of program goals. The second decision

is the nature of and extent to which an expanded range of services can be made available to targeted students by classroom teachers (e.g., Curriculum Compacting, Enrichment Clusters, Mentorship Programs for advanced students). Services such as Robotics Club; History Day Competition; Math League; Music, Art, and Drama clubs; or any other organized, interest-based grouping that focuses on a specific talent area falls within the scope of most special program goals. These types of opportunities reflect a total school talent development perspective, and they are especially valuable for a student or small group that has a high degree of potential, but only in a particular area of interest. It is important to convey to parents that this expanded range of services is, in fact, part of the special program opportunities that fall under the purview of the gifted program.

This second decision about an expanded range of services also has implications for special program administrative personnel. If we expect classroom teachers to participate in the services mentioned above, and if we hope to offer a robust range of extra-curricular activities geared toward talent development, it is essential to have a program coordinator that plans and "grows" such services, monitors the effectiveness of the services, maintains student records, and communicates talent development progress with parents. All teachers involved in the expanded range of services should believe they are an integral part of the program rather than a random provider of an extracurricular activity. They should be aware of the program mission and goals, participate in staff development that focuses on talent development, and attend "gifted program" meetings. Their accomplishments should be described in program brochures, reported in program announcements and newsletters, and recognized in special events about program activities. The program coordinator helps to create an expanded range of services that are an essential part of a total talent development program.

The RIS/GPS respects and includes students who earn high scores on traditional measures of cognitive ability, but a major variation from traditional identification practices is that this system leaves room in the Talent Pool for students who show their potentials in other ways. The percentage of total students in the Talent Pool and the corresponding proportions of students identified through test and non-test criteria can and should be modified based on the resources and goals of the individual program involved.

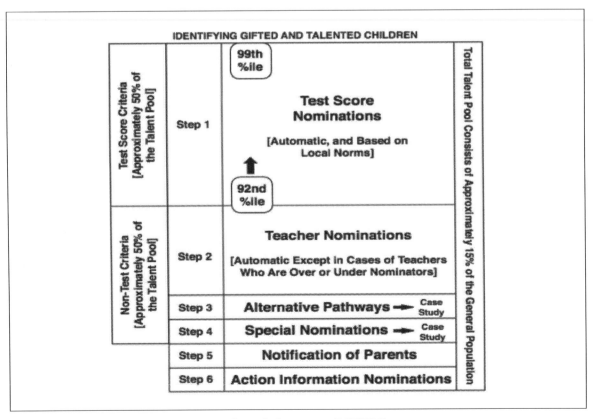

**Figure 4.** The Renzulli Identification System for Gifted Programs (RIS/GPS).

## Steps in Forming the Talent Pool

A team of school personnel, including teacher(s) of the gifted, classroom teachers, administrators, and pupil personnel specialists (e.g., counselor, school psychologist, social worker), should be responsible for managing the Talent Pool selection process. This group can be thought of as the Review and Selection Team. Any and all information related to the selection process should be made available to all members of the team and a case study approach should be used to review each set of student records. On some occasions, it will be necessary to seek supplementary information about a student and to request that non-team members meet with the team to provide additional information. It is important for all persons on the team (and parents and the general faculty as well) to understand that ***instruments provide information, but people make decisions!*** A multiple-criteria approach means that simply setting arbitrary cut-off points or adding up points from various instruments cannot make decisions. Informed human judgment is crucial for an identification system that (1) seeks to develop diverse talent potentials in diverse segments of the school population and (2) is geared toward services that place a premium on developing creative productivity rather than mere advanced lesson learning.

## Step 1: Academic performance and test score nominations.

Academic performance based on end-of-year grades for the past two years and the most recent total verbal and total numerical scores from district-wide achievement tests are the first two criteria used in forming the Talent Pool. In a 15% Talent Pool example, students who score at or above the 92nd percentile on either verbal or numerical sections of the achievement test should automatically be placed in the Talent Pool. In schools that serve diverse populations, it is also recommended that a non-verbal cognitive ability test be used in addition to standard achievement tests or aptitude tests. A very big caution, however, is in order here: There is a good deal of controversy about the effectiveness of non-verbal tests for increasing the proportion of minority students in programs for the gifted (Lohman, 2005; Naglieri & Ford, 2003, 2005). Until more definitive studies are conducted, we should treat non-verbal test scores as another piece of information in the overall decision-making process rather than a substitute for regular cognitive ability tests and school performance. Lohman has argued forcefully that

(1) admission to programs for the gifted should be guided by evidence of aptitude for the particular types of advanced instruction that can be offered by schools; (2) the primary aptitudes for development of academic competence are current knowledge and skill in a domain, the ability to reason in the symbol systems used to communicate new knowledge in the domain, interest in the domain, and persistence; (3) inferences about aptitude are most defensible when made by comparing a student's behavior to the behavior of other students who have had similar opportunities to acquire the skills measured by the aptitude tests; however, (4) educational programming and placement should be based primarily on evidence of

current accomplishment. (Lohman, in press, p.1)

Lohman further argues that comparisons should only be made between students who share similar learning opportunities or background characteristics. It is for this reason that this identification system recommends the use of *local norms* (i.e., calculated by school and grade level). Our goal is to identify the most promising students in *each* school and at *each* grade level who are the best candidates for supplementary services. Since we are not admitting students from other school districts or states, it does not make sense to engage in national comparisons. The use of national norms invariably results in the under-representation of minorities and students whose potentials may be manifested in non-traditional ways.

Students who score below the 92$^{nd}$ percentile, but who have demonstrated "straight A" academic performance in their end-of-year grades should also be considered eligible for gifted program services unless the selection team notes unusual discrepancies between test scores and grades. Or there may be cases in which high-scoring students do not have high grades due to underachievement or personal or social issues. In such cases, before determining which services are appropriate, additional *individual* assessment and record review should be carried out to determine if factors such as underachievement, a learning disability, personal or family problems, or difficulty with timed group tests are giving an inaccurate picture of the student's potential. Individual intelligence tests administered by a qualified examiner are needed when discrepancy information is found in the types of assessment mentioned above. This approach will

help to control the expensive and time-consuming use of individualized testing, thereby meeting the economy goal of this identification system.

Scores from the most recent regularly administered standardized achievement or aptitude test can be used for this purpose; however, we recommend that admission to the Talent Pool be granted on the basis of either a high verbal *or* a high mathematics score. This approach will enable students who are high in verbal or mathematical ability (but not necessarily both) to gain admission. Programs that focus on special talent areas such as music, art, drama, or leadership should use non-test criteria (see Step 2) as major indicators of above-average ability in a particular talent area. In a similar fashion, whenever test scores are not available or there is some question as to their validity, the non-test criteria recommended in the following steps should be used. This approach is especially important when considering primary age students, disadvantaged populations, or culturally and linguistically different groups.

The conclusion of Step 1 should be the creation of a list of names with an approximately equivalent number of students selected from each grade level. Through team discussions and negotiations, this list should represent approximately one-half of the predetermined number of "slots" in the Talent Pool.

## STEP 2: TEACHER NOMINATIONS.

If we were using nothing but test scores to identify a 15% Talent Pool, the task would be ever so simple. Any child who scores above the 85$^{th}$ percentile (using local norms) would be placed in the Talent Pool. In this identification system, however, we have made a commitment to "leave some room" for students whose potentials may not be reflected in standardized tests. This approach guarantees that all traditionally bright youngsters will automatically be selected, and they will account for approximately 50% of the Talent Pool. This process also guarantees admission to bright underachievers.

In order to minimize paperwork on the parts of classroom teachers, the first activity in Step 2 is to provide classroom teachers with a list of the names of students from their class who have already been selected for the Talent Pool in Step 1. After being provided with a brief training activity on the use of teacher rating forms (see Appendix B at the end of the chapter), teachers are asked to complete ratings on *other* students (i.e., other than those already selected in Step 1) whom they might consider for admission to the Talent Pool. In other words, teachers should be informed about all students who have gained entrance through test score nominations so that they will not have to complete ratings for students who have already been admitted. Step 2 allows teachers to nominate students who display characteristics that are not easily determined by tests (e.g., high levels of creativity, task commitment, unusual interests, talents, or special areas of superior performance or potential).

The instrument recommended for teacher ratings is the *Scales for Rating the Behavioral Characteristics of Superior Students* (SRBCSS; Renzulli, Smith, White, Callahan, Hartman, Westberg, Gavin, Reis, Siegle, & Sytsma Reed, 2010). These scales are the most thoroughly researched and widely used teacher-rating instrument in the

world (Renzulli, Reis, Gavin. & Sytsma Reed, 2009). The scales are now available in an online version, (www.renzulliscales.com) which allows for ease of rating, and, more importantly (because this system recommends the use of local norms[2]), the online version automatically calculates local norms as well as individual student profiles. Local norms should be calculated on a broad achievement range of students across the grade levels targeted to be identified before the scales are used to nominate high potential and gifted students.

Most schools use the three scales that correspond to the Three-ring Conception of Giftedness (Learning, Motivation, and Creativity); however, employing one or a combination of the other scales (Leadership, Reading, Mathematics, Science, Technology, Music, Art, Drama, Communication: Precision, Communication: Expression, and Planning) may be appropriate for programs focusing on special areas of talent or for categorical programs such as Future Problem Solving, Web Quest, or Math-Counts. Table 1 includes examples of how these rating scales may be used to nominate students for special topic programs by matching program goals and targeted skills to relevant rating scales. Once again, local norms based on school and grade-level

---

2. National norms for SRBCSS-III are not offered because we do not believe that national information is meaningful or appropriate since student populations differ from school district to school district and even between and among schools in the same district. Accordingly, we believe that local norms should be calculated for a broad achievement range of students across the grade levels targeted to be identified. The step-by-step procedure for calculating local norms (percentile ranks) is outlined in Appendix E of the manual for SRBCSS (Renzulli, Smith, White, Callahan, Hartman, Westberg, Gavin, Reis, Siegle, & Sytsma Reed, 2010) or, if you are using the online version of the Scales, it is calculated for you.

Table 1. Matching SRBCSS scales to program goals.

| Program | Program Goals | Rating Scales to Use |
|---|---|---|
| Future Problem Solving (FPS) | • Increase creative thinking abilities<br>• Improve analytical thinking skills<br>• Stimulate an interactive interest in the future<br>• Extend perceptions of the real world<br>• Explore complex societal issues<br>• Refine communication skills—written, verbal, and technical<br>• Promote research<br>• Integrate problem-solving into the curriculum<br>• Encourage cooperative, responsible group membership<br>• Offer authentic assessment | • Creativity<br>• Motivation<br>• Leadership |
| WebQuest | To develop the following skills:<br>• Comparing<br>• Classifying<br>• Inducing<br>• Deducing<br>• Analyzing errors<br>• Constructing support<br>• Abstraction<br>• Analyzing perspectives | • Technology<br>• Planning<br>• Learning<br>• Reading |
| MathCounts | • Challenge students' math skills<br>• Develop their self-confidence,<br>• Reward them for their achievements | • Mathematics<br>• Motivation<br>• Communication: Precision |
| National History Day | • Engage students in the process of discovery and interpretation of historical topics<br>• Combine creativity and scholarship | • Learning<br>• Motivation<br>• Creativity<br>• Planning<br>• Communication:Precision<br>• Communication:Expressive |

ratings are used rather than state, regional, or national norms; and each scale is considered a categorical data point. *In other words, scores from the scales should never be added together or averaged.*

With the exception of teachers who are over-nominators or under-nominators, nominations from *teachers who have received training in this process* are accepted into the Talent Pool on a par

value with test score nominations. We do not refer to students nominated by test scores as the "truly gifted" and the students nominated by teachers as the moderately or potentially gifted. Nor do we make any distinctions in the opportunities, resources, or services provided other than the normal individualization that should be a part of any program that attempts to meet unique needs and potentials. Thus, for example, if a student gains entrance on the basis of teacher nomination because he or she has shown advanced potential for creative writing, we would not expect this student to compete on an equal basis in an advanced math class with a student who scored at or above the 92nd percentile on a math test. Nor should we arrange program experiences that would place the student with talents in creative writing in an advanced math cluster group. *Special programs should first and foremost respect and reflect the individual characteristics that brought students to our attention in the first place.*

In cases of teachers who are over-nominators, the selection team can and should request that teachers rank order their nominations for review (i.e., place the scales in a pile from high to low) and return them to the selection team. Procedures for dealing with under-nominators or non-nominators will be described in Step 4.

### STEP 3: ALTERNATE PATHWAYS.

Most schools using this identification system make use of test scores and teacher nominations, and in most cases, the majority of the Talent Pool will come from these two criteria.

Alternate pathways are optional, locally determined by individual schools, and pursued in varying degrees by individual school districts. Alternate pathways generally include parent nominations, peer nominations, self-nominations, specialized tests (e.g., creative writing, spatial or mechanical ability), product evaluations, or virtually any other procedure that might lead to *initial* consideration by a selection team. A large number of instruments for gathering alternate

pathway information are available in the identification literature. (A good source for information about traditional testing instruments can be found in *Assessment of Children: Cognitive Applications* [Sattler, 2001] and reviews of instruments specifically related to gifted programs can be found in *Instruments Used in the Identification of Gifted and Talented Students* [Callahan, Hunsaker, Adams, Moore, & Bland, 2005].) A few examples of instruments that can be used for parent, peer, and product evaluation are included in Appendix C at the end of the chapter. The language of the cover letter for "Things My Child Likes to Do" is written in a way that seeks parent input about particular strength areas, but it does not place the parent in the awkward position of favoring or jeopardizing their child's designation as a "gifted" student. It is, of course, important and ethically responsible for teachers to put the results from the use of this instrument (described in the cover letter) to use, whether or not the child is placed in the Talent Pool. This information should always be shared with classroom teachers and periodically monitored to determine if appropriate attention is given to information about special interests or activities.

Sensitive issues need to be addressed whenever we open the door to parent input. Objectivity is always a concern when parents are asked to rate their own child, and it is for this reason that the parent rating scale mentioned above is not characterized as a "gifted instrument." Examples of representative behaviors associated with each scale item are included so that we can avoid, at least to some extent, the surplus interpretation that parents may bring to the ratings.

There are even more important issues related to parent input, primarily school districts that allow scores obtained through private testing to be submitted for consideration in the identification process. Assuming that reputable psychologists are administering the tests,[3] there is the issue of parents who are wealthy enough to afford private testing; and even in cases where private testing may be underwritten by the school district, there is the issue of parent savvy—simply knowing that the service is available and making the arrangements to have one's child tested. Since private testing is frequently a function of program history that has become accepted tradition, or even school board policy, the only way we can guard against unfair advantage is to make certain that (1) all parents are made aware of and have access to equivalent testing offered by or supported by the school, (2) inferences about test results are only made by comparing a student's behavior to the behavior of other students who have had similar opportunities to acquire the skills measured by the test, and (3) no single piece of identification information be used as the sole gatekeeper for admission decisions. The major difference between alternate pathways on the one hand (Step 3) and test score and teacher nomination on the other (Steps 1 and 2) is that alternate pathways are not automatic. In other words, students nominated through one or more alternate pathways will become the subjects of a case study by the Review and Selection Team, after which a selection decision will be made. In most cases the team carries

out a case study that includes examination of all previous school records; interviews with students, teachers, and parents; and the administration of individual assessments (as needed) that may be recommended by the team. In some cases, students recommended on the basis of one or more alternate pathways can be placed in the Talent Pool on a trial basis.

A local planning committee or the Review and Selection Team should make decisions about which alternative pathways might be used. Some consideration should also be given to variations in grade level. For example, self-nomination is more appropriate for students who may be considering advanced classes at the secondary level. Peer nomination is particularly useful for program services that focus on particular talent areas such as technology, music, or drama, and students themselves are sometimes better at revealing which students have natural or "street smart" leadership potential.

## STEP 4: SPECIAL NOMINATIONS (SAFETY VALVE NO. 1).

Special nominations represent the first of two "safety valves" in this identification system. This procedure involves preparing grade-level lists of all students who have been nominated through one of the procedures in Steps 1 through 3 and circulating these lists to all previous year teachers. The directions sent with the lists are as follows:

> These lists contain the names of all students who have been nominated for the Talent Pool for the forthcoming year. Will you please review the lists and send us the names of any students you have previously taught who are not on the lists, but

---

3. We are reminded of a newspaper article that made reference to a local psychologist who was popularly known as "Dr. 130!" For the right fee, he would automatically make a child gifted by giving him or her an IQ of 130 or higher.

who you think should be considered for Talent Pool membership.

Teachers should *not* be required to give a reason for their special nominations at this time. Busy schedules may discourage teachers from preparing justifications "on the spot." A later meeting or request that teachers complete a set of rating scales can also help to insure that invitations for special nominations are not ignored by busy teachers.

This procedure allows previous year teachers to nominate students who have not been recommended by their present teacher, and it also allows gifted education teachers to make recommendations based on their own previous experience with students who have already been in the Talent Pool or students they may have encountered as part of enrichment experiences that have been offered in regular classrooms. This process also allows special topic teachers (e.g., music, art, physical education) or teachers who have had responsibilities for special programs (e.g., Future Problem Solving, National History Day) to have opportunities for input into the nomination process. These teachers often observe students in non-traditional learning environments, and, therefore, they are excellent talent scouts for a variety of creative, practical, and motivational strengths. Faculty orientation about such opportunities is, of course, very important for gaining such input.

The Special Nomination step allows for a final review of the total school population and is designed to circumvent the opinions of present year teachers who may not have an appreciation for the abilities, styles, or even the personality of a particular student. This one last "sweep" through the population also helps to pick up students who

may have "turned off" to school or developed patterns of underachievement as a result of personal or family problems. This step also helps to overcome the general biases of any given teacher who is an under-nominator or a non-nominator. As with the case of alternate pathways, special nominations are not automatic. Rather, a case study is carried out, and the final decision rests with the selection team.

## STEP 5: NOTIFICATION AND ORIENTATION OF PARENTS.

A letter of notification and a comprehensive description of the program should be forwarded to the parents of all Talent Pool students indicating that their youngster has been placed in the Talent Pool for the year. The letter does not indicate that a child has been certified as "gifted," but rather explains the nature of the program and extends an invitation to parents to an orientation meeting. At this meeting, a description of the Three-ring Conception of Giftedness should be provided, as well as an explanation of the differences between "high achieving giftedness" and "creative productive giftedness." It is important to emphasize that both types of giftedness are important and will be addressed in the program. What should also be emphasized is that creative productive giftedness is the type that represents the way that the larger society has recognized persons of significant accomplishment (Treffinger & Renzulli, 1986).

The meeting with parents should also provide an explanation of all program policies, procedures, and activities. Parents should learn about how admission to the Talent Pool is determined, that selection is carried out on an annual basis, and that changes in Talent Pool membership might take place during the year as a result of evaluations of student participation and progress. Parents are also invited to make individual appointments whenever they feel additional information about the program in general, or their own child, is required. A similar orientation session should be provided for students, with emphasis once again being placed on the services and activities being provided. Parents are *not* told that their children are "the gifted," but through a discussion of the Three-ring Conception and the procedures for developing general and specific potentials, they should come to understand that the development of gifted behaviors is a program goal as well as part of their own responsibility.

### STEP 6: ACTION INFORMATION NOMINATIONS (SAFETY VALVE NO. 2).

In spite of our best efforts, this system will occasionally overlook highly creative students or students talented in a specific area, who, for one reason or another, are not selected (but should have been) for Talent Pool membership. To help overcome this problem, a process called Action Information Nomination is used, and all teachers are provided with an orientation related to spotting unusually favorable high-interest topics in the regular curriculum.

*Action information* can best be defined as the dynamic interactions that occur when a student becomes extremely interested in or excited about a particular topic, area of study, issue, idea, or event that takes place in school or the non-school environment. It is derived from the concept of

performance-based assessment, and it serves as the second safety valve in this identification system. The transmission of an Action Information Message (see Appendix D) does not mean that a student will automatically be placed in the Talent Pool. It does, however, serve as the basis for a careful review of the situation to determine if any types of special services are warranted. Action Information Messages are also used within Talent Pool settings (i.e., pull-out groups, advanced classes, cluster groups) to make determinations about the pursuit of individual or small group investigations (Type III Enrichment in the Triad Model). In order for the Special Nomination process to work effectively, all school personnel should be provided with an orientation to "talent spotting" situations where the initiation and transmission of an Action Information Message may be warranted. Transmission to the Review and Selection Team or to someone in the school and/or community that might provide guidance, serve as a mentor, or help the student to follow up in his or her area of interest are obligations that accompany the use of Action Information Messages in the effort to leave no stone unturned in helping young people develop their potential talents. In programs based on the Schoolwide Enrichment Model (Renzulli & Reis, 1997), we also provide a wide variety of in-class enrichment experiences that might result in recommendations for special services through the Action Information process. This process is facilitated through the use of a teacher training activity that can be used to orient teachers in the use of the Action Information Message (Renzulli & Reis, 1997).

## Processing Identification Information: Keeping it Organized and Communication-Friendly

Despite our initial admonitions against emphasizing administrative "tidiness" at the expense of multiple sources of data identifying young people's talents, it is nonetheless important to keep all sources organized in a coherent manner that enhances communication among stakeholders. We recommend placing a summary sheet, such as the one presented in Figure 5, at the very top of each student's file. This allows a concise condensation of the multiple measures used in the identification process that is clearly visible to anyone who accesses the information.

Another possible way to summarize multiple criteria into a meaningful format for decision making is to use the following steps, developed by Lohman and Renzulli (see also Chapter 12). This process incorporates verbal, quantitative, and non-verbal CogAT scores, math and reading achievement scores, and SRBCSS Learning Ability, Creativity, and Motivation scales in the review and selection process.

## Seven Step Identification System (Lohman & Renzulli, 2007)

1.  Enter percentile ranks (PRs) from the three CogAT batteries (Verbal, Quantitative,

### Renzulli Identification System: Information Summary Form

Name:_____  Date:_____

School:_____  Grade:_____

**I. Academic Performance**
A. Achievement Test Scores (Most Recent Achievement Test Scores

|  | Test | Date | Raw Score | Grade Equiv. | Local %ile |
|---|---|---|---|---|---|
| Verbal |  |  |  |  |  |
| Numerical |  |  |  |  |  |
| Non-verbal |  |  |  |  |  |

**B. End of Year Grades for Past 2 Years**

| Subject | Year 1 | Year 2 | Subject | Year 1 | Year 2 |
|---|---|---|---|---|---|
| Reading |  |  | Music |  |  |
| Mathematics |  |  | Art |  |  |
| Language Arts/English |  |  | Foreign Language |  |  |
| Social Studies |  |  | Other: |  |  |
| Science |  |  | Other: |  |  |

**II. Teacher Ratings** [Scales for Rating the Behavioral Characteristics of Superior Students (SRBCSS) ]

| Scale | Score | Group Mean | Scale | Score | Group Mean |
|---|---|---|---|---|---|
| Learning |  |  | Technology |  |  |
| Motivation |  |  | Artistic |  |  |
| Creativity |  |  | Musical |  |  |
| Leadership |  |  | Dramatic |  |  |
| Reading |  |  | Communication I |  |  |
| Mathematics |  |  | Communication II |  |  |
| Science |  |  | Planning |  |  |

**III. Alternative Pathways**

|  | Scale | Summary of Strengths |
|---|---|---|
| Parent Rating |  |  |
| Peer Rating |  |  |
| Product Rating |  |  |

**IV. Special Nominations**

Figure 5. Summary information sheet for review and selection process.

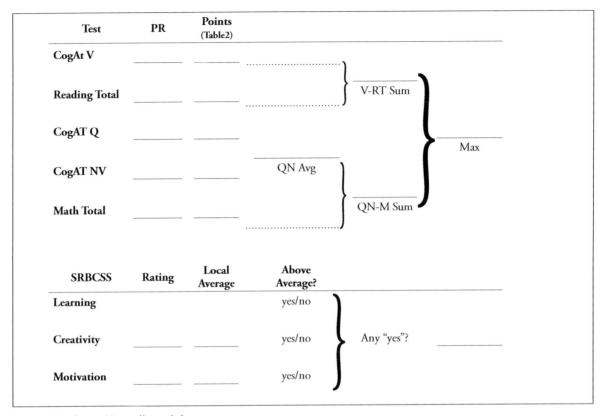

**Figure 6.** Lohman/Renzulli worksheet.

and Nonverbal) in the first column of the worksheet in Figure 6.

2. Convert Percentile Ranks (PRs) to points (Standard Age Scores) following Table 2. Enter these points into the worksheet.

3. Average the points for the Quantitative and Nonverbal batteries. Enter this value on the worksheet in the QN Avg space.

4. Sum the points for CogAT Verbal and Reading Total and enter this value in the **V-RT Sum** space on the worksheet.

5. Sum the points for the CogAT Quant-Nonverbal Composite (from step 3) and Mathematics Total and enter this value in the **QN-M Sum** space on the worksheet.

6. Take the **higher value** of **V-RT** and **QN-M** and enter it on the **Max** space of the worksheet.

7. Enter ratings for the three SRBCSS scales.

**Table 2.** Conversion Chart for CogAT Scores

| Use to convert PR from any test or CogAT SAS scores to points | | |
|---|---|---|
| Points | PR | SAS |
| 1 | 80-83 | 113-115 |
| 2 | 84-88 | 116-119 |
| 3 | 89-92 | 120-123 |
| 4 | 93-95 | 124-127 |
| 5 | 96-97 | 128-131 |
| 6 | 98 | 132-135 |
| 7 | 99 | 136-139 |
| 8 | 99+ | 140+ |

8. Compute the average teacher rating on each of the three SRBCSS scale for the group of students who were nominated for the program.

The point totals for the composite verbal/reading total and the composite quant/nonverbal/mathematics total can now be used to identify students. Figure 7 assumes that cut points are set at the 80th and 96th PRs.

Category I: Superior reasoning and achievement. Rated as highly capable, motivated, or creative by their teachers

Category II: Superior reasoning and achievement. Not rated as highly by their teachers on any one of the three major scales of the SRBCSS

Category III: Somewhat lower but strong reasoning abilities (between 80th and 96th PR) on one of the ability-achievement composites. Rated as highly capable, motivated, or creative by their teachers

Category IV: Good but not exceptional abilities (between 80th and 96th PR). Not rated as unusually capable, motivated, or creative by their teachers

For a more detailed description of this system of multiple-criteria identification and appropriate educational services for children who fall under the four categories mentioned above, see Chapter10.

CLOSING THOUGHTS

The most important factor that should be addressed when considering any identification system is the consistency that should exist between and among (1) the conception/definition of giftedness selected by a school or district, (2) the congruence between the conception/definition and the criteria used in the identification process, and (3) the goals and types of services that constitute the day-to-day activities that students will pursue in a special program. This consistency or "flow"

| | | TEACHER RATING ON LEARNING, MOTIVATION, OR CREATIVITY | |
|---|---|---|---|
| | | BELOW AVERAGE TEACHER RATINGS | ABOVE AVERAGE TEACHER RATINGS |
| COGAT VERBAL + READING T. OR COGAT QN + MATH T. | 8 OR MORE POINTS (≥96TH PR) | II | I |
| | 2 – 7 POINTS (80TH – 95TH PR) | IV | III |

Figure 7. Using CogAT, achievement test scores, and teacher ratings.

between conception, identification, and programming is so important that it might be viewed as "the golden rule" of gifted education! The material covered in any special program should reflect the purposes or mission of gifted education and the characteristics that brought particular students to our attention through a systematic identification process. Intimately related to the development an identification system is the selection of one or more organizational models that determine how we group students and move them around a pedagogical model that will guide instructional practices regardless of how students are grouped or organized for special program services.

Finally, we would like to close by again pointing out that simplistic single-score identification systems cannot provide us with the rich information necessary in making decisions on how to best provide services to develop children's unique talents and gifts. Choosing to implement a multiple-criteria identification system harnesses the best

theoretical evidence about talent development across the lifespan. It also provides avenues for traditionally under-represented student populations to participate in special programming, thus enhancing social equity. The chapter details how implementing such a system is not only desirable, but practically feasible as well. As educators move to the implementation stage of any decision-making innovation process, we hope this chapter has provided a practical roadmap as well as resources to guide a successful implementation of a flexible and fair identification system. We believe that the focus of tradition and expediency that has characterized gifted program identification must give way to expanded conceptions and innovative approaches to identification. These expanded approaches may not be as "tidy" or expedient as past practices, but they will help our field fulfill its promise of developing outstanding talent in more young people and increasing society's reservoir of creative and productive adults.

### REFERENCES

Betts, G., & Kercher, J. J. (2009). The Autonomous Learner Model for the Gifted & Talented. In J. S. Renzulli, E. J. Gubbins, K. S. McMillen, R. D. Eckert, & C. A. Little, *Systems and models for developing programs for the gifted and talented* (2nd ed., pp. 49–102). Mansfield Center, CT: Creative Learning Press.

Borland, J. (2004). *Issues and practices in the identification and education of gifted students from under-represented groups* (Research Monograph 04186). Storrs, CT: The University of Connecticut, The National Research Center of the Gifted and Talented.

Callahan, C., Hunsaker, S., Adams, C., Moore, S., & Bland, L. (2005). *Instruments used in the identification of gifted and talented students* (Research Monograph 95130). Storrs, CT: The University of Connecticut, The National Research Center of the Gifted and Talented.

Dai, D. Y. (2010). *The Nature and nurture of giftedness: A new framework for understanding gifted education.* New York: Teachers College Press.

Delcourt, M., Dewey, C., & Goldberg, M. (2007). Cognitive and affective learning outcomes of gifted elementary school students. *Gifted Child Quarterly, 51*(4), 359–381.

Field, G. B. (2009). The effects of using Renzulli Learning on student achievement: An investigation of internet technology on reading fluency, comprehension, and social studies. *International Journal of Emerging Technology, 4,* 29–39.

Frasier, M. M., & Passow, A. H. (1995). *A review of assessment issues in gifted education and their implications for identifying gifted minority students* (Research Monograph 95204). Storrs, CT: The University of Connecticut, The National Research Center of the Gifted and Talented.

Gardner, H. (1983). *Frames of mind.* New York: Basic Books.

Lohman, D. F. (2005). Review of Naglieri and Ford (2003): Does the Naglieri Nonverbal Ability Test identify equal proportions of high-scoring White, Black, and Hispanic students. *Gifted Child Quarterly , 49*(1), 19–28.

Lohman, D. F., & Renzulli, J. S. (2007). A simple procedure for combining ability test scores, achievement test scores, and teacher ratings to identify academically talented children. Retrieved from http://faculty.education.uiowa.edu/dlohman/

Naglieri, J., & Ford, D. (2003). Addressing underrepresentation of gifted minority students using the Naglieri Nonverbal Ability Test (NNAT). *Gifted Child Quarterly, 47*(2), 155–161.

Naglieri, J., & Ford, D. (2005). Increasing minority children's participation in gifted classes using the NNAT: A response to Lohman. *Gifted Child Quarterly, 49*(1), 29–36.

Reis, S. M., & Purcell, J. H. (1993). An analysis of content elimination and strategies used by elementary classroom teachers in the curriculum compacting process. *Journal for the Education of the Gifted, 16*(2), 147–170.

Reis, S. M., & Renzulli, J. S. (2004). Current research on the social and emotional development of gifted and talented students: Good news and future possibilities. *Psychology in the Schools, 41*(1), 119–130.

Reis, S. M., & Renzulli, J. S. (2005). *Curriculum compacting: An easy start to differentiating for high potential students.* Waco, TX: Prufrock Press.

Reis, S. M., Westberg, K. L., Kulikowich, J. M., & Purcell, J. H. (1998). Curriculum compacting and achievement test scores: What does the research say? *Gifted Child Quarterly, 42*, 123–129.

Renzulli, J. (1977). *The enrichment triad model: A guide for developing defensible programs for the gifted and talented.* Mansfield Center, CT: Creative Learning Press.

Renzulli, J. (1978). What makes giftedness? Re-examining a definition. *Phi Delta Kappan, 60*, 180–184.

Renzulli, J., Gubbins, E. J., McMillen, K., Eckhart, R., & Little, C. (Eds.). (2009). *Systems and models for developing programs for the gifted and talented* (2nd ed.). Mansfield Center, CT: Creative Learning Press.

Renzulli, J., & Reis, S. (1994). Research related to the Schoolwide Enrichment Triad model. *Gifted Child Quarterly, 38*, 7–20.

Renzulli, J., & Reis, S. (1997). *The Schoolwide Enrichment Model: A how-to guide for educational excellence* (2nd ed.). Mansfield Center, CT: Creative Learning Press.

Renzulli, J. S., Reis, S. M., Gavin, M. K., & Sytsma Reed, R. E. (2009). An investigation of the reliability and factor structure of four new scales for rating the behavioral characteristics of superior students. *Journal of Advanced Academics, 22*(1), 84–108

Renzulli, J., Smith, L., & Reis, S. (1982). Curriculum compacting: An essential strategy for working with gifted students. *Elementary School Journal*, 174–175.

Renzulli, J., Smith, L., White, A., Callahan, C., Hartman, R., Westberg, K., Gavin, M. K., Reis, S., Siegle, D., & Sytsma Reed, R. (2010). *Scales for rating the behavioral characteristics of superior students. Technical and administration manual* (3rd ed.). Mansfield Center, CT: Creative Learning Press.

Rogers, E. (1962). *Diffusion of innovations.* New York: Free Press.

Sattler, J. (2001). *Assessment of children: Cognitive applications* (4th ed.). Austin, TX: Jerome M. Sattler, Publisher, Inc.

Sternberg, R. (1985). *Beyond IQ: A triarchic theory of human intelligence.* Cambridge, UK: Cambridge University Press.

Sternberg, R., & Davidson, J. (Eds.). (2005). *Conceptions of giftedness* (2nd ed.). Cambridge, UK: Cambridge University Press.

Treffinger, D., & Renzulli, J. (1986). Giftedness as potential for creative productivity: Transcending IQ scores. *Roeper Review, 8*(3), 150–154.

Winner, E. (1996). *Gifted children: Myths and realities.* New York: Basic Books.

## Appendix A
## A Bibliography of Resources for Conceptions and Definition of Giftedness and Talent Development

Borland, J. H. (2005). Gifted education without gifted children: The case for no conception of giftedness. In R. J. Sternberg and J. E. Davidson (Eds.), *Conceptions of giftedness* (2nd ed.) (pp. 1–19). New York: Cambridge University Press.

Brody, L. E. & Stanley, J. C. (2005). Youths who reason exceptionally well mathematically and/or verbally: Using the MVT:D4 model to develop their talents. In R. J. Sternberg and J. E. Davidson (Eds.), *Conceptions of giftedness* (2nd ed.) (pp. 20-37). New York: Cambridge University Press.

Feldman, D. H. & Benjamin, A. C. (1986). Giftedness as the developmentalist sees it. In R. J. Sternberg and J. E. Davidson (Eds.), *Conceptions of giftedness* (pp. 285–305). New York: Cambridge University Press.

Field, G. B. (2009). The effects of the use of Renzulli Learning on student achievement in reading comprehension, reading fluency, social studies, and science. *International Journal of Emerging Technologies in Learning, 4*(1), 23–28.

Gagné, F. (2005). From gifts to talents: The DMGT as a developmental model. In R. J. Sternberg and J. E. Davidson (Eds.), *Conceptions of giftedness* (2nd ed.) (pp. 98–119). New York: Cambridge University Press.

Renzulli, J. S. (2005). The Three-ring conception of giftedness: A developmental model for promoting creative productivity. In R. J. Sternberg and J. E. Davidson (Eds.), *Conceptions of giftedness* (2nd ed.) (pp. 246–279). New York: Cambridge University Press.

Renzulli, J. S., & Delcourt, M. A. B. (1986). The legacy and logic of research on the identification of gifted persons. *Gifted Child Quarterly, 30,* 20–23.

Robinson, N. M. (2005). In defense of a psychometric approach to the definition of academic giftedness. In R. J. Sternberg and J. E. Davidson (Eds.), *Conceptions of giftedness* (2nd ed.) (pp. 280–294). New York: Cambridge University Press.

Stanley, J. C. & Benbow, C. P. (1986). Youths who reason exceptionally well mathematically. In R. J. Sternberg and J. E. Davidson (Eds.), *Conceptions of giftedness* (pp. 361–387). New York: Cambridge University Press.

Sternberg, R. J. (1986). A triarchic theory of intellectual giftedness. In R. J. Sternberg and J. E. Davidson (Eds.), *Conceptions of giftedness* (pp. 223–243). New York: Cambridge University Press.

Tannenbaum, A. J. (1986). Giftedness: A psychosocial approach. In R. J. Sternberg and J. E. Davidson (Eds.), *Conceptions of giftedness* (pp. 21–52). New York: Cambridge University Press.

Walters, J. & Gardner, H. (1986). The crystallizing experience: Discovering an intellectual gift. In R. J. Sternberg and J. E. Davidson (Eds.), *Conceptions of giftedness* (pp. 306–331). New York: Cambridge University Press.

## APPENDIX B

## SRBCSS TRAINING ACTIVITY FOR TEACHERS: MATHEMATICS CHARACTERISTICS

**TASK No. 1:**   Individually, select the letter of a key concept that you believe most closely matches each item.
**TASK No. 2:**   In a small group, discuss specific examples of when you have observed each behavior in a student.

| Key Concepts | | |
|---|---|---|
| A. Multiple illustrations | E. Mental manipulation | H. Readily absorbs |
| B. Finds challenge pleasurable | F. Diverges from the ordinary | I. Strives to understand |
| C. Organizer | G. Variety of methods | J. Seeks solutions |
| D. Numeracy | | |

### The student . . .

1.   is eager to solve challenging math problems. (A problem is defined as a task for which the solution is not known in advance.)    _____

2.   organizes data and information to discover mathematical patterns.    _____

3.   enjoys challenging math puzzles, games, and logic problems.    _____

4.   understands new math concepts and processes more easily than other students.    _____

5.   has creative (unusual and divergent) ways of solving math problems.    _____

6.   displays a strong number sense (e.g., makes sense of large and small numbers, estimates easily and appropriately).    _____

7.   frequently solves math problems abstractly, without the need for manipulatives or concrete materials.    _____

8.   has an interest in analyzing the mathematical structure of a problem.    _____

9.   when solving a math problem, can switch strategies easily, if appropriate or necessary.    _____

10.  regularly uses a variety of representations to explain math concepts (written explanations, pictorial, graphic, equations, etc.).    _____

Answer Key

| | | |
|---|---|---|
| 1. J | 5. F | 9. G |
| 2. C | 6. D | 10. A |
| 3. B | 7. E | |
| 4. H | 8. I | |

## Appendix C

### Examples of Special Nomination Forms to Use for Multiple Criteria Identification

"Things My Child Likes To Do"

Cover Letter

To:        Parent/Guardian of _____

From:

Subject:    Things My Child Like To Do

One of the major goals of our overall school program is to provide each child with an opportunity to develop his or her individual strengths and creative thinking abilities. We also would like to provide your child with an opportunity to do some work in an area of study that is of personal interest to him or her. In other words, we would like to supplement our basic curriculum with experiences that are interesting, challenging, and enjoyable to individual children.

Although the work that your child does in school gives us many opportunities to observe his or her strengths and areas of interest, the activities that your children pursues at home can also help us to find ways for enriching his or her overall school program. For this reason, we are asking you to complete the attached questionnaire and return it to us at your earliest convenience.

The attached questionnaire contains 14 items. Each of the items deals with a general type of interest or activity that you may or may not have seen in your child. The interests or activities might be the results of school assignments, extracurricular, club activities such as Girl Scouts or 4-H Club projects or other activities in which your child has developed an interest. It will, of course, be very helpful if you can jot down specific examples of your child's interests or activities in the right-hand column of the questionnaire.

If you should have any questions about this questionnaire, please contact the person whose contact information is listed below. We very much appreciate your assistance is helping us to provide the very best possible educational program for your child.

*Note.* Items used in this instrument were originally developed as *Things My Child Likes to Do* by James R. Delisle, 1979, University of Connecticut, which was derived and adapted from *Scales for Rating the Behavioral Characteristics of Superior Students* by J. S. Renzulli, R. K. Hartman, and C. M. Callahan, as appeared in "Teacher identification of superior students," Exceptional Children, 1971, 38, 211–214, 243–248.

## "Things My Child Likes To Do"

Your Name_____ Child's Name _____

Child's Age _____ Child's School _____ Today's Date_____

| | Seldom or Never | Some-times | Quite Often | Almost Always | Example from your own child's life |
|---|---|---|---|---|---|
| 1.My child will spend more time and energy than his/her age-mates on a topics of his/her interest. | | | | | |
| 2. My child is a "self-starter" who works well alone, needing few directions and little supervision. | | | | | |
| 3. My child sets high personal goals and expects to see results from his/her work. | | | | | |
| 4. My child gets so involved with a project that (s)he gives up other pleasures in order to work on it. | | | | | |
| 5. My child continues to work on a project even when faced with temporary defeats and slow results. | | | | | |
| 6. While working on a project (and when it is finished), my child knows which parts are good and which parts need improvement. | | | | | |
| 7. My child is a "do-er" who begins a project and shows finished products of his/her work. | | | | | |
| 8. My child suggests imaginative ways of doing things, even if the suggestions are sometimes impractical. | | | | | |
| 9. When my child tells about something that is very unusual, (s)he expresses himself/ herself by elaborate gestures, pictures, or words. | | | | | |
| 10. My child uses common material in ways not typically expected. | | | | | |

*Note.* Items used in this instrument were originally developed as *Things My Child Likes to Do* by James R. Delisle, 1979, University of Connecticut, which was derived and adapted from *Scales for Rating the Behavioral Characteristics of Superior Students* by J. S. Renzulli, R. K. Hartman, and C. M. Callahan, as appeared in "Teacher identification of superior students," *Exceptional Children,* 1971, 38, 211–214, 243–248.

| | | | | | |
|---|---|---|---|---|---|
| 11. My child avoids typical ways of doing things, choosing instead to find new ways to approach a problem or topic. | | | | | |
| 12. My child likes to "play with ideas," often making up situations that probably will not occur. | | | | | |
| 13. My child finds humor in situations or events that are not obviously funny to most children his/her age. | | | | | |
| 14. My child prefers working or playing alone rather than doing something "just to go along with the group." | | | | | |

*Note.* Items used in this instrument were originally developed as *Things My Child Likes to Do* by James R. Delisle, 1979, University of Connecticut, which was derived and adapted from *Scales for Rating the Behavioral Characteristics of Superior Students* by J. S. Renzulli, R. K. Hartman, and C. M. Callahan, as appeared in "Teacher identification of superior students," Exceptional Children, 1971, 38, 211–214, 243–248.

Peer Referral Form – Anne Udall, copyright pending

Teacher's Name _____

I'm going to ask you to think of your classmates in a different way than you usually do. Read the questions below and try to think of which child in your class fits best each question. Think of the boys and girls, quiet kids and noisy kids, best friends and those with whom you don't usually play. You may only put down one name for each question. You may leave a space blank. You can use the same name for more than one question. You may not use your teacher's name or names of other adults. Please use first and last name. You do not have to put your name down on this form, so you can be completely honest.

1.  What boy OR girl learns quickly, but doesn't speak up in class very often?
    _____

2.  What girl OR boy will get interested in a project and spend extra time and take pride in his or her work?
    _____

3.  What boy OR girl is smart in school, but doesn't show off about it?
    _____

4.  What girl OR boy is really good at making up dances?
    _____

5.  What boy OR girl is really good at making up games?
    _____

6.  What girl OR boy is really good at making up music?
    _____

7.  What boy or girl is really good at making up stories?
    _____

8.  What girl OR boy is really good at making up pictures?
    _____

9.  What boy OR girl would you ask first if you needed any kind of help at school?
    _____

10. What girl OR boy would you ask to come to your house to help you work on a project? (Pretend that there would be someone to drive that person to your house).
    _____

Anne Udall, Vice President for Professional Development, Northwest Evaluation Association

**APPENDIX D: ACTION INFORMATION MESSAGE FORM**

ACTION INFORMATION MESSAGE

GENERAL
CURRICULUM AREA _____

ACTIVITY OR TOPIC _____

IN THE SPACE BELOW, PROVIDE A BRIEF DESCRIPTION OF THE INCIDENT OR SITUATION IN WHICH YOU OBSERVED HIGH LEVELS OF INTEREST, TASK COMMITMENT OR CREATIVITY ON THE PART OF A STUDENT OR SMALL GROUP OF STUDENTS. INDICATE ANY IDEAS YOU MAY HAVE FOR ADVANCED LEVEL FOLLOW-UP ACTIVITIES, SUGGESTED RESOURCES OR WAYS TO FOCUS THE INTEREST INTO A FIRST-HAND INVESTIGATIVE EXPERIENCE.

TO:

FROM:

DATE:

☐ PLEASE CONTACT ME.

☐ I WILL CONTACT YOU TO ARRANGE A MEETING.

J.S.R. '81

Received _____

of Interview
h Child _____

Child Was
volved in _____

Renulli, J. S., & Reis, S. M. (1997). *Schoolwide Enrichment Model.* Mansfield Center, CT: Creative Learning Press.

## CHAPTER 2 STUDY GUIDE

**Prompt 1** *Knowledge*

Explain in your own words how the identification system described in this chapter is consistent with the conception of giftedness also presented in this chapter.

**Prompt 2** *Opinion*

Explain why the first order of business for anyone seeking to serve gifted and talented students must be to decide on a conception of definition of giftedness.

**Prompt 3** *Affect*

This chapter presents six considerations in developing an identification system. Which of these have been especially well addressed or egregiously ignored in your school setting? What reactions did this cause among you and your colleagues?

**Prompt 4** *Experience*

Describe any experience you or a colleague has had with the innovation process presented in this chapter. Based on the experience described as well as the material in this chapter, explain why it is important to address all aspects of the innovation process.

**Prompt 5** *Preconception/Misconception*

Many people claim that excellence, equity, and economy cannot be achieved simultaneously. Yet Renzulli and Reis insist in this chapter that all three goals can be met through the identification system they have proposed. Explain how their system meets the three criteria

# MULTICULTURAL THEORY AND GIFTED EDUCATION: IMPLICATIONS FOR THE IDENTIFICATION OF TWO UNDERREPRESENTED GROUPS

DONNA Y. FORD, VANDERBILT UNIVERSITY

## GIFTED EDUCATION'S ALBATROSS: UNDERIDENTIFICATION AND UNDERREPRESENTATION

*A mind is a terrible thing to waste and erase.*

(Ford, 2010)

All of education is mired in controversy, tension, and contention to some degree or another. On a daily basis, policy makers and decision makers discuss and debate how best to educate students, especially low-performing students, who are disproportionately Black and Hispanic and, as such, culturally different from the *status quo*. As with special education overidentification and overrepresentation, few topics and issues are as polemical and entrenched as the underidentification and subsequent underrepresentation of Black and Hispanic students in gifted education. Every report and study on gifted education demographics reveals the disturbing finding that Black and Hispanic students are sorely underrepresented in gifted education.[1]

Underrepresentation has been our field's albatross. First and foremost, dating back perhaps to the scholarship of Martin Jenkins in the 1930s, every report and study has shown that Black students are underrepresented in gifted education by almost 50%, followed by Hispanic students (almost 40%). Ford, Grantham, and Whiting's (2008) review of the literature revealed that underreferrals by teachers and counselors, followed by testing and assessment issues, are the quintessential barriers. They contend that deficit thinking (racial stereotypes, prejudice, and discrimination) prevents educators from recognizing, appreciating, and validating the gifts and strengths of Black and Hispanic students.

For obvious reasons, underidentification and underrepresentation matter in the short and long run. Regardless of race and culture, students who are gifted but underidentified and inadequately served have a great(er) probability of becoming turned off —unmotivated and disengaged—which contributes to underachievement in a myriad ways (e.g., low grades, low test scores, poor participation,

---

1. While this chapter focuses on gifted education, the same issues are evident and prevalent in Advanced Placement (AP) classes.

poor attendance, dropping out) and the omnibus achievement gap (Ford, 2010, 2011b).

Relatedly and importantly, as most of our federal definitions of gifted have championed, gifted education is a need, not a privilege. Gifted students want and require an education that is responsive (i.e., understanding, affirming, and respectful) to their intelligence, academics, and creativity. Every educator and informed caregiver knows that when gifts are not identified and not nurtured, they atrophy (Ford, 2010, 2011b). For a large number and/or percentage of unidentified and unserved gifted students, underachievement and academic apathy is pervasive—and expected; these students suffer, as does the larger society, when their potential is unrecognized and denied. The cost—regardless of how it is defined, conceptualized, and calculated—is great.

However, the picture and outcomes do not have to remain bleak; there are a number of theories that offer information, guidance, and hope. Ford, Moore, and Trotman Scott (in press) and Ford and Trotman Scott (2010) present several theories and frameworks that help understand and change the underidentification/representation of Black students in gifted education. In this chapter, I focus on one theory in particular, primarily relying on the scholarship of James Banks.

This chapter presents an overview of central issues and barriers to Black and Hispanic representation in gifted education programs and is a clarion call to make changes, including the support and adoption of multicultural theory to both understand and eliminate underidentification and underrepresentation of gifted Black and Hispanic students. The chapter's underlying or guiding question is this: How can multicultural theory be used to efficaciously address the underidentification and underrepresentation of students who differ from the mainstream?

## GIFTED EDUCATION'S PERFECT STORM

In a recent report released by the Educational Testing Services, Kirwin, Braun, Yamamoto, and Sum (2009) discussed the notion of the "perfect storm" as it relates to forces impacting our nation's future and what places us at risk for implosion. A perfect storm is an expression that describes an event where a rare combination of circumstances drastically aggravates a situation, problem, and/or issue. In this chapter, this situation is the underidentification of Black and Hispanic students as gifted and their subsequent underrepresentation in gifted education. That is, I consider how underidentification and underrepresentation of Black and Hispanic students as gifted is influenced and aggravated or exacerbated by ever-changing student demographics, unchanging teacher/educator demographics, and theories and policies that are not only stagnant (resistant to change) but also acultural (i.e., void of culture, colorblind). Frankly, despite changes in the general student population, changes in gifted education classes/programs are not evident. This lack of change is unacceptable, indefensible, and potentially illegal. In this discussion of the twin and inseparable issues of underidentification and under-representation, I hone in on how multicultural education theory by James Banks informs underidentification and underrepresentation and, ideally or ultimately, holds promise for change—for understanding and reversing this long-standing national problem, our field's albatross and perfect storm.

## CIRCUMSTANCE ONE: CHANGING STUDENT DEMOGRAPHICS

To say that our nation is more culturally diverse[2] and different than ever before is no understatement or trivial fact. As the proverbial and idealized "land of opportunity," the United States may be the most culturally diverse *and* culturally different nation in the world. Depending on one's views about race and culture and about those whose background differs from our own, racial and attendant views and reactions to cultural differences offer either promise or peril. At present, too few individuals and groups, including students, appear to hold cultural differences in high regard. Instead, they frequently operate under colorblind and assimilationist perspectives. Yet, tensions between racial and cultural groups in schools, colleges, and communities are reported *ad nauseum* in the media, as well as in personal stories and narratives. Nationally, prejudice and discrimination, in the forms of hate crimes and racial profiling, are but two examples that are relevant to this chapter, but space limitations hinder the amount of attention that can be devoted to it.

U. S. census data from 2010 reveal that, within every region defined by the census and in a majority of the states, the population of school age children who are non-White or are racially different from populations in positions of power and privilege has increased in terms of both number and proportion. This trend has also been verified by the most recent data from the U. S. Department of Education (2011). As of 2009, public schools are made up of Asian and Pacific Islanders (4.9%), African-American/Blacks (16.5%), Hispanic/Latinos (21.4%), and American Indian/Alaska Natives (1.2%) (see U.S. Department of Education, 2011, Table A-3.2, p. 147). Conversely, White students in public schools are consistently on the decline (55.4% as of 2009). In 1989, White students were 67.9% of public school populations (p. 154). In addition to racial changes, data indicate that the percentage of students who speak a language other than English at home is 23.7%, reflecting a persistent increase and a trend that is expected to continue (see Table A-6-1, p. 162).

## CIRCUMSTANCE TWO: UNCHANGING EDUCATOR DEMOGRAPHICS

Changes in the racial demographics of our nation's public school is not mirrored in or reflected by teacher demographics. During the 2007-08 school year, White teachers represented about 85% of the teaching force. This percentage is similar to previous years, including 1999-2000 (U.S. Department of Education, 2011; see p. 92). In *Other People's Children*, Delpit (1995) argued that cultural differences between culturally different students and White teachers contribute to and maintain the achievement gap and their poor educational experiences and outcomes, especially for Black males and females. Cultural clashes and mismatches—prevalent in communication, values, attitudes, beliefs, and behavior—between White teachers and their culturally different students, chiefly given the aforementioned data, contribute to lower and negative expectations of Black

---

2. The terms *culturally different* and *diverse* are not used synonymously in this chapter. Every group has a culture, thus all of society and every classroom are culturally diverse. Instead, the fundamental issue is "cultural difference," which contributes to disharmony, misunderstanding, miscommunication, and so much more

and Hispanic students, even if they are gifted or high achieving.

Further, and directly related to this chapter, cultural mismatches must not and cannot be ignored as influencing underidentification (especially underreferral) and underrepresentation (Ford et al., 2008). Specifically, every study has demonstrated that teachers systematically and consistently underrefer Black students for gifted education identification and services; about half of studies reveal underreferral for Hispanic students. With this in mind, in many venues, I have argued and advocated for training in multicultural education so that educators working with gifted students become culturally competent. With such preparation (e.g., in college coursework and professional development), educators are less likely to engage in deficit thinking, which prevents them from having high and positive expectations for Black and Hispanic students (Ford, in press; Ford & Grantham, 2003). Multicultural education theory, described later, when implemented with integrity, can contribute significantly and meaningfully to the recruitment and retention of Black and Hispanic students in gifted education.

## CIRCUMSTANCE THREE: ACULTURAL THEORIES OF GIFTED

As important as demographics are, especially in setting the context for this chapter, this data alone does not and cannot adequately explain the poor presence of Black and Hispanic students in gifted education. A look at theories is essential. A number of theories of what it means to be "gifted" exist. Three popular ones were written during the 1980s (Gardner, 1985; Renzulli, 1986; Sternberg,

1988). I have supported and advocated for these theories in my work, as they appear to be the most culturally responsive. Their authors have been strong supporters of increasing access and equity in gifted education, continuously extolling educators to remove barriers and gatekeepers. Beyond their scholarship (e.g., instruments, publications, theories, programs), too few other theories in gifted education are culturally inclusive and responsive. Instead, they are frequently acultural—to wit, culture (attitudes, beliefs, values, customs and traditions) and cultural differences are treated as tangential, if considered at all in their development and application (Ford, 2010, 2011a).

One might ask why colorblindness or cultureblindness matters in the identification and representation of culturally different students. Theories are analytical tools for understanding, explaining, and making predictions about a given subject matter and population. They are useful for providing a model or framework for understanding thinking, emotions/feelings, decisions, and behaviors. Theories guide beliefs, decisions, practice, and policies. Thus, theories of gifted that are acultural/colorblind fail to shed light on giftedness and its manifestation among Black and other culturally different groups. As Sternberg (2007) asserted, what is deemed as and valued as gifted in one culture may not be valued and viewed as gifted in another culture. This begs the question of the appropriateness and utility of applying such theories to populations on whom they were not developed or normed or considered. In practice, these theories can contribute to educators failing to see and appreciate giftedness among traditionally underidentified students. Consider, for example, that language is one of the first characteristics or signs that teachers look for when considering who is gifted (or not). A Black and/or Hispanic student who is not proficient in English may be perceived as not having a strong vocabulary. For the Black student, his or her primary language might be African American English Vernacular; for the Hispanic student, it may be Spanglish. Neither may be bilingual, but they are fully capable of speaking traditional English with formal instruction. Another example is drawn from the voluminous research indicating the Hispanic and Black students often come from communal or collectivist cultures. They prefer working with others, helping others, socializing, and so forth. However, teachers may see them as not being independent and self-sufficient, which is often deemed to be another characteristic of being gifted. In Ford (2011b), dozens of other examples are shared, including a case study where the culture between a Black student and teacher clashes. This failure to recognize, understand, value, and respect cultural differences manifests itself in underreferral and perhaps even disbelief and disagreement when a Black or Hispanic student is successfully identified as gifted based on district and/or state criteria (Ford et al., 2008).

Just as important, acultural or colorblind theories contribute to practices that are often unfair and ineffective at challenging and changing underidentification. For instance, theories help to determine the (a) choice of tests and instruments for identification, (b) policies and procedures for labeling (referral, cutoff scores, selection criteria), and (c) programs and services options (e.g., pull-out classes, resource rooms, gifted education centers, self-contained classrooms).

## WHERE DO WE GO FROM HERE? MULTICULTURAL THEORY AS ONE WAY TO ADDRESS UNDERIDENTIFICATION AND UNDERREPRESENTATION

Multiculturalism grew out of the desegregation era and civil rights struggles of the 1960s and is a response to the changing demographics of our nation, as described earlier. With *Brown v. Board of Education of Topeka* in 1954 and the *Civil Rights Act of 1964,* discrimination and segregation in schools was legally prohibited. In particular, Title VI of the 1964 Civil Rights Act prohibits discrimination in schools: "no person in the United States shall, on the ground of race, color, or national origin, be excluded from participation in, be denied the benefits of, or be subjected to discrimination under any program or activity receiving federal financial assistance" (Public Law 82-352 [78 Stat. 241]). This includes gifted education, which are the most racially and culturally homogeneous programs in our schools; they represent a form of *de facto* segregation. Clearly, they must become desegregated and integrated.

More than ever before, educators are confronted with the important and necessary task of addressing the educational and achievement issues and needs of a very culturally different student population. Practices traditionally and/or consistently found to be efficacious with middle class White students may not be appropriate and useful with other racial and cultural groups. James Banks (e.g., 1999, 2008; Banks et al., 2010), a leader and the father of multicultural education, contends that multicultural education plays a momentous and non-negotiable role in creating a more democratic and equitable society, a nation that lives up to the promise of being the land of opportunity for all. He states that an important goal of the schools should be to forge a common nation and destiny from our tremendous cultural and language diversity and associated differences. To forge a common destiny, educators must respect and build upon the cultural strengths and characteristics that students from different racial and cultural groups bring to school and the (gifted) educational enterprise.

Founded in 1991, the National Association for Multicultural Education (NAME) was created to formally recognize, promote, and advance this culturally-grounded educational field. Their definition of multicultural education (National Association for Multicultural Education, 2003) is presented in Table 1. A sample of key tenets includes:

- Principles and Values. "Multicultural education is a philosophical concept built on the ideals of freedom, justice, equality, equity, and human dignity as acknowledged in various documents . . . It affirms our need to prepare students for their responsibilities in an interdependent world. It recognizes the role schools can play in developing the attitudes and values necessary" for a democratic and equitable school and larger society (National Association for Multicultural Education, 2003).

- Cultural Differences: Multicultural education theory presents a balance between understanding cultural similarities and differences *and* encouraging and supporting individuals to maintain and broaden their own culture and cultural perspectives.

Multiculturalism "values cultural differences and affirms the pluralism that students, their families, their communities, and teachers reflect" (National Association for Multicultural Education, 2003).

- Social Justice and Antidiscrimination: Multicultural education theory holds at its core the principle of eradicating racial and cultural stereotypes. Multiculturalism confronts and challenges all forms of discrimination in schools and society through the promotion of democratic principles of equity and social justice. Teachers and students must critically analyze oppression, privilege, and power relations in their classrooms, schools, communities, and the larger society (National Association for Multicultural Education, 2003).

- Equitable Educational Opportunity: Recognizing that equality and equity are not the same thing, multicultural education theory endeavors to offer all students an equitable educational opportunity. This aspect is in line with Horace Mann's (1848, 1935) notion that education is the great equalizer[3] and Carter G. Woodson's (1939/1990) major concern and diatribe that Blacks have been (and continue to be) miseducated. The American Library Association presents a brief and informative discussion of the difference between

---

3. More specifically, Horace Mann stated that education, beyond all other devices of human origin, is the great equalizer of the conditions of men, the balance wheel of the social machinery.

Table 1. National Association for Multicultural Education Definition of Multicultural Education. (National Association for Multicultural Education [2003]).

**DEFINITION OF MULTICULTURAL EDUCATION**

Multicultural education is a philosophical concept built on the ideals of freedom, justice, equality, equity, and human dignity as acknowledged in various documents, such as the U.S. Declaration of Independence, constitutions of South Africa and the United States, and the Universal Declaration of Human Rights adopted by the United Nations. It affirms our need to prepare student for their responsibilities in an interdependent world. It recognizes the role schools can play in developing the attitudes and values necessary for a democratic society. It values cultural differences and affirms the pluralism that students, their communities, and teachers reflect. It challenges all forms of discrimination in schools and society through the promotion of democratic principles of social justice.

Multicultural education is a process that permeates all aspects of school practices, policies and organization as a means to ensure the highest levels of academic achievement for all students. It helps students develop a positive self-concept by providing knowledge about the histories, cultures, and contributions of diverse groups. It prepares all students to work actively toward structural equality in organizations and institutions by providing the knowledge, dispositions, and skills for the redistribution of power and income among diverse groups. Thus, school curriculum must directly address issues of racism, sexism, classism, linguicism, ablism, ageism, heterosexism, religious intolerance, and xenophobia.

Multicultural education advocates the belief that students and their life histories and experiences should be placed at the center of the teaching and learning process and that pedagogy should occur in a context that is familiar to students and that addresses multiple ways of thinking. In addition, teachers and students must critically analyze oppression and power relations in their communities, society and the world.

To accomplish these goals, multicultural education demands a school staff that is culturally competent, and to the greatest extent possible racially, culturally, and linguistically diverse. Staff must be multiculturally literate and capable of including and embracing families and communities to create an environment that is supportive of multiple perspectives, experiences, and democracy. Multicultural education requires comprehensive school reform as multicultural education must pervade all aspects of the school community and organization.

Recognizing that equality and equity are not the same thing, multicultural education attempts to offer all students an equitable educational opportunity, while at the same time, encouraging students to critique society in the interest of social justice.

"equity" and "equality."[4] These terms and notions are similar but also so very different.

- Curricular Infusion: "Multicultural education is a process that permeates all aspects of school practices, policies and organization as a means to ensure the highest levels of [rigor and] academic achievement for all students. . . . school curriculum must directly address" "isms"—racism, sexism, classism, linguicism, ablism, ageism, heterosexism—as well as religious intolerance and xenophobia (National Association for Multicultural Education, 2003). This type of education is based on the assumption that there is no single correct interpretation of events and history. Instead, curriculum achieves relevance by stressing comparative analysis through different cultural viewpoints and experiences.

- Self-Image: Multicultural theory helps racially and culturally different students develop a positive self-image (i.e., self-concept, self-esteem, racial identity) by providing substantive knowledge about the histories, cultures, accomplishments, and resilience of racially and culturally different individuals and groups (National Association for Multicultural Education, 2003. The enhanced self-image is not colorblind; it focuses on racial identity and pride. Multicultural theory also lets White students know, appreciate, revere, and value the reality that other racial groups

have played a pivotal role in our nation's history *and* their lives.

In an interesting body of work, Kincheloe and Steinberg (1997) presented a taxonomy of multiculturalism and multicultural education ranging from conservative multiculturalism to critical multiculturalism (see Table 2). The typology reminds us that views about culture and culturally different students and groups vary. There is no definitive theory of multiculturalism. Each type is not just about beliefs and assumptions, but also responses to differences. The most rigorous type is critical multiculturalism, where I place Banks' theory.

## JAMES BANKS' THEORY OF MULTICULTURAL EDUCATION: IMPLICATIONS FOR IMPROVING IDENTIFICATION AND REPRESENTATION

*If Americans are to embrace diversity, the conscious and unconscious expressions of racism within our society must be identified and done away with.*
(Hilliard & Pine, 1990, p. 7).

As just noted, multicultural education is an idea and an ideal, an educational reform movement, and a process (Banks, 1999, 2008). As both an idea and ideal, multicultural education seeks to create equitable educational opportunities for all students, not just those from different racial, cultural, and social class groups. Multicultural education endeavors to create equitable educational opportunities for all students by changing the total school environment so that it will reflect the variety of cultures and groups in a society and in our nation's classrooms. Multicultural education is a process because its goals are ideals that teach-

4. See http://www.ala.org/ala/aboutala/offices/oif/iftoolkits/toolkitrelatedlinks/equalityequity.cfm

**Table 2.** Kincheloe and Steinberg's Taxonomy of Multiculturalism and Multicultural Education. (Adapted from http://en.wikipedia.org/wiki/Multicultural_education)

| TYPES AND DIMENSIONS OF MULTICULTURAL EDUCATION | SAMPLE OF PRIMARY ASSUMPTIONS |
|---|---|
| **CONSERVATIVE MULTICULTURALISM** | 1. Low-performing students and their families from culturally different backgrounds blamed for their poor performance.<br>2. White culture and standards are the norm. Whiteness is not included in notions of culture—it is an invisible barometer of normality.<br>3. Content of curriculum is decided by the dominant culture. Intelligence and achievement tests used uncritically to measure students' acquisition of academic content and student cognitive ability.<br>4. Culturally different groups are studied as add-ons to the dominant culture, outsiders who must assimilate.<br>5. The existing social order is fair and equitable. |
| **LIBERAL MULTICULTURALISM** | 1. Multicultural education should be based on a notion of "sameness" or colorblindness. Everyone is the same.<br>2. Racial inequality exists because of a lack of or differences in the opportunity structure.<br>3. Abstract individualism is central to Western social organization -- all humans can succeed with hard work and if given a chance or opportunities; we are free agents responsible for our own success or failure. Fails to consider covert forms of racism and norms devised around dominant cultural values.<br>4. Multicultural curriculum is safe and trivial (e.g., foods, celebrations) with little integration of the curriculum. Studies of racism and other injustices are viewed as divisive.<br>5. Whiteness viewed and valued as the norm. |
| **PLURALIST MULTICULTURALISM** | 1. Shares numerous features with liberal multiculturalism, but it focuses more on difference and tougher issues than liberal multiculturalism.<br>2. Still de-contextualized in that it fails to problematize whiteness and norms of the dominant group.<br>3. Recognizes that despite laws, social injustices exist and education should address stereotypes and prejudices.<br>4. Race and ethnicity (unlike class and sexism) viewed as private matters, with little connection to the larger and complicated/complex structures of patriarchy, classism, and white privilege and supremacy.<br>5. Curriculum involves learning about the "other"—their knowledge, values, beliefs, and patterns of behavior—rather than about self as a cultural being. Cultural tourism is common.<br>6. Education should promote cultural pride and identity. |

Table 2 continued.

| LEFT-ESSENTIALIST MULTICULTURALISM | 1. Cultural differences are central to multiculturalism. Racial groups possess a specific and even unique set of cultural characteristics. <br> 2. Cultural differences are often romanticized and exoticized in ways that position "difference" in a distant past of social/cultural authenticity. This process removes various groups from history, culture, and power relations, keeping them fixated in a primeval past. Contemporariness is lacking. <br> 3. Political correctness disrupts honesty, change, and progress in the curriculum and interchanges. <br> 4. The curricula invert traditional stereotypes and truth claims, resulting in a multicultural education that, as moralistic reductionism, fails to understand and address the subtlety of racism and injustices. <br> 5. Subjugated knowledge is important in this context, but it is often romanticized as a pure manifestation of natural truth. In this way, it can be passed along as a new authoritarian canon. <br> 6. Cultural knowledge from their viewpoint of racially and culturally different groups needs to be studied as both separate and integrated phenomena— separate from white, male, middle/upper class, and heterosexual experience and yet inseparable from them at the same time. |
|---|---|
| CRITICAL MULTICULTURALISM | 1. Problems, realities, and representations of race, class, gender, and sexuality are grounded in larger complex/complicated social issues, events, and struggles. <br> 2. A multicultural curriculum is part of a larger effort to transform the social, cultural, and institutional structures that generate these representations and perpetuate oppression. <br> 3. Race, class, gender, sexual differences exist in the context of power and privilege that favors Whites. <br> 4. Justice already exists but needs to be distributed more equitably. <br> 5. Progress can be realized in the cultivation of critical thinking, ethical/moral reasoning, and problem solving. <br> 6. A homogeneous community grounded on consensus (e.g., one view point) is less able to criticize the injustice and exclusionary practices that undermine it. <br> 7. Cultural clashes and pathology often come from recognizing difference but not interactions with individuals who are different and oppressed. <br> 8. Multicultural education is based on a respect for differences; social groups are listened to—their perspectives, values, and experience. <br> 9. The lives and experiences of different groups are interconnected such that we are all accountable to each other. <br> 10. Multiple traditions of knowledge must be acknowledged and taught. <br> 11. Multicultural curriculum explores the social construction of whiteness and effects of whiteness should be critically examined; thus, the curriculum is changed in significant ways; students learn about themselves and others. <br> 12. Whites' experience must be problematized as the 'norm' or standard of truth, health, right, etc.; it must not remain the invisible standard by which other cultural groups are measured. |

ers and administrators must constantly strive to achieve. Below, I describe and expound on Banks' dimensions of multicultural education (see Ford, 2011b for an extensive treatise)

Fundamentally, multicultural education supports the belief that students' backgrounds and experiences must be the center of their education. According to Banks (1999, 2008), multicultural education is a means to ensure the highest levels of academic achievement for all students. In other words, multicultural education promotes ethical and equitable decision making and critical thinking, while moving toward cultural pluralism. As described next, in the larger scheme, Banks' multicultural theory endeavors to substantially reform schools and the context for learning and achieving.

## BANKS' DIMENSIONS OF MULTICULTURAL EDUCATION

Banks' five dimension of multicultural education are (1) content integration, (2) the knowledge construction process, (3) prejudice reduction, (4) an equity pedagogy, and (5) an empowering school culture and social structure (Banks, 1995a, 2008; Ravitch, 1990). *Content integration* concerns the extent to which teachers use examples and content from a variety of cultures to illustrate key ideas, concepts, generalizations, and issues within their content or subject areas and disciplines. It is a virtually uncontested truth that when the curriculum is personally relevant and meaningful, students' interest and engagement increase. Worded differently and applied through a cultural lens, culturally different students have been found to psychologically and physically dropout of school

when it is personally and culturally irrelevant and disconnected from their lives and immediate community and from real-world issues (Bridgeland, Dilulio, & Morison, 2006). This applies particularly to gifted Black students, many of whom have expressed greater interest in school when it is multicultural and, thus, more interesting and relevant (Ford, 2010; Ford, in press; Harmon, 2002). This increased engagement maintains and/or improves learning, which results in higher achievement and outcomes (e.g., grades, test scores, attendance, participation, motivation). With higher performance and a demeanor or persona of interest and motivation, more Black and Hispanic students may be referred by their teachers for screening, identified as gifted, and receive services. Of course, teachers and other educators who have received formal and comprehensive preparation in multicultural education are better equipped to implement all of what this dimension entails by infusing high quality multicultural content into the curriculum.

The *knowledge construction process* describes how teachers help *all* students to understand, investigate, and interrogate how biases, frames of reference, and perspectives affect how knowledge is constructed, validated, and utilized. Students are empowered—they learn how to build knowledge in this dimension (Banks, 1996, 1999, 2008). Gifted students, who are frequently inquisitive and independent or self-sufficient learners, thrive in classrooms that challenge their mindsets and thinking; they thrive in classrooms that value and promote critical thinking.

When students are gifted and culturally different, educators must address their academic and cultural interests and needs through the dual lens of rigor and relevance. The Bloom-Banks model, created by Ford and Harris (1999) and updated by Ford (2011b), presents sample lesson plans that are high level in multicultural content *and* high level in critical thinking. Essentially, when the curriculum interrogates mainstream ideas and concepts—for example, using multicultural materials and content—culturally different students are more likely to be academically invested, to participate more and ask more questions. Such investment is likely to increase teachers' expectations of them. It makes sense that when the curriculum is multicultural, when students read and learn about their own racial group and heritage, they will be more interested in what is taught. With interests come higher achievement; with higher achievement, educators will likely increase their expectations of Black and Hispanic students.

*Prejudice reduction,* the third dimension, describes lessons and activities teachers use to help all students develop positive attitudes toward those who are different from them racially and culturally. This dimension is designed to reduce stereotypes, prejudice, and discrimination. I believe that the goal should not be prejudice reduction but rather prevention and elimination (Allport, 1954; Dovidio, & Gaertner, 2000; Dovidio, Glick, & Rudman, 2005; Merton, 1968).

Lessons and teaching materials that include content about different racial and cultural groups help gifted students to develop more positive inter-group attitudes, behaviors, and relations. This change is most likely to take place when positive images of different or non-traditional groups are in the materials and when multicultural materials are used in a consistent and sequential way (Banks, 1995b, 2008; Ford, in press). Prejudice reduction (and prevention and elimination) fosters classroom and school harmony. It creates, reinforces, and values a sense of community in which every student feels safe, is a valued, and believes that he or she is welcomed and an invaluable class member. Thus, students from all backgrounds work in a cooperative, communal spirit in which differences are recognized, valued, and respected.

This dimension's focus on reducing prejudiced attitudes and behaviors can inform and assist with both the recruitment and retention of Black and Hispanic students in gifted education classrooms. Specifically, as I have written and kvetched about in a number of venues, these two student groups repeatedly feel lonely, alienated, and isolated in predominantly White gifted classes and activities. Believing that they may be "the only one" or an anomaly, Black students have refused to enroll in gifted education classes and services, or once enrolled, they may refuse to stay (Davis, 2010; Ford, 2010). However, it is possible to be "the only one" or one of few Black and Hispanic gifted students and still feel a sense of belonging when he or she has positive, supportive relationships with White classmates and educators.

As both professionals and adults, teachers must also work on reducing their stereotypes and prejudices, which will improve their expectations and referrals of Black and Hispanic students for gifted education. When professional development and courses in higher education focus on recognizing biases and prejudice reduction and elimination, educators learn more about stereotypes, biases, and discriminations in themselves and others, as well as in curriculum and instruction (Ford, in press). Here, educators strive to abolish stereotypes and injustices in order to be culturally competent with their students.

An *equity pedagogy* exists when teachers modify their teaching or instructional styles to facilitate the academic achievement of students from different racial and cultural groups (Banks & Banks, 1995; Banks et al., 2010). For example, the academic achievement of African-American and Hispanic students has been shown to improve when cooperative teaching activities and strategies, rather than competitive ones, are used in instruction. Boykin's Afro-centric cultural style model, based on a number of studies, demonstrates the importance of matching teaching and culturally-based learning styles (Boykin, 1986; Boykin, Tyler, & Miller, 2005). Teachers who understand, respect, and teach to the vervistic (i.e., energetic, lively, enthusiastic, and movement-oriented), verbally-oriented, and communal learning styles, preferences, and needs of many Black students are likely to increase students' engagement, confidence, learning, and achievement (Ford, 2011a and 2011b; Ladson-Billings, 2009; Shade, Kelly, & Oberg, 1997). Adding more social and group activities and implementing a family environment are just two ways to address the communal orientations of Black and Hispanic students. Using tactile and kinesthetic activities will be responsive to verve and movement orientations. And adding debates, speeches, and other oral strategies adapts to the strong oral tradition of African Americans. All too often, to the untrained eye and mind, learning differences are viewed as learning deficits! Educators do not recognize and appreciate the

styles of Hispanic and Black students, resulting in underreferral. As with the previous examples, I am convinced that improved student engagement, relevance, and performance can contribute to higher teacher expectations, increased identification, and reduced underrepresentation in gifted programs.

The final dimension, an *empowering school culture and social structure,* develops when the culture and organization of the school are transformed to enable students from different racial and cultural groups to experience equity in social status and education, which includes access to gifted education. Its implementation consists of attention to (a) the attitudes, beliefs, practices, and behaviors of teachers and administrators to eliminate deficit thinking and practices (Valencia, 2010); (b) the curriculum and course of study (Ford, 2010, 2011b); (c) assessment and testing procedures (e.g., Naglieri & Ford, 2003); and (d) the teaching styles and strategies used by teachers (Boykin, 1986; Boykin et al., 2005). The school culture, however, cannot change unless teachers, counselors, psychologists, and administrators (all educators) get formal, on-going, and substantive preparation to become culturally competent. This preparation can be in the form of courses and professional development. Preparation to become culturally competent eliminates both individual and institutional racism, be they intentional or unintentional (Allport, 1954; Dovidio, Glick, & Rudman, 2005; Merton, 1968), that pose barriers to accessing gifted education (and AP classes) for Black and Hispanic students.

## SUMMARY

*Multicultural education is for all children, not just for African-American and Hispanic students.*

While Banks' multicultural education theory (dimensions and curricular infusion model) is often discussed in the context of K–12 school settings, specifically with curriculum, his theory has broader utility in discussions of gifted underidentification and underrepresentation, as demonstrated in this chapter and by Ford (2011b).

For education to be multicultural education and responsive to Black and Hispanic students and to achieve its equity-minded purposes for such students, along with their caregivers, teachers, administrators, and the larger community, there must be (1) a learning environment that supports positive interracial contact, (2) a rigorous multicultural education (curriculum and instruction), (3) positive and high teacher/educator expectations, (4) unwavering administrative support, and (5) continuous and in-depth courses and professional development. As Leibowitz, Bozalek, Rohleder, Carolissen, and Swartz (2010) asserted, this training may be uncomfortable and may need to be uncomfortable, but a pedagogy of discomfort can be effective at moving us out of complacency and colorblindnesss/cultureblindness to proactively, efficaciously, and equitably address real students, real issues, real problems, and real needs. The need to be culturally responsive in curriculum, instruction, and assessment is real—and long overdue.

Black and Hispanic students are victims of benign neglect. They are seldom deemed gifted, and their gifts and talents are often unrecognized, misunderstood, and devalued. Educators can tinker with referral and identification criteria, which is too commonplace. However, the meaningful and necessary goal of desegregating gifted education must be more serious, proactive, and deliberate. Eliminating de facto segregation will consist of bucking the status quo and taking risks to bring about change—that is, to stop doing business as usual. Cosmetic changes to identification procedures (e.g., using different cut-offs, criteria, and/or tests) will never solve the problem of underidentification and underrepresentation in gifted education programs and AP classes. Ultimately, what is required is a change in belief and value systems and the practices that ensue from those belief and value systems. It is so very clear that past and current practices have been futile as Black students and Hispanic students are inequitably represented in gifted education (and AP classes). And too little has changed, perhaps due to an allegiance to and/or ignorance of culture and cultural differences by educators in gifted education. Our students have changed; we must change; our current practices, which have clearly been ineffective, must change. Multicultural theory holds much promise for facilitating the equitable identification and representation of Hispanic and Black students in gifted education.

## REFERENCES

Allport, G. (1954). *The nature of prejudice*. Reading, MA: Addison-Wesley.

Banks, J. A. (1995a). Multicultural education: Historical development, dimensions, and practice. In J. A. Banks & C. A. M. Banks (Eds.). *Handbook of research on multicultural education* (pp. 3–24). New York: Macmillan.

Banks, J. A. (1995b). Multicultural education: Its effects on students' racial and gender role attitudes. In J. A. Banks & C. A. M. Banks (Eds.). *Handbook of research on multicultural education* (pp. 617–627). New York: Macmillan.

Banks, J. A. (Ed.). (1996). *Multicultural education, transformative knowledge and action*. New York: Teachers College Press.

Banks, J. A. (1999). *An introduction to multicultural education* (2nd ed.). Boston: Allyn and Bacon.

Banks, J. A. (2008). *An introduction to multicultural education* (4th ed.). Boston: Ally and Bacon.

Banks, C.A.M. & Banks, J. A. (1995). Equity pedagogy: An essential component of multicultural education. *Theory Into Practice, 34* (3), 151–158.

Banks, J. A., Cookson, P., Gay, G., Hawley, W. D., Irvine, J. J., Nieto, S., Schofield, J. W., & Campbell, D. E. (2010). *Choosing democracy: A practical guide to multicultural education* (4th ed.). Boston: Allyn and Bacon.

Boykin, A. W. (1986). The triple quandary and the schooling of Afro-American children. In U. Neisser (Ed.), *The school achievement of minority children*. Hillsdale, NJ, Lawrence Erlbaum Associates: 57–91.

Boykin, A. W., Tyler, K. M., & Miller, O. A. (2005). In search of cultural themes and their expressions in the dynamics of classroom life. *Urban Education, 40*, 521–549.

Bridgeland, J. M., Dilulio Jr., J. J., & Morison, K. B. (2006). *Perspectives of high school dropouts*. Washington, DC: Gates Foundation.

Davis, J. A. (2010). *Bright, talented, & Black: A guide for families of African American gifted learners*. Tempe, AZ: Gifted Potential Press.

Delpit, L. (1995). *Other people's children*. New York: The New Press.

Dovidio, J. F., & Gaertner, S. L. (2000). Aversive racism and selection decisions. *Psychological Science 11*(4), 315–319.

Dovidio, J. F., Glick, P. G., & Rudman, L. (Eds.). (2005). *On the nature of prejudice: Fifty years after Allport*. Malden, MA: Blackwell.

Ford, D. Y. (in press). *Multicultural gifted education: Rationale, models, strategies, and resources* (2nd ed.). Waco, TX: Prufrock Press.

Ford, D. Y. (2010). *Reversing underachievement among gifted Black students: Theory, research and practice* (2nd ed.). Waco, TX: Prufrock Press.

Ford, D. Y. (2011a). Closing the achievement gap: Gifted education must join the battle. *Gifted Child Today, 31*(1), 31–35.

Ford, D. Y. (2011b). *Multicultural gifted education*. (2nd ed.). Waco, TX: Prufrock Press.

Ford, D. Y., Grantham, T. C., & Whiting, G. W. (2008). Culturally and linguistically diverse students in gifted education: Recruitment

and retention issues. *Exceptional Children,
74*(3), 289–308.

Ford, D. Y., & Harris III, J. J. (1999). *Multicultural gifted education.* New York: Teachers College Press.

Ford, D. Y., Moore III, J. L., & Trotman Scott, M. (in press). Key theories and frameworks for improving the recruitment and retention of African American students in gifted education. *Journal of Negro Education.*

Ford, D. Y., & Trotman Scott, M. (2010). Under-representation of African American students in gifted education: Nine theories and frameworks for information, understanding, and change. *Gifted Education Press Quarterly, 24*(3), 2–6.

Gardner, H. (1983). *Frames of mind: The theory of multiple intelligences.* New York: Basic Books.

Harmon, D. A. (2002). They won't teach me: The voices of gifted African American inner-city students. *Roeper Review, 24,* 68–75.

Hilliard, A., & Pine, G. (1990, April). Rx for racism: Imperatives for American's schools. *Phi Delta Kappan,* 1–7.

Kincheloe, J., & Steinberg, S. (1997). *Changing multiculturalism.* London: Open University Press.

Kirwin, I., Braun, H., Yamamoto, K., & Sum, K (2009). *A perfect storm: Three changes facing our nation's future.* Princeton, NJ: Educational Testing Service.

Ladson-Billings, G. (2009). *Dreamkeepers: Successful teachers for African-American children.* San Francisco, CA, Jossey Bass.

Leibowitz, B., Bozalek, V., Rohleder, P., Carolissen, R., & Swartz, L. (2010). "Ah, but the whiteys love to talk about themselves": Discomfort as a pedagogy for change. *Race, Ethnicity and Education. 13*(1), 83-100.

Mann, H. (1848). Twelfth annual report of Horace Mann as Secretary of Massachusetts State Board of Education. Retrieved on September 6, 2011, from http://www.tncrimlaw.com/civil_bible/horace_mann.htm

Mann, H. (1935). The Curriculum and the Negro child. *Journal of Negro Education, 4*(2) p. 163.

Merton, R. K. (1968). *Social theory and social structure.* New York: The Free Press

Naglieri, J. A., & Ford, D. Y. (2003). Addressing under-representation of gifted minority children using the Naglieri Nonverbal Ability Test (NNAT). *Gifted Child Quarterly, 47,* 155-160.

National Association for Multicultural Education. (2003). *Definition of multicultural education.* Retrieved September 4, 2011, from http://nameorg.org/position-statements/

National Education Association. (2000). Walk the talk. *NEA Today, 18*(8), 1-3.

Public Law 82-352 (78 Stat. 241).

Ravitch, D. (1990). Multiculturalism: E Pluribus Plures, *American Scholar, 59*(3), 337-354.

Renzulli, J. S. (1986). The three-ring conception of giftedness: A developmental model for creative productivity. In R. J. Sternberg & J. E. Davidson (Eds.). *Conceptions of giftedness,* (pp. 53-92). New York: Cambridge University Press:

Shade, B. J., Kelly, C., & Oberg, M. (1997). *Creating culturally responsive classrooms.* Washington, DC: American Psychological Association.

Sternberg, R. J. (1988) *The triarchic mind: A new theory of human intelligence.* New York: Penguin.

Sternberg, R. J. (2007). Cultural concepts of gifted. *Roeper Review, 29*(3), 160-165.

United States Census Bureau. (2010). 2010 census data. Retrieved from http://2010.census.gov/2010census/data/

United States Department of Education. (2010). Condition of Education 2011. Washington, DC: Author.

Valencia, R. R. (2010). *Dismantling contemporary deficit thinking: Educational thought and practice.* New York: Routledge.

Woodson, C. G. (1933/1990). *The mis-education of the Negro.* Trenton, NJ: Africa World Press.

## Chapter 3 Study Guide

**Prompt 1** *Knowledge*

Summarize in your own words the five dimensions of multicultural education posited by Banks.

**Prompt 2** *Opinion*

Drawing from any of the explanations of multicultural education presented in this chapter, what aspect or aspects of multicultural education seem most essential to you to affect a change in the way students are identified as gifted?

**Prompt 3** *Affect*

The author of this chapter clearly feels both frustration and hope when faced with the current underrepresentation of Black and Hispanic students in gifted programs. Which feeling seems to dominate the author's affect in this chapter? Which feeling dominates your affect as you consider the issues raised?

**Prompt 4** *Experience*

Describe the experience you have had with each of the three circumstances described by Ford that contributes to the *perfect storm* gifted education now faces.

**Prompt 5** *Preconception/Misconception*

Some educators believe that acting in an acultural (i.e., void of culture, colorblind) manner will ameliorate issues related to diversity in schools, such as the underrepresentation of Black and Hispanic students. Why would this attitude make it difficult or not for educators to play an important role in forging a common destiny for our nation from its tremendous diversity?

# CHAPTER 4

# CHARACTERISTICS OF GIFTED CHILDREN AS A GUIDE TO IDENTIFICATION

SALLY KRISEL, HALL COUNTY SCHOOLS & THE UNIVERSITY OF GEORGIA

Throughout history there has been curiosity about and interest in those whom societies have deemed "gifted." Ancient Romans selected their most promising leaders and soldiers very early in their lives and provided them with specialized schooling. How were those gifted young statesmen and fighters selected? Standardized tests? No, surely the Roman nobles and teachers observed qualities in those young boys that suggested great promise; educational decision makers recognized exceptional traits and behaviors in some children, and they provided advanced training to further develop those aptitudes. It was ancient Rome's version of gifted education.

But cultures varied in their beliefs about exceptional ability and times changed. Ancient Greeks and medieval Europeans believed that great intellect was a divine gift that enabled one to understand great truths about the universe. As interest in science flourished in the 19th century, Sir Francis Galton concluded that heredity was the prime determinant of genius (Tannenbaum, 1983).

Just as cultures and the talent areas valued by those cultures have changed, so have the prevailing theories regarding the nature and development of giftedness—and so, too, have the prevailing practices used to identify gifted children. We will examine both here and consider implications for adopting identification practices that are theoretically sound, equitable, and that can guide the development of appropriately challenging instruction for students with gifts and talents.

## GIFTEDNESS THEORY

It should be noted that, even today, there is no singular, generally accepted "theory of giftedness." Instead, there are many concepts, all of which attest to an increasingly complex understanding of extraordinary human potential, that is, giftedness as a multifaceted phenomenon that includes both cognitive and affective qualities and is influenced by both social and psychological contexts.

These modern theories have roots, of course, in earlier traditions that over time proved to be inadequate. In some cases, identification procedures based on traditional theories of intelligence failed to provide a sense of predictive validity. Also, there was a growing awareness that (a) these more limited conceptions of

75

giftedness—and the resultant procedures used to place children in gifted programs—failed to assess the skills, knowledge and/or aptitudes possessed by significant numbers of potentially gifted individuals, and (b) these overlooked individuals were disproportionately members of minority groups and/or were economically disadvantaged or of limited English proficiency. As theorists and practitioners worked to resolve these problems with earlier conceptions of giftedness, our understanding of the phenomenon became richer.

## THE TRADITIONAL PARADIGM

No conception of giftedness has been as pervasive as the one proposed by Lewis Terman in the 1920s. His longitudinal studies of high IQ subjects had a profound and lasting influence on both educators and the general public. The landmark studies, along with Terman's work in developing the *Stanford Binet Intelligence Scale*, led to a popular concept of giftedness and adoption of assessment techniques that dominated the field of gifted education for most of the 20th century.

Even though Binet's test was never designed to assess a person's absolute "giftedness," many psychologists began assuming that this is what the tests were really measuring. There was confusion in the field of psychology in the early to mid-1900s about the meaning of IQ scores, or mental ability test scores in general. Harvard psychologist E. G. Boring, in an effort to define the term *intelligence*, famously announced in 1923 that intelligence is whatever is measured by intelligence tests (Boring, 1923, p. 35).

It is no wonder that educators followed suit in the over-interpretation and attachment of meaning

to the scores obtained on such tests. By defining exceptional ability solely in terms of the types of verbal, figural, and quantitative reasoning assessed by the *Stanford Binet*, Terman set the stage for the enduring use of standardized intelligence tests as the preferred measure of giftedness (Jenkins-Friedman, 1982).

As Terman followed his 1300 subjects into adulthood, however, he had to admit that intellect (as measured by the *Stanford Binet*) and later life accomplishments were "far from perfectly correlated" (Terman, cited in Barbe & Renzulli, 1975, p. 19). Clearly there were other abilities that predicted professional attainment at least as well as the intellectual abilities measured by standardized tests.

If standardized tests of mental ability and academic achievement were not reliable predictors of extraordinary accomplishments later in life, what then did they tell us about children? By the 1970s the limitations of these standardized measures in the identification process were clear. In the upper score ranges, standardized tests of aptitude and achievement simply predict the scores on similar tests (Wallach, 1976). They also correlate well with grades (Munday & Davis, 1974), but they fail to identify individuals who are most successful once they leave the school learning environment. Since the concept of giftedness must look beyond the schoolhouse door, identification procedures used to identify gifted students must surely include measures other than IQ and academic achievement. They must, it would seem, also include assessment of those other characteristics possessed by students who later distinguish themselves through real-world accomplishments.

## FAILURE OF THE TRADITIONAL PARADIGM

In addition to the theoretical shortcoming described above (i.e., the failure of scores on standardized tests to correlate with achievement of adult eminence), the traditional paradigm was proving inadequate in another important way, this one related to equity. As early as 1950, the Educational Policy Commission called for an end to discriminatory practices that reduced educational opportunities for gifted minority students. Since that time, considerable discussion and research have been devoted to understanding the causes of the underrepresentation of a wide range of atypical students in programs for the gifted. These populations include certain racial and/or cultural minorities (e.g., Blacks, Hispanics, and Native Americans); economically disadvantaged students; children with limited English proficiency; children from rural and inner-city areas; underachievers; and children with disabilities and/or behavior problems.

The most frequently cited explanations for this persistent problem were associated with standardized tests: test bias and the inappropriateness of identification procedures that relied on only one or two (often similar) measures to assess a complex phenomenon (Baldwin, 1985; Bernal, 1981; Hilliard, 1991). There was increasing tension in a field that seemed stuck on the notion that giftedness equals a score (or two) on standardized tests of mental ability and/or achievement, while there was growing sensitivity to the fact that standardized tests were inadequate measures of the complex phenomenon we call "giftedness" and that reliance on those tests was particularly detrimental to children from underserved populations.

Early attempts to resolve the dissonance between an outdated theory and a desire for more equitable identification practices included use of compensatory techniques, quotas and separate criteria for gifted program eligibility, all of which failed to address the underlying problem: that giftedness is intricate and multifaced. Yet we continue to try to "force fit" children who demonstrate their exceptional abilities in a hundred different ways into narrow operational definitions, grounded in old theories, that suggest a fixed or static nature of intelligence, that is, "Giftedness equals an IQ of 135."

The dilemma is graphically depicted in Figure 1. At the center of the old paradigm is the narrow, limited definition, often a cut-off score on a particular test. Around the inner circle are shapes representing the wonderful diversity of gifts we see in children with different strengths, children from different economic, linguistic, and cultural backgrounds. Some of those children, regardless of their potential, simply will not be successful in the one-size-fits-all identification procedure. Further, the narrow definition promotes identification practices that do not yield enough diagnostic data to plan appropriate curricular and programming responses for any of the children, even those who are able to demonstrate their abilities in the limited ways available to them.

To move identification practices beyond reliance on standardized tests that measured only a limited array of verbal and logical reasoning abilities, educators needed richer, more explicit theories about the nature of giftedness.

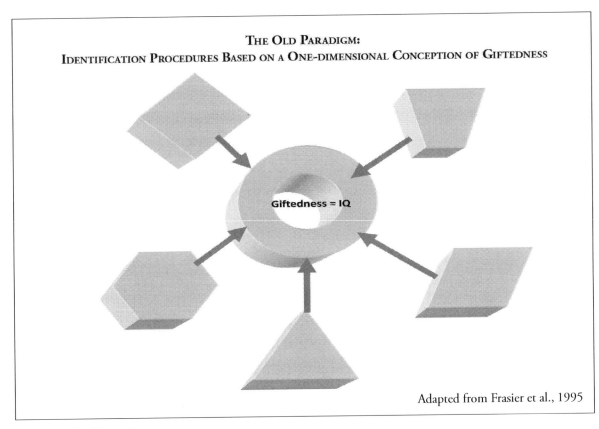

**Figure 1.** The old paradigm.

## THE PROMISE OF NEW PARADIGMS: A CONSTRUCT DEFINITION

Newer theories that began to emerge called attention to a broad slate of traits and behaviors that contribute to the development of giftedness. *The National Report on Identification* (Richert, Alvino, & McDonnell, 1982) described a strong trend toward broadening definitions of giftedness to include multiple abilities and factors. One of the earliest and most important contributors to this trend was Torrance (1964) who argued that high levels of creativity are evidence of superior intellectual functioning and constitute a component of giftedness.

Using factor analytic verification, Guilford (1977) proposed an elaborate structure of the intellect model. He theorized that five mental operations (cognition, memory, divergent production, convergent production, and evaluation) converted five types of content (e.g., figural, semantic) into six types of products, resulting in as many as 150 discrete factors of intelligence!

Using a simpler conceptual model, Renzulli (1978), too, emphasized components of giftedness (as opposed to general intelligence) and helped focus attention more on behaviors and less on psychometrics. His three-ring concept presented giftedness as the interaction between above-average ability, creativity, and task commitment. By naming specific, equally important abilities that combine to predict gifted potential, Renzulli helped educators make the transition to a new paradigm for identifying giftedness, one that was useful in assessing the abilities of a more diverse population of students. Renzulli's work also stressed the developmental nature of giftedness. By reminding educators that giftedness emerges through the interaction of innate abilities and learning or experience, he encouraged stronger programmatic emphasis on talent development.

The idea that the specific behaviors included in newer theories of giftedness might manifest themselves differently in different children was promoted by Baldwin (1978). She developed an extensive list of culturally-sensitive characteristics of giftedness, including resilience to overcome environmental hardships, sensitivity and alertness to movement, intense loyalty to a peer group, and a high sense of moral obligation, religion, and tradition. Unless teachers were taught to recognize evidence of these traits as cognitive and creative strengths, Baldwin argued, they would interfere with the identification of gifted African-American students.

Gardner (1983) and Sternberg (1985) also recommended the recognition of discrete cognitive abilities in the identification of giftedness, and both recognized the impact that culture plays on the display of these abilities. Gardner's multiple intelligences (MI) theory defined intelligence as a set of abilities that allow an individual to solve problems or create products that are meaningful in a particular cultural setting. His approach was that of a cognitive scientist, relying less on factor analysis and more on clinical and neurological studies to describe a variety of intelligences, seven of which were named in the original theory: linguistic, logical-mathematical, spatial, musical, bodily-kinesthetic, interpersonal and intrapersonal. According to Gardner (1985), each intelligence is relatively autonomous—an idea that had important implications for the field of gifted education

as it continued to struggle with antiquated identification practices (i.e., overreliance on measures of "general intelligence") and the one-size-fits-all approach to programming for gifted students.

Sternberg also warned against the practice of trying to capture a concept as complex as intelligence with a single test score. His triarchic theory of human intelligence proposed multiple sources of giftedness and defined three main kinds: analytic, synthetic, and practical abilities. Sternberg's theory also included an information-processing component that described how executive processes contribute to the development of the three general categories of intellectual ability.

The importance of an adequate definition of giftedness had also been emphasized by Hoge (1988, 1989). He noted that while generally accepted theoretical definitions of giftedness included a variety of cognitive, creative, motivational, and personality traits, schools continued to rely almost solely on IQ tests to identify gifted students. Hagen (1980) also described giftedness as a construct, not a directly observable (or measurable) trait of an individual, but one that could be inferred based on assessment of observable characteristics. Leung (1981) called such characteristics "absolute attributes of giftedness," noting that they are observed universally across time and cultures. He distinguished core attributes from *"specific behaviors"* or manifestations of the traits in particular contexts or settings. What was needed, according to Hoge (1989), was a clear statement specifying the traits, aptitudes, and behaviors associated with the giftedness construct before appropriate assessment procedures could be developed and sound decisions made about labeling and placement.

Frasier's (1994, 1995) work contributed to this clear delineation of traits to be observed and assessed when making inferences about children's intellectual potential.

She and her colleagues at the University of Georgia developed a research-based assessment plan and staff development model to improve identification and education of gifted students from economically disadvantaged families and English language learners (Frasier et al.,1994). This study, part of The National Research Center on the Gifted and Talented Project at the University of Georgia, contributed to our understanding of giftedness as a psychological construct

The giftedness construct was defined as a set of traits, aptitudes, and behaviors that, while universally associated with talent potential, may be displayed differently in different individuals as a result of the social and cultural contexts in which they occur (Passow & Frasier, 1996). The characteristics and behaviors associated with the construct could be measured, and the sum of those measurements provided the indirect measure of the construct itself.

A helpful analogy of this concept is a cutaway image of a tree, one in which we can see both above and below the ground. In reality, all we can see when we look out at a tree is the above-the-ground portion. We cannot actually see the root system. But from the health and vitality of the tree's branches, from the rate of the tree's growth, we can draw some inferences about the depth and strength of its roots. In similar fashion, we can neither see nor measure directly a child's creative and cognitive abilities. But knowledgeable teachers can carefully and sensitively observe the *above-the-ground* behaviors and then draw inferences

about what those observable (and measurable) characteristics might mean in terms of the child's exceptional abilities, the "roots" or core attributes of giftedness. If, however, we fail to recognize the connection between core attributes and the ways that some children might manifest those abilities, we are likely to overlook children who would benefit from gifted program services.

The basic elements of the giftedness construct, as defined by Frasier (1995), were motivation, intense (sometimes unusual) interests, communication skills, problem-solving ability, memory, curiosity/inquiry, insight, reasoning, imagination/creativity, and humor. (See Figure 2 and, at the end of the chapter, Appendix A.)

Each of these widely accepted attributes of giftedness might have a variety of expressions, depending on students' individual differences, cultural, economic or language backgrounds.

For example, extraordinary communication skills, often operationally defined in traditional identification procedures as advanced vocabulary and/or reading and writing ability, might be conceptualized differently for a child who has limited proficiency in the English language or from an educationally disadvantaged background. Consider this acrostic poem written by Carla, a struggling fourth-grade student, after only two years of English language instruction:

> **H**ow wonderful it was
> **O**n the boat
> **N**ear the mouth of the river at
> **D**awn. The sun was pointing at me
> **U**nder the roof of the boat. The
> **R**iver was wonderful when the sun was
> pointing at me

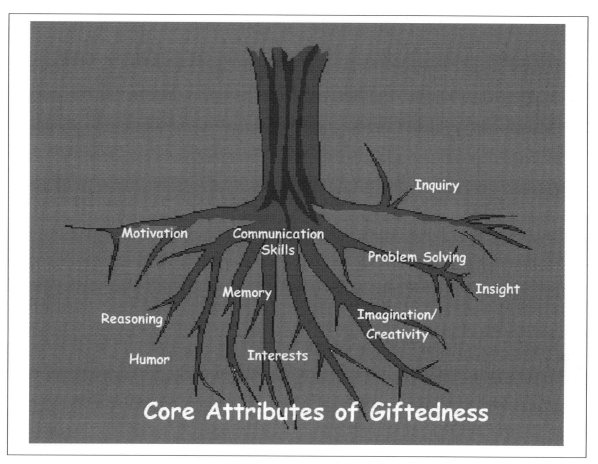

**Figure 2.** Core attributes of giftedness.

And the boat was soft on the water,

**S**oft, very soft, on the water.

(Robisheaux, 1997)

Even though Carla had poor grades and appeared to be at risk academically, this example certainly suggests that it is possible for a child to communicate effectively and powerfully without advanced vocabulary or polished writing skills. The vocabulary used in the poem is not advanced for a typical fourth grader. Yet, even with limited opportunity to learn English, when given the chance to express herself creatively, Carla was able to create beautiful imagery and evoke emotion from the reader. Advanced vocabulary? No, not really. Extraordinary communication skill?

Absolutely! But it is displayed in a way that can't be measured on a multiple choice test.

And there are other symbol systems through which one might communicate. Ask yourself these questions: "Is it possible to demonstrate extraordinary communication skills with no language at all? What if the symbol system is math or music or movement?" Isadora Duncan (1927), considered by many to be the creator of modern dance, once said, "If I could tell you what it meant, there would be no point in dancing it."

To improve identification of gifted students from underserved populations, teachers were trained to recognize a child's unusually effective communication skills using a variety of symbol systems, such as verbal, nonverbal, mathematical, or artistic. In turn, each element of the construct definition was examined through the lens of individual differences, particularly those differences that are likely to result when children have had limited opportunity to develop their gifts because of poverty or because expression of their abilities is filtered through a cultural or linguistic context.

Another clear example of varied manifestations of the same core attribute of giftedness is seen when we look more closely at the trait of intense curiosity. Traditional checklists used for gifted program referrals almost always include the item "Asks a lot of questions." While it is true that many gifted children do ask a lot of questions, they are more likely to demonstrate curiosity in this way if they are proficient in the language of the classroom and if they have been raised in a home where it is all right, even desired and rewarded, for children to interact with adults in this fashion.

But what about children who have not yet mastered the language well enough to feel comfortable asking their teachers questions in class. And what about children who have been taught not to question adults? Garrison (1989), for example, pointed out that in American Indian cultures, students learn primarily by observation with very little verbal explanation and little or no questioning of teachers or elders. Because bright children from these groups do not ask their teachers a lot of questions, it does not mean that they are not curious. Instead teachers must become more sensitive to other demonstrated skills of inquiry, and they must value those alternative expressions of the core attribute. (See Figure 3.)

When teachers and other educational decision makers learn to recognize a variety of *above-the-ground* expressions of the same core attributes of giftedness, they have taken the first steps toward effectively advocating for potentially gifted children from a variety of cultural and economic backgrounds, and they have a foundation on which to build equitable multiple-criteria identification procedures.

By defining giftedness dynamically and honoring different expressions of the same core attributes, the possibilities for students from all groups to demonstrate advanced potential are increased. In turn, the construct definition is constantly enriched and made more accurate. In Figure 4 giftedness is now defined in terms of core traits, aptitudes, and behaviors. The wonderful diversity we see within the gifted population is again represented by the smaller geometric shapes. But this time factors influencing the development and manifestation of gifts and talent in differing sociocultural contexts are recognized and they are accommodated in the methods used to identify gifted students for special programming. Thus, there is reciprocal influence between our growing understanding of how giftedness is exhibited and valued in various contexts and the universal construct definition.

## TEACHERS AS TALENT SCOUTS: RECOGNIZING GIFTEDNESS IN THE CLASSROOM

Central to the new understanding of giftedness is the role that teachers play in recognizing talent in their students because classroom teachers' advocacy is often the first step in a referral process that may result in gifted program placement.

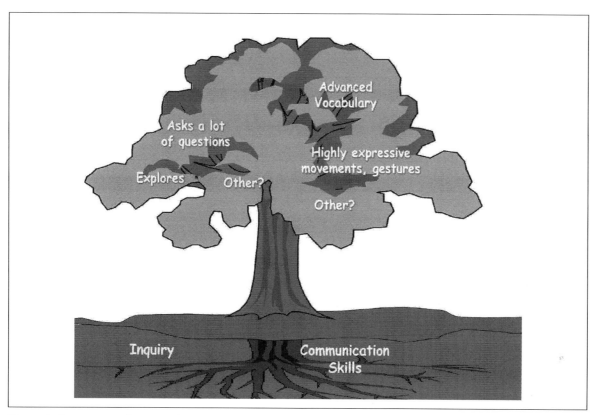

**Figure 3**. Expressions of core attributes.

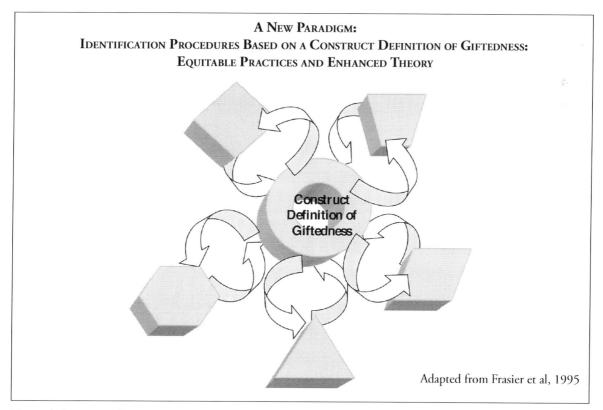

**Figure 4**. A new paradigm.

Frasier et al. (1995) developed an observation form to help teachers recognize varied expressions of the traits, aptitudes, and behaviors (TABs) associated with giftedness. This form, called *Panning for Gold*, which may be found in Appendix A, is a practical and effective tool for teachers who are called upon to nominate children for gifted program consideration.

An instrument such as the *Panning for Gold* observation form, when used with regular classroom and special area teachers who have had training on the principles behind it, provides what Frasier et al. (1995) called a "new window for looking at gifted children." It encourages teachers to take a proficiency view of children, actively watching for indicators of advanced abilities that might manifest themselves in a variety of ways. Thus, these teachers become more skilled talent scouts, accurate nominators for gifted program consideration, and effective advocates for potentially gifted children from diverse backgrounds.

Even if access to a formal gifted program were not an issue, the teacher's failure to recognize intellectual strengths in some children would be of serious concern because of the impact it would have on the teacher's interaction with those children and with curricular decisions. It has frequently been found that children for whom teachers have higher expectations are given a wider range of classroom activities and that these activities tend to be of a higher interest level. When teachers underestimate children's potential because they fail to recognize the TABs associated with giftedness, the result can be insufficient performance expectations and curricular stimulation (Blatchford, Burke, Farquhar, Plewis, & Tizard, 1989; Rist, 1970).

This type of differential curricular coverage sets up a deleterious cycle for potentially gifted youngsters because low-level learning activities give students few opportunities to demonstrate advanced abilities and do not contribute to the development of gifted behaviors. In addition, the child who is very bright but has not been recognized as such is likely to become bored quickly with a basic-skills, drill-and-practice approach, and may engage in even more of the negative behaviors that initially caused the classroom teacher to underestimate his or her intellectual potential. Consequently, atypical gifted children are likely to remain in classroom environments that do little to develop their potential and, in fact, make it less likely that teachers will recognize their abilities and proceed with gifted program nomination. Failure to recognize and develop talent in young children with advanced abilities is associated with negative outcomes in cognitive, academic, social, and emotional development (Neihart, Reis, Robinson, & Moon, 2002).

With classroom teachers so frequently playing the role of gatekeeper and with our growing awareness of the potential tragedy, both to individuals and to our society, when talent goes unrecognized, it is imperative that all educators be trained to recognize intellectual ability in the many ways it might be manifested. An evidence-based practice such as using the *Panning for Gold* observation form in the early stages of the nomination/talent search process is a promising first step.

Research in this area (Borland, 1978; Brighton, Moon, Jarvis, Hocket, 2007; Ciha, Harris, Hoffman, & Potter, 1974; Cornish, 1968; Jacobs, 1972; Pegnato & Birch, 1959) has consistently found that teachers without special training in characteristics of gifted students tend to rely on their implicit notions of giftedness (e.g., those children who are performing very well in their regular classroom curriculum). Since some children who are not performing well in school (or in other ways do not match teachers' implicit theories of giftedness) may indeed have very high aptitude for reasoning or creative productivity, a referral process which has no teacher training component is seriously flawed. Professional learning activities should include information on the construct definition of giftedness, how each core attribute may be observed in students from different cultural backgrounds, and what the characteristics may look like when viewed through the lens of poverty or from the perspective of specific talent areas.

However, a full understanding of the giftedness construct with all of its richness and contextual variety means also knowing which characteristics may *not* be relevant in the search for talent. The work of Gear (1978) and others (Dusek & Joseph, 1983; Krisel, 2000; Pegnato & Birch, 1959; Siegle, & Powell, 2004) has demonstrated the need to educate teachers about the characteristics of gifted students, but it may be equally important to provide explicit instruction about student characteristics potentially causing their evaluation to be biased— noncognitive traits that are not necessarily good indicators of potential giftedness, but that may influence teachers' assessment of intellectual ability. A number of studies indicate that the expectancies teachers form about their students' intellectual and academic skills may be based on information that is not relevant to the competency under consideration (Brighton at al.,

2007; Brophy, 1983; Braun, 1976; Cooper, 1979; Dusek, 1975; Dusek & Joseph, 1983; Harris & Rosenthal, 1985). The factors that may cause bias include characteristics as irrelevant to intellectual potential as the popularity or ethnicity of children's names (Demetrulias, 1990; Dusek & Joseph, 1983; Garwood, 1976; Harari & McDavid, 1973). A number of studies show that teachers develop differential expectancies of students' academic potential based on the students' race (Dusek & Joseph, 1983; Tom, Cooper, & McGraw, 1984; Wong, 1980) and socioeconomic status (Dusek & Joseph, 1983; Tom & Cooper, 1986).

Past performance, as indicated by previous standardized test scores and report card grades, influences teachers' assessments of children's abilities (Matuszek & Oakland, 1979). When an official diagnostic label (e.g., learning disabled or behavior disordered) accompanies records of past performance and behavioral descriptions from report cards, the effects on teacher expectancies appear to be particularly pronounced. Certain social behaviors reported in children's cumulative records also influence teachers' perceptions of students' intelligence (Murrone & Gynther, 1991). For example, if the child comes from a disadvantaged background, undesirable school behaviors are strongly associated with poor cognitive ability (Marjoribanks, 1978).

Numerous studies (Clifford & Walster, 1973; Elovitz & Salvia, 1982; Kenealy, Frude, & Shaw, 1988) have shown that the physical appearance of children affects teachers' judgments as to the children's intelligence, social competence, popularity, confidence, and leadership ability. Certain temperament characteristics in children are also associated with teachers' inaccurate estimations the mental abilities of their students (Krisel, 2000). These factors may keep some children from being considered for gifted program placement, even though they possess the cognitive, motivational, or creative potentials that would allow them to benefit from such a program. Understanding the factors that affect teachers' perceptions of students' mental abilities is an important part of comprehending (and subsequently improving) the referral process used to nominate children for gifted programs. These misconceptions should be addressed directly during training on the characteristics that are in fact associated with extraordinary potential—the traits, aptitudes and behaviors associated with the giftedness construct.

## RECOGNIZING TALENT IN SPECIAL POPULATIONS

The original *Panning for Gold* observation form and related training were developed to assist educators in identifying gifted children from special populations (i.e., those who are from minority or economically disadvantaged families and areas and/or those who are of limited English proficiency). The concept of *above-the-ground* manifestations (i.e., characteristics that are observable and measurable) of core attributes varying from student to student because of cultural or linguistic differences, as illustrated by the tree analogy in Figure 3, proved to be a key component in the State of Georgia's gifted education reform efforts that began with a National Research Center on the Gifted and Talented Project at the University of Georgia (Frasier et al., 1994) and resulted in extraordinary growth in the number of minority children identified as gifted—a 570% increase in the number of Hispanic students and a 206% increase

in the number of African-American students over a nine-year period (Georgia Department of Education, 2005).

With training, teachers began to recognize that an Hispanic student's demonstrated desire to communicate effectively using Standard American English (even though the student's written and spoken English skills might not be as strong as those of native English-speaking classmates) and the rapid progress in language acquisition that resulted may indeed be a better indicator of the core attribute of *Communication* than any single snapshot of language skills that could be obtained on a standardized test. Similarly, the African-American student whose experiences have been limited by poverty may not have the same large storehouse of information that bright children from educationally advantaged homes have, but if that youngster knows the names of every major rap artist and can recite the lyrics of dozens of songs perfectly, is he not demonstrating exceptional *Memory?* While it might be more readily recognizable as an indicator of potential giftedness when exceptional memory has been applied to historical events and number facts, the core attribute is the same, regardless of manifestation. And taking a proficiency view of students such as these, focusing on their strengths as opposed to what they cannot yet do well, has a profound effect on the curricular and programmatic opportunities that may be made available.

Focusing clearly on the characteristics of giftedness (i.e., the TABs of the giftedness construct and the varied ways each can be revealed) also helps teachers see beyond the challenges faced by twice exceptional students to recognize their gifts. Typical of gifted children without a learning disability, for example, the Gifted LD child may possess a wide range of *Interests*. Often they are unusual or intense interests about specific topics. However, many times those passions are more easily seen in non-school activities or in areas in which the child can circumvent his or her learning disability. While gaps in basic skills or organizational problems may make it difficult for the Gifted LD child to pursue his or her passions independently (and these are undoubtedly classroom management and instructional concerns), it is the wise and sensitive teacher who gets to know the struggling child well enough to capitalize on those intense interests to make school more engaging and, to the greatest degree possible, subsume necessary remediation through a focus on the student's interests and strengths.

When teachers assume that the only gifted students in their classes are those who reveal their abilities in ways that reflect the teachers' (often uninformed) implicit definitions of giftedness, atypical gifted students from underserved populations are denied access to the kinds of services they need to fully develop their talents.

## RECOGNIZING SPECIFIC ACADEMIC TALENT

Clear delineation of the traits, aptitudes, and behaviors that, while universally associated with talent potential, may manifest themselves differently in different individuals as a result of social and cultural contexts provided a new window for observing potential giftedness in special populations. Classroom teachers and gifted program leaders have found (Krisel, personal communication) the concept of core attributes of giftedness, however, to be equally helpful in considering how the same core trait might look different

in dissimilar disciplines or talent areas. In other words, the TABs associated with giftedness will manifest differently if the talent domain is visual arts or music than if the talent domain is mathematics or language arts.

Might the science teacher, for example, be trained to recognize potential giftedness in his or her classroom by observing for domain-specific indicators of elements of the giftedness construct? Display of *Motivation*, for example, is likely to be discipline-specific. Few students are equally enthusiastic about the study of all subject areas, but potentially gifted young scientists would be highly enthusiastic about science and are likely to demonstrate persistence in completing assignments, lab work, and self-selected projects in science. And exceptional *Insight* might be evident when a student accurately and precisely predicts the results of lab experiments.

Move down the hall to the social studies class, and a teacher might observe that same core attribute of *Insight* when a student is able to compare the points of view of a variety of people who lived during various historical events at a level that is well beyond those of his classmates. He may be particularly adept at historical analyses of primary documents and their significance. Same core attribute, different revelation.

While exceptional communication skills are most often associated with language arts, mathematics teachers should be trained to be alert for evidence of the *Communication* facet of the giftedness construct. It may be seen when a student effectively uses non-mathematical terms associated with mathematics operations; when she skillfully models situations using oral, written, concrete, pictorial, and/or graphical methods; or when she appreciates the value and role of mathematical notation to a degree not often seen among that age group. The gifted young artist, on the other hand, may demonstrate advanced *Communication* ability by conveying powerful images in works of art, creating meaningful—perhaps spiritually or politically motivated—artwork, or creating understandable connections to the viewer without the use of words at all.

*Reasoning*, often thought of most easily in terms of mathematics, can also be demonstrated in discipline-specific ways. The advanced thought processes of young writers are readily apparent when they use the argumentative or persuasive mode effectively or when they use logical approaches to determine the appropriate meaning of words, phrases, or statements from figurative or technical contexts. The trained art teacher will recognize the same core attribute when a young painter judges visual weights of shapes, colors, empty spaces, and visual lines and counterbalances large shapes with intense color.

*Imagination/Creativity*, too often associated only with the arts, is an important characteristic of giftedness in all disciplines. In the science classroom, students with exceptional potential may develop unique procedures or display ingenuity in using available supplies to investigate scientific questions. They may see unique connections between topics or concepts and use these ideas to generate novel investigations. Our most gifted young mathematicians may experiment with solutions to math problems not suggested by the teacher, or they may use math to attempt to find

solutions for personal or societal problems. Same core attribute, different revelation.

## IMPLICATIONS FOR IDENTIFICATION

Why is it important for educators to have a clearer understanding of the characteristics of able learners and how those traits might manifest themselves in a particular discipline? Not only must teachers' internal templates of gifted students be made more accurate, but they must also understand how to create curriculum and programmatic opportunities for all students to demonstrate advanced abilities in the areas associated with the giftedness construct. Throughout the school day, numerous opportunities exist to create a match between characteristics of students, teacher expectations, and requirements of the learning environment.

In order to make appropriate referrals for gifted program services, it is important to consider the effects of the environment on the student's behavior. In other words, we must continue to estimate to what extent traditional school environments and curricula serve as gateways to the referral process for some students and act as barriers for the emergence and recognition of gifted behaviors for others.

What should curriculum look like if we are using it to help teachers recognize and develop exceptional talent? Picture the math classroom that gives students opportunities to exhibit—indeed one that *requires* them—the characteristics described above:

- a classroom in which students experiment with novel solutions to math problems,

88

- a classroom in which students use math to try to solve personal or societal problems,

- a classroom in which students use oral, written, concrete, pictorial and/or graphical methods to explain their work.

Math worksheets are not likely to elicit that kind of student activity, are they? No, students have to be engaged in meaningful problem solving. They have to be talking about math, trying new approaches, debating alternative solutions. In other words, the classroom has to be filled with teaching and learning activities that very consciously mirror the traits, aptitudes, and behaviors associated with giftedness!

Again, picture a classroom, this time an English language arts classroom, in which students are demonstrating extraordinary reasoning. They are testing the validity of their assertions by examining the evidence. They debate which organizational structure is most appropriate for purpose, audience, content, and type of composition. When we picture student behaviors like these, we see them in the context of challenging reading and writing assignments or lively debates and the like; it's awfully hard to draw out characteristics of giftedness by asking students to underline all the nouns on a worksheet or to memorize vocabulary words. Teachers will only have opportunities to observe and assess exceptional abilities in the content area if the curriculum is rich and authentic! Our classrooms provide a window for viewing those indicators of potential—*if* the opportunity exists!

## CONCLUSIONS

For over half a century, educators and decision makers have been calling for an end to the tragic waste of talent that occurs when potentially gifted youngsters go unrecognized and unserved in gifted programs (Educational Policies Commission, 1950). A major factor that has been identified as contributing to this loss of talent is the weakness of a nomination and referral process that does not include well-trained, culturally sensitive teachers as the front-line referrers and advocates for possible gifted program participation. Without adequate understanding of the theories of giftedness, often lacking practical tools and procedures for helping them recognize and document characteristics of potential giftedness observed in their classrooms, even our most dedicated teachers are not adequately prepared to help eliminate once and for all an outdated identification paradigm that relies on assessment of those cognitive and academic skills most easily measured be standardized tests.

However, newer theories of giftedness have called attention to a much broader array of traits and behaviors that contribute to the recognition of giftedness. In these newer views, giftedness is most often presented as a psychological construct (i.e., a set of traits, aptitudes, and behaviors that may manifest themselves differently in different individuals) often as a result of the social and cultural contexts in which the giftedness occurs. Equitable identification procedures, including appropriate teacher nominations, depend on a clear understanding of these traits, aptitudes, and behaviors associated with this view of giftedness as a construct.

To improve identification practices, there is value in clearly defining the traits, aptitudes, and behaviors associated with the giftedness construct theory and to providing teachers with clearer examples of what these behaviors may look like in the classroom setting. Observable characteristics of students with gifts and talents, the core attributes of the giftedness construct, provide the best foundation for developing procedures to help school personnel recognize students who would likely benefit from gifted education programming. Additionally, these universal traits help educators appropriately consider the cultural, economic, and environmental factors that should guide thoughtful assessment procedures when considering nominees for gifted program participation.

With a commitment toward recognizing and embracing the idea that core attributes of giftedness can be found in children from all economic, cultural, or ethnic backgrounds, teachers should be trained and assisted in the creation of rich, challenging instructional settings that allow them to more effectively observe for indicators of potential giftedness and develop that potential. To give students the best opportunities to demonstrate advanced abilities, classroom curriculum must be rich enough and rigorous enough to elicit those behaviors every day.

Secondly, these core attributes should be used to guide the selection of a variety of objective and subjective assessment measures that provide different ways for students to demonstrate gifted characteristics and for professionals to observe and document those abilities. Using procedures through which it carefully considers all assessment information, a team of committed educators can then make decisions related to gifted program placement and services.

Finally, that comprehensive profile of assessment data serves as the basis for assigning and/or developing program options for addressing the exceptional needs of students with gifts and talents. And what are those advanced learning needs? Once again we turn back to giftedness theory, specifically newer construct-related conceptions of giftedness. Defensible services provided for young people who have been identified as gifted differ from the excellent curriculum we want for all students in the same ways that gifted learners differ from the general population. To a greater degree that is practical in the regular classroom, gifted education programming should give highly-able students opportunities to explore their *interests*, further develop intrinsic *motivation* by pursuing self-selected tasks in depth, practice a variety of advanced *communication* skills, develop and use *logical* and *creative problem solving*, *investigate*, and *create*. We have come full circle: the traits, aptitudes, and behaviors elucidated in modern giftedness theory are the same traits that guide identification procedures and best practice in gifted education programming.

## REFERENCES

Baldwin, A. Y. (1978). Curriculum and methods —What is the difference? In A. Y. Baldwin, G. H. Gear, & L. J. Lucito (Eds.), *Educational planning for the gifted: Overcoming cultural, geographic, and socioeconomic barriers* (pp. 37–49). Reston, VA: Council for Exceptional Children.

Baldwin, A. Y. (1985). Programs for the gifted and talented: Issues concerning minority populations. In F. D. Horowitz & M. O'Brien (Eds.), *The gifted and talented: Developmental perspectives* (pp. 223–249). Washington, DC: American Psychological Association.

Bernal, E. M. (1981). *Special problems and procedures for identifying minority gifted students.* Paper presented for The Council for exceptional Children Conference on the Exceptional Bilingual Child, New Orleans, LA. (ERIC Document Reproduction Service No. ED 203 652)

Blatchford, P., Burke, J., Farquhar, C., Plewis, I., & Tizard, B. (1989). Teacher expectations in infant school: Associations with attainment and progress, curriculum coverage and classroom interaction. *British Journal of Educational Psychology, 59*(1), 19–30

Boring, E.G. (1923) Intelligence as the tests test it. *New Republic, 36,* 35–37.

Borland, J. (1978). Teacher identification of the gifted: A new look. *Journal for the Education of the Gifted, 1,* 22–32.

Braun, C. (1976). Teacher expectation: Sociopsychological dynamics. *Review of Educational Research, 6*(2), 185-213.

Brighton. C. M., Moon, T. R., Jarvis, J. M., Hockett, J. A., (2007). *Primary grade teachers' conceptions of giftedness and talent: A case-based investigation.* Storrs, CT: University of Connecticut, National Research Center on the Gifted and Talented. [RM 07232]

Brophy, J. E. (1983). Research on the self-fulfilling prophecy and teacher expectations. *Journal of Educational Psychology, 75,* 631–661.

Ciha, T., Harris, R., Hoffman, C., & Potter, M. 1974. Parents as identifiers of giftedness, ignored but accurate. *Gifted Child Quarterly, 18,* 191–195.

Clifford, M., & Walster, E. (1973). The effect of physical attractiveness on teacher expectations. *Sociology of Education, 46(2),* 248–258.

Cooper, H. M. (1979a). Pygmalion grows up: A model for teacher expectation communication and performance influence. *Review of Educational Research, 49,* 389

Cooper, H. M. (1979b). Some effects of preperformance information on academic expectations. *Journal of Educational Psychology, 71,* 95–109.

Cornish, R. (1968). Parents', teachers', and pupils' perception of the gifted child's ability. *Gifted Child Quarterly, 34,* 14.

Demetrulias, D. M. (1990). Ethnic surnames. *Educational Research Quarterly, 14*(3), 2–6.

Duncan, I. (1927). *My life.* New York: Boni and Liveright.

Dusek, J. (1975). Do teachers bias children's learning? *Review of Educational Research, 45,* 661–684.

Dusek, J. B., & Joseph, G. (1983). The bases of teacher expectancies: A meta-analysis. *Journal of Educational Psychology, 3,* 327–346.

Educational Policies Commission (1950). *Education of the gifted.* Washington, DC: National Education Association and American Association of School Administrators.

Elovitz, G. P., & Salvia, J. (1982). Attractiveness as a biasing factor in the judgments of school psychologists. *Journal of School Psychology, 20,* 339–345.

Frasier, M. M., Martin, D., Garcia, J., Finley, V., Frank, E., Krisel, S., & King, L. (1995). *A new window for looking at gifted students.* Athens, GA: University of Georgia, National Research Center on the Gifted and Talented.

Frasier, M. M., & Passow, A. H. (1994). *Toward a new paradigm for identifying talent potential.* Storrs, CT: University of Connecticut, National Research Center on the Gifted and Talented. [RM 94111]

Gardner, H. (1983). *Frames of mind.* New York: Basic.

Garrison, L. (1989). Programming for the gifted American Indian student. In C. J. Maker & S. W. Schiever (Eds.), *Critical issues in gifted education: Defensible programs for cultural and ethnic minorities* (pp. 116–127). Austin, TX: Pro-Ed.

Garwood, S. (1976). First-name stereotypes as a factor in self-concept and school achievement. *Journal of Educational Psychology, 68,* 482–487.

Gear, G. (1978). Effects of training on teachers' accuracy in the identification of gifted children. *Gifted Child Quarterly, 22,* 990–97.

Guilford, J. P. (1977). *Way beyond the IQ.* Buffalo, NY: Bearly.

Hagen, E. (1980). *Identification of the gifted.* New York: Teachers College Press.

Harari, H., & McDavid, J. (1973). Name stereotypes and teachers' expectations. *Journal of Educational Psychology, 65,* 222–225.

Harris, M. J., & Rosenthal, R. (1985). Mediation of interpersonal expectancy effects: 31 meta-analyses. *Psychological Bulletin, 97,* 363–386.

Hilliard, A. G. (1991). The learning potential assessment device and instrumental enrichment as a paradigm shift. In A. G. Hilliard (Ed.), *Testing African American students: Special re-issue of The Negro Educational Review* (pp. 220–208). Morristown, NJ: Aaron Press.

Hoge, R. D. (1988). Issues in the definition and measurement of the giftedness construct. *Educational Researcher, 17*(7), 12–16, 22.

Hoge, R. D. (1989). An examination of the giftedness construct. *Canadian Journal of Education, 14*(1), 6–17.

Jacobs, J. (1972). Teacher attitude towards gifted children. *Gifted Child Quarterly, 16,* 23–26.

Jenkins-Friedman, R. (1982). Myth: Cosmetic use of multiple criteria. *Gifted Child Quarterly, 26,* 24–26.

Kenealy, P., Frude, N., & Shaw, W. (1988). Influence of children's physical attractiveness on teacher expectations. *Journal of School Psychology, 128,* 373–383.

Krisel, S. C. (2000). *An investigation of temperament factors as influence on teacher perceptions of potential giftedness in economically disadvantaged students.* Unpublished doctoral dissertation. Athens, GA: University of Georgia.

Krisel, S. (1995). [Georgia Department of Education: Referrals, Referral Sources, and Results]. Unpublished raw data.

Leung, E. K. (1981, February). *The identification and social problems of gifted bilingual bicultural children.* Paper presented at The Council for Exceptional Children Conference on the Exceptional Bilingual Child, New Orleans, LA.

Marjoribanks, K. (1978). Teacher perceptions of student behavior, social environment, and cognitive performance. *Journal of Genetic Psychology, 133,* 217–228.

Matuszek, P., & Oakland, T. (1979). Factors influencing teachers' and psychologists' recommendations regarding special class placement. *Journal of School Psychology, 17,* 116–125.

Munday, L. A., & Davis, J. C. (1974). *Varieties of accomplishment after college: Perspectives on the meaning of academic talent.* Iowa City, IA: American College Testing Program. [Research Report No. 62]

Murrone, J., & Gynther, M. D. (1991). Teachers' implicit "theories" of children's intelligence. *Psychological Reports, 69,* 1195–1201.

Neihart, M., Reis, S. M., Robinson, N. M., & Moon, S. M. (2002). *The social and emotional development of gifted children: What do we know?* Waco, TX: Prufrock Press.

Passow, A. H., & Frasier, M. M. (1996). Toward improving identification of talent potential among minority and disadvantaged students. *Roeper Review, 18,* 198–202.

Pegnato, W., and Birch, J. 1959. Locating gifted children in junior high school. *Exceptional Children, 26,* 303–304.

Renzulli, J. S. (1978). What makes giftedness? Reexamining a definition. *Phi Delta Kappan, 60,* 180–184; 261.

Richert, E. S., Alvino, J., & McDonnell, R. (1982). *The national report on identification: Assessment and recommendations for comprehensive identification of gifted and talented youth.* Sewell, NJ: Educational Information and Resource Center, for US Department of Education.

Rist, R. (1970). Student social class and teacher expectations: The self-fulfilling prophecy in ghetto education. *Harvard Educational Review, 40,* 411–451.

Robisheaux, J. (1997). Presentation at OERI/OBEMLA initiative on LEP students with outstanding abilities. Retrieved April 2, 2011, from http://www.ed.gov/pubs/TalentandDiversity/talent.html

Siegle, D., & Powell, T. (2004). Exploring teacher biases when nominating students for gifted programs. *Gifted Child Quarterly, 48,* 21–29.

Sternberg, R. (1985). *Beyond IQ.* Cambridge: Cambridge University Press.

Tannenbaum, A. J. (1983). *Gifted children: Psychological and educational perspectives.* New York: Macmillan.

Terman, L. M. (1975). The discovery and encouragement of exceptional talent. In W. B. Barbe & J. S. Renzulli (Eds.), *Psychology and education of the gifted* (pp. 6–20). New York: Halsted Press.

Tom, D., Cooper, H., & McGraw, M. (1984). The influence of student background and teacher authoritarianism on teacher expectations. *Journal of Educational Psychology, 76,* 259–265.

Tom, D., & Cooper, H. (1986). The effect of student background on teacher performance attributions: Evidence for counterdefensive patterns and low expectancy cycles. *Basic and Applied Social Psychology, 7*(1), 53–62.

Torrance, E. P. (1964). *Education and the creative potential.* Minneapolis, MN: University of Minnesota Press.

Wallach, M. (1976). Tests tell us little about talent. *American Scientist, 64,* 57–63.

Wong, M. C. (1980). Model students? Teachers' perceptions and expectations of their Asian and white students. *Sociology of Education, 53,* 226–246.

**APPENDIX A: PANNING FOR GOLD**

## Nomination for Gifted Program Consideration
## Record of Observations
## TAB's Descriptors

Use the following definitions and descriptions of **traits**, **aptitudes**, and **behaviors** (TAB's) associated with gifted potential to help you observe children.

| Motivation | Interests | Communication Skills | Problem-Solving Ability | Memory |
|---|---|---|---|---|
| *Evidence of desire to learn* | *Intense (sometimes unusual) interests* | *Highly expressive and effective use of words, numbers, symbols* | *Effective, often inventive strategies for recognizing and solving problems* | *Large storehouse of information on school or non-school topics* |
| **Description:** Forces that initiate, direct, and sustain individual or group behavior in order to satisfy a need or attain a goal<br>Student may:<br>• demonstrate persistence in pursuing/completing self-selected tasks ( may be culturally influenced; evident in school or non-school activities)<br>• be an enthusiastic learner<br>• aspire to be somebody | **Description:** Activities, avocations, objects, etc., that have special worth or significance and are given special attention<br>Student may:<br>• demonstrate unusual or advanced interests in a topic or activity<br>• be beyond age group<br>• pursue an activity unceasingly | **Description:** Transmission and reception of signals or meanings through a system of symbols (codes, gestures, language, numbers)<br>Student may:<br>• demonstrate unusual ability to communicate (verbally, physically, artistically)<br>• use particularly apt examples, illustrations, or elaborations | **Description:** Process of determining a correct sequence of alternatives leading to a desired goal or to successful completion of a task<br>Student may:<br>• demonstrate unusual ability to devise or adapt a systematic strategy for solving problems and to change the strategy if it is not working<br>• create new designs, invent | **Description:** Exceptional ability to retain and retrieve information<br>Student may:<br>• already know<br>• need only 1-2 repetitions for mastery<br>• have a wealth of information about school or non-school topics<br>• pay attention to details<br>• manipulate information well |

| Inquiry | Insight | Reasoning | Imagination/Creativity | Humor |
|---|---|---|---|---|
| *Questions, experiments, explores* | *Quickly grasps new concepts and makes connections; senses deeper meaning* | *Logical approaches to figuring out solutions* | *Produces many ideas; highly original* | *Conveys and picks up on humor* |
| **Description:** Method or process of seeking knowledge, understanding, or information<br>Student may:<br>• ask unusual questions for age<br>• play around with ideas<br>• demonstrate extensive exploratory behaviors directed toward eliciting information about materials or situations | **Description:** Sudden discovery of the correct solution following incorrect attempts<br>Student may:<br>• demonstrate exceptional ability to draw inferences<br>• appear to be a good guesser<br>• be keenly observant<br>• see many unusual, diverse relationships<br>• integrate ideas and disciplines | **Description:** Highly conscious, directed, controlled, active, intentional, forward-looking, goal-oriented thought<br>Student may:<br>• make generalizations<br>• use metaphors and analogies<br>• think things through in a logical manner<br>• think critically<br>• come up with plausible answers | **Description:** Process of forming mental images of objects, qualities, or situations which aren't immediately apparent to the senses. Problem solving through non-traditional patterns of thinking<br>Student may:<br>• show exceptional ingenuity in using everyday materials<br>• have wild, seemingly silly ideas | **Description:** Ability to synthesize key ideas or problems in complex situations in a humorous way; exceptional sense of timing in words and gestures<br>Student may:<br>• have a keen sense of humor (may be gentle or hostile)<br>• see unusual relationships<br>• demonstrate unusual emotional depth<br>• demonstrate sensory awareness |

## TAB's Observation Sheet

Student's Name: _____

Completed by: _____

School: _____  Grade Level: _____

Relationship to student: _____

Date: _____

**Directions:** Use the spaces below to identify basic traits, aptitudes, and behaviors (TAB's) displayed by this student. Provide specific anecdotal information in the appropriate areas. See descriptions above.

| **Motivation**<br>*Evidence of desire to learn* | **Interests**<br>*Intense (sometimes unusual) interests* | **Communication Skills**<br>*Highly expressive and effective use of words, numbers, symbols* | **Problem-Solving Ability**<br>*Effective, often inventive strategies for recognizing and solving problems* | **Memory**<br>*Large storehouse of information on school or non-school topics* |
|---|---|---|---|---|
| | | | | |
| **Inquiry**<br>*Questions, experiments, explores* | **Insight**<br>*Quickly grasps new concepts and makes connections; senses deeper meaning* | **Reasoning**<br>*Logical approaches to figuring out solutions* | **Imagination/Creativity**<br>*Produces many ideas; highly original* | **Humor**<br>*Conveys and picks up on humor* |
| | | | | |

## CHAPTER 4 STUDY GUIDE

**Prompt 1** *Knowledge*

Explain in your own terms the relationship between a core attribute and its manifestation within contextual differences.

**Prompt 2** *Opinion*

Why, in your opinion, did the application of ideas presented in this chapter have such an extraordinary effect on the identification of children from minority populations in Georgia? How might this effect be transferred to your own state?

**Prompt 3** *Affect*

In applying the ideas from this chapter, teachers often felt some initial anxiety. What would be the sources of this anxiety? What would your initial reaction be if you were asked to apply these ideas? Eventually teachers became quite enthusiastic about these ideas. What would be the sources of that enthusiasm? Do you believe you and your colleagues would experience this same change? Why or why not?

**Prompt 4** *Experience*

Select any three of the ten core attributes described in this chapter and brainstorm how they would be manifested in a particular group of students with whom you have contact. This group of students can be based on ethnicity, age, career goals, or any other variable.

**Prompt 5** *Preconception/Misconception*

Explain why it is important for teachers to go beyond their implicit impressions of what giftedness is and to study core attributes and their manifestations in order to become excellent talent scouts.

# Section II.

# Professional Foundations

# IDENTIFICATION OF THE GIFTED:
# AN OVERVIEW OF LEGAL ISSUES

KRISTEN R. STEPHENS, DUKE UNIVERSITY
JOHN DUDLEY, THE UNIVERSITY OF SOUTHERN MISSISSIPPI
FRANCES A. KARNES, THE UNIVERSITY OF SOUTHERN MISSISSIPPI

## INTRODUCTION

The federal government has been slow to respond to the needs of the gifted in our country. While a mandate for the identification of disabled students exists at the federal level, the lack of a federal mandate for the gifted leaves the responsibility for identifying and serving these students to the discretion of each state. Currently, only 26 states have a mandate for identifying gifted learners. Inevitably, the inconsistency in identification procedures and educational services for the gifted across states and even among districts within the same state creates an environment ripe for disputes between parents and schools. When parents and schools cannot resolve issues pertaining to the identification of gifted students and/or admission process into specialized programs for the gifted, steps of dispute resolution should be employed. The focus of this chapter is to review these steps and to provide information on selected due process hearings and court cases that have occurred addressing the identification and/or admission processes for gifted learners. Examining such

cases is important due to the absence of federal protections for gifted students. In the absence of a mandate, legal recourse is often the only option that parents of gifted children have to secure appropriate educational services. However, many cases involving gifted students do not make it past the "due process" hearing level because of these limited protections and lack of legal precedence or law/policy to support a strong case if litigated. Since very few "gifted" cases are litigated, one has to examine due process hearings to get a better idea of the "issues" that are commonly in dispute involving gifted students.

### IDENTIFICATION AND THE STATE OF THE STATES

Though the federal government can establish parameters that guide state educational policy, states have considerable freedom in setting their own policies that directly impact the education of gifted students. While Local Education Agencies (LEAs) typically desire some flexibility in order to establish those procedures that best meet the needs of their respective student population, too much leeway can lead to misinterpretation or misrepresentation of the law and/or policy, thus creating a mass of inconsistencies across the state.

The State of the States Report is a publication of the Council of State Directors in Gifted Education and National Association for Gifted Children (NAGC, 2009). It provides a biannual summary of the status of gifted education across individual states.[1] Among those states responding,

- 28 mandate the identification of gifted students, but only 6 states provide full funding to support this mandate;

- 26 require specific criteria/methods to identify gifted students, with 21 of these using a multiple criteria model to identify gifted students;

- 17 report that all LEAs in their state identify gifted and talented students;

- 16 mandate the age at which gifted and talented students must be identified;

- 21 collect information on the numbers of students identified as gifted and talented (among those that do collect demographic data, Caucasians represented the majority of gifted students in all but three states [Texas, Hawaii and Nebraska]); and,

- 43 do not place a cap on the percent of students a district may identify for the gifted and talented program. Two states that do set such caps are Maine (5% cap) and Washington (2.314% cap).

The variations between states and ambiguity within policies make the area of gifted identification particularly difficult for parents and educa-

tors to understand and navigate. And conflicting understandings and expectations between parents and schools can lead to formal disputes. (Chapter 6 in this volume offers additional discussion on ambiguity within policies in gifted identification.)

## METHODS FOR RESOLVING DISPUTES

While some states have legislation and/or state board of education policy that establishes when and how gifted students are to be identified, court cases and administrative hearings are other sources by which procedural guidelines, methods, and related policy are developed (Gallagher, 2002). When there is a disagreement between a family and a school regarding identification—or any other educational issue—negotiation, mediation, and due process should be sought first to resolve disputes, with litigation being a final consideration. Descriptions of each of these processes follow.

### NEGOTIATION

Negotiation is the informal process by which parties discuss a problem in an effort to reach a compromise. Typically, negotiation begins at the level at which the dispute arises, which is often the classroom teacher (Karnes & Marquardt, 1997). If negotiations at this level are unsuccessful, involvement by others up the administrative ladder—the principal, the superintendent, or even the school board may be necessary.

In order to prepare for the negotiation process, both parties must be well informed about the state and local rules, regulations, and policies that govern identification of the gifted. Both parents

---

[1] Additional information regarding the status of gifted education across states can be found at the Davidson Institute for Talent Development at http://www.davidsongifted.org/db/StatePolicy.aspx

and school and district personnel should retain detailed records of all meetings and correspondence during the negotiation process (Karnes and Marquardt, 1997). If negotiation is unsuccessful, mediation may be the next course of action.

## MEDIATION

Mediation is a voluntary, nonadversarial process that allows disputing parties to meet with an impartial, third-party facilitator in order to reach an agreement. In the 1997 reauthorization of the Individuals with Disabilities Education Act (IDEA), states were mandated to offer mediation as an option to individuals requesting a due process hearing.

According to respondents of the 2008–2009 State of the States Report (NAGC, 2009), mediation is required by state law for issues involving gifted education in 8 states (Alabama, Delaware, Florida, Kansas, Louisiana, New Mexico, Pennsylvania, and West Virginia).

Provisions regarding mediation cited in the 1997 amendments to IDEA include the following:

- Mediation must be voluntary and not delay or deny a parent's request for a due process hearing.
- A qualified, impartial mediator who is trained in effective mediation techniques must conduct the mediation.
- The state must maintain a list of qualified mediators who are knowledgeable in the laws and regulations regarding the provision of special education and related services.
- The mediator must be selected at random from a list or the parties may agree on the selection of a qualified mediator.
- The mediation sessions must be scheduled in a timely manner and held at a location convenient to both parties.
- Discussions that take place during the mediation process must be confidential and may not be used as evidence in any subsequent due process hearings or civil proceedings.
- The mediated agreement must be put in writing.
- All costs related to the mediation process are the responsibility of the state.

In the 2004 reauthorization of IDEA, these mediation requirements from the 1997 Act remained, with the only clarification being made to the confidentiality and written agreement requirements. For instance, the written agreement is described as a legally binding agreement that is enforceable in any State court of competent jurisdiction or in a district court of the United States.

Encouraged by the effectiveness of alternative dispute resolution mechanisms, both federal and state governments continue to provide financial support through legislation to establish mediation opportunities (Karnes, Troxclair, & Marquardt, 1998). However, if an agreement cannot be reached through mediation, the next step, if available, is due process.

## DUE PROCESS

Due process is a procedure by which an aggrieved party has an opportunity to be heard by an impartial hearing officer. Due process hearings have several common requirements across states. These include

- timely notice to all parties involved that a hearing has been scheduled;
- opportunity to present evidence, witnesses, and oral arguments to an impartial hearing officer;
- opportunity to have counsel present;
- an oral or written record of the proceedings; and
- a written decision from the hearing officer based on the arguments presented at the hearing (Karnes, Troxclair, & Marquardt, 1998).

Locating hearing officer decisions is not an easy process. There is no federal mandate for the collection of such data (Ahearn, 2002). Furthermore, most states retain confidentiality of proceedings by deleting the names of the children, parents, and hearing officers involved, and many records are not kept for extended periods of time. In those states where gifted and talented programs are housed under "exceptional children," the statutory mandates of IDEA regarding due process hearings are typically followed unless otherwise specified. In addition to federal requirements, some states have adopted their own regulations or developed guidelines and policies in regard to due process procedures for students with disabilities (Ahearn, 2002). Those states that specifically cite provisions for due process hearings within their state rules, regulations, or legislation regarding the education of gifted and talented students are:

- Alabama
- Connecticut
- Florida
- Louisiana
- New Mexico[2]
- North Carolina
- Pennsylvania
- West Virginia

The 2008-2009 State of the States Report (NAGC, 2009) indicates that ten states offer the right to due process to the gifted under state special education law. Data regarding due process hearings compiled from an inquiry to state departments of education and extensive Internet research reveal that due process hearings are not widely used to resolve issues pertaining to gifted education (Karnes, Stephens, and McHard, 2007). Of the 40 states responding to the inquiry, only 11 (Alabama, Florida, Illinois, Iowa, Kansas, Louisiana, New Jersey, New York, Pennsylvania, Rhode Island, and Texas) reported due process hearings between 1990 and 2006 pertaining to gifted education. Two states (Connecticut and West Virginia) noted due process hearing requests involving gifted education, but these never progressed to a hearing.

## SUMMARIES OF SELECTED DUE PROCESS HEARINGS ON IDENTIFICATION ISSUES

The selected hearings presented here show that parents often use due process rights to resolve

---

[2] Gifted children fall under the umbrella of exceptional children. All the applicable rules for children with disabilities apply to gifted children except child find (the process by which children are initially referred for potential services) in private schools, home schooled children, those enrolled in state supported schools, or children in detention and correctional facilities; and when a child receiving specific services under special education needs to be removed from those services for disciplinary reasons and given some other services, instead, special education law requires that certain procedures be followed.

disputes pertaining to identification. More often than not, hearing officers sided with the school district on program eligibility and identification, with Pennsylvania reporting the most hearings (over 30). Many of Florida's hearings involved the implementation of PLAN B, a plan to increase minority participation in programs for the gifted.[3]

Following is an overview of selected due process hearing decisions related to identification issues in gifted education.

### FLORIDA.

*Leon County School Board* (1998)—This case raised the issue of whether the Individualized Education Plan (IEP) for a student would provide a Free and Appropriate Education (FAPE) and, specifically, whether the student was entitled to be enrolled in the district's gifted program on the basis of being a member of an underrepresented racial or ethnic group or by having limited English proficiency (PLAN B). The student was Asian, of Sri Lankan origin, and bilingual. The administrative law judge found that Asian/Pacific Islanders as a category were well represented proportionally in the gifted program and that it had not been demonstrated by a preponderance of evidence that the student was of limited English proficiency. Thus the student could not be recommended to the gifted program on the basis of PLAN B.

---

[3] In 1991, the state of Florida ordered school systems to develop a second plan (PLAN B, as it came to be known) to increase minority participation in programs for the gifted. PLAN B allowed districts to accept minority or low-income students into the gifted program without having the required IQ score of 130 as long as these children showed other signs of giftedness. In 2002, PLAN B was amended and racial/ethnic background was excluded as a category for eligibility under PLAN B.

*School Board of Palm Beach County* (2000)—A mother of an eight-year-old filed a request for due process seeking a determination that her son be eligible for the gifted program based upon his partial IQ score of 135 on the verbal component. The mother's request was denied because the child had not demonstrated the need for a special program and had not achieved the required score on a gifted characteristics checklist that was also required for eligibility determination.

*Miami-Dade County School Board* (2002)—Parents alleged that the school district improperly denied their fifth-grade autistic child a place in the gifted program for which, they asserted, he was eligible under the PLAN B criteria. The district explained to the parents that as of December 12, 2001, they had stopped using the race and ethnicity factors for evaluating students under PLAN B, but that it was still considering limited English proficiency and low socio-economic status. Since the student was neither, he was not eligible for the gifted program under PLAN B. Furthermore, he was not eligible under PLAN A because his IQ was below the cutoff prescribed by the state. The administrative law judge found that the student was ineligible for the district's gifted education program.

### NEW JERSEY.

*Lower Camden County Regional School District Number One* (1999)—Parents of a thirteen-year-old with a subtle learning disability challenged the decision of the local school board to deny the student participation in the school district's academically gifted and talented enrichment class. Students with disabilities must meet the same cutoff score for entry into the gifted and talented program as their non-disabled peers. The parents contended that the student was gifted with a potential higher than was demonstrated due to the subtle learning disability in speech and language and motor coordination. The district contended that the student would be easily frustrated by the extensive writing, rapid pace, and keyboarding skills of the gifted program and felt the student would not function well in the class. Since the student was performing well academically, he did not qualify for special accommodations. The administrative law judge affirmed the decision of the board of education, thus dismissing the parents' appeal.

### PENNSYLVANIA.

*Tulpehocken Area School District* (1999)—A father rejected an IEP team's decision that his sixteen year-old daughter did not qualify as an eligible child according to the gifted criteria. The hearing officer ordered that the student continue program and placement in regular education as currently designed because she did not qualify as mentally gifted. The father filed a Notice of Appeal excepting to the entire hearing officer's decision. The appeals panel affirmed the hearing officer's decision and dismissed the parent's exceptions.

*Williamsport Area School District* (2000)—Parents of a second-grader requested a due process hearing following a disagreement with the district about appropriate identification. The hearing officer's decision stated that the student did not meet the criteria under current Pennsylvania definition of mentally gifted and, therefore, did not require gifted education. The parents filed exceptions to this decision. Specifically, the parents questioned

how the student was evaluated for possible giftedness in light of a suspected learning disability. The appeals panel affirmed the hearing officer's decision, asserting that the student was well served in the regular classroom without specially designed instruction.

*Maple Newtown School District* (2000)—Parents of a third-grade student initiated a due process hearing after their daughter was found to be ineligible to participate in the district's gifted program. The hearing officer ordered that the student should continue in her current placement and that the educational program supplied to the student should be at her appropriate instructional level. The parents presented exceptions to the hearing officer's decision. The appeals panel denied the parent's exceptions.

*Lower Merion School District* (2001)—Parents requested a due process hearing to challenge the district's determination that their daughter was not eligible for the gifted program. The hearing officer ordered that the student did not meet the criteria for inclusion under the current Pennsylvania definition of mentally gifted and, therefore, did not require gifted education. The parents exceptions were procedural and substantive as follows:

1) the failure of the process to consider the report of the parents' expert;

2) the failure to consider testimony from the parents' independent and neutral expert;

3) the failure to provide documents within five days pursuant to the five day disclosure rule;

4) the failure to grant continuance so that the parents may supplement and/or complete record with consideration of

the independent and neutral expert's report on child's giftedness;

5) failure of expert witness to meet, test, and/or personally interview the student;

6) failure of the expedited due process hearing to interview, meet, and/or confer with child's classroom teachers and failure to call classroom teachers to testify; and

7) failure to permit the parents continuance to allow time for the presentation of an independent educational evaluation report relative to an evaluation scheduled for student by parents' independent educational expert.

The district's response urged the appeals panel to affirm the hearing officer's decision. The exceptions of the parents were dismissed and the hearing officer's decision affirmed.

*Hempfield School District* (2002)—In a dispute regarding a student's eligibility under Pennsylvania's gifted education regulations, a hearing officer determined that

1) the student did not qualify for specially designed gifted education;

2) the student's parents were not entitled to reimbursement for an independent educational evaluation;

3) the student was not entitled to compensatory education; and

4) the district's policy for identifying gifted students under the gifted education regulations was not flawed.

The parents filed exceptions to this decision. The appeals panel affirmed the hearing officer's decision, but modified the order indicating that the district should retest the student using the Raven's

Progressive Matrices and the WISC-III with the Symbol Search replacing the Coding Test. The district filed a petition for review of the panel's order with the Commonwealth Court of Pennsylvania. The panel's order was stayed pending a determination of the appeal to the courts.

*Wilson School District* (2005)—Parents of a nine-year-old sought an evaluation to determine eligibility for the gifted program. Evaluation revealed the student was high functioning, but not gifted. The hearing officer found that the preponderance of the evidence overwhelmingly supported this conclusion since the parents only put forth subjective assessment to challenge the decision.

*Haverford School District* (2005)—After being identified as gifted, parents of a student filed a request for a due processing hearing seeking compensatory education for previous years when the student had not qualified for the gifted program. A hearing officer determined the parents were not entitled to compensatory education, reimbursement for independent evaluations, or any other relief. The parents filed exceptions to the hearing officer's decision. The appeals panel unanimously affirmed the hearing officer's orders.

### RHODE ISLAND.

*Pawtucket School Committee* (1997)—A parent argued that she was in the best position to evaluate her child and that she should have the choice of whether or not to enroll her son in the gifted program. The student in this case had not achieved a high enough score to be admitted into the gifted program, even though he had been tested several times. The commissioner concluded that the school had the right to reasonably classify students and found nothing unreasonable about the classification methods used. The judgment not to admit the student into the gifted program was therefore sustained.

### TEXAS.

*Longview Independent School District* (1993)— A parent petitioned for a review before the State Commissioner of Education alleging that his daughter was improperly denied entrance into the gifted and talented program. Specifically, the parent claimed that the district's identification procedures did not meet the state guidelines. The district afforded relief to the student allowing her to participate in the gifted and talented program, but she did not enroll. The parent's appeal was dismissed for mootness of issue.

These examples show that courts are willing to grant a good deal of deference to the decisions of hearing officers. Parents face an uphill battle in trying to get these decisions changed.

Due to the confidentiality of most due process proceedings, it is difficult to determine how many parents, when dissatisfied with a hearing officer's decision, decide to take further action in advocating for their child through litigation. Since school systems have overwhelmingly prevailed on issues of identification in due process hearings, it can be assumed that some of these parents have sought relief through district courts. Regardless, parents do report the need for increased information and support with regard to hearing and complaint procedures (Opuda, 1999), as well as assurances that the due process system will not harm their long-term relationships with schools. Such fears

may deter parents from using any dispute resolution mechanism.

### LITIGATION

As mentioned previously, litigation should be the last option pursued, as it is the most costly and time-consuming method for resolving a dispute. Zirkel (2004; 2005) suggested that when reviewing case law on gifted students, two distinct categories should be considered: (1) "gifted alone," meaning those students eligible for gifted education without any other special legal protection, and (2) "gifted plus," or those students who are gifted but are also eligible for other federal, legal protections (e.g., students with disabilities under IDEA and minority gifted students under Title IV of the Civil Rights Act).

In both instances—"gifted alone" and "gifted plus"—decisions dealing with gifted education provisions have favored school districts, particularly in states with permissive gifted education legislation. In "gifted plus" cases, courts have had a tendency to focus on a child's disability rather than his or her academic or intellectual strengths (Zirkel, 2004). For the purpose of this chapter, we present only "gifted alone" cases as they specifically pertain to the topic at hand—gifted child education—and the children depicted in these cases do not fall under federal protections (i.e., IDEA).

### SELECTED CASES ADDRESSING IDENTIFICATION ISSUES

Court cases involving the identification of gifted students have addressed a wide range of issues including reimbursement for educational evaluation; challenges to evaluation procedures, assessment instruments, and eligibility criteria; and perceived discriminatory practices. Following are summaries of select cases that are representative of these issues. For the most part, school districts have prevailed in these disputes.

## REIMBURSEMENT FOR INDEPENDENT EDUCATIONAL EVALUATION.

IDEA (Individuals with Disabilities Education Act) includes a provision that allows parents to obtain an independent educational evaluation at the school district's expense whenever parents disagree with an evaluation provided by the district. Since gifted students (except those with diagnosed learning disabilities) are not included in IDEA, parents of gifted children have unsuccessfully pursued reimbursements for such evaluations.

In *Ford v. Long Beach Unified School District* (2002), parents challenged a district's determination that their daughter was not disabled despite the fact that she scored high on IQ tests, but was doing very poorly in school. The parents believed that their daughter was entitled to services under IDEA due to a central auditory processing disorder. They relied on a California regulation that makes students eligible for services if they have a severe discrepancy between intellectual ability and achievement. The parents challenged the assessments given by the district and their right for reimbursement for an independent evaluation. The Ninth Circuit U.S. Court of Appeals found that the district's assessments were adequate and that the parents were responsible for the cost of any independent evaluations.

In a similar case, a parent demanded that his daughter receive an independent evaluation at the district's expense and that he be reimbursed for his attorney's fees pursuant to IDEA (*Huldah A. v. Easton Area School District*, 1992). The Pennsylvania Commonwealth Court affirmed the special education appeals panel's decision, which indicated that gifted children do not fall under the protections of IDEA; therefore, the plaintiff was not entitled to an independent evaluation at the school district's expense or the reimbursement of attorney fees.

## IDENTIFICATION PROCESS.

Some cases have challenged the process by which school systems identify gifted students. Many complainants have used civil rights laws to support their argument.

In Alabama, *Lee v. Lee County Board of Education* (2007) addressed the disproportionate majority of Black students in special education and the underrepresentation of such students in gifted and talented programs. The U.S. District Court ordered the superintendents of Alabama to rectify the problem. Revisions to the procedures and policies related to pre-referral, referral, evaluation, and eligibility criteria were made by the state board of education; teachers were provided with extensive training; and monitoring of special education plans and programs across local school districts was initiated, resulting in annual progress reports. As a result of these provisions, Black student enrollment in gifted education doubled from 1999 to 2007.

In *Rosenfeld v. Montgomery County Public Schools* (2001), parents of two students in Maryland challenged various procedures and policies the school system used to select students for participation in the gifted and talented program. The parents claimed the policies and procedures discriminated against students who were not members of "preferred" minority groups by creating different, less stringent admission criteria for such minority students. As a result of this practice, White and Asian students were at a disadvantage in competing for the limited number of spaces available in the program. The parents sought injunctive relief under the Equal Protection Clause of the Fourteenth Amendment and under Title VI of the Civil Rights Act.

The U.S. District Court sided with the school system, indicating that both students involved lacked standing to challenge the admissions policy. One student lacked standing because her prospective injury was not imminent enough to meet the constitutional requirement of injury, and the other student's claim for injunctive relief was barred because he had already been accepted into the International Baccalaureate (IB) program at his high school, which was considered the "gifted program." On appeal, the circuit court affirmed the district court's decision.

In the Pennsylvania case, *Lisa H. v. Board of Education* (1982), two students who were evaluated but not selected to participate in the gifted program claimed that the Pennsylvania Code that defines gifted and talented individuals was unconstitutional under both the United States and Pennsylvania Constitutions. They argued that the gifted and talented program infringed upon their fundamental property right to a free, public education appropriate to their needs. The plaintiffs also argued that the program excluded them from available educational instruction without just cause, provided them with an education inferior

to that afforded to students in the program, and resulted in the expenditure of fewer tax dollars on their education than on the education of students categorized as gifted.

The Pennsylvania Commonwealth Court found that education is not among the rights, either implicitly or explicitly, that is guaranteed under the Federal Constitution. In addition, the court held that the state constitution does not confer an individual with the right to a particular level or quality of education, but only requires the legislature the duty of providing a thorough and efficient system of schools throughout the state. Further, the court held that the plaintiffs did not use their right to due process prior to seeking litigation. The defendants' objections were sustained and the case dismissed.

In *Williamson County Board of Education v. C.K.* (2007), the use of outside testing results was challenged by a school. C.K. had been tested by an outside educational firm, scoring a 143 on the WISC-III (Wechsler Intelligence Scale for Children, Third Edition)(99th percentile). In light of his poor grades and diagnosed ADHD, C.K.'s parents urged the school to develop an IEP for their son. The school felt that C.K. did not qualify for an IEP. Finding that the WISC-III test score was three years old, the school board demanded a new test be administered by school officials. C.K. scored a 121 on this test. The board then concluded that C.K.'s needs were being met in a general education setting. The parents asked for an administrative hearing, claiming that C.K. had been denied a Free and Appropriate Education (FAPE) because he was never given an IEP. The school board argued that the outside testing results should never have been considered. However, the U.S. District Court for the Middle District of Tennessee found that as a matter of law, the school board cannot reject outside testing without showing why that testing should not be used. The court could find no such evidence provided by the school board.

In Pennsylvania, the gifted education guidelines (Pennsylvania Department of Education, 2004) state that a child is considered gifted if (1) the student "has an IQ of 130 or higher" and (2) displays "multiple criteria . . . indicat[ing] gifted ability" (22 Pa. Code § 16.1 [d]). In *E.N. v. M. School District* (2007), parents challenged the school system's decision that their six-year-old, first grader was not eligible for the gifted program based on his IQ test scores (Composite score of 131 on the *Kaufman Brief Intelligence Scale, 2nd Edition* and a Full Scale IQ score of 124 on the Wechsler Intelligence Scale for Children, Fourth Edition [WISC-IV]). The school report indicated that he had scored significantly lower on those WISC-IV components that address processing speed. In an argument against the use of rigid IQ standards, the parents specifically cited the research of Mary Frasier (as cited in Coleman, 2003) that states "[w]hen identification procedures require the use of 'cut scores' and/or formulas that combine scores from a variety of measures into a single score (i.e., an IQ score combined with an achievement score and a performance score from a checklist), we violate sound statistical methods and the data are no longer valid" (p. 3)." However, the court noted that the regulations do provide some flexibility by providing that "[a] person with an IQ score lower than 130 may be admitted to gifted programs when other educational criteria in the profile of

the person strongly indicate gifted ability" (22 Pa. Code § 16.1 [d]).

The parents in this case also requested compensatory education for their child for the time he was not receiving gifted services. The Pennsylvania Commonwealth Court found no errors of law with the district's determination that the petitioner's child was not eligible for the gifted program.

It should be noted that researchers have closely examined the issue of slow processing speed on the WISC-IV (NAGC, 2010). In the WISC-IV, the weight given to processing skills in calculating Full Scale IQ doubled in comparison to earlier versions of the scale, while the weight assigned to reasoning skills was reduced. Since advanced reasoning skills, not processing speed, best identify gifted children, a deflation of full scale IQ scores may occur among gifted children on the WISC-IV (NAGC, 2010). In a recent position paper on the issue, the National Association for Gifted Children (2010) recommends that Full Scale IQ scores from the WISC-IV not be required for admission into gifted programs. Instead, it is advised that the General Ability Index (GAI) be used for this purpose. (Harcourt Assessments, the publisher of the WISC-IV, provides GAI tables on their Web site at http://harcourtassessments.com/hai/Images/pdf/wisciv/WISCIVTechReport4.pdf)

As many of the above cases show, parents have had little success trying to apply the protections afforded under IDEA to their gifted child, which isn't surprising since gifted students (with the exception of those students who also have a diagnosed learning disability) are not acknowledged in this legislation.

## IDENTIFICATION AND THE OFFICE FOR CIVIL RIGHTS

The Office for Civil Rights (OCR) in the U.S. Department of Education is designated to enforce five federal civil rights laws. The laws prohibit discrimination pertaining to color, national origin, race, sex, disability, and age in activities and programs receiving federal assistance. Ensuring equal access to education and promoting educational excellence is the mission of OCR. The major responsibilities of OCR include investigating complaints, compliance reviews, and providing technical assistance to institutions to achieve voluntary compliance with OCR standards (Karnes and Marquardt, 1994).

Three major studies have been reported on the investigations of OCR involving gifted students (Karnes and Marquardt, 1994; Karnes, Stephens, & McHard, 2007; Karnes, Troxclair, & Marquardt, 1998). From 1985-1991, there were forty-eight letters of finding pertaining to the gifted (Karnes and Marquardt, 1994), and OCR data from 1992–1995 revealed thirty-eight cases involving the gifted (Karnes, Troxclair & Marquardt, 1998). From 2000–2006, Karnes, Stephens, and McHard (2007) reported fifty-six letters of findings from twenty-five states. During this time, Florida had the highest number of investigated complaints (7). The major issues from 2000-2006 were identification and admissions to programs.

It must be emphasized that there are no quotas or percentages of protected classes of students in gifted education set forth by OCR. Rather school districts must prove that their policies do not discriminate against these students. Some guidelines school systems might take into consideration to ensure compliance follow.

- Appoint a bi-racial committee to establish guidelines for screening and identification procedures that do not discriminate on the basis of race, color, disability, gender, and age.

- Determine the eligibility criteria, including multiple criteria for eligibility and multiple assessment measures.

- Inform all parents, students, and the community about the screening and identification procedures and program(s).

- Provide staff development on an annual basis for all certified school personnel about the characteristics, nature, and needs of all gifted and talented students.

- Use nondiscriminatory screening criteria and procedures that are directly related to the purpose of the gifted program.

- Ensure that all approved assessment instruments/measures are validated with respect to the population for whom they are being used, that the instruments/measures accurately assess the abilities/skills intended to be measured, and that the abilities/skills are consistent with the definition of the gifted used at the local/state level.

- Monitor by race, disability, gender, and age the number of students nominated and identified in each individual school in the district to determine that discrimination does not occur.

- Initiate change, if and when needed.

• Appoint a bi-racial appeals committee for the district.

OCR has worked in many ways to represent and protect gifted students from underserved populations. In 2000, OCR collaborated with a state educational agency to ensure that all students with outstanding abilities had access to gifted and talented programs (OCR, 2000). In addition, OCR commissioned a study in 2002 by the National Academy of Sciences entitled Minority Students in Special and Gifted Education (Donovan & Cross, 2002). This report examined the underrepresentation of minority students in programs for the gifted and made recommendations to increase participation.

The OCR has proven to be a viable vehicle for resolving discrimination on issues involving race, color, national origin, sex, disability, and age in programs and activities receiving federal assistance. Karnes and Marquardt (1994) emphasized that complainants can delineate the issues, provide information, and discuss proposed solutions without worrying about technical court procedures.

## CONCLUSION

As evidenced by many of the arguments brought forth in the courts regarding gifted and talented education, there continues to be a high degree of misunderstanding about the rights of gifted students under the law. Parents have attempted (unsuccessfully) to use the protections afforded to students with disabilities under IDEA to support their arguments for FAPE, compensatory education, and the development of IEPs. However, gifted students (except those with a diagnosed

learning disability) are excluded from this federal legislation.

To further compound the issue, only about half of the states have a mandate for the identification of gifted students, and in those states with a mandate, disparities in identification procedures vary across school systems. It is no wonder that parents of the gifted are often confused about the educational responsibilities of school systems to identify and serve gifted students.

With no federal mandate and few, if any, court cases to set legal precedence, no guiding structures exist by which states can establish their own sound policies and regulations for gifted students. Parents are left to navigate the appropriateness of their child's education alone, and school systems will continue to prevail in disputes due to ambiguous state policies regarding methods for identifying and serving gifted students that often "lack teeth" or assurances of enforceability. In other words, policies are only as good as the mechanisms in place to ensure that school districts are accountable to them. There must be state oversight to ensure the fidelity of identification procedures at the school district level.

A clear definition for an "appropriate" education for gifted students needs to be established. In addition, equitable and accurate screening, identification, and program eligibility criteria/procedures must be determined. There has been a tendency to focus on the objective in identifying students—a test score—which is easily quantified and helps "sort" students. But, are some gifted students being missed? Those with undiagnosed learning disabilities? Those who are not fluent in English? Those from low socio-economic circumstances?

Comprehensive standards, sound policies, and carefully monitored accountability mechanisms are all needed to ensure that schools across the country are sufficiently identifying gifted students across all populations.

Perhaps more subjective means (i.e., teacher observations and parent reports) may be more successful in identifying gifted students. If this is the case, how can teachers become more adept in recognizing those behaviors and traits that are characteristic for gifted students? How can teachers move beyond their biases and perceived stereotypes to recognize potentially gifted students? It is also important to note that the creation of any law and policy pertaining to the identification of gifted students must involve teachers as a key stakeholder. Teachers must be involved from the beginning of such policy conversations to ensure

clarity in interpretation, long term sustainability, and "buy-in."

Even though the use of multiple-criteria is required in many states when identifying gifted students, the reality is that "multiple-criteria" has come to mean the use of many methods to gather information, and this rarely translates into the use of ALL collected data to make an informed decision regarding program eligibility. The fact remains that some data is considered above and beyond all others, and as a result, we are probably missing many gifted students who would thrive in specialized programs. As such, it is quite possible that legal disputes, particularly those involving constitutional challenges (Fourteenth Amendment), will continue with regard to how students are identified for gifted programs.

## REFERENCES

Ahearn, E. (2002, April). Due process hearings: 2001 update. Retrieved on July 31, 2006, from http://www.projectforum.org/docs/due_process_hearings_2001.pdf

Coleman, M. (2003). *The identification of students who are gifted.* Arlington, VA: ERIC Clearinghouse on Disabilities and Gifted Education. (ERIC Document Reproduction Service No. ED480431)

Donovan, M. S., & Cross, C. T. (Eds.) (2002). *Minority students in special and gifted education.* Washington, DC: National Academies Press.

Gallagher, J. J. (2002). *Society's role in educating gifted students:* The role of public policy. [Monograph]. Storrs, CT: National Research Center on the Gifted and Talented. (ERIC Document Reproduction Service No. ED476370)

Individuals with Disabilities Education Act Amendments of 1997, 20 U.S.C. § 1400 et seq. (1997).

Individuals with Disabilities Education Improvement Act of 2004, 20 U.S.C. § 1400 et seq. (2004).

Karnes, F. A., & Marquardt, R. G. (1994). Gifted education and discrimination: The role of the Office for Civil Rights. *Journal for the Education of the Gifted, 18,* 87–94.

Karnes, F. A., & Marquardt, R. G. (1997). *Know your legal rights in gifted education.* Reston, VA: Council for Exceptional Children. (Eric Reproduction Document Service No. ED415590)

Karnes, F. A., Stephens, K. R., & McCard, E. (2007). Legal issues in gifted education. In F. A. Karnes and K. R. Stephens (Eds.), *Gifted education* [Tentative Title]. Columbus, OH: Pearson Merrill/Prentice Hall.

Karnes, F. A., Troxclair, D. A., & Marquardt, R. G. (1998). Due process in gifted education. *Roeper Review, 20,* 297–301.

National Association for Gifted Children. (2009). *The state of the states report.* Washington, DC: Author.

National Association for Gifted Children. (2010). *Position statement: Use of the WISC-IV for gifted identification.* Retrieved April 26, 2011, from http://nagc.org/uploadedFiles/WISC%20IV%20Position%20Paper.pdf

Office for Civil Rights. (2000). Annual report to Congress. Retrieved August 9, 2006, from http://www.ed.gov/about/offices/list/ocr/AnnRpt2000/edlite-index.html

Opuda, M. J. (1999). A comparison of parents who initiated due process hearings and complaints in Maine. (Doctoral dissertation, Virginia Polytechnic Institute And State University, 1999). *Dissertation Abstracts International, 60,* 1081.

Pennsylvania Department of Education. (2004). *Gifted guidelines.* Harrisburg, PA: Author. Retrieved August 3, 2006, from http://www.pagiftededucation.info/pdf/GiftedGuidelines.pdf

Zirkel, P. A. (2004). The case law on gifted education: A new look. *Gifted Child Quarterly, 48,* 309–314.

Zirkel, P. A. (2005). *The law on gifted education* (Rev. ed.). [Research Monograph 05178R].

Storrs, CT: The National Research Center on
the Gifted and Talented.

## COURT CASES

E. N. v. M. School District, 928 A.2d 453 (Pa.
Commw. Ct. 2007).

Ford v. Long Beach Unified School District, 291
F.3d 1086 (9th Cir. 2002).

Huldah A. v. Easton Area School District, 601
A.2d 860 (Pa. Commw. Ct. 1992).

Lee v. Lee County Board of Education, 476 F.
Supp. 2d 1356, 2007 U.S. Dist. (M.D. Ala.
2007).

Lisa H. v. Board of Education, 447 A.2d 669 (Pa.
Commw. Ct. 1982).

Rosenfeld v. Montgomery County Public
Schools, 41 F. Supp. 2d 581, 1999 U.S. Dist.
2940 (D. Md. 1999).

Williamson County Board of Education, v. C.
K., No. 3:07-0826, U.S. Di

# ADDITIONAL RESOURCES

## WEB SITES

**Center for Gifted Education Policy (CGEP):** www.apa.org/ed/cgep.html

Housed in APA's Education Directorate, CGEP generates public awareness, advocacy, clinical applications, and cutting-edge research ideas regarding children and adolescents with special gifts and talents.

**Consortium for Appropriate Dispute Resolution in Special Education (CADRE):** www.directionservice.org/cadre

Provides technical assistance to state departments of education on implementation of the mediation requirements under IDEA '97. CADRE also supports parents, educators, and administrators in dispute resolution.

**Genius Denied:** www.geniusdenied.com/StatePolicy.aspx

Provides information about respective state policies in gifted education.

**National Association of State Directors of Special Education:** www.nasdse.org/index.cfm

Helps state agencies promote and support specially designed instruction and related services for children and youth with disabilities.

**National Research Center on Gifted and Talented Education (NRC/GT):** www.nrcgt.org

Funded by the Jacob K. Javits Gifted and Talented Students Education Act, NRC/GT is a nationwide cooperative of researchers, practitioners, policy makers, and other persons and groups that have a stake in developing the performance and potentials of young people from preschool through postsecondary levels.

**U.S. Department of Education's Office for Civil Rights:** www.ed.gov/ocr

Ensures equal access to education and promotes educational excellence throughout the nation through enforcement of civil rights.

**State of the States Report:** www.nagc.org/index.aspx?id=10

Presents a biannual snapshot of how states regulate and support programs and services for gifted students.

## SUGGESTED READINGS

Gallagher, J. J. (1994). Current and historical thinking on education for gifted and talented students. In P. O'Connell-Ross (Ed.), *National excellence: A case for developing America's talent. An anthology of readings.* Washington, DC: Office of Educational Research and Improvement. (ERIC Document Reproduction Service No. ED372584)

Gallagher, J. J. (Ed.). (2004). *Public policy in gifted education.* Thousand Oaks, CA: Corwin.

Karnes, F. A., & Marquardt, R. G. (1991). *Gifted children and legal issues in education: Parents' stories of hope.* Scottsdale, AZ: Great Potential.

Karnes, F. A., & Marquardt, R. G. (2000). *Gifted children and legal issues: An update.* Scottsdale, AZ: Great Potential.

Karnes, F. A., & Marquardt, R. G. (2003). Gifted education and legal issues: Procedures and recent decisions. In N. Colangelo & G. A. Davis (Eds.), *Handbook of gifted education* (pp. 590–603). Boston: Allyn & Bacon.

Landrum, M. S., Katsiyannis, A., & DeWaard, J. (1998). A national survey of current legislative and policy trends in gifted education: life after the national excellence report. *Journal for the Education of the Gifted, 21*, 352–371.

O'Connell-Ross, P. (2003). Federal involvement in gifted and talented education. In N. Colangelo and G. A. Davis (Eds.), *Handbook of gifted education* (pp. 604–608). Boston: Allyn & Bacon.

Russo, C. J., & Harris, J. J. (1996). Gifted education and the law: A right, privilege, or superfluous? *Roeper Review, 18*, 179–182.

Shaunessy, E. (2003, Summer). State policies regarding gifted education. *Gifted Child Today, 26*, 16-22.

Stephens, K. R. (2000, January/February). Gifted education and the law. *Gifted Child Today, 23*, 30–37.

## CHAPTER 5 STUDY GUIDE

Prompt 1 *Knowledge*

Distinguish among the four means for resolving disputes related to gifted identification (i.e., negotiation, mediation, due process, litigation) as described in this chapter.

**Prompt 2** *Opinion*

The authors believe that litigation should be saved to use as a last resort by families to solve disputes with schools. Do you agree with this? Why or why not?

**Prompt 3** *Affect*

Select any of the due process cases described in this chapter. Describe and defend your emotional reactions to the case.

**Prompt 4** *Experience*

Keeping in mind confidentiality requirements, describe any experience you or a colleague have had with any of the levels of dispute discussed in this chapter (i.e., negotiation, mediation, due process, litigation). Explore the degree to which the suggestions or requirements, as given in this chapter, for the level you of dispute you experienced were followed.

**Prompt 5** *Preconception/Misconception*

Select one of the court cases described in this chapter that had an outcome that was surprising to you (e.g., the Pennsylvania case, *Lisa H. v. Board of Education*, in which it was found that there is not a constitutional right to an education). Explain why the finding of the court was surprising to you.

# POLICY PERSPECTIVES ON GIFTED EDUCATION

SCOTT L. HUNSAKER, UTAH STATE UNIVERSITY
PAUL SHEPHERD, GRANITE SCHOOL DISTRICT, SALT LAKE CITY, UT

Policy in gifted education, especially as it pertains to the identification of gifted students, is the domain of state and local educational agencies (Irby & Lara-Alecio, 2002). These policies "often determine the educational fates of many gifted children" (Gallagher, 2002, p. 1), yet many educators and parents ignore the role policy plays in their students' and children's lives. As Gallagher laments, "These policies, [teachers and parents] believe, are created by powerful people geographically and psychologically distant from them, and result in abstract rules and obscure language that does not concern them or the children who are their main interest" (p.1). Because policy emanates from legislation, court cases, administrative rules, or professional standards (Gallagher, 2002), teachers and parents may feel some justification in their attitude toward policy. Yet doing so can have dire consequences for their children. Because, as Gallagher notes, policies are really "social hypotheses" (p. 6), they can have unintended effects, for good or for ill. When those effects are for ill, they will continue until the causal policy is removed from the books. As Gallagher points out, "Old policies can be like unwelcome houseguests who overstay their visit, but continue to stay around until someone tells them to go" (p. 27).

Reis (1989) has quipped that "policy is a term used by many but defined by few" (p. 402). Fortunately, one of the few is a leading scholar in gifted education, who has defined policy thus, "Social policy creates the rules and standards by which scarce resources are allocated to meet almost unlimited social needs" (Gallagher, 2002, p. 1; see also, Gallagher, 2006; and Moon & Roselli, 2000). This definition supplies the outline for the remainder of this chapter, in which we will first explore the need claims of gifted education, followed by a presentation on the allocation of resources, and finishing with a discussion of the establishment of rules.

## CLAIMING NEED

According to Stone (2002), "Need is the most fundamental political claim" (p. 86). Need claims can be based on a number of dimensions. The most basic needs, of course, are those related to physical survival. We as humans have certain minimal biological requirements for sustaining life. These needs would tend to be absolute and direct—meaning that they must be fulfilled for survival to be ensured and that it is quite obvious when these needs are or are not being met.

Some needs, on the other hand, are more symbolic, drawing their meaning from a social context rather than a physical necessity. These needs are defined in accordance with societal standards, norms, and customs. Fulfillment of such needs is more difficult to assess because they are more instrumental, enabling us to do important things in the future or making up for mistakes in the past, rather than satisfying our need to survive in the here and now (Stone, 2002).

In discussing the purposes of program evaluation of gifted programs, Callahan and Caldwell (1997) identify "documenting the need for the program" (p. 3) as essential. Under this rubric, they list three basic assumptions about programs for the gifted:

> (a) that a group of students who can appropriately be identified as gifted and talented exists, (b) that these individuals have educational needs which are different from those of students who are not identified as gifted and talented, and (c) that the educational needs of the identified students are not currently being met by the regular school program. (pp. 3-4)

These same three functions are also at the heart of establishing policy for gifted education. The first of these functions is what Gallagher (2002) calls the *eligibility question* and refers to questions such as "How are gifted students defined?" (p. 9),

and "Which children will be identified as gifted students and become eligible for available special education services?" (p. 1). At this point, according to the most recent *State of the States* report (National Association for Gifted Children [NAGC] & Council of State Directors of Programs for the Gifted [CSDPG], 2009), only 41 states have a definition of giftedness, with intellectual giftedness being the focus of the bulk of these definitions. However, the majority of these states do not require specific identification processes. This has been and will continue to be the major policy decision, according to Reis (1989), in gifted education at the national, state, and local levels.

Stone (2002) points out that "policy is centrally about classification and differentiation, about how we do and should categorize in a world where categories are not given" (p. 380). Relative to gifted education, much has been made of the concept of giftedness as a social construction rather than as something real (see, for example, Borland, 1996; Sapon-Shevin, 2003), yet, if we follow Stone's point, all policy is based on social construction—the creation of categories that do not exist in physical reality. The articulation of the construct, then, is much more important in policy setting, and this is no easy matter.

The definition itself of giftedness is unclear to many people. In 2008, then President of NAGC, Dr. Del Siegle, called for more clarity in the definition of the term. Siegle (2008) asserted that lack of clarity in defining giftedness led to a specific policy issue—the difficulty of lobbying for support of gifted learners. Stephens (2008) joins Siegle in lamenting the lack of clarity and specificity in policies for gifted education, including definitions, stating that it creates problems for local education agencies in establishing identification and services.

While this lack of clarity is problematic in policy formulation and advocacy, it may have another kind of utility and serve a purpose within the educational system. Scott (1998) describes a phenomenon in which policy within organizations acts as a buffer between environmental pressures and core technology of the organization. This phenomenon is referred to as *loose coupling*. One way it plays out at the state or district level is that the system establishes policies to satisfy environmental concerns and pressures (in this case, the concern for addressing the educational need of a gifted child), while leaving the fundamental actions in the classroom unchanged. Patrons concerned about the needs of gifted students will be directed to state and district policies in support of such services that satisfy their concern. Yet daily classroom operation remains largely unaffected by the policy. The policy acts as a buffer, providing stability within the organization without reallocating resources and disrupting current structures and programs. Viewed in this context, it is no surprise that definitions lack clarity or policy does not directly translate into program services. While serving organizational stability and functioning however, it creates a persistent problem in serving the legitimate special needs of the child.

Reis (1989) predicts that a consensus definition will never be reached. Cramond (2004) furthers this prediction when she points out that we've had an official federal definition of giftedness since 1972, and yet this has not lead to a unity of vision about gifted education services. She points out the

diversity of definition "allows representation of various viewpoints, consideration of diverse abilities, and expansion of the field" (p. 16). It could be debated that Siegle and Cramond are arguing about different types of definitions—theoretical and official, respectively—but Siegle uses a policy matter to defend his viewpoint, while Cramond uses a theoretical argument to support hers. However, Bélanger and Gagné (2006), arguing from both a theoretical and a policy perspective, seem to come down on the side of Siegle about the need for consensus on definition, but also lament that it will likely never be reached.

Stone (2002) specifically discusses the advantages of having either precise policy rules or flexible ones. She points out that precise policies "ensure fairness by treating likes alike, eliminate arbitrariness and discrimination in officials' behavior, create predictability for citizens, [and] symbolize the rule of law" (p. 292). While all of these outcomes seem desirable, Stone also points out that less precise, but more flexible, policies "ensure fairness by allowing sensitivity to contextual and individual differences, allow officials to respond creatively to new situations, create efficiencies by letting officials use their knowledge of particular situations, [and] symbolize ideals and aspirations of community, which are necessarily vague" (p. 292). The debate, then, in gifted education, from a policy perspective ought not necessarily be about the precision of the definition but about which we value more: precision or flexibility.

Even this distinction is fraught with difficulty, according to Stone (2002), because neither a perfectly precise nor a perfectly flexible policy is possible. Suggesting that a balance between the two be sought is also somewhat naïve, as is the search for a neutral rule. Such solutions are difficult because, with the balanced rule, we would be seeking to "eliminate unnecessary discretion" (p. 292), thereby setting ourselves up for debate about what is unnecessary; and with the neutral rule we'd be blithely ignoring that fact that "all rules benefit some people and harm others, however trivial the effects may be" (p. 295). Paradoxically, Stone criticizes the former solution because it causes debate and the latter solution because it avoids debate.

Clearly, debate will occur, creating a condition acknowledged by Stone and articulated by Gallagher (2006) that what will be done is that which is "best for the school or education department at the moment" (p. 212). Stephens (2008) decries this condition, stating that "policy development in gifted education has been driven by world events, perceived crises, and even the economy. As a result, a reactive rather than a proactive approach to addressing the needs of gifted students has ensued" (p. 404).

While proactivity in general is considered desirable, it may be important to remember that the policy-making environment is by definition a reactive environment. If policy is formulated based on need, then policy itself is a reaction to a need that exists or develops. A republican form of government is designed to react to the emerging needs of the citizenry. While frustrating to experts and professionals, care must be taken to acknowledge that legislative and administrative processes exist to arbitrate conflicting societal needs and those processes are necessarily reactive. Purcell (1994) has, in fact, shown a primacy for economic considerations in gifted policy development, demonstrating

that philosophical considerations do not have the impact both critics and supporters of gifted education might wish they would have. It would seem that the first proactive stance we could take in the development of gifted policy would be to understand the ambiguous, reactive nature of policy development in the political arena.

Another issue in establishing the existence of gifted children as a group with needs, as suggested by Callahan and Caldwell (1997), is the inductive process by which categories are created. According to Stone (2002), "We categorize by selecting important characteristics and asking whether the object to be classified is substantially like other objects in the category" (p. 164). This process is certainly followed in the identification of gifted students. Yet it is not without controversy either, as Callahan (1996) has pointed out. Lists of characteristics of gifted children were originally derived from the seminal work of Stanford University's Dr. Lewis Terman (1925) and his *Genetic Studies of Genius*, which investigated children who could primarily be said to exhibit intellectual giftedness. Yet these lists are often applied to children being assessed for artistic or social or other gifts. Further, multiple lists of the traits of gifted individuals have been developed, occasionally with overlap, but often not, so that the chances of any particular child being identified as gifted may depend on the list being used at his or her school. Further, the research basis of these lists is not always apparent.

Gallagher (1996) asserts that there does exist a group of children who "learn faster, remember more, or solve problems better than other students the same age" (p. 234) and draws upon evidence from genetics to sustain his argument. While it could clearly be debated whether or not this is the list of characteristics of giftedness we're searching for to aid us in establishing policy, it also raises the debate of whether or not giftedness is a physical reality.

Callahan and Caldwell (1997) indicate that the two final tasks for establishing the need for a program are to determine what the needs of the target population are and whether those needs are being met or not. Stone (2002) suggests that policy is created because "we have a suspicion, or a fear, or even some suggestive evidence that bad things will happen, but we do not know for sure" (p. 236). Some make needs arguments based on threats to the physical survival of gifted individuals. For example, some posit that dropping out of school (Rimm, 1995), substance abuse (Tieso, 1999), juvenile delinquency (Brooks, 1985), and suicide (Delisle & Galbraith, 2002) are distinctive problems among gifted students. While gifted students have certainly been known to face these issues, (see, for example, Cross, Gust-Brey, & Ball, 2002; Hansen & Toso, 2007), other scholars (Cornell, 1992; Irvine, 1987; Matthews, 2006) have demonstrated that the rates for gifted students are actually much lower than for other populations.

Regardless of whether or not these issues are really a problem for gifted-level learners, as Stone (2002) points out, "These kinds of facts are simply not the ones that matter in politics. . . . What communities decide about when they make policy is meaning, not matter" (p. 379). Or, as Gallagher (2006) states, "In policy decisions, values can trump facts when the final decisions are made" (p. 221).

Debates about meaning are, of course, related to the symbolic, relative, instrumental needs discussed earlier. One of the most frequently used arguments in favor of gifted education is the "enlightened self-interest" (Gallagher, 1991, p. 177) argument. Gallagher states this argument quite straightforwardly,

> This is one fundamental reason for wanting to provide special challenges for these gifted youngsters now in our public schools. The more they can accomplish, in school and beyond, the more benefits accrue to *all of us*. That is why investment in appropriate programs for highly able students is enlightened self-interest. There need be no apology for asking what is in the national self-interest, as well as in our own personal and professional best interest. (p. 178, emphasis in the original)

Clark (2008) has more recently and more sanguinely made a similar argument:

> The consequences of ignoring the needs of the brightest and most promising among us can be devastating. If society is to move forward, find solutions to overwhelming problems it faces throughout the world, realize its goals for peaceful coexistence of all humankind, and ensure the very continuation of its existence on this planet, we need the ideas our brightest minds can produce, and we will continue to need them far into the future. Such minds do not come fully formed at birth; giftedness must be nurtured. (p. 5)

Clark asserts that such contributions to the advancement of society come "in overweighted

125

proportion from gifted individuals" (p. 8). Clark later returns, however, to a physical need argument, "When human beings are limited and restricted in their development, we run the risk of creating both physical and psychological dysfunction" (p. 7).

Borland (1996), however, returns us to the central question about the meanings of our policy actions when he asks, "If one is helping one group and hurting another, do the demands of equity require one to stop helping the first group" (p. 139)? Sapon-Shevin (1996) extends this argument when she writes, "I am pained by the idea of *any* child who is rejected, unhappy, or unsupported in school. But focusing on the pain and difficulties of one particular group of students unnecessarily limits our scope and sense of responsibility" (p. 206). Gallagher (1996) counters with a statement of the societal meanings he draws from the discussion about the needs of various groups of students: "To argue for educational services for bright children is not an argument for inequity but rather a recognition that inequity will be unlikely to be cured by forcing a false equity upon people" (p. 246).

Within the preceding paragraph, it is apparent that one of the values used to establish or reject the need claims for the gifted student population is the concept of equality of equity. Further, from the preceding paragraph, it is clear that different individuals interpret the concepts differently. It would seem a simple task to define equality as a mathematical concept. Yet, "mathematics has only limited ability to identify what is equal in society" (Meyerson, 2002, p. 93). This idea is supported by Justice Willis Van DeVanter, who states, "A classification having some reasonable basis does not

offend against [the Equal Protection Clause of the U. S. Constitution] merely because it is not made with mathematical nicety" (cited in Meyerson, 2002, p. 91).

Other ways of thinking about equality or equity are needed. As Moon and Rosselli (2000) explain,

> Perhaps the most important cultural influences on gifted education are those related to educational philosophies . . . The *egalitarian* philosophy holds that the primary purpose of education is to create similar outcomes for all students . . . Thus an important educational goal in an egalitarian culture is the reduction of individual differences. In contrast, an *equal opportunity* culture values equality of opportunity more than equality of outcomes and recognizes that providing equal opportunities may actually increase the differences between individuals . . . A core education value in an equal opportunity culture is adapting instruction to meet individual needs. In an egalitarian culture, achieving excellence beyond age-group norms is discouraged. In an equal opportunity culture, achieving excellence beyond age-group norms is encouraged to the extent that resources are available. (p. 503, emphasis in the original)

The difference in the two equity arguments explained in the preceding quote can be illustrated through Clark's (2008) statement: "When we speak of equity, we must agree that having equal opportunity does not mean having the *same* opportunity. Equity means making experiences available that are uniquely appropriate to each individual"

(p. 6, emphasis in the original). Felicitously, in making her own distinction related to the term equal, Sapon-Shevin (2003) states,

> We need to distinguish between 'equal' education, meaning the same—the same curriculum, the same standards, the same teaching methods, the same evaluation—and an 'equally good' education, one responsive to each child as an individual, an education planned by a group of people who know the child well and can envision exciting possibilities for his or her education. (p. 139)

It appears that there is some common ground of values upon which proponents and opponents of gifted education may discuss the needs of gifted learners.

Clearly, claiming need for gifted students through defining giftedness, determining the needs of the population, and instituting a process for identification of the individuals to directly benefit from services is a political process. "In political life," Stone (2002) asserts, "precisely because it is so hard to draw clear lines about things that matter, fights arise at the lines and are about the lines" (p. 312), and, further, that "to claim need is to claim that one should be given resources or help because they are essential" (p. 86). In doing this, even in good faith, one creates "innocent victims" (Meyerson, 2002, p. 108). So the debate really is not about definitions, but about values.

## ALLOCATING RESOURCES

The system for allocating resources represents the mediation of dominant values and metavalues

within society. Values are beliefs that one specific mode of conduct is preferable to the opposite mode of conduct (Rokeach, 1973). Values are neither completely stable nor unstable within a society. They exist along a continuum of relative importance for each individual or group. A metavalue is a "concept of the desirable" (Hodgkinson, 1983, p. 43) so entrenched that it is beyond dispute. Such metavalues that are commonly shared and accepted in society create stability. However, factors such as time, context, and individual differences lead to differing prioritization of these values. Decisions on how resources are allocated reflect the tension among metavalues and evolving or changing priorities within the value system. Liberty and equality are examples of entrenched metavalues that may exist in tension within society. For example, greater societal prioritization for liberty may lead to greater inequalities, while greater prioritization of equality may necessarily result in limiting choices and reducing liberty. While both metavalues are embraced, time, context, and individual preference mediate which metavalue is dominant at any given moment in society.

As discussed previously, tension may exist within society about the equality of equity. Egalitarian values of equal treatment for all exist in creative tension with conceptualizations of equal opportunity for all. Thus, resource allocation policy issues dealing with identification and programming for gifted students are framed within the context of these two values. Government budgets become statements of policy priorities (Fowler, 2004). Laws are adopted and regulations passed that go unfunded. Often these laws and regulations exist in tension with one another and reflect the overall tensions among competing values in society. Those that are funded represent the priorities and compromises in mediating the competing needs and values.

Equity analysis presents a useful framework with which to understand state and federal funding for the needs of the gifted. Baker (2001) suggests that resource allocation for the gifted can be understood in terms of horizontal or vertical equity frames. Horizontal equity could best be understood as "equal treatment of equals" (p. 6) and is based on the assumption that if one group of students is similar to another group, they should receive similar resources. It is often applied to analysis of general populations on school funding disparities. Vertical equity may be understood in terms of "unequal treatment of unequals" (p. 6). This framework recognizes that some students may require more resources in order to attain a comparable education, so it is assumed equitable to provide additional resources for a special population. Using both forms in an analysis of the Texas school system, Baker analyzed funding efforts for adequacy within districts (vertical equity). Combining this with a horizontal equity analysis, Baker was also able to analyze funding across districts within the state, demonstrating that wealth-related disparities and urban-rural disparities existed. He argued that the use of equity analysis in this manner may provide a useful advocacy tool.

In education, states play the major role in policy development and resource allocation. Because the federal role is more visible through the media and public discussion, the state level role is often ignored or misunderstood (Fowler, 2004). The allocation structure in states distributes responsibility for resource allocation between branches of government. The legislative branch enacts statutes and sets budgets. The executive branch (including the governor and state and local boards of education) establishes the rules and regulations under which resources are distributed and provides accounting procedures. The judicial branch ensures that statutes and rules and regulations meet constitutional guidelines and provides oversight on protected class issues. Resources allocated for identification and programming for gifted and talented students are the result of complex interactions between actors in these branches of government as well as the input and negotiation of other institutional and organizational actors such as unions, education and parent associations, and non-education interest groups.

Firestone (1989) describes this complex political process as an "ecology of games" (p. 18). In this conception, organizations and individuals are all understood in terms of the games played to secure resources. The games of each organization will differ as their values, objectives, and goals differ. Where organizations can cooperate or negotiate to benefit collective interests, coalitions will form, power will be exercised, and resources will be acquired. Where enduring differences persist, organizations will conflict. An ecology represents the set of organizational stakeholders with an interest in a given issue or arena of conflict. Because of the inherent complexity in the competition for finite resources, policy development and resource allocation have a non-rational dimension. Instead of policy formulation and funding for the gifted proceeding in a rational way from identifying needs to establishing programs to address those needs, competition for resources leads to compromises and negotiations between stakeholders with competing interests. In our democratic system, the compromises often result in a disjointed or asynchronous approach to addressing the issues and needs of the gifted. This asynchrony will manifest itself in a variety of ways. For example, requirements to identify gifted students may not have concomitant requirements to provide services for those identified, and mandates to provide assessment and services may not have resources attached to fund the mandate.

## MANDATES

In analyzing societal progress toward identifying the needs of gifted children and addressing them in education, one must distinguish between those statutes, rules, and regulations that exist without the necessary resources to implement and those that come with attached resources. The allocation of resources is a real measure of societal commitment and priorities. The Davidson Institute for Talent Development (2010), in its analysis of state gifted education policy, classified states into five categories along two indices: programming and funding. The states were classified as follows:

1. gifted programming is not mandated and gifted funding is not available (twelve states);

2. gifted programming is not mandated, but gifted funding is available (five states);

3. gifted programming is mandated, but gifted funding is not available (six states);

4. gifted programming is mandated and partially funded by the state (twenty-one states); or

5. gifted programming is mandated and fully funded by the state (six states).

If one were to examine the number of states where gifted programming is mandated (33 states), the assumption could be made that gifted education receives wide policy support in the United States. However, compared with the understanding that only six states fully fund gifted education, a different perspective on support for the needs of the gifted emerges.

## FUNDING SCHEMES

Methods for funding provide tacit information regarding societal perceptions of the gifted. Different methods of funding have implications regarding identification and conceptualization of giftedness. Baker and Friedman-Nimz (2003), after review of National Center for Educational Statistics 1998-99 Public School Finance Program data and subsequent data provided by the National Association for Gifted Children State Legislative Policy Task Force in 2002, described five methods of funding for the gifted; pupil weights, flat grants, resource based, percentage equalization, and discretionary grants.

Pupil weights provide supplemental funding allocated per identified student. In such mechanisms, a gifted child might be weighted 1.12, providing an additional 12% for that child over basic funding. State regulations for qualification for funding and required accounting procedures would necessitate identification processes and guidelines that are explicit. Rules and regulations developed by the executive branch might reduce local flexibility in identification. Other difficulties may arise in several ways. First, in smaller districts, there may not be a sufficient number of students to generate useful levels of funds to address student need. Also, since supplemental funds are combined with general funds, they provide more flexible use at district and school levels. Such use may or may not directly benefit the intended recipients (Baker & Friedman-Nimz, 2003). Eight states used pupil weights for funding in the 1998-99 school year.

Flat-grant funding is based on a fixed funding amount per student and may be allocated either per identified student or per total student population. For example, a supplemental amount may be provided for each identified student or based on an established percentage of the population. In the latter case, this would mean establishing a percentage based on total population and assuming fixed distribution across districts. For example a state may provide a $200 flat grant for 3% of the student population in each district. The underlying assumption is that giftedness would be evenly distributed among districts. This distribution may lead to the development of arbitrary and inflexible cut levels in identification processes, such that students in the top 3% may qualify for funding through the state allocation, but any students over the 3% limit would not, even though any real differences between students in the top 3% and those just below may be statistical artifacts only. It also creates a problem similar to pupil weights, as some districts may not have sufficient numbers of students to generate an adequate level of funding (Baker & Friedman-Nimz, 2003). In the 1998-99 school year, 13 states used flat grant funding.

Resource-based funding allocates money based on a specific education resource, usually teaching staff, but sometimes classroom units. An allocation might be made to provide a teacher for every 1000 enrolled students. An advantage to this approach is that it does not necessarily imply a set percentage of students to be served, giving greater flexibility in identification and participation in programming. A disadvantage is that, when based on personnel, it ignores the other costs of education including supplies, textbooks, and transportation (Baker& Friedman-Nimz, 2003). In 1998-99, seven states used resource-based mechanisms to fund gifted education.

Percentage-based funding provides reimbursements from the state to districts based on prior year expenditures for the program. Such funding may provide more flexibility and local discretion in identification and programming. The state sets guidelines on what is reimbursable and generally reimburses what the state can afford in a given year. An advantage to this approach is that it can accommodate considerable cost differences across districts and recognizes that giftedness may vary between districts as well as costs in providing appropriate programming. Baker and Friedman-Nimz (2003) point out that the higher marginal costs for educating students, even gifted students, may be inferred in districts with high rates of poverty or significant numbers of limited English proficient students. This funding mechanism could provide significant flexibility in identification and participation in programs. One state used percentage-based funding in 1998-99.

Discretionary grants are awarded to districts by application to the state, often on a competitive basis. In 1998-99, eleven states used discretionary funding as the sole basis for funding gifted education (Baker

& Friedman-Nimz, 2003). The most common use for these mechanisms is to promote new programs or staff development. Discretionary grants rarely support ongoing operations. The most obvious policy implication is that this form of funding is generally intended to encourage innovation and therefore provides some discretion in identification.

## Evolving Authority in Policy and Resource Allocation–The Federal Role

Since the development of common schools in the United States, the policy environment has changed dramatically. This change is partly due to the shift of the economy of the United States from agrarian to industrial and the shift from decentralized government to greater centralization at the state and federal level, but also due to shifts in thinking regarding how much influence and what kind of influence each level of government should exert (Swanson &, King, 1997; Elmore, 1993). The common school emerged in an agricultural economy when the communities being served were small and the governance structure resembled the town meeting. As industrialization emerged, greater centralization and coordination was needed and bureaucracy emerged in an effort for efficient organization. Bureaucratic patterns of educational governance evolved within this broader societal change to professionalize the operation of schools and to "free education from politics" (Tyack, 1974, p. 25). With the growth and sophistication of the teaching profession in the 20th century, professional control grew substantially. States began to exert influence through compulsory education laws, certification standards, and

school district consolidation. The concentration of groups by homogeneous social economic status and ethnicity between the suburbs and urban areas also led to the civil rights suits and litigation that led to increased state and federal legislation and policy.

Perceived deterioration in the quality of student achievement became a national concern in the 1970s and 80s and evolved into an educational reform movement that looked to state and federal level reform to stop the decline in performance. For example, the 1983 Nation at Risk report declared, "If an unfriendly foreign power had attempted to impose on America the mediocre educational performance that exists today, we might well have viewed it as an act of war. As it stands, we have allowed this to happen to ourselves" (U.S. Department of Education, 1983, p. 5). Within the context of national concerns over equity and quality, identification policy and resource allocation for the needs of the gifted also evolved. In the next two decades identification policy would center on both quality and diversity.

As attention focused on educational reform and the disparities between urban and suburban school performance, state and federal policy prioritized gifted policy relative to these concerns. In 1972, the Marland Report provided the first federal or national definition of giftedness and continues to influence state and local identification policy. The report expanded the definition to include both high performance and potential for high performance and provided a specific list of abilities consisting of general intellectual ability, specific academic aptitude, creative or productive thinking, leadership, visual and performing arts, and psychomotor ability (Marland, 1972). Dai (2010) suggests that this approach was pragmatic and reflected the recognition that giftedness was more complex and diverse than previously recognized. Other recommendations from the report also mirrored the societal priorities in the 1970s. Consistent with national concerns for equity, the report stated that only a small fraction of gifted population was receiving appropriate educational services and argued that gifted services inherently helped the disadvantaged. Quality concerns were likewise emphasized in the conclusions by pointing to inadequate services, lack of qualified educators, and funding shortages. The Nation at Risk report (U.S. Department of Education, 1983) articulating the national concern over the quality of educational services also recommended an increased federal role in identifying and providing services for the gifted.

Not surprisingly then, the most substantial federal policy initiative for the gifted emerging from this period also reflected the broader national priorities. The Jacob Javits Gifted and Talented Student Education Act was enacted in 1988 to support research on effective methods of testing, identification, and programming; award grants to educational entities that focus on underrepresented students; and provide grants for program implementation. The Javits program must be funded each year by the Congress. It was funded at $7.46 million in 2009 (NAGC, 2010) and remains the main federal involvement in gifted education. The program funding fell from .02% in 2008 to approximately .01% of the federal education budget in 2009 ($7.5 million of the $59.2 billion education budget). The grant focus reflects the broader

societal focus and priorities in which it was enacted by continuing to support initiatives for greater equity and quality programming.

In the decade since 2000, the federal role seems to be moving again toward greater centralization through enactment of legislation such as "No Child Left Behind." The focus of this legislation was to bring all children to grade-level proficiency. While making some provision for the education of gifted children, critics have argued that the resources and attention are geared toward students below grade level. Since sanctions are imposed on schools with students who fail to meet proficiency levels, educators focus resources on bringing children to proficiency and provide scant attention to the growth of students already above proficiency levels (Winerip, 2006). With the growing national concern over security and economic competitiveness, science, technology, engineering, and mathematics (STEM) initiatives are beginning to influence policy formulation. It is likely that policy formulation will evolve to address the national concern to spur innovation. A report issued by the National Science Board (2010), *Preparing the Next Generation of Stem Innovators: Identifying and Developing our Nation's Human Capital*, concludes that the U.S. has failed to identify and develop our most promising students, crippling the nation's ability to produce the next generation of innovators. The National Association for Gifted Children (2010) quickly issued a press release praising the report for noting the clear need to identify talent in economically disadvantaged communities and among minority students, two sectors that for far too long have been overlooked.

132

The last decade demonstrates that policy and resource allocation continue to be influenced by metavalues and societal prioritizations. Gifted policy and resource allocation in the recent past have evolved within a context of growing state and federal centralization and national priorities on equity and efficiency. This policy and resource allocation will continually evolve as these priorities are mediated. The allocation of resources will continue to reflect a negotiation of competing interests and values representing societal prioritizations. Those having a stake in seeing effective education policies emerge for the gifted would be well advised to attend to the context and complexity of the resource allocation processes and participate at all levels to advocate for the educational needs of the gifted.

## ESTABLISHING RULES

Given this complexity, it is not surprising, that scholars in gifted education would claim that "there is no single model that provides a pattern for other states to follow (Passow & Rudnitski, 1993, p. vii) as far as education for the gifted is concerned. Passow and Rudnitski claim that "we found as many strong statements as weak ones; as many well-constructed statements of commitment as well intentioned statements of conciliation" (p. xix). Brown, Avery, VanTassel-Baska, Worley, and Stambaugh (2006) further characterize the condition of gifted education policy at the state level as "diffuse and idiosyncratic" (p. 11). Still, states are encouraged to "learn from each other's legislation and regulations, borrowing language, concepts provisions and ideas from one another" (Passow &

Rudnitski, p. x). Following from this, four major policy areas that affect gifted identification in the states have been identified and will be discussed in the remainder of this chapter: (1) rationale for gifted programming, (2) definition of giftedness, (3) mandates for identification and programming, and (4) identification procedures.

## RATIONALE FOR GIFTED PROGRAMMING

Passow and Rudnitski (1993) offer that a statement of rationale or philosophy for gifted programs can serve as a driving force for action. "When clearly expressed," they state, "the philosophy conveys an unclouded message to educators, parents, and the community as to how gifted education is viewed by policymakers" (p. xii).

Clark (2008) has posited several potential rationale statements that can be used singly or in combination to justify identification and programming for gifted and talented students. These statements are summarized in Table 1 on the following page. Not all these rationale statements are equally valued by champions of gifted education. Passow and Rudnitski (1993), for example, aver:

> The rationale for identifying and nurturing the gifted must be grounded in a meaningful commitment to develop the talent potential of all children to the maximum extent possible, including those who have manifested potential for outstanding achievement. Put in this framework, the rationale for educating gifted and talented children would not rest on some perceived external economic, military, or social threat, but on the conviction that the nature and needs of the gifted require

Table 1. Rationale Statements for the Identification and Nurturance of Gifted and Talented Students. (All quotations are from Clark [2008].)

| PERSPECTIVE | RATIONALE |
|---|---|
| Right to Learn | "Giftedness" is a label used to indicate a high level of intelligence; it has a dynamic quality that can be furthered only by participation in learning experiences that challenge and extend the child's level of intelligence, ability, and interest. (p. 6) |
| Equal Opportunity | The school, as an extension of society's principle of equity, purports to provide an equal educational opportunity for all children so they can develop their intellect and talents to the fullest potential. Because all children must, therefore, be educated at their level of development, it is against the principles of a just society to refuse gifted and talented children the right to educational experiences appropriate to their developed level of ability. (p. 7) |
| Individual Cost | When human beings are limited and restricted in their development, we run the risk of creating both physical and psychological dysfunction. (p. 7) |
| Talent Development | Society gains from the greatest advancement of all the abilities and from the highest development of all the talents of all its members, whatever their areas of strength. (p. 7) |
| Individual Differences | Gifted youngsters often think differently and have different interests than their age-mates. They usually enter school having already developed many basic skills, sometimes to high levels. They have areas of interest that have developed into advanced areas of knowledge. (p. 8) |
| Individual Growth | When the needs of the gifted and talented are recognized and the educational program is designed to meet their needs, these students make significant gains in achievement, and their sense of s is enhanced. (p. 8) |
| Societal Benefit | Contributions to society in all areas of human endeavor come in over-weighted proportion from gifted individuals. (p. 8) |

differentiated educational experiences if they are to fulfill their promise. (p. 70)

However, nearly contemporaneous with this report was a warning by Sternberg (1996) that, without appropriate identification and programming for the gifted, our nation would be "in the same position with respect to innovation as we are in with respect to natural resources—dependent on other nations" (p. 171). Sternberg's statement seems almost prophetic when the recent report released by the National Science Board (2010) is

considered. This report calls for the identification and development of the talented students who will become the future innovators in science, technology, engineering, and mathematics as an "economic imperative" (p. 7). Advocates for gifted education are then left in a quandary because ignoring the support and reasoning of such a distinguished group as the National Science Board could be ill-advised for those lobbying for well-crafted gifted education policy.

## Definition of Giftedness

Definitions are critical because they should drive identification procedures. Issues relating to definition were previously discussed in the "Claiming Need" section of this chapter. However, a few further thoughts relative to official definitions as they are stated in policy are worthwhile here.

Bélanger and Gagné (2006) take a mathematical approach to what they call "the prevalence issue" (p. 132). They suggest that four factors should be considering when determining a definition of giftedness:

1. the minimum threshold—the percentage of the total population at which the boundary between membership and nonmembership will be placed,

2. the number of criteria—the various forms of giftedness and talent that will be included in the definition,

3. the disjunctive or conjunctive perspectives—whether the various traits must be manifest singly or in combination with other traits, and

4. the correlations between criteria—an understanding of the overlap between traits.

Each of these factors has an impact on how many students will be identified as gifted and talented.

Passow and Rudnitski (1993) take a more conceptual approach to the definition. They charge that "few state definitions reflect the existing knowledge base about the nature and diversity of human talent" (p. 70). Instead, issues about percentile rank cut-offs or space availability in programs tend to drive definition considerations. Pulling from the guidelines for the definition produced by the state of New Hampshire, Passow and

Rudnitski suggest evaluating an official state definition by employing six questions as follows:

1. Does the definition reflect contemporary knowledge of the nature and diversity of human talents and abilities?

2. Does the definition take into account the importance of environmental impact and developmental differences?

3. Does the definition describe giftedness in relation to meaningful, well-documented personal traits and characteristics?

4. Does the definition reflect appropriately the variability of human performance over time or in various situations?

5. Does the definition take into account the possibility of expanding human talents or ability through effective instructional interventions? Does it recognize that many, perhaps all, important components of giftedness might be nurtured?

6. Does the definition provide a clear and effective foundation for practical instructional planning, rather than merely leading to categorical inclusion or exclusion decisions?

States are in the practice of changing their definition from time to time. However, the changes usually do not reflect an understanding of the types of questions asked in the New Hampshire list. Rather, they represent a fine tuning of the federal definition first proposed in 1972 (Stephens & Karnes, 2000).

## Mandating Identification and Programming

The place of mandates within gifted education policy has already been discussed in the "Allocating Resources" section of this chapter. When a state has a mandate, the basic idea is that local education agencies will take a required action. Such mandates are seen as protection of the program in question. The degree to which mandates actually provide such protection in gifted education has been called into question in times of economic downturn. Even states with mandates have experienced some reduction in services when budgets are cut. However, gifted programs in states with mandates seem not to be targets for such cuts to the same extent as programs in states without mandates (Brown et al., 2006).

In gifted education, some mandates require identification and services, while others require only identification (Brown et al., 2006). As with any policy statement, the terms used in a mandate can be open to interpretation and construed in various ways. Further, a mandate is only a beginning as far as quality identification and services are concerned. The strongest mandates create a clear flow from definition to identification to services and are supported by sufficient funding. However, strong state mandates also tend to limit local options, as stricter controls for identification and programming are often put into place (Passow & Rudnitski, 1993).

Another aspect of the mandate issue is whether or not states should place gifted education under the auspices of special education. The logic is that the protections and requirements afforded special education students would then extend to gifted students, as both are groups that deviate from the norm in a similar manner, but in different directions. Russo, Harris, and Ford (1996) point out that such thinking "often generates mixed results" (p. 181). Unless mandate law specifically gives

them to gifted students, the mere association within a state special education department will not secure those protections and rights to the gifted students.

## IDENTIFICATION PROCEDURES

First and foremost, identification practices should be driven by the definition of giftedness. Within this general statement, Passow and Rudnitski (1993) suggest that a strong policy on identification procedures "would provide both flexibility and guidance" (p. 27) for local education agencies and would help local personnel view identification as an on-going, continuous process rather than as a one-time event. Their review of then current policies indicated a range of policies between these two poles, with some states setting restrictive rules about score cut-offs or percentages of students permitted to be identified and other states providing little or no guidance at all. In a later review, Landrum, Katsiyannis, and DeWaard (1998) found a similar range. Gallagher and Coleman (1994) identified the barriers that may explain the reticence of some states to be more flexible in their identification policies. These barriers include a concern that such policies would result in an increase in the number of students served without an attendant increase in resources to serve them and a fear of parental pressure to include unqualified students in the program as well.

It is also important to consider in policy the roles to be played by various educators in the identification procedures. Teachers are seen as an integral part of the process in many policies because of their intimate knowledge of the student in the school setting. School psychologists are also required by some state policies to be involved because of their ability to interpret test score data from a professional perspective (Brown et al., 2006; Passow & Rudnitski, 1993).

Arguably the most salient issue relative to establishing rules for identification procedures in gifted education is the issue of the underidentification of students from economically disadvantaged and minority populations (Brown, 1997; Matthews, D. J., Subotnik, R. F., & Horowitz, F. D, 2009; McBee, 2006). Brown, Avery, VanTassel-Baska, Worley, and Stambaugh (2006) insist that without policies that support nontraditional assessment, many underrepresented populations will continue to go unnoticed. Brown and her colleagues also point out that even for those states that have such policies in place, no effort has been made to evaluate the effectiveness of the policies in yielding more representative membership in gifted programs. However, in one policy analysis study, Gallagher and Coleman (1994) indicate that state policies do not appear to be preventing students from traditionally underserved populations from being served. However, demographic data indicate that students from these populations are not being served. Further, a policy analysis of the state of Texas conducted by Baker (2001) has demonstrated that, despite the laudable efforts by the state, "there remains a likelihood that economi-cally disadvantaged students will not have access to opportunities" (p. 11). While state policies may be written in such a way as to permit inclusion of traditionally underrepresented populations, implementation at the local level is problematic, according to Gallagher and Coleman. They insist that this practice will continue to be the case until states provide substantial resources and technical assistance in the implementation of identification procedures.

While the definition of policy articulated by Gallagher (2002), that "social policy creates the rules and standards by which scarce resources are allocated to meet almost unlimited social needs" (p. 1), provided the outline for this chapter, we have recognized throughout the discussion in the chapter that policy is more complex than even this statement. We assume a level of rationality to policy that may not actually be there. Gallagher is right that policy creates rules and standards for the allocation of resources. However, the negotiations and conflict inherent in the competing interests of groups result in policy that is not necessarily coherent. The policy environment is complex. Existing policy is more the result of compromise and negotiation. It is not a rational approach, but rather a patchwork quilt approach with different quilters contributing wildly diverging pieces to the fabric. That is the nature of life in a democratic society.

## REFERENCE

Baker, B. D. (2001). Measuring the outcomes of state policies for gifted education: An equity analysis of Texas school districts. *Gifted Child Quarterly, 45,* 4–15.

Baker, B. D., Friedman-Nimz, R. (2003). Gifted children, vertical equity, and state school finance policies and practices. *Journal of Education Finance, 28,* 523–556.

Bélanger, J., & Gagné, F. (2006). Estimating the size of the gifted/talented population from multiple identification criteria. *Journal for the Education of the Gifted, 30,* 131–163.

Borland, J. H. (1996). Gifted education and the threat of irrelevance. *Journal for the Education of the Gifted, 19,* 129–157.

Brooks, R. (1985). Delinquency among gifted children. In J. Freeman (Ed.), *The psychology of gifted children: Perspectives on development and education* (pp. 297–308). New York: Wiley.

Brown, C. N. (1997). Gifted identification as a constitutional issue. *Roeper Review, 19,* 157–160.

Brown, E., Avery, L., VanTassel-Baska, J., Worley, B. B., II, & Stambaugh, T. (2006). A five-state analysis of gifted education policy. *Roeper Review, 29,* 11–23.

Callahan, C. M. (1996). Critical self-study of gifted education: Healthy practice, necessary evil, or sedition? *Journal for the Education of the Gifted, 19,* 148–163.

Callahan, C. M., & Caldwell, M. S. (1997). *A practitioner's guide to evaluating programs for the gifted.* Washington, DC: National Association for Gifted Children.

Clark, B. (2008). *Growing up gifted: Developing the potential of children at home and at school.* Upper Saddle River, NJ: Pearson.

Cornell, D. G. (1992). High intelligence and severe delinquency: Evidence disputing the connection. *Roeper Review, 14,* 233–236.

Cramond, B. (2004). Can we, should we, need we agree on a definition of giftedness? *Roeper Review, 27,* 15–16.

Cross, T. L., Gust-Brey, K., & Ball, P. B. (2002). A psychological autopsy of the suicide of an academically gifted student: Researchers' and parents' perspectives. *Gifted Child Quarterly, 46,* 247–264.

Dai, D. Y. (2010). *The nature and nurture of giftedness: A new framework for understanding gifted education.* New York: Teachers College Press.

Davidson Institute for Talent Development (2010). *Gifted education policies.* Retrieved from http://www.davidsongifted.org/db/StatePolicy.aspx.

Delisle, J., & Galbraith, J. (2002). *When gifted kids don't have all the answers: How to meet their social and emotional needs.* Minneapolis, MN: Free Spirit.

Elmore, R. F. (1993). School decentralization: Who gains? Who loses? In J. Hannaway & M. Carnoy (Eds.), *Decentralization and school improvement* (pp. 33–54). San Francisco: Jossey-Bass.

Firestone, W. A. (1989). Educational policy as an ecology of games. *Educational Researcher, 18,* 18–24.

Fowler, F.C. (2004). *Policy studies for educational leaders: An introduction.* New Jersey: Pearson Prentice Hall.

Gallagher, J. J. (1991). Programs for gifted students: Enlightened self-interest. *Gifted Child Quarterly, 35,* 177–178.

Gallagher, J. J. (1996). A critique of critiques of gifted education. *Journal for the Education of the Gifted, 19,* 234–249.

Gallagher, J. J. (2002). *Societies role in educating gifted students: The role of public policy.* Storrs, CT: University of Connecticut, National Research Center on the Gifted and Talented. [RM 02162]

Gallagher, J. J. (2006). *Driving change in special education.* Baltimore, MD: Paul H. Brookes.

Gallagher, J., & Coleman, M. R. (1994). *A Javits project: Gifted education policies study program final report.* Chapel Hill, NC: University of North Carolina at Chapel Hill, Gifted Education Policy Studies Program.

Hansen, J. B., & Toso, S. J. (2007). Gifted dropouts: Personality, social, family, and school factors. *Gifted Child Today, 30*(4), 30–41.

Hodgkinson, C. (1983). *The philosophy of leadership.* Oxford, England: Basil Blackwell.

Irby, B. J., & Lara-Alecio, R. (2002). Educational policy and gifted/talented, linguistically diverse students. In J. A. Castellano & E. I. Díaz (Eds.), *Reaching new horizons: gifted and talented education for culturally and linguistically diverse students* (pp. 265–281). Boston: Allyn & Bacon.

Irvine, D. J. (1987). What research doesn't show about gifted dropouts. *Educational Leadership, 44*(6), 79–80.

Landrum, M. S., Katsiyannis, A., & DeWaard, J. (1998). A national survey of current legislative and policy trends in gifted education: Life after the National Excellence Report. *Journal for the Education of the Gifted, 21,* 352–371.

Marland, S. P., Jr. (1972). *Education of the gifted and talented: Report to the Congress of the United States by the U.S. Commissioner of Education and background papers submitted to the U.S. Office of Education,* 2 vols. Washington, DC: U.S. Government Printing Office. (Government Documents Y4.L 11/2: G36)

Matthews, M. S. (2006). Gifted students dropping out: Recent findings from a southeastern state. *Roeper Review, 28,* 216–23.

Matthews, D. J., Subotnik, R. F., & Horowitz, F. D. (2009). A developmental perspective on giftedness and talent: Implications for research, policy, and practice. In F. D. Horowitz, R. F. Subotnik, & D. J. Matthews (Eds.), *The development of giftedness and talent across the life span* (pp. 209–225). Washington, DC: American Psychology Association

McBee, M. B. (2006). A descriptive analysis of referral sources for gifted identification by race and socioeconomic status. *Journal of Secondary Gifted Education, 17,* 103–111.

Meyerson, M. (2002). *Political numeracy: Mathematical perspectives on our chaotic constitution.* New York: W. W. Norton & Company.

Moon, S. M. & Rosselli, H. C. (2000). Developing gifted programs. In K. A. Heller, F. A. Mönks, & R. A. Sternberg, R. F. Subotnik (Eds.), *International handbook of giftedness and talent* (2nd ed., pp. 499-521). Amsterdam: Elsevier.

National Association for Gifted Children (2010, September 15). National panel of experts: U.S. is squandering its most promising students. Retrieved from http://www.nagc.org/index.aspx?id=1484

National Association for Gifted Children & Council of State Directors of Programs for the Gifted. (2009). *2008–2009 state of the states in gifted education: National policy and practice data*. Washington, DC: Authors.

National Science Board. (2010). *Preparing for the next generation of STEM innovators: Identifying and developing our nation's human capital*. Arlington, VA: Author.

Passow, A. H., & Rudnitski, R. A. (1993). *State policies regarding education of the gifted as reflected in legislation and regulation*. Storrs, CT: University of Connecticut, National Research Center on the Gifted and Talented. [CRS No. 93302]

Purcell, J. H. (1994). *The status of programs for high ability students: Executive summary*. Storrs, CT: University of Connecticut, National Research Center on the Gifted and Talented. [CRS No. 94305]

Reis, S. M. (1989). Reflections on policy affecting the education of gifted and talented students: Past and future perspectives. *American Psychologist, 44*, 399-408.

Rimm, S. B. (1995). *Why bright kids get poor grades and what you can do about it*. New York: Crown.

Rokeach, M. (1973). *The nature of human values*. New York: Free Press.

Russo, C. J., Harris, J. J., III, & Ford, D. Y. (1996). Gifted education and the law: A right, privilege, or superfluous? *Roeper Review, 18*, 179–182.

Sapon-Shevin, M. (1996). Beyond gifted education: Building a shared agenda for school reform. *Journal for the Education of the Gifted, 19*, 194-214.

Sapon-Shevin, M. (2003). Equity, excellence, and school reform: Why is finding common ground so hard? In J. H. Borland, *Rethinking gifted education* (pp. 127–142). New York: Teachers College Press.

Scott. W. R. (1998). *Organizations: Rational, natural, and open systems* (4th ed). Upper Saddle River, New Jersey: Prentice-Hall.

Siegle, D. (2008). The time is now to stand up for gifted education: 2007 NAGC presidential address. *Gifted Child Quarterly, 52*, 111–113.

Stephens, K. R. (2008). Applicable federal and state policy, law, and legal considerations in gifted education. In S. I. Pfeiffer (Ed.), *Handbook of giftedness in children: Psychoeducational theory, research, and best practice* (pp. 387–408). New York: Springer.

Stephens, K. R., & Karnes, F. A. (2000). State definitions of the gifted and talented revisited. *Exceptional Children, 66*, 219-238.

Sternberg, R. J. (1996). The sound of silence: A nation responds to its gifted. *Roeper Review, 18*, 168–172.

Stone, D. A. (2002). *Policy paradox: The art of political decision making*. New York: W. W. Norton.

Swanson, A. D., & King, R. A. (1997). *School finance: Its economics and politics* (2nd ed.). New York: Longman.

Terman, L. M. (1925). *Mental and physical traits of a thousand gifted children: Genetic studies of genius, Vol. 1*. Stanford, CA: Stanford University Press.

Tieso, C. (1999). Meeting the socio-emotional needs of talented teens. *Gifted Child Today, 22*(3), 38–43.

Tyack, D. B. (1974). *The one best system: A history of American urban education*. Cambridge, MA: Harvard University Press.

United States Department of Education. (1983). *A nation at risk: The imperative for educational reform*. Washington DC: Author.

Winerip, M. (2006, April 5). No child left behind? Ask the gifted. The New York Times. Retrieved from http://www.nytimes.com/2006/04/05/nyregion/05education.html?pagewanted=1

# CHAPTER 6 STUDY GUIDE

**Prompt 1** *Knowledge*

> Define the term *policy* in your own words.

**Prompt 2** *Opinion*

> Do you believe a consensus definition of giftedness and talent is needed to establish a need claim for gifted and talented children? Why or why not?

**Prompt 3** *Affect*

> Many educators express frustration and confusion when working within the policy environment, yet the authors suggest that educators should embrace the policy environment as it exists as a manifestation of the democratic processes upon which our nation was founded. What has been your emotional experience in working for policy adoption, implementation, or change? How does this experience lead you to agree or disagree with the authors?

**Prompt 4** *Experience*

> Describe any experience you or a colleague has had in working for better policy related to identification of gifted students. To what degree does the experience illustrate the ideas presented in this chapter?

**Prompt 5** *Preconception/Misconception*

> The authors cite a number of policy experts in asserting that, in policy, values are more important than facts. How might this idea be used to more effectively advocate for sound identification practices for gifted learners?

# PROFESSIONAL MEASUREMENT STANDARDS AND IDENTIFICATION

CAROLYN M. CALLAHAN, UNIVERSITY OF VIRGINIA

For those trying to create a system for identifying gifted and talented students, perhaps the most central and difficult challenge is evaluating and selecting the data-collection instruments upon which decisions will be made. In the field of gifted education, instruments used to nominate, screen, and identify[1] students range from intelligence or achievement tests (in which student characteristics are derived from scores reflecting correctness or relative merit of a response) to rating scales, inventories, or checklists requiring observers or informants to assess student characteristics. These instruments include published, standardized, objective instruments (such as tests and standardized rating scales) as well as locally constructed performance assessments, portfolio rating scales, and teacher and parent rating scales or checklists. For this chapter, the term "test" will be used to include any of these assessment tools. And for ease of reading, the term "gifted" will be used for all gifts and

talents ranging from intellectual and scholastic to the fine and performing arts.

In order to make responsible choices from the many measurement tools and to appropriately interpret the results of the administration of those instruments, test users, be they administrators, teachers, counselors or psychologists, must carefully evaluate the test according to the standards that educational and psychological professional organizations offer. The most comprehensive set of standards are those presented by the American Educational Research Association (AERA), the American Psychological Association (APA), and the National Council on Measurement in Education (NCME) in the *Standards for Educational and Psychological Testing* (*The Standards*; 1999). These standards were established to guide developers in producing tests that would meet the criteria for excellence in assessment and to help users determine whether a given instrument merits use for a particular purpose. Responsible test users and educators making decisions about selecting students to receive special services will take care to evaluate all instruments (professionally published

---

1. To the degree that assessment data is also used after the student has been identified as needing services for further discussions of placement, the same standards and criteria are applicable.

and locally developed) used in that process against *The Standards*.

A second, important set of standards test users should consider are those offered in the Code of Professional Responsibilities in Educational Measurement (NCME Ad Hoc Committee on the Development of a Code of Ethics, 1995). Because many of the responsibilities outlined in the Code reflect and extend *The Standards*, particularly in providing more detail, a table at the end of this chapter supplements this discussion of *The Standards*.

## CAUTIONS

The authors of the *Standards for Educational and Psychological Testing* note that accepting a test or other evaluation instrument for use in decision making does not depend on the satisfaction of every standard offered, nor can one use a checklist to choose the instrument that satisfies the most standards. In other words, not all standards are created equal, with those pertaining to validity carrying greatest weight. Further, one must consider the "state of the art" in the fields of measurement and gifted education, the degree to which a standard has been satisfied by the test developer or independent evidence gathered by the local user, available alternative assessment tools, and the feasibility of meeting the standard for local purposes. *The Standards'* creators also warn that blanket claims made by the authors of tests and the users of tests that "the standards have been satisfied" should be viewed with caution. Rather, tests developers and users are on firmer ground when they provide evidence and documents that allow users to judge for themselves the claims that the standards have been met. One can never assume that conclusions

drawn by test authors in their manuals about the test are the best interpretation of evidence.

## STANDARDS FOR EDUCATIONAL AND PSYCHOLOGICAL TESTING (THE STANDARDS)

*The Standards* are grouped into 15 categories divided into three overarching groups: Test Construction, Evaluation, and Documentation; Fairness in Testing; and Testing Applications. Every one of the standards is important, but review of all of the standards for test development and use are beyond the purview of this chapter. Those standards most relevant and critical for selecting and using instruments in the identification of gifted students will be highlighted throughout the discussion following, along with examples from practice.

## THE OVERARCHING STANDARDS FOR TEST USERS

While *The Standards* give considerable attention to the test development and evaluation process (to be discussed in detail in the text that follows), the obligations of the test user are summarized emphatically in Standards 11.1 and 11.2:

> Prior to the adoption and use of a published test, the test user should study and evaluate the materials provided by the test developer. . . . When a test is to be used for a purpose for which little or no documentation is available, the user is responsible for obtaining evidence of the test's validity and reliability for this purpose. (AERA, APA, & NCME, 1999)

It is clear from these standards that the use of tests based on "recommendations" from other school districts or by choosing from a menu of tests in state guidelines is not professionally defensible. The responsibility for tailoring an identification process, including the selection of appropriate instruments, rests at the level where the definition of giftedness is operationalized, which varies from state to state and district to district. State guidelines vary considerably in degree of specificity and the degree to which a definition has been put into action. When specific instruments are named or identification procedures are explicitly delineated in state rules, regulations, or guidelines, then the state has done the job of operationalizing the definition. But when terms such as creativity or aptitude are used in state definitions and choice of instruments and procedures for using data in identification are left to the school district, then those charged with identification must first agree on the meaning of terms.

## VALIDITY

Without question, the most important set of standards against which a test should be judged are those related to validity:

> Validity refers to the degree to which evidence and theory support the interpretation of test scores entailed by the proposed users. Validity is, therefore, the most fundamental consideration in developing and evaluating tests. The process of validation involves accumulating evidence to provide a sound scientific basis for the proposed score interpretation. It is the interpretations of test scores required by the proposed uses that are evaluated, not the test itself. When test scores are used or interpreted in more

than one way, each intended interpretation must be validated. (AERA, APA, NCME, 1999, p. 9)

As this definition of validity suggests, those who ask, "Is this test valid?" are not asking the right question. The more appropriate question is, "Can the scores from this instrument be used validly for this proposed purpose?" Or more specifically in the case of gifted identification, "Can the scores from this instrument be used validly to make decisions regarding giftedness?" This definition clearly points to two central concepts. First, in making a decision about using a test for identifying gifted students to receive gifted services, users must be clear on exactly how their interpretation of the scores derived from the instruments are to be used. Before the evaluation of an instrument or set of instruments can even begin, the decision maker must have an explicit statement of the construct or constructs to be measured. For example, a proposed interpretation of a test score that presumably measures the construct of intelligence must be accompanied by a clear rationale for how that construct is defined for use in identifying gifted students and what that construct looks like. An instrument that would yield valid assessments of intelligence as defined by the conception of intelligence as a unitary and verbally-based concept underlying the construct of giftedness would not yield scores that validly assess the dimensions of intelligence as defined by Gardner (1983) or Sternberg (1986).

It is also unwise to assume that the title of a test gives sufficient guidance in assessing the validity. For example, an achievement test with a subtest entitled "mathematics" may focus on computation, problem solving, or mathematical concepts.

The potential user should review the test specifications contained within the technical manual and the items to ensure the underlying aspects of mathematical achievement measured by the test match those that correspond to the mathematical achievement and thinking described in the operationalization of the construct of giftedness that is being assessed.

The second, and equally important, dimension of the definition of validity is the use to which the scores will be put. If the purpose of assessment is to make a decision about a student's identification for the purpose of receiving services, then the test user must look for evidence that the scores predict success in the particular type of service that will be offered—data that may be hard to find in a test's technical manual. When that data is not provided by the test developer, it is the responsibility of the test user to collect such data to ensure that appropriate decisions are being made regarding student identification and placement.

To judge the appropriate use of test scores, the user must be able to discern that evidence has been provided by the test developer or must conduct studies locally to demonstrate that an argument can be made that the use of the scores for the designated purpose is supported. For example, in reviewing the *Raven's Progressive Matrices* (Raven, 2003) or the *Naglieri Non-Verbal Ability Test* (NNAT, Naglieri, 1996) for the purpose of identifying a student to receive gifted services, the test user must look for evidence that higher scores on these non-verbal tests predict greater success in the services to be offered than lower scores or that students who score below a pre-determined cutoff score would not be likely to succeed in the

program, while those that score above that point would likely succeed. If the technical manual or the relevant literature that is reviewed does not provide such evidence, then the user must seek to establish those relationships empirically, and in the interim warn those making placement decisions to consider the information with careful attention to pertinent data from other sources. Lohman, Korb, and Lakin (2008), for example, caution that non-verbal, spatial assessments may be adequate for predicting success in non-verbal domains but are not appropriate for identifying students for placement in gifted services with a focus on verbal or linguistic curricula.

Attention to these critically important standards leads to the conclusion that scores from an instrument appropriate for placement of students in one type of gifted program or service may not be appropriate for placement in a different program or for recommending a different service. Simply using a creativity test or an assessment of spatial abilities as a tool to increase the identification rates of minority students because they earn higher scores on those assessments than other types of assessments is not warranted if the scores used for identification do not relate to the definition of giftedness and the instructional program or its intended outcomes. Further, beyond pilot use of any instrument, the test user must create and maintain databases over time that verify the prediction strength of using the instrument for gifted identification purposes.

While test developers are responsible for collecting and describing relevant evidence and related rationales for using an instrument for the purposes they outline in their presentation of the

---

**SELECTED VALIDITY STANDARDS**

**Standard 1.1**[*] A rationale should be provided for each recommended interpretation and use of test scores, together with a comprehensive summary of the evidence and theory bearing on the intended use or interpretation. (p. 17)

**Standard 1.2** . . . and the construct that the test is intended to assess should be clearly described. (p. 17)

**Standard 1.4** If a test is used in a way that has not been validated, it is incumbent on the user to justify the new use, collecting new evidence if necessary. (p. 18)

**Standard 1.15** When it is asserted that a certain level of test performance predicts adequate or inadequate criterion performance, information about the levels of criterion performance associated with given levels of test scores should be provided. (p. 21)

**Standard 1.16** When validation relies on evidence that test scores are related to one or more criterion variables, information about the suitability and technical quality of the criterion should be provided. (p. 21)

**Standard 1.18** When statistical adjustments, such as those for restriction of range or attenuation, are made, both adjusted and unadjusted coefficients, as well as the specific procedure used in the adjustment should be reported. (pp. 21–22)

**Standard 13.2** In educational settings, when a test is designed for multiple purposes, evidence of the test's technical quality should be provided for each purpose. (p. 145)

**Standard 13.5** In educational settings, reports of group differences in test scores should be accompanied by relevant contextual information, where possible, to enable meaningful interpretation of those differences. (p. 148)

**Standard 13.9** When test scores are intended to be used as part of the process for making decisions about educational placement, or implementation of prescribed educational plans, empirical evidence documenting the relationship among particular test scores, the instructional programs, and desired student outcomes should be provided. When adequate empirical evidence is not available, users should be cautioned to weigh the test results accordingly in light of other relevant information about the student. (p. 147)

[*] In this chapter the standard numbers from the original document have been maintained so that the reader may easily access the commentary that accompanies the standard. Further, rather than give the full reference following each standard, only page numbers are provided.

---

instrument, test users are ultimately responsibility for determining whether the evidence provided fits the setting and purposes for which they intend to use the tests. Further, when the setting (e.g., grade level/age, population, etc.) or intended use differs from those which have been evaluated by the test developer, there is an additional, special burden on the test user to collect and evaluate the evidence of validity with those different populations in the various settings. An instrument developed for use with middle class students may not be appropriate for use in predicting the success of students from impoverished environments. It is important to understand that sometimes our assumptions about the predictive validity of some instruments are not supported by data. For example, there is evidence that some standardized aptitude test scores (e.g., SAT scores) overpredict the success of Black, Latino, and American Indian students in college—contrary to popular belief (Nalchik, 2008). Frasier, Garcia, and Passow (1995) concluded that "when bias in predictive validity did occur, it most often favored low income socioeconomic, disadvantaged ethnic minority children, or other low scoring groups" (p. 4).

As noted above, any instrument used in the gifted identification process should be scrutinized for evidence of validity. Specifically, there should be evidence that the scores obtained from an instrument contribute to an evaluation of gifted behaviors as well evidence of the degree to which the scores predict performance in related educational services. Therefore, it is the responsibility of the school district to identify data from the test developers or other users or collect data relating to the validity of teacher nomination forms or rating scales, parent nomination forms, peer nomination forms, or other locally constructed instruments such as alternative assessments or portfolio rating scales. That is, if a teacher rating scale is used in the screening and identification process, the school district should examine the degree to which students who receive higher ratings on the teacher rating scale are associated with higher achievement levels in the services provided. When an instrument such as a teacher rating scale plays a pivotal role in creating the pool of students for further screening, evidence of validity for that purpose is critical.[2] Similarly, if performance assessments or portfolios are used as a means of providing additional information about student potential, the degree to which the performance assessment scores reflect the construct that is being measured and the degree to which those scores predict performance in the gifted program setting should be assessed. Using scores from instruments which have not been subject to the important scrutiny of validation in making identification and placement decisions leaves the process open to criticism and is not ethically (and perhaps not legally) defensible.

When we collect evidence on the degree to which an instrument predicts success and/or benefits of receiving gifted services, then we must take care to collect data on success that allows us to statistically determine not just "success" or "nonsuccess," but the level of success (see earlier comments about establishing data bases for scrutinizing test scores for validity for the purposes for which they are being used locally). We should also seek to determine whether any cut-off scores or screening scores truly are predictive of student success in a gifted program. If students scoring below a cut-off score would be equally successful in achieving the goals of the gifted program, then the use of the cut-off score for screening, identification, and/ or placement is not justifiable.

As mentioned above, when examining tests' technical manuals to make decisions about the instruments to be used in the process of identification of gifted students, validity evidence relevant to the population to be considered is important. In the case of gifted student populations, the predictability of test scores for a restricted group of

2. Note that even though teacher rating scales and/or nomination forms may play pivotal roles, it is not appropriate to use only a teacher nomination form or rating scale to create a pool for further screening for reasons discussed in Chapter. 14.

students who have already been screened through the use of other test scores form a unique group. The predictability of success in the program for the screened group may be considerably lower. If test developers provide statistically adjusted data (i.e., adjusting for attenuation) on a group with a restricted range (such as the gifted) there may be an inflated estimate of the validity for selection purposes. Queries as to the unadjusted correlations will yield a more reasonable estimate of validity. (See also the standards in the section on Scales and Norming.)

## RELIABILITY

Second only to validity in the consideration of a test's worth is the reliability of the scores derived from the test. Reliability refers to the "consistency of such measurements when the testing procedure is repeated on a population of individuals" (AERA, APA, & NCME, 1999, p. 25). A student's test score or teacher rating is highly unlikely to be exactly the same from one testing or rating occasion to another, even under the most controlled conditions. Nor is it likely that two teachers would rate a student exactly the same. These differences in test scores or ratings stem from errors that may be inherent in the external environment (e.g., distractions during the testing period, scoring subjectivity, rater subjectivity) or from variations in the examinee (e.g., on one occasion the student may feel more stress or be more anxious because her mother has reminded her of the crucial decisions about placement in a gifted program made on the basis of test scores, the student may be luckier in guessing one day, a teacher may be feeling more

positively disposed toward her class on one day than on another because of variables associated with behavior unrelated to those on the rating scale or checklist). The errors affecting reliability are different from those affecting validity because they are random and non-systematic.[3] The more random error in a test score, the less useful the score is in decision making because of reduced confidence in its consistency. For example, we would be very uncomfortable in using a test score that indicated a student was scoring at the 85th percentile if we knew his score might vary 10 percentile points from one testing occasion to another.

A test score or a rating is considered the best estimate of the true score or the score an individual would receive if there were no random error at all (Observed Score = True Score + Error). The developer of a test or rating scale or checklist thus has the responsibility to create instruments that are as free as possible from these measurement errors. There is also a professional obligation to report an estimate of potential error in the test score and to provide guidance in helping users estimate the range of scores one could expect if the student were to be tested on several occasions, were to be rated by different raters, or were to take alternate forms of the test.

It is very common in the identification of gifted students to use subscores from a battery of standardized achievement tests or aptitude tests. For example, the scores from the Reading Comprehension, Language and/or Math subtests of the Iowa Tests of Basic Skills (Hoover, Dunbar, & Frisbie, 2001) or just the Math Concepts and Math Problem Solving subtests

---

3. Changes in scores that result from learning, maturation, or development are not considered error.

may be used when considering a student for placement. Or the Verbal score of the Cognitive Abilities Test (Lohman & Hagen, 2001) may be used in evaluating a student. If the subscores are to be used, then the individual reported score reliability data should be considered in determining their appropriateness.

Reliability estimates are derived in several ways. Each approach reflects different estimates of error and may vary greatly for the same test. Thus, in evaluating the reliability associated with a test, as in evaluating validity, the way in which the test score will be used is an important consideration. Commonly reported indices of reliability are test-retest (stability), parallel forms (equivalence), internal consistency, and inter-rater reliability. Errors that affect an examinees performance on two different occasions are estimated by indices of stability. Errors that come from the lack of equivalence of items on two forms of the same test are estimated by parallel-forms reliability estimates. Errors that come from lack of consistency in the way the items measure the underlying construct relate to internal consistency. And errors that come from differences in raters (e.g., two teachers rating the same student on a teacher rating scale) or scoring (e.g., of a performance assessment) are estimated by inter-rater reliability.

*The Standards* authors note that in cases where individuals are classified (e.g., gifted or not gifted), some measurement errors are more critical than others and that errors and variation around the "cut score" are more serious than errors in scores far above or below that point. Estimates of reliability are not consistent across all scores on a given instrument, and often scores on a standardized test are least reliable at the extremes of the distribution. In other words, test scores that fall in the upper range, like those typical of gifted students, are less reliable than those test scores that fall in the middle part of the distribution (around the $50^{th}$ percentile). Of course, the goal is to provide a test score that would be as free from the influence of random error as possible. The issues of errors in the extremes of a distribution (above the $90^{th}$ percentile) thus make identification procedures that make fine distinctions, say between a student who scores at the $92^{nd}$ percentile and one who scores at the $95^{th}$ percentile, indefensible.

---

**SELECTED RELIABILITY STANDARDS**

**Standard 2.1** For each total score, subscore, or combination of scores that is to be interpreted, estimates of relevant reliabilities and standard errors of measurement or test information functions should be reported. (p. 31)

**Standard 2.4** Each method of quantifying the precision or consistency of scores should be described clearly and expressed in terms of statistics appropriate to the method. The sampling procedures used to select examinees for reliability analyses and descriptive statistics on these samples should be reported. (p. 32)

**Standard 2.11** If there are generally accepted theoretical or empirical reasons for expecting that reliability coefficients, standard error of measurement, or test information functions will differ substantially for various subpopulations, publishers should provide reliability data for each major population for which the test is recommended. (p. 34)

As important as the reliability index that is reported for a test is the standard error of measurement (SEM) or the index of how much one might expect a score to vary from one testing occasion to another, from one form of the test to another, or from one rater to another. The SEM depends on the reliability as well as the standard deviation, or variability, in a distribution of test scores. It is affected by the amount of error in a test and the range of test scores of those who are being tested, which is an important concern when examining scores in a restricted population such as those being considered for gifted services.

The issue of attenuation or restricted range of scores is also particularly important. One cannot assume that the SEM given for the entire sample on whom the reliability estimate was calculated will be the same in the higher end of the distribution (Harvill, n.d.). Scores at the extreme of a distribution are more prone to error than scores near the average; hence the SEM will be greater. Test users must take this fact under consideration, as there will be more variability in repeated testings or across forms or raters, resulting in the need to interpret those scores using larger confidence intervals.[4]

## MODIFYING TESTS OR RATING SCALES

In determining which instruments will be used for screening or selection, a school district may decide to modify a test by selecting only certain items or re-arranging items, or the district may edit a rating scale to make it shorter or easier to complete. For example, teachers may be asked to complete the Creativity Scale of the *Scales for Rating the Behavioral Characteristics of Superior Students* (Renzulli, Smith, White, Callahan, Hartman, & Westberg, 2002) in isolation from the other three scales which were used in estimating reliability and validity. In the original work of the authors, the four original scales were completed by teachers as one packet; hence teachers' scores may have been affected by the items preceding those on the scale selected, either in a positive or negative way. That is, reading and reacting to one item or subscale may affect how the teacher rates a student on second item or subscale. Teachers who are asked to complete the scales in isolation will not be affected by prior sets of items and, therefore, may not have the same response to items. *The Standards* explicitly warn that any alteration of the original form may affect scores, normative information, and score reliability and validity. If teachers complete a long and complex rating scale comprised of items from several existing scales, a fatigue factor may make the inter-rater reliability, the stability, or the internal consistency estimates of the reliability of the scale lower than those reported in the technical information reported by the test developers.

Many experts in the field of gifted education have recommended the use of performance and portfolio assessments in the identification of gifted students (see summary in Borland, 2008). It is critical that the users of such assessments take the same

---

4. A confidence interval is used to express the degree of confidence we have that if we tested a student over and over, his or her scores would fall within a given range. If the confidence interval is given as 95% for a range of scores, we are saying that if you were to test that student over and over the probability of the score falling outside that range would be only 5%. Some use confidence interval to express the idea that you can be confident with a given level of certainty that the student's true score falls in the range given.

care to ensure that the reliability indices of these assessments meet acceptable levels and that the variability in scorer ratings, in particular, be calculated and taken into account when the data is considered as part of a student profile. Satisfactory levels of reliability depend on the careful development of scoring protocols and training raters in the use of the protocols in rating assessments.

In choosing instruments for the screening and identification of very young gifted children using intelligence tests, aptitude tests, or achievement tests, it is particularly important to consider the reliability of the assessments, as the stability of the scores for young children is often considerably less than that of older children. Further, indices of reliability that have been calculated across a large range of examinees in age, grade, or level of performance will overestimate the reliability for a narrower range of students. As emphasis on identifying young gifted children (in the primary grades) increases, it is very important to consider the carefully developed guidelines on assessment offered by the National Association for the Education of Young Children

and National Association of Early Childhood Specialists in State Departments of Education (2003)[5].

## SCALES AND NORMS

The interpretation of data for a screening and identification process is most often premised on the assumption that the students to be identified for services are achieving or have the potential to achieve at a level beyond that of the general stu-

---

[5]The fundamental recommendations of the NAEYC and NAECS/SDE parallel those of NCME /APA standards in calling for ethical use of test, use of tests for intended purposes, and the use of instruments of high quality. More specific to the testing of young children are recommendations that the assessment is developmentally appropriate and important for the age of the child being assessed, that assessment evidence is gathered in realistic settings, that multiple sources of evidence be collected over time, and that data from assessments be used to improve learning. In particular, the guidelines caution that individually administered, norm-referenced testing be limited.

Where We Stand on Curriculum, Assessment, and Program Evaluation National Association for the Education of Young Children (NAEYC) and the National Association of Early Childhood Specialists in State Departments of Education (NAECS/SDE) http://www.naeyc.org/files/naeyc/file/positions/StandCurrAss.pdf

---

| SELECTED STANDARDS ON MODIFYING TESTS OR RATING SCALES |
| --- |
| **Standard 2.10** When subjective judgment enters into test scoring, evidence should be provided on both inter-rater consistency in scoring and within-examinee consistency over repeated measurements. (p. 33) |
| **Standard 2.12** If a test is proposed for use in several grades or over a range of chronological groups and if separate norms are used for each grade level or age groups, reliability should be provided for each age or grade population. (p. 34) |
| **Standard 4.15** When additional test forms are created by taking a subset of the items in an existing test form or by rearranging its items and there is sound reason to believe that scores on these forms may be influenced by item contexts effects, evidence should be provided that there is no undue distortion of norms for the different versions or of score linkages between them. (p.58) |

dent population (hence, in need of programmatic and/or curricular adjustments to make their educational programs suitable to their level of performance). Thus, the scores students achieve on various instruments are compared in some way to either norms provided by the test developers or calculated locally.

In making determinations about the performance of a student relative to other students, educators also may compare scores across different forms of the same test, different administrations of the same test, or across tests designed to measure different constructs. For example, in creating profiles of students, educators may translate all scores from the IQ tests; the reading, language arts, math concepts, and math problem solving subtests of a standardized achievement test; teacher ratings, and performance assessments into percentile scores, stanines, or other standard scores.

Standard 4.18 clearly charges test publishers with providing up-to-date and appropriate norms; however, the user of the test is responsible for ensuring that the derived scores they use (percentiles,

standard scores, etc.) are based on up-to-date norms. Because updating norms is an expensive process, it is likely that not all tests considered for use in the identification process will provide normative scores based on current samples. The test user also has responsibility for ensuring the norms are current and based on samples representative of the sample on which decisions are being made (age, gender, socio-economic status, geographic distribution, and ethnicity). For example, the *Raven's Progressive Matrices* has been renormed on American subjects since its original development in Britain, but the most recent norms must be carefully examined for currency and the population on which the norming was based. Further, research on the Raven indicates that over time, scores increase; so the older the normative base, the more likely the scores underestimate relative performance (Raven, 1989). The *Ross Test of Higher Cognitive Processes* (Ross & Ross, 1976), sometimes recommended as a non-verbal assessment of thinking skills was developed in 1976, and the norms were based on identified gifted students and have not been updated

---

**SELECTED STANDARDS ON NORMING**

**Standard 4.6** Reports of norming studies should include precise specifications of the population that was sampled, the sampling procedures and participation rates, any weighting of the sample, the dates of testing and, descriptive statistics. (p. 55)

**Standard 4.18** If a publisher publishes norms for use in test score interpretation, then so long as the test remains in print, it is the publisher's responsibility to assure the test is renormed with sufficient frequency to permit continued accurate and appropriate score interpretations. (p. 59)

**Standard 13.4** Local norms should be developed when necessary to support test users' intended interpretations. (p. 146)

**Standard 13.15** In educational settings, reports of group differences in test scores should be accompanied by relevant contextual information, where possible, to enable meaningful interpretation of these differences. Where appropriate contextual information is not available, users should be cautioned against misinterpretation. (p.148)

since the test was first developed. In this instance, the norms are not reflective of today's populations, and all test users should develop local norms if the test is going to be used as part of an identification process.

One of the principles underlying the identification and placement of gifted students is that these students "require services or activities not ordinarily provided by the schools" (U. S. Department of Education, 1993, p. 26). Hence, the curriculum and programming opportunities that are available to all students (presumably based on the characteristics of the general student population in a school) will determine which students need services beyond the general education program. Therefore, a student might be very similar to all students in one setting, but be distinctly more advanced than students in another setting. Parents and educators may become confused around the concept that a student may be "gifted" in one setting, but not another. This confusion stems from the emphasis on *labeling* rather than *services*. The underlying focus of the screening and selection and placement process should not be on the label of giftedness, but whether the criterion of needing a curriculum and/or opportunities beyond those of the traditional setting is met–whether the recommendation be enrichment or acceleration of a curriculum or mentoring or early admission to school. This focus leads to the important issue of local norms. A school district that accepts the notion that gifted services should be provided to those who are in need of modifications to address educational needs not met by the general education program will likely need local norms to help determine which students need services. Large test

companies often provide such norms for standardized group aptitude tests and achievement tests (e.g., the CogAT and the ITBS) if such norms are requested. For other tests, the test manual may provide direction in creating norms or it may be the responsibility of the test users to determine when local norms are needed and how they will be constructed. Teacher rating scales and other non-standardized instruments should also be interpreted in light of local norms.

## INTERPRETATION OF NORMS

As noted above, the reliability, validity and standard error of measurement may be affected by creating another form of a test that is a subset of the items of an existing test, re-arranging items, or a combination of several instruments. These characteristics (reliability, validity, SEM) may also be affected by using an instrument in a way other than the purpose for which the test was developed. Norms may also be influenced by such modifications. Hence, Standard 4.15 (p. 58) suggests that when such modification are made to an instrument, the test user should verify that normative data is not affected by the modifications or exercise extreme caution in interpretation.

## FAIRNESS IN TESTING AND TEST USE

Use and interpretation of test scores of students from differing races, cultures, and language groups; different genders; students with handicapping conditions; and different socioeconomic groups may present unique circumstances that should be considered in the when establishing of processes and procedures for identifying and placing students in

---

**SELECTED STANDARDS ON FAIRNESS AND TEST USE**

**Standard 7.1** When credible research reports that test scores differ across examinee subgroups for the type of test in question, then to the extent feasible, the same forms of validity evidence collected for the examinee population as a whole should also be collected for each relevant subgroup. (p. 80)

**Standard 7.3** When credible research reports that differential item functioning exists across age, gender, racial/ethnic, cultural, disability, and/or linguistic groups in the population of test takers in the domain measured by the test, test developers should conduct appropriate studies when feasible [and report the results of those and other such studies in their test manuals]. (p. 81)

**Standard 7.10** When the use of a test score results in outcomes that affect the life chances or educational opportunities of examinees, evidence of mean test score differences between relevant subgroups of examinees should, where feasible, be examined for subgroups for which credible research reports mean differences for similar results. Where mean differences are found, an investigation should be undertaken to determine that such differences are not attributable to a source of construct underrepresentation or construct irrelevant variance. . . . The test user bears responsibility for uses with groups other than those specified by the test developer. (p.83)

---

services for gifted students. In particular, the sensitivity of assessments for these children and adolescents dictates that test users not be misled by false claims or fall prey to unwarranted assertions about the validity, reliability, or norms for tests.

Of particular concern to those involved in the process of identifying students from racial/ethnic minorities or Limited English Speaking students is the possible misinterpretation and unfounded assumptions that may come from the use of non-verbal assessments. For example, it is often assumed that verbal tests are biased and discriminatory in assessing the aptitude and achievement of minority students, and the use of non-verbal assessments will lead to a higher proportion of minority students identified as gifted. However, research on at least one such instrument, the NNAT, does not always support that assertion in the case of Black and Latino students (Lohman, 2005a), and research on the Raven's Advanced Matrices suggest that sex differences may exist favoring males on that instrument (Colom & Abad, 2007).

While such data do not condemn a test or warrant abandoning its use, they do suggest that assumptions made about the underlying constructs and interpretations of the validity of test scores are not equal across subgroups and should be taken into account in interpreting test scores. (See Chapter 12 for addition discussion on this topic.)

## RIGHTS AND RESPONSIBILITIES OF TEST TAKERS

*The Standards* are explicit on the rights of test takers. They are designed to ensure that all test takers have the same opportunity to receive information about tests and the testing situation, are given the opportunity to fully understand the meaning and implications of testing, and are protected from inappropriate disclosure of testing outcomes. As with all high stakes or categorical testing, students and the parents/guardians of students who are tested for possible placement in a gifted program are entitled to full disclosure about the process and the results of testing.

---

**SELECTED STANDARDS ON RIGHTS OF TEST TAKERS**

**Standard 8.6** Test data maintained in data files should be adequately protected from improper disclosure. Use of facsimile transmission, computer networks, and other electronic data processing . . . should be restricted to situations in which confidentiality can be reasonably assured. (p. 88)

**Standard 8.8** When score reporting includes assigning individuals to categories, the category should be chosen carefully and described precisely. The least stigmatizing labels, consistent with accurate representation, should always be assigned. (p. 88)

**Standard 8.13** In educational testing programs . . . test takers are entitled to fair consideration and reasonable process . . . in resolving disputes about testing. (p. 89)

---

We have all been alerted to the dangers of identitfy theft that come with the increased access to electronic data. We should be equally concerned about the possible revelation of student data to persons who should not have access to data collected during the testing process. In particular, admonitions to use test data in making instructional decisions does not justify distribution of that data through unprotected modes, nor does it suggest that data that is not used for instruction should be shared simply because "it is in the same file."

Another consideration to the students should be in the ways labels are used. While the label "gifted" does carry some cache with parents and some students, we should also be aware that the label seems also to designate those who are not selected to receive services as "ungifted" or "not gifted." Seeking to identify students for services or to use phrases which imply the decision relates to a need for special educational programming will diminish the negative association with a "failure" to be identified.

Finally, these standards support the need for a formal appeals process that is public and clearly delineated in terms of process, individuals who are to be involved, and the need for independence

from the original decision-making group. Members of the original decision-making committee should not serve on the appeals committee as this is considered a conflict of interest in which the original decision is defended rather than given a non-partisan hearing.

## USE AND INTERPRETATION OF TEST SCORES

All of the standards discussed thus far in one way or another have implications for the use and interpretation of test scores in identifying gifted students and placing them in appropriate services. There are several other standards that represent good practice in the use and interpretation of test scores that warrant attention.

The very complex nature of cognitive and achievement assessment requires close attention by those who are charged with test administration and test interpretation. Directions for administration of standardized assessments must be followed very carefully. Otherwise the resultant scores will have no meaning. Further, interpretation of standard scores, percentiles, and standard errors of measurement are often flawed and leave parents and students confused or misled. Some come away believing the test score the child has received is an absolute measure of the construct; others come away confused as to why, with the confidence band they had been given, the child was not identified as gifted. As an example of a negative consequence, sharing a test on an assessment of intelligence when a child has not been identified for a gifted program may leave the impression with a parent (or a teacher) that the child is "not gifted" and result in lowered expectations for performance and subsequent treatment that would discourage high levels of performance or high aspirations. The individual who has responsibility for test score interpretation must be able to explain the ways in which the scores have been used in making decisions that accurately reflect the construct measured and the meaning of scores. Users should also dispel any interpretations of test

---

### SELECTED STANDARDS RELATED TO TEST USE AND INTERPRETATION OF TEST SCORES

**Standard 11.3** Responsibility for test use should be assumed by or delegated only to those individuals who have the training, professional credentials, and experience necessary to handle this responsibility. Any special qualifications for test administration or interpretation specified in the test manual should be met. (p. 114)

**Standard 11.15** Test users should be alert to potential misinterpretations of test scores and to possible unintended consequences of test use; users should take steps to minimize or avoid foreseeable misinterpretations and unintended consequences. (p. 116)

**Standard 11.16** Test users should verify periodically that their interpretations of test data continue to be appropriate given any significant changes in their population of test takers, their modes of test administration, and their purposes in testing. (p. 117)

**Standard 11.7** Test users have the responsibility to protect the security of tests, to the extent that developers enjoin users to do so. (p. 115)

**Standard 11.20** In educational . . . settings, a test score should not be interpreted in isolation; collateral information that may lead to alternative explanations for the examinee's tests performance should be considered. (p 117)

**Standard 12.11** Professionals and others who have access to test materials and test results should ensure the confidentiality of the test results and testing materials, consistent with legal and professional requirements. (p. 132–133)

**Standard 12.13** Those who select tests and draw inferences from test scores should be familiar with the relevant evidence of validity and reliability of inventories used and should be prepared to articulate a logical analysis that supports all facets of the assessment and the inferences made from the assessment. (p. 133)

**Standard 12.19** The interpretation of test scores or patterns of test battery results should take cognizance of the many factors that may influence a particular outcome. (p. 134)

**Standard 13.7** In educational settings, a decision or characterization that will have a major impact on a student should not be made on the basis of a single test score. Other relevant information should be taken into account if it will enhance the overall validity of the decision. (p.14)

scores as absolutes, but instead present them as the best estimate at a given point in time. The person interpreting test scores should also have sufficient background—formal training and experiential, if needed—to explain the ways in which environmental or cultural differences in groups may have affected test scores and their interpretation in the identification process. As the population demographics in schools shift rapidly, those responsible for the identification of gifted students need to regularly re-evaluate the tests, rating scales, and other instruments used in the identification process to ensure that they remain valid, reliable, and non-biased. The lack of representation of traditionally underserved groups of students in gifted programs (Black, Latino/Latina, English Language Learners, etc.) can be attributed to some degree of failures to attend to these standards and those relating to score interpretation and norms discussed earlier.

As mentioned above, the use of performance assessments is receiving attention as a means of ensuring opportunities for students to display gifted behavior that might not be tapped through traditional assessments. The scores or ratings on such assessments can be open to question if the directions for administration are not carefully followed and scorers are not trained or do not have the appropriate content and process knowledge to score the tests accurately and reliably.

Screening, identifying, and placing gifted learners is a very high stakes process. Hence, the instruments used should be available to some parents and students and not others. School officials should take all steps necessary to protect the tests from distribution to anyone in the public or to educators within the system whose children may

be taking the tests. If the school district has a suspicion that some examinees have had access to a particular test, it behooves the school to consider choosing a new test for the screening or identification process.

These standards reflect the many admonitions in the literature on identification of gifted and talented students to use multiple measures and to collect data from multiple sources in making decisions about the identification of these students. NO instrument has sufficient reliability or validity to warrant its use alone in making such decisions. Test score data should be considered in conjunction with data derived from school records (grades), classroom observations, teacher reports or rating scales, or other indicators of student performance or potential in the area of giftedness for which the student is being screened.

## WHERE TO LOOK FOR THE INFORMATION ON WHETHER OR NOT A TEST MEETS THE STANDARDS

The most common source of information on published instruments is the Mental Measurements Yearbooks. The Yearbooks are available in hard copy or online, and the reviews are particularly valuable because the reviewers present their evaluations in light of the professional standards and other available instruments developed for the same assessment purposes. When consulting test reviews from any sources, it is very important to remember there are no perfect tests of any construct, but it is the obligation of the test user to choose the best available instrument. Validity for the intended use of the test should be the primary criterion, and then users should implement and interpret test scores in light of all available information about its characteristics. The Mental Measurements Yearbooks and reviews of tests in professional journals are important sources of professional interpretations of test qualities; however, there are other professional resources such as school psychologists and counselors or persons in a district's research or testing office who can assist in interpreting the test's technical manual, which should be consulted before using any test. Finally, choosing non-standardized, non-published instruments for use places the burden for providing evidence of technical quality on the test user.

## REFERENCES

American Educational Research Association, the American Psychological Association, and the National Council on Measurement in Education. (1999). *Standards for Educational and Psychological Testing*. Washington, DC: Author.

Borland, J. H. (2008). Identification. In J. A. Plucker & C. M. Callahan (Eds.), *Critical issues and practices in gifted education: What the research says* (pp. 261–280). Waco, TX: Prufrock Press.

Colom, R. & Abad, F. J. (2007). Advanced progressive matrices and sex differences: Comment to Mackintosh and Bennett. *Intelligence, 35*, 183.

Frasier, M. M., Garcia, J. J., & Passow, A. H. (1995). A review of assessment issues in gifted education and their implications of identifying gifted minority students (Report No. RM 95203). Storrs: National Research Center on the Gifted and Talented, University of Connecticut.

Gardner, H. (1983). *Frames of mind: The theory of multiple intelligences*. New York: Basic Books.

Harvill, L. M. (n.d.) An NCME instructional module on standard errors of measurement. Retrieved March 27, 2009 from http://www.ncme.org/pubs/items/16.pdf.

Hoover, H. D., Dunbar, S. B., & Frisbie, D.A. (2001). *Iowa Tests of Basic Skills*. Itaska, IL: Riverside.

Lohman, D. F. (2005a). Review of Naglieri and Ford (2003): Does the Naglieri Nonverbal Ability Test identify equal proportions of high-scoring White, Black, and Hispanic students? *Gifted Child Quarterly, 49*, 19–28.

Lohman, D. F. (2005b). The role of nonverbal ability tests in identifying academically gifted students: An aptitude perspective. *Gifted Child Quarterly, 49*, 111–138.

Lohman, D. F., & Hagen, E. P. (2001). *Cognitive Abilities Test*. Itaska, IL: Riverside.

Lohman, D.F., Korb, K. A., & Lakin, J. M. (2008). Identifying academically gifted language-learners using non-verbal tests: A comparison of the Raven, NNAT, and CogAT. *Gifted Child Quarterly, 52*, 275-296.

National Association for the Education of Young Children and National Association of Early Childhood Specialists in State Departments of Education (2003). *Early childhood curriculum, assessment and program evaluation*. Retrieved April 4, 2009 from http://www.naeyc.org/about/positions/pdf/pscape.pdf.

NCME Ad Hoc Committee on the Development of a Code of Ethics (1995). *Code of professional responsibilities in educational measurement*. Retrieved April 4, 2009 from http://www.natd.org/Code_of_Professional_Responsibilities.html.

Naglieri, J. A. (1996). *Naglieri Non-Verbal Ability Test*. San Antonio, TX: Harcourt Brace Educational Measurement

Raven, J. C. (1938). *Standard progressive matrices*. London: H. K. Lewis.

Raven, J. C. (1989). The Raven Progressive Matrices: A review of national norming studies and ethnic and socioeconomic variation within the United States. *Journal of Educational Measurement, 26*, 1–16.

Raven, J., Raven, J.C., & Court, J.H. (2003). *Manual for Raven's Progressive Matrices and Vocabulary Scales. Section 1: General overview.* San Antonio, TX: Harcourt Assessment. Practitioner

Renzulli, J. S., Smith, L.H., White, A. J., Callahan, C. M., Hartman, R. K., & Westberg, K. A. (2002). *Scales For Rating the Behavioral Characteristics of Superior Students* (Revised Edition). Mansfield Center, CT: Creative Learning Press.

Ross, J. D., & Ross, C. M. (1976). *Ross Test of Higher Cognitive Processes.* Novato, CA: Academic Therapy.

Sternberg, R. J. (1986). A triarchic theory of intellectual giftedness. In R. J. Sternberg & J. Davidson (Eds.), *Conceptions of giftedness* (pp. 223–243). Cambridge: Cambridge University.

U. S. Department of Education. (1993). *National excellence: A case for developing America's talent.* Washington, DC: U. S. Government Printing Office.

**RESPONSIBILITIES FROM THE CODE OF PROFESSIONAL RESPONSIBILITIES IN EDUCATIONAL MEASUREMENT (NCME, 1995)***

### RESPONSIBILITIES OF THOSE WHO SELECT ASSESSMENT PRODUCTS AND SERVICES

Those who select assessment products and services for use in educational settings, or help others do so, have important professional responsibilities to make sure that the assessments are appropriate for their intended use. Persons who select assessment products and services have a professional responsibility to:

3.1 Conduct a thorough review and evaluation of available assessment strategies and instruments that might be valid for the intended uses.

3.2 Recommend and/or select assessments based on publicly available documented evidence of their technical quality and utility rather than on unsubstantiated claims or statements.

3.3 Disclose any associations or affiliations that they have with the authors, test publishers, or others involved with the assessments under consideration for purchase and refrain from participation if such associations might affect the objectivity of the selection process.

3.4 Inform decision makers and prospective users of the appropriateness of the assessment for the intended uses, likely consequences of use, protection of examinee rights, relative costs, materials and services needed to conduct or use the assessment, and known limitations of the assessment, including potential misuses and misinterpretations of assessment information.

3.5 Recommend against the use of any prospective assessment that is likely to be administered, scored, and used in an invalid manner for members of various groups in our society for reasons of race, ethnicity, gender, age, disability, language background, socioeconomic status, religion, or national origin.

3.6 Comply with all security precautions that may accompany assessments being reviewed.

3.7 Immediately disclose any attempts by others to exert undue influence on the assessment selection process.

3.8 Avoid recommending, purchasing, or using test preparation products and services that may cause individuals to receive scores that misrepresent their actual levels of attainment.

### RESPONSIBILITIES OF THOSE WHO ADMINISTER ASSESSMENTS

Those who prepare individuals to take assessments and those who are directly or indirectly involved in the administration of assessments as part of the educational process, including teachers, administrators, and assessment personnel, have an important role in making sure that the assessments are administered in a fair and accurate manner. Persons who prepare others for, and those who administer, assessments have a professional responsibility to:

* Reprinted by permission; © 1995, National Council on Measurement in Education

4.1 Inform the examinees about the assessment prior to its administration, including its purposes, uses, and consequences; how the assessment information will be judged or scored; how the results will be kept on file; who will have access to the results; how the results will be distributed; and examinees' rights before, during, and after the assessment.

4.2 Administer only those assessments for which they are qualified by education, training, licensure, or certification.

4.3 Take appropriate security precautions before, during, and after the administration of the assessment.

4.4 Understand the procedures needed to administer the assessment prior to administration.

4.5 Administer standardized assessments according to prescribed procedures and conditions and notify appropriate persons if any nonstandard or delimiting conditions occur.

4.6 Not exclude any eligible student from the assessment.

4.7 Avoid any conditions in the conduct of the assessment that might invalidate the results.

4.8 Provide for and document all reasonable and allowable accommodations for the administration of the assessment to persons with disabilities or special needs.

4.9 Provide reasonable opportunities for individuals to ask questions about the assessment procedures or directions prior to and at prescribed times during the administration of the assessment.

4.10    Protect the rights to privacy and due process of those who are assessed.

4.11    Avoid actions or conditions that would permit or encourage individuals or groups to receive scores that misrepresent their actual levels of attainment.

### RESPONSIBILITIES OF THOSE WHO SCORE ASSESSMENTS

The scoring of educational assessments should be conducted properly and efficiently so that the results are reported accurately and in a timely manner. Persons who score and prepare reports of assessments have a professional responsibility to:

5.1 Provide complete and accurate information to users about how the assessment is scored, such as the reporting schedule, scoring process to be used, rationale for the scoring approach, technical characteristics, quality control procedures, reporting formats, and the fees, if any, for these services.

5.2 Ensure the accuracy of the assessment results by conducting reasonable quality control procedures before, during, and after scoring.

5.3 Minimize the effect on scoring of factors irrelevant to the purposes of the assessment.

5.4 Inform users promptly of any deviation in the planned scoring and reporting service or schedule and negotiate a solution with users.

5.5 Provide corrected score results to the examinee or the client as quickly as practicable should errors be found that may affect the inferences made on the basis of the scores.

5.6 Protect the confidentiality of information that identifies individuals as prescribed by state and federal laws.

5.7 Release summary results of the assessment only to those persons entitled to such information by state or federal law or those who are designated by the party contracting for the scoring services.

5.8 Establish, where feasible, a fair and reasonable process for appeal and rescoring the assessment.

### RESPONSIBILITIES OF THOSE WHO INTERPRET, USE, AND COMMUNICATE ASSESSMENT RESULTS

The interpretation, use, and communication of assessment results should promote valid inferences and minimize invalid ones. Persons who interpret, use, and communicate assessment results have a professional responsibility to:

6.1 Conduct these activities in an informed, objective, and fair manner within the context of the assessment's limitations and with an understanding of the potential consequences of use.

6.2 Provide to those who receive assessment results information about the assessment, its purposes, its limitations, and its uses necessary for the proper interpretation of the results.

6.3 Provide to those who receive score reports an understandable written description of all reported scores, including proper interpretations and likely misinterpretations.

6.4 Communicate to appropriate audiences the results of the assessment in an understandable and timely manner, including proper interpretations and likely misinterpretations.

6.5 Evaluate and communicate the adequacy and appropriateness of any norms or standards used in the interpretation of assessment results.

6.6 Inform parties involved in the assessment process how assessment results may affect them.

6.7 Use multiple sources and types of relevant information about persons or programs whenever possible in making educational decisions.

6.8 Avoid making, and actively discourage others from making, inaccurate reports, unsubstantiated claims, inappropriate interpretations, or otherwise false and misleading statements about assessment results.

6.9 Disclose to examinees and others whether and how long the results of the assessment will be kept on file, procedures for appeal and rescoring, rights examinees and others have to the assessment information, and how those rights may be exercised.

6.10 Report any apparent misuses of assessment information to those responsible for the assessment process.

6.11 Protect the rights to privacy of individuals and institutions involved in the assessment process.

CHAPTER 7 STUDY GUIDE

**Prompt 1** *Knowledge*

Select any one of the *programming* standards listed in this chapter and explain the evidence you would expect to see showing that the standard has been met by a school, school district, or state.

**Prompt 2** *Opinion*

In your opinion, which of the *programming* standards for identification is most frequently violated? What evidence do you have that this is so? Why does this occur?

**Prompt 3** *Affect*

Both sets of standards place a great deal of responsibility on educators for both their knowledge and their skills. Do you feel adequately prepared to carry out these responsibilities? If so or if not, what follow-up actions do you need to take to address your feelings?

**Prompt 4** *Experience*

Consider the identification processes in your school, school district, or state (or, if your school, school district, or state has none that you know of, find a description of another set of processes). Select three of the *programming* standards and three of the *teacher preparation* standards. Assess, based on your personal experience, the degree to which each standard is met by the process you're reviewing.

**Prompt 5** *Preconception/Misconception*

A recent effort was made by the National Association for Gifted Children to align the *programming* standards and the *teacher preparation* standards. Why was this effort worthwhile or not as far as identification of gifted students is concerned?

# THE IMPACT OF PROFESSIONAL STANDARDS IN GIFTED EDUCATION ON THE IDENTIFICATION OF GIFTEDNESS & TALENT

Mary L. Slade, James Madison University

## INTRODUCTION

When it comes to the practice of gifted and talented education, perhaps nothing is quite as controversial, expensive, and time consuming as student identification. The goal of gifted education programming is to evaluate students' academic and socio-emotional needs in order to provide appropriately differentiated educational services. Therefore, gifted learners must be assessed in order to determine eligibility and placement in appropriately differentiated educational services (Hansford, Bonar, Scally, & Burge, 2001). Albeit necessary, student identification can be plagued by negative influences that deter the efficiency of practices.

When it comes to the identification of giftedness and talent in school-age children, there are a phenomenal number of factors that influence the efficacy of day-to-day practice at the levels of individual student and institution. Policy, funding, and advocacy are just some of the many external factors that impact the identification of giftedness and talent in school-age children. Internal factors that influence the formal identification of gifted-

ness in any individual include race, linguistics, gender, and age—to name a few. All too often, chance or luck may also play into the individual identification of any given child. But perhaps there are no greater requisite influences on the practice of identifying giftedness and talent than competence and knowledge in gifted education. Therefore, efficacious identification paradigms, procedures, and policies are rooted in theoretical constructs and empirical data.

Two sets of professional standards in gifted education exist to codify the best practices in the implementation of gifted and talented education programming as evidenced by both theoretical constructs and empirical findings. A standard is described as a designated level of performance against which program success is measured (Worthen, Sanders, & Fitzpatrick, 1997). The initial set of standards developed for gifted education consist of the National Association for Gifted Children (NAGC) Pre-K–12 Gifted Program Standards that were drafted in 1998 to provide guidance in the development, administration, and evaluation of gifted education programming at the building, district, and state levels. In 2010 the original pre-K–12 gifted education programming standards were revised as well as aligned more closely with the now existent professional standards for teacher education preparation programs. The significant differences in the more recent set of standards Include (1) a greater emphasis on diversity, (2) an emphasis on evidence-based practices, and (3) alignment with the teacher education preparation program standards. The revised document consists of six standards that encompass effective programming, including (1) learning and development, (2) assessment, (3) curriculum planning and instruction, (4) learning environments, (5) programming, and (6) professional development.

A second set of national standards that impact gifted education are the National Council for Accreditation of Teacher Education (NCATE) approved joint professional standards for teacher education preparation programs in gifted education authored by NAGC and the Council for Exceptional Children (CEC) in 2006. These standards are used to guide the content and competencies that make up the foundations of the curriculum of teacher education and professional development programs in the field of gifted education. Both documents provide the benchmarks for effective gifted education programming against which the efficacy of all practice should be measured.

Given that the standards in gifted education both for programming and teacher preparation provide a framework on which to delineate the best practices of the assessment of giftedness and talent in school-age children, they are used as a frame of reference for the discussion of student identification contained in this chapter. Therefore,

the impact of these professional standards on the procedural implementation of rigorous identification paradigms is the subject of this chapter. The standards will be discussed as touchstones for recommended practice in the design, implementation, and evaluation of the identification of giftedness and talent.

## THE IMPACT OF THE NAGC PRE-K–12 GIFTED PROGRAM STANDARDS ON ASSESSMENT

The impact of student identification is evident throughout the NAGC Pre-K–12 Gifted Education Program Standards document (see Appendix A). For example, student identification is directly related to the need for curricular and instructional modifications and adaptations as it assesses students' educational strengths, weaknesses, and needs. The mere process of identifying students and subsequently labeling them as gifted and talented has socio-emotional implications, including impacting their self-esteem and identity formation. Further, we know that labeling students can also affect peer and family dynamics for the targeted student. Identification is a critical component of all aspects of gifted education programming as well as an important entity in and of itself. Thus throughout the standards programming document there are implications for the significance of student identification on every aspect of gifted education. However, the essence of recommended student identification practice is most prominent when discussed as one of the six standards that make up the educational programming standards framework called "Assessment," which is described as the provision of information regarding identification, learning progress and outcomes, and the evaluation of programming for students with gifts and talents in all domains (NAGC, 2010b).

As part of the standard on assessment, both student outcomes and accompanying evidence-based practices are provided in order to shape practice as well as provide specific outcomes necessary to the effective practice of student identification. For the purpose of this chapter, three student outcomes and the eleven accompanying evidence-based practices will serve as the infrastructure to a more comprehensive and detailed discussion of student identification of giftedness and talent. In other words, the outcomes promote the requisite parts of the identification process. Each of the evidence-based practices accompanying student outcomes is presented below in order to guide a broader discussion of related information regarding student identification. Supporting research for evidence-based practices is published in a separate document (NAGC, 2010b). This manuscript is contained in Appendix B. Specifically, the outcomes guide not only the development of identification practice, but also serve as benchmarks from which to measure the effectiveness of the same.

## THE ACCESSIBILITY OF A COMPREHENSIVE ASSESSMENT SYSTEM

The first identification student outcome falling under the assessment standard calls for equal access of all students to a comprehensive assessment system that promotes environments whereby students are able to demonstrate diverse characteristics and behaviors related to their giftedness. Two evidence-based practices are associated with this student outcome.

**Practice 2.1.1.** "Educators develop environments and instructional activities that encourage students to express diverse characteristics and behaviors that are associated with giftedness" (NAGC, 2010a).

Giftedness is expressed in terms of behavior. Giftedness is not a unitary trait, and, therefore, a confluence of behaviors reflects one's giftedness or talent. In fact, it is the sustained behavior over time and environments that best denotes giftedness or talent. However, the behavior only occurs when supported by nurturing environments. In classrooms, nurturing environments consist of appropriate curricular and instructional practices, rigor, understanding, and values that accept and welcome giftedness or talent. Without the appropriate support systems, gifted behavior is hidden. Giftedness and talent do not occur in a vacuum!

Without appropriate environmental circumstances and nurturing, giftedness and talent lie unrealized. In other words, when giftedness is not fully actualized, then it remains merely as the raw potential that is not developed. Students at this phase of talent development are just as much in need of gifted education programming as those students for whom some level of nourishment and support has already taken place. This level of self-actualization of one's own giftedness or talent is thus emerging and must be identified as such versus being dismissed because of current levels of performance. The right environment can support potential and assist in the realization process.

**Practice 2.1.2.** "Educators provide parents [and] guardians with information regarding diverse characteristics and behaviors that are associated with giftedness" (NAGC, 2010a).

Schools must communicate with parents in a collaborative effort to identify giftedness and talent. In fact, parents are excellent purveyors of information about gifted behavior in their own children. Because they watch their children develop over time, they have the added advantage, when compared to teachers, of seeing sustained behavior across years and many diverse environments. It is particularly important that parents recognize giftedness in their children as it promotes understanding and acceptance. Further, parents who understand their child's giftedness are the strongest advocates for appropriate services and placements in educational programming and settings.

## ASSESSMENT EVIDENCE OF EXCEPTIONALITIES OR POTENTIAL GUIDES INSTRUCTIONAL MODIFICATIONS

The second student outcome related to identification under the assessment standard highlights the relationship of assessment data not only to eligibility and placement in educational services, but also to guide curricular and instructional practice. Six evidence-based practices illustrate how this goal might be accomplished best.

**Practice 2.2.1.** "Educators establish comprehensive, cohesive, and ongoing procedures for identifying and serving students with gifts and talents. These provisions include informed consent, committee review, student retention, student reassessment, student exiting, and appeals procedures for both entry and exit from gifted program services" (NAGC, 2010a).

Comprehensive procedures for student identification must include, at the very least, provisions for informed consent, student retention, student reassessment, student exiting, and appeals procedures (NAGC, 2010b). All policies and procedures for student identification and placement must strive to protect the rights of students (Hansford et al., 2001). The establishment of student rights during student identification is advantageous for several reasons (Hansford et al., 2001). Sound policies and procedures lead to more equitable identification and placement of students. Equally important is the need for regular reassessment to assist in the realignment of educational placements and academic decision making to changing student needs. While student eligibility may not change over time, the learner's needs most certainly will change. Original determination of placement in services as well as provisions for curricular and instructional adaptations need to be reconsidered to best fit the student's current level of needs. In order to determine the continuation of the best placement in services as well as related educational planning, reassessment must be conducted regularly in order to gain information about the educational needs of gifted and talented students.

Equally important to having comprehensive and cohesive identification procedures is the existence of written documentation of the same, which serves not only to inform constituency groups, but also to establish the policies and procedures from which daily practice must emanate. Consider that informed consent, student retention, exiting, and appeals procedures are the written contract for student identification between the school district and

170

the community regarding student rights during identification and any subsequent reevaluation. This information serves the school district as well, given that student identification can present the threat of litigation to the practice of gifted education programming. Written procedures help to establish requisite content as well as clarify the need for revisiting the documentation regularly for currency. The standards for written documentation illustrate the minimum expectations for distributing polices regarding student identification to the educational and community constituencies. Written documentation not only serves to distribute information, but improves the likelihood that the policies will be consistently enforced.

Finally, it is imperative that identification policies and procedures be reviewed and revised regularly. Any set of policies and procedures that dictate practice as well as protect students' rights must be current and reflect up-to-date knowledge and practice in the field of gifted education. Annual review allows the institution to make appropriate changes to existing policies as well as the format for distribution. Perhaps an excess number of appeals or complaints can be avoided with the addition of information or clarification of existing policy descriptions. Parents and their children are entitled to the necessary information that facilitates the student identification process. Educators are equally in need of being up-to-date on the policies and procedures that dictate their practice of student assessment.

**Practice 2.2.2.** "Educators select and use multiple assessments that measure diverse abilities, talents, and strengths that are based

on current theories, models, and research" (NAGC, 2010a).

Regarding what we use to identify giftedness and talent, evidence-based practice insists that instrumentation used for student assessment to determine eligibility for gifted education services must measure diverse abilities, talents, strengths, and needs in order to provide students an opportunity to demonstrate any giftedness or talent (NAGC, 2010b). When a variety of instruments is used in the student identification process, there is an improved opportunity for students to demonstrate any of their strengths. On the other hand, the use of one or two scores to illustrate students' strengths can lead to missed opportunities to demonstrate giftedness and talent in a specific area that was not properly assessed or assessed at all. Further, a narrow assessment of giftedness and talent will lead to insufficient information on which to base student placement in necessary services.

A comprehensive assessment paradigm looks at the constructs of giftedness such as ability, creativity, and motivation, but also should include other aspects of the student's inclination for learning such as interests and learning styles. Patterns in emerging interests or concentrated motivation in areas of passion can aid in the eligibility decisions for gifted services.

Similarly, identification instrumentation must reflect sensitivity to a diverse population, which enhances the possibility that giftedness is found in the broadest spectrum of students. Further, when the greatest number of talents and strengths are included in the search for giftedness, better assessment data are collected. This diversity of student data improves the appropriate translation of assessment data regarding student eligibility for placement in appropriate services and for curriculum and instructional modifications.

Equally important is the consideration of finding potential versus actualized giftedness and talent. Therefore, when selecting appropriate assessment instrumentation, a critically important consideration is its best fit to the developmental nature of talent (Landrum & Shaklee, 2000). Some instruments are better suited for recognizing the potential of talent while others clearly assess current performance. Both are important to the student identification process.

Identification procedures as well as instrumentation must be based in current theory and research (NAGC, 2010b). Empirical and theoretical knowledge in the field of gifted education is relatively new and constantly evolving. New research and theory within the field and in related areas are constantly impacting the principles and practices in gifted and talented education. Student identification in particular is impacted by ongoing investigations into brain research, conceptions of intelligence, the use of traditional and non-traditional assessments, and a working knowledge of culturally fair and unbiased instrumentation and identification procedures. Thus it is imperative that the student identification policies, procedures, instrumentation, and processes undergo constant reconsideration and updating as a result of the ever changing body of knowledge and recalculation of theoretical frameworks. Our understanding of these factors is augmented by new information and theories that guide our identification of gifted and talented students.

**Practice 2.2.3.** "Assessments provide qualitative and quantitative information from a variety of sources, including off-level testing, are nonbiased and equitable, and are technically adequate for the purpose" (NAGC, 2010a).

Assessment data should represent an appropriate balance of reliable and valid quantitative and qualitative measures (Landrum & Shaklee, 2000). When recognizing the significance of multiple sources and multiple methods, it follows that the most appropriate type of methodology must be employed. Typically, methodologies are either qualitative or quantitative in nature. Both are critically important in order to best assess the varied criteria involved in giftedness and talent. Foremost, the decision to use a particular type of methodology should be due to a true fit to the target data source. For example, one must consider whether a portfolio of creative work or a test of creativity best suits the type of data desired. One is an assessment of creative productivity while the other measures creative thinking. When a variety of sources are used, then qualitative and quantitative methodologies will be necessary. Only reliable and valid methodologies of either origin should be employed in the assessment of giftedness and talent.

Off-grade level testing occurs when student scores on standardized instrumentation are interpreted at levels beyond current chronological age and grade placement. In other words, students' performance scores are compared to students with similar scores regardless of age and grade placement. This allows for a more accurate interpretation of a student's level of performance. Above grade-level performance is indicative of giftedness and talent. Further, this specificity of information best guides educational planning and placement in appropriate levels of services for gifted students.

Attending to the technical adequacy of any instrument used in student identification, including representative student populations present in the sample used to determine the instrument's reliability and validity, remains as important as selecting instrumentation that is a best match to the construct it purports to measure. Student identification is impacted both by the technical adequacy of instruments as well as the most current theory and research on which they are predicated (Handsford, et al., 2001). (See also Chapter 7 of this volume.) Careful alignment must exist between the accepted definition of giftedness, the related instruments, as well as the technical adequacy of the instrumentation used with gifted and talented students.

Ultimately, it is the use by education professionals of instruments in student identification that matters most to the success of a good fit of gifted education programming to individual gifted students. When instrumentation is used correctly and different measures are considered in a careful accompaniment of assessment procedures, data is more likely to fully describe the strengths of students in a meaningful way. Hansford et al. (2001) indicate that updated and current instruments lead to district practices and procedures that are appropriate for their students. Inevitably this leads to less time and resources spent on student appeals and processes of exiting misidentified students from gifted education services. Further, the likelihood that traditionally overlooked gifted students will be appropriately assessed is improved by the use of the most current and updated identification paradigm.

**Practice 2.2.4.** "Educators have knowledge of student exceptionalities and collect assessment data while adjusting curriculum and instruction to learn about each student's developmental level and aptitude for learning" (NAGC, 2010a).

Another significant consideration in the selection of assessment instrumentation is that the data collected during student identification informs the eligibility of services as well as the nature of services provided to target students (NAGC, 2010b). The more comprehensive and diverse the instrumentation employed, the better the assessment data translates into meaningful changes in educational programming that addresses students' needs. Therefore, the instrumentation adopted for the collection of student assessment data must be sensitive to the many aspects of giftedness that help facilitate eligibility and, more importantly, necessary instructional decisions.

The student identification process should seek to encourage the student to demonstrate any strength, aptitude, or ability that warrants gifted education services. It follows then that a profile consisting of diverse student data will reveal more about potential giftedness and talent than any one or two standardized scores would provide. Further, a diverse set of data will provide more guidance in the subsequent curricular and instructional decisions involved in student placement of services.

Identification is a vital component of gifted education programming. More importantly, the appropriate design and implementation of the identification framework has the potential to drive gifted education programming. A good fit between the identification of students' strengths and the best determination of related educational services is the essence of effective gifted education. Therefore, it is critical that identification is conceptualized based on theory and research, as well as practiced according to high quality standards. This translation of empirical and theoretical constructs to meaningful practice is essential to quality identification of giftedness and talent in students

Student assessment that best determines eligibility as well as facilitates educational programming must reflect a comprehensive view of the student and not rely on a limited view associated with a single score (Callahan & McIntire, 1994). The best way to comprehensively represent student assessment data is in a profile. More importantly, it is the analysis and synthesis of assessment data within the profile that best guides student identification. The student profile portrays an extensive view of the constructs of giftedness and related factors that influence realization of potential into performance. It is the collection, collation, and analysis of data for individual students that best describe the advantage of a student profile (Hansford et al., 2001) over other compilation systems such as the matrix. A profile is recommended over the use of a matrix that translates assessment data into ratings or scores that limit the meaningful interpretation of data and instead compares students to one another on an artificial scale. In fact, Callahan and McIntire (1994) caution against the use of matrices in interpreting student assessment results in deference to moving toward the case study approach.

The more information that is accumulated from the assessment process, the better the decisions that are made regarding eligibility, placement,

and subsequent instructional planning. Therefore, an assemblage of student assessment with individual strengths and needs must be developed to plan appropriate intervention (Landrum & Shaklee, 2000). Determining student eligibility and placement in services constitutes data-driven decision making. The ease and efficacy of making these decisions depend on the quality of the data collected as well as how the data are organized. Careful alignment of student data allows the information "to tell a story" about current performance and full potential. Each of the standards associated with this guiding principle further clarifies the need for thoughtful assessment data assemblage within a meaningful structure.

**Practice 2.2.5.** "Educators interpret multiple assessments in different domains and understand the uses and limitations of the assessments in identifying the needs of students with gifts and talents" (NAGC, 2010a).

Our understanding and conceptualization of giftedness and talent is evolutionary. There is no universally accepted definition of giftedness, which points to the lack of agreement on our understanding of the construct of giftedness. However, it is generally accepted that since there is no true test of giftedness, instruments that measure the various constructs of giftedness must be employed. Because there is no unitary construct supporting giftedness or talent, several instruments are required in order to fully assess the integrated factors that influence giftedness or talent. Assessment data should come from multiple sources and include multiple assessment methods (NAGC, 2010b). The fundamental purpose of the assessment of giftedness is that students should be given every available opportunity to demonstrate giftedness, rather than merely considered in or out of a gifted program. In order to practice this type of assessment, multiple sources and multiple methods are required in order to produce such possibilities or opportunities to find giftedness or talent. Therefore, a construct such as achievement can be associated with several sources of data and methods. For example, a student's current level of achievement can be assessed via a standardized test as well as curriculum-based assessment.

Giftedness or talent is not a unitary trait. Multiple data sources are needed in order to assess a variety of criteria that in their totality define giftedness or talent. Likewise, no one measure can adequately determine eligibility in gifted education programming. Instead, several measures must be used to identify the various criteria that result in the assessment of giftedness or talent. Data analysis across multiple sources explains giftedness, as well as related factors such as underachievement or twice-exceptionality. Different sources of data will indicate potential versus performance as well. (The importance of assessing both potential and performance were discussed earlier in the chapter.)

A critical consideration for the use of multiple data assessment methods is that assessment of different types of giftedness and talent necessitate different data sources best found by a variety of methods. Intellectual giftedness is more likely to be assessed by standardized testing. On the other hand, performing arts aptitude is often measured by performance or portfolio assessment. When identifying different types of giftedness, different assessment methods must be employed. In

determining an individualized assessment plan, one must surmise the type of giftedness or talent suspected for any given student in order to appropriately match methodology to the specific domain of talent. Information regarding the type of talent in need of assessment must be sought during the referral or nomination phase of assessment.

Similarly, multiple data assessment methods are critically important to the success of student identification of giftedness and talent. Not only are multiple data sets important for completely understanding giftedness, but various types of data are essential. Different assessment methods produce various kinds of information. For example, it is as important to know a students' achievement via a test score as it is to know about related academic behaviors in the classroom.

In spite of the potential for additional costs and time consumption associated with the use of multiple instruments for data collection, the benefits of providing multiple opportunities to demonstrate giftedness and talent are noteworthy (Hansford et al., 2001). First, diverse and comprehensive student assessment will result in a more equitable student identification process. For example, multiple opportunities to demonstrate giftedness and talent provide greater access to gifted education programming to populations of students that might otherwise be overlooked. Second, instructional decisions are more effective and efficient when based on comprehensive information regarding student strengths and weaknesses. The costs of reassessing students who are not identified during the first assessment or misidentifying students who don't perform well in gifted education programming are diminished greatly with the initial investment of diverse assessment instruments and practices.

**Practice 2.2.6.** "Educators inform all parents and guardians about the identification process. Teachers obtain parental or guardian permission for assessments, use culturally sensitive checklists, and elicit evidence regarding the child's interests and potential outside of the classroom setting" (NAGC, 2010a).

Identification paradigms must promote cultural responsiveness and fairness to a diverse pool of potentially gifted students. For example, identification instrumentation and other assessments must be responsive to students' economic conditions, gender, linguistic differences, developmental differences, disabilities, and other factors that mitigate against fair assessment practices (Landrum & Shaklee, 2000). The practice of using culturally sensitive or fair instrumentation and practices improves the outcomes of assessment as it includes otherwise overlooked students as well as accurately portrays students needs in terms of educational services for both strengths and weaknesses. In essence, when instrumentation is employed, it should be accessible and responsive to the student rather than limit or inhibit the chances of recognizing giftedness and talent. There must be an acceptance of the realization that, in order for instrumentation to be culturally fair, different assessments may need to be used for various constituents.

The most important aspect of accessibility in student identification is the selection of assessment instruments and identification processes that are not only responsive to the unique needs of any population with whom it is used, but also

respectful of differences as well. In other words, student assessment must be appropriate to the entire diverse student population including all ethnic, racial, socio-economic, and linguistic groups of students. This includes use of native language.

The assessment administration used may also need to be differentiated based on the related needs of the students' circumstances in life. For students with linguistic differences, this may mean conducting assessment in the student's native language. For students with disadvantaged economic backgrounds, assessment may be based on recognizing potential rather than more mature talent.

### IDENTIFIED STUDENTS REFLECT THE DIVERSITY OF THE TOTAL LOCAL STUDENT POPULATION

The final assessment standard student outcome discussed in this chapter emphasizes the desired goal of recognizing all potential gifted and talented students as a result of the assessment process. Three evidence-based practices describe how to realize this universally desired aspiration.

**Practice 2.3.1.** "Educators elect and use non-biased and equitable approaches for identifying students with gifts and talents, which may include using locally developed norms or assessment tools in the child's native language or in nonverbal formats" (NAGC, 2010a).

The practice of constructing local or group norms for instrumentation allows the comparison of individual student's assessment results against the local population versus the national sample used in constructing standardized equivalents of student scores. In particular when the local population within a district is unique or relatively unduplicated in available standardized testing, local norms provide comparisons amongst students that are more equitable and at least representative of the local population of students. The construction of local norms can be completed after widespread distribution of instrumentation within a school district across the same grade level.

Just as it is important to use local norms to interpret test results, all identification assessments should be provided in a language in which the student is most fluent, if available (NAGC, 2010b). When communications are written or spoken in the students' native language, there is greater potential for participation in the process. Equally important, however, is that the instrument is able to elicit all of the necessary information intended with accuracy. When instrumentation reflects the students' strongest language, there is greater occasion for the data to reflect accurately students' strengths and interests. Further, if an instrument is going to measure what is intended with reliability and validity, then the content and administration of the instrument should be conducted in the students' strongest language. Using the student's strongest language for assessment purposes will lead to fewer false negatives in the eligibility process as well as produce more accurate indicators of student strengths and weaknesses for facilitating educational interventions associated with gifted education programming.

**Practice 2.3.2.** "Educators understand and
    implement district and state policies designed
    to foster equity in gifted programming and
    services" (NAGC, 2010a).
    Due to a lack of federal and often state legislation that serves students' rights in gifted education,

written documentation provides schools with local policy in the absence of such at other levels. When provided to key stakeholders, such as parents, identification policies and procedures can support unbiased educational decision making that is dictated by policy and not the individuals making the determination of eligibility. In fact, the approval of the documentation and its contents by the local school board lends credibility to their acceptance and perhaps even support by local school personnel.

**Practice 2.3.3.** "Educators provide parents and
    guardians with information in their native
    language regarding diverse behaviors and
    characteristics that are associated with gifted-
    ness and with information that explains the
    nature and purpose of gifted programming
    options" (NAGC, 2010a).

School personnel should be sure to make available gifted education information, in particular identification policies and procedures, in multiple languages in order to create the possibility that all constituents understand the information. Widespread distribution of the documentation will improve the chances that it is read. Possible distribution avenues include brochures, the Internet, and posting in all schools.

### THE IMPACT OF PROFESSIONAL TEACHER EDUCATION STANDARDS IN GIFTED EDUCATION ON IDENTIFICATION

The preparation and accompanying training of educators in gifted education are supported by the Teacher Knowledge & Skills Standards for Gifted and Talented Education (see Appendix C). The joint publication between the National Association for Gifted Children (NAGC) and the Council for Exceptional Children (NAGC & CEC, 2006) highlights the requisite knowledge and skills related to teacher preparation in the field of gifted and talented education. The National Council for the Accreditation of Teacher Educators has adopted the standards to empower teacher preparation programs to develop educational interventions that best develop teachers ready to meet the challenges of gifted students. NAGC also recommends (Johnson, 2008) the use of the national standards to dictate professional development programs for existing educators who already have initial licensure in education but did not receive specialized training in gifted and talented education. Training can be provided to existing educational staff via conferences, workshops, institutes, college coursework, and professional development programs.

The standards document (NAGC & CEC, 2006) is comprised of knowledge and skill standards for ten components of the field, one of which is titled "Assessment." This component is associated with three knowledge standards and four related skill standards in regard to the identification of giftedness and talent. Key knowledge and skills are necessary for effective decision making and practice by professional educators when engaging in student assessment—in particular, when considering student eligibility, placement, and curriculum and instructional needs. In order to best inform policy, procedure, and practice in student identification, only educators with the most current and pedagogically sound knowledge about gifted education must be involved in the process.

The knowledge and skill standards minimally define the requisite scholarship for practitioners in student identification.

The professional standards are based on the theoretical, empirical, and practice-based literature. Johnsen (2008) notes that the literature base suggests that assessments are essential to professional decision making regarding identification, monitoring academic performance, as well as when adjusting instruction. Based on the literature, seven observations influence student identification and educational placement processes:

1. Multiple measures and alternative assessments are recommended given the diverse nature of giftedness and talent;

2. Specific measures have been designed and should be used to measure different types of giftedness and talent;

3. The identification process must match the program of services provided by an individual school district;

4. Assessments that reach all students, including those typically underserved, include dynamic assessment, peer nomination, nonverbal tests, alternative screenings, performance assessment, problem-based tasks, observations, as well as other qualitative assessments;

5. In order to best identify underserved students, assessment administrators must be able to measure language proficiency, examine tests for bias, as well as know how to recognize gifted behavior outside of school-related activities;

6. Non-traditional measures of academic progress include authentic tasks, portfolios,

rubrics, and performance-based assessments; and

7. The results of assessments that measure student progress are warranted in order to adjust instruction, place students in appropriate educational environments, and for academic acceleration.

In order to preserve the integrity of any student identification system, the teachers and other staff involved in the process must be prepared. Essentially the content of the standards (NAGC & CEC, 2006) states that educators must understand thoroughly the processes and procedures of assessment as well as the equitable and non-biased use of assessment in gifted education. Further, the standards guide the educators' decision making about curricular and instructional adaptations based on assessment data. The focus of this section of the chapter is the impact of the professional standards on student identification in gifted education.

## KNOWLEDGE STANDARDS

Student identification is a journey and not a destination, requiring participants to constantly solve problems and make decisions based on acquired assessment data. Therefore, educators are called upon to have requisite knowledge on which to draw when engaged in the process of student identification. Identification demands a series of decisions that must be made on behalf of the various constituency groups to be served by gifted and talented programming. For example, educators must call upon the most current related knowledge in the field in order to decide how to employ the relevant multiple assessment sources and methods, choose appropriate assessments,

match instrumentation to specific needs, interpret assessment data in order to determine eligibility and service placement, and translate data into curricular and instructional modifications. Therefore, possessing current knowledge on student identification and the related issues of assessment and measurement are critical to the success of student identification.

The knowledge standards contain the necessary information required by educators to understand, practice, and evaluate the identification procedures used for the assessment of giftedness and talent. Teachers employed to work directly with gifted education must possess the knowledge outlined within these standards. Accompanying each standard is a set of questions that educators must contemplate during the data-driven decision making required in the process of student identification.

**Knowledge Standard 1.** "Processes and procedures for the identification of individuals with gifts and talents" (NAGC & CEC, 2006)

In order for teachers to fully participate in student identification, they must possess the basic procedural knowledge of the process. This includes a full understanding of every aspect of the nomination or referral, assessment, eligibility, placement, and appeals stages of identification. Specifically, teachers must understand "the process of identification, legal policies, and ethical principles of measurement and assessment related to referral, eligibility, program planning, instruction, and placement for individuals with gifts and talents, including those from culturally and linguistically diverse backgrounds" (Johnsen, 2008, p. 16).

Teachers must be made aware of the strengths and weaknesses of the various approaches to student identification. The best identification paradigm is open or inclusive and, therefore, allows for the opportunity or opportunities to find giftedness and talent. Any approach to assessment that limits students is a closed approach. Practices that can hinder or limit the identification process is the practice of arbitrary weighting of criteria, use of a matrix, or establishing hurdles that inhibit multiple source and multiple methods. Richert (1997) comments that the purpose of multiple methods and sources is "to have a variety of measures complement each other in order to discover gifted potential that a single measure might not indicate" (p. 82).

**Questions for effective practice.** Educators must be prepared to answer the following questions in regard to the student identification system used in their school district.

1. What is the current definition of giftedness?
2. What data sources and methods will provide the best opportunity for students to demonstrate their giftedness?
3. What assessments match the constructs of giftedness and talent as outlined in the adopted definition?
4. What tests already are administered by the school district?
5. What other tests are available within the school district?
6. What alternative assessments are warranted?
7. How do the adopted assessments drive placement?

8. What assessment data are available to facilitate curricular and instructional modifications?

**Knowledge Standard 2.** "Uses, limitations, and interpretation of multiple assessments in different domains for identifying individuals with exceptional learning needs, including those from diverse backgrounds" (NAGC & CEC, 2006)

It is important for educators to know measurement theory and practices in order to interpret assessment results and recognize the appropriate uses and limitations of a variety of assessments (Johnsen, 2008). It is important that the educator use "a variety of appraisals so that schools can find students in different talent areas and at different ages" (U. S. Department of Education [DOE], 1993, p. 26). Similarly, schools must seek variety, looking through a range of disciplines for students with diverse talents (U. S. DOE, 1993). In order for all students of all backgrounds to have equal access to gifted education programming, the student identification process as well as the related instrumentation must be free of bias (U. S. DOE, 1993). Because giftedness and talent can appear differently in different people and at different times for any given person, the identification system must be fluid or address the varying rates of development and diverse interests that change over time as students mature (U. S. DOE, 1993). It is recommended that, in addition to other constructs of giftedness and talent, motivation, in particular, be taken into account during the identification process due to its importance in developing accomplishment. Equally important is the identification of potential that represents talents not readily obvious due to lack of full realization or actualization of talent (U. S. DOE, 1993).

The use of multiple criteria, in particular, to identify giftedness and talent is important for several reasons (Shore, Cornell, Robinson, & Ward, 1991). First, this practice reduces the likelihood that twice exceptional learners or gifted students with underachievement will be missed by assessments that rely on a single score or limited criteria. Secondly, an identification system that uses multiple criteria rather than relying on individual measures of any construct is more psychometrically sound. Third, multiple criteria include the chances of more non-traditional students being included in gifted education programming. And finally, Shore et al. found that multiple criteria are better than reliance on measures of scholarship for identifying students for services in specialized disciplines such as the arts.

**Questions for effective practice.** Educators must be prepared to answer the following questions in regard to the student identification system used in their school district.

1. How does the sample of students on which the test was normed adequately represent the student populations of the schools where it will be used?

2. What level of technical adequacy exists for each standardized measure used in student identification?

3. What types of sources best produce the desired data?

4. What different domains of giftedness and talent are represented in the adopted definition of giftedness and talent?

5. What assessment instruments will address the unique learning needs of typically underserved populations of gifted and talented students?

6. How do designated assessment methods (traditional and non-traditional) address the unique learning needs of typically underserved populations of gifted and talented students?

7. How will a student profile best represent the multiple sources and measures employed during student identification?

**Knowledge Standard 3.** "Uses and limitations of assessments documenting academic growth of individuals with gifts and talents" (NAGC & CEC, 2006)

In an age of high-stakes testing, all too often student and educator performance is based solely on the results of assessments that measure student progress according to criterion-referenced testing. It is the intent that students' academic growth can be assessed according to the possession of specific knowledge for a given grade level and age group. Therein lies the limitation for assessing students who are gifted and talented, as their current academic performance as well as progress must be assessed using off-grade level measurement.

**Questions for effective practice.** Educators must be prepared to answer the following questions in regard to the student identification system used in their school district.

1. What is the baseline level of performance for the students who are gifted and talented?

2. Do the targeted assessments allow for measuring high-end growth?

3. Is off-grade level testing necessary for gifted and talented students (based on the baseline information)?

4. How can gifted and talented students engage in off-grade level assessment?

5. How can current assessments be used for off-grade level assessment?

6. What additional or supplemental assessments must be used for off-grade level assessment?

### SKILL STANDARDS

In addition to a current knowledge base, teachers involved in student identification for giftedness and talent must possess accompanying professional skills. These standards contain the foundational skills required to engage in successful student identification. The skills must accompany the knowledge base covered in the knowledge standards. The skill standards are discussed below. Along with each standard are some recommendations for best practices that support effective skill performance.

**Skill Standard 1**. "Use non-biased and equitable approaches for identifying individuals with gifts and talents, including those from diverse backgrounds" (NAGC & CEC, 2006)

Traditionally underserved populations of gifted and talented students were ignored by assessment methods and instruments that were not equitable and, therefore, denied access to services. Although assessment approaches may be appropriate for some students, it could be biased toward others. For example, culturally or economically diverse students may not be represented in the sample used to norm

an instrument. Or, the language itself could preclude students' successful performance because of linguistic differences. Shore et al. (1991) suggest that tests that are less dependent on English mastery are more likely to help identify students with linguistic and other cultural differences. Linguistically sensitive assessment practices are more equitable identification processes because they increase access to gifted education programming for students otherwise missed by traditional assessment procedures.

**Recommended best practices.** In applying the skill standard, the related best practices can support performance. The educator should:

1. Read the technical adequacy information, including the normative sampling, for any instrument used in student identification for giftedness and talent.

2. Determine an appropriate fit of any identification approach to the target student.

3. Determine an appropriate fit of any identification approach to the domain of giftedness or talent under consideration.

4. Use alternative assessments only when necessary rather than for the sake of doing so.

**Skill Standard 2**. "Use technically adequate qualitative and quantitative assessments for identifying and placing individuals with gifts and talents" (NAGC & CEC, 2006)

Educators must make use of only technically adequate measures to engage in the search for giftedness and talent. Both qualitative and quantitative measures have technical adequacy or reliability, validity, and representative sampling. No assessment method should be used without the appropriately documented technical adequacy for the targeted student group. One of the best ways to determine technical adequacy for the specific contingency group is to determine local norms.

**Recommended best practices.** In applying the skill standard, the related best practices can support performance. The educator should:

1. Determine which constructs of giftedness and talent are best suited for qualitative or quantitative methodology.

2. Select only technically adequate methodology for use in student identification.

3. Select assessment methodologies that use data from both qualitative and quantitative assessments to determine eligibility as well as make placement determinations.

**Skill Standard 3**. "Develop differentiated curriculum-based assessments for use in instructional planning and delivery for individuals with gifts and talents" (NAGC & CEC, 2006)

Curriculum-based assessment is the evaluation of student behavior, knowledge, and skill based on the students' performance within the current curricula in which they are working. Gifted and talented students work in advanced curricula that are differentiated from grade-level curriculum and instruction. For gifted learners, who are often working in enriched and accelerated curriculum, this type of assessment monitors student progress as well as determines the appropriate levels of elevated outcomes. The curriculum-based assessment assists educators in grading but also in making subsequent curriculum decisions.

Assouline (1997) describes a curriculum decision as one that "requires information about an individual's achievement within a curriculum domain. The information then guides decisions about which curriculum the learner needs (p. 90)." Curriculum-based assessment data should also inform educators about the necessary adjustment of instructional pace and rate of learning for any gifted and talented learner. The purposeful use of accelerative strategies should be based on evidence of current student status and some prediction of where in the scope and sequence of curriculum a student should be placed for a rigorous learning experience.

**Recommended best practices.** In applying the skill standard, the related best practices can support performance. The educator should:

1. Use pre-testing to establish mastery of grade-level curricula.

2. Base curricular and instructional adaptations, modifications, and supplants on a student's current performance and related needs.

3. Use curriculum-based assessments to document academic growth or progress.

**Skill Standard 4**. "Use alternative assessments and technologies to evaluate learning of individuals with gifts and talents" (NAGC & CEC, 2006)

In addition to the use of curriculum-based assessments, teachers should use alternative assessments to evaluate learning status as well as academic progress. For specific domains of giftedness and talent—for example, creativity—alternative assessments may be best suited to evaluating student progress in learning. Alternative assessments typically require a student to produce a product, performance, or demonstration. The alternative assessments can take the form of presentations, portfolios, performance-based assessments, or problem resolutions, to name a few.

Not only do alternative assessments provide performance measures for grading student learning, but they also inform subsequent curricular and instructional recommendations for a differentiated learning experience. As teachers make adjustments in the depth, breadth, and complexity of a learning experience, alternative assessments are best suited to gauging students' progress toward the intended elevated outcomes. Further, the assessment results dictate the subsequent learning experiences based on requisite knowledge, skill, and advanced learning.

**Recommended best practices.** In applying the skill standard, the related best practices can support performance. The educator should:

1. Use alternative assessments to evaluate student performances, demonstrations, and products.
2. Match alternative assessments to appropriate student performances and products to evaluate students' mastery of the curriculum.
3. Use alternative assessments to guide subsequent curricular and instructional changes.

## CONCLUSION

The practice of student identification is critical to the overall effectiveness of gifted education programming. Not only does identification determine eligibility for differentiated education services, but also matches learners' needs to the accompanying curriculum and instructional modifications associated with gifted and talented education. Therefore, a strong and efficacious student identification process can enhance gifted education programming.

Perhaps the best way to assure the integrity of the student identification process is to base practice on the highest standards used by a knowledgeable and skillful staff. The NAGC Pre-K–12 Programming Standards (NAGC, 2010a) and the NAGC-CEC Teacher Knowledge and Skill Standards for Gifted and Talented Education (NAGC & CEC, 2006) serve as benchmarks for effective student identification to effective practice and efficient staff decision making. The standards impact practice by setting the context and levels of effectiveness.

The standards for performance and staff preparedness can be used to facilitate the initial development or subsequent revision of any student identification system, serving as benchmarks for success. Similarly, the standards may serve as the criteria for ongoing evaluation of student assessment initiatives. Further, the standards can be used in initiatives to expand existing gifted education programming. For example, in attempts to gain funding to improve this area of gifted education programming, the standards can serve to justify the need to enhance existing practices to meet national standards for minimal competency. Most importantly, the standards translate to practice that is meaningful and beneficial to gifted learners by facilitating their access and experience in gifted education programming.

## REFERENCES

Assouline, S. G. (1997). Assessment of gifted children. In N. Colangelo & G. A. Davis (Eds.), *Handbook of gifted education* (second edition). Boston: Allyn & Bacon.

Callahan, C. M., & McIntire, J. A. (1993). *Identifying outstanding talent: In American Indian and Alaskan native students.* Washington, DC: Office of Educational Research and Improvement.

Landrum, M. S., & Shaklee, B. D., Eds. (2000). *The National Association for Gifted Children (NAGC) Pre-K–12 gifted education program standards.* Washington, DC: National Association for Gifted Children.

Hansford, S. J., Bonar, A. M., Scally, J. M., & Burge, N. A. (2001). Student identification. In M. S. Landrum, C. M. Callahan, & B. D. Shaklee (Eds.), *Aiming for excellence: Gifted program standards.* Waco, TX: Prufrock Press.

Johnsen, S. K. (2008). Professional standards for teachers of students with gifts and talents. In M. Kitano, D. Montgomer, J. Van Tassel-Baska, & S. K. Johnsen (Eds), *Using the national gifted education standards for pre-k–12 professional development.* Thousand Oaks, CA: Corwin Press.

NAGC (2010a). Pre-K–12 gifted education programming standards. Washington, DC: National Association for Gifted Children.

NAGC (2010b). Research support for student outcomes and alignment with the NAGC-CEC/TAG Teacher Preparation Standards and the 1998 NAGC Gifted Program Standards. Washington, DC: National Association for Gifted Children.

NAGC & CEC (2006). Teacher preparation standards in gifted and talented education. Washington, DC: National Association for Gifted Children.

Richert, E. S. (1997). Excellence with equity in identification and programming. In N. Colangelo & G. A. Davis (Eds.), *Handbook of gifted education* (2nd edition). Boston: Allyn & Bacon

Shore, B. M., Cornell, D. G., Robinson, A., & Ward, V. S. (1991). *Recommended practices in gifted education: A critical analysis.* New York: Teachers College Press.

U. S. Department of Education. (1993). *National excellence: A case for developing America's talent.* Washington, DC: Author.

Worthen, B. R., Sanders, J. R., & Fitzpatrick, J. L. (1997). *Program evaluation: Alternative approaches and practical guidelines* (2nd edition). New York: Longman.

APPENDIX A

PRE-K–12 GIFTED EDUCATION PROGRAM STANDARDS (NAGC, 2010A)*

## Gifted Education Programming Standard 2: Assessment

### Introduction

Knowledge about all forms of assessment is essential for educators of students with gifts and talents. It is integral to identification, assessing each student's learning progress, and evaluation of programming. Educators need to establish a challenging environment and collect multiple types of assessment information so that all students are able to demonstrate their gifts and talents. Educators' understanding of non-biased, technically adequate, and equitable approaches enables them to identify students who represent diverse backgrounds. They also differentiate their curriculum and instruction by using pre- and post-, performance-based, product-based, and out-of-level assessments. As a result of each educator's use of ongoing assessments, students with gifts and talents demonstrate advanced and complex learning. Using these student progress data, educators then evaluate services and make adjustments to one or more of the school's programming components so that student performance is improved.

| Standard 2: Assessment | |
|---|---|
| Description: Assessments provide information about identification, learning progress and outcomes, and evaluation of programming for students with gifts and talents in all domains. | |
| **Student Outcomes** | **Evidence-Based Practices** |
| 2.1. *Identification*. All students in grades PK-12 have equal access to a comprehensive assessment system that allows them to demonstrate diverse characteristics and behaviors that are associated with giftedness. | 2.1.1. Educators develop environments and instructional activities that encourage students to express diverse characteristics and behaviors that are associated with giftedness. |
| | 2.1.2. Educators provide parents/guardians with information regarding diverse characteristics and behaviors that are associated with giftedness. |
| 2.2. *Identification*. Each student reveals his or her exceptionalities or potential through assessment evidence so that appropriate instructional accommodations and modifications can be provided. | 2.2.1. Educators establish comprehensive, cohesive, and ongoing procedures for identifying and serving students with gifts and talents. These provisions include informed consent, committee review, student retention, student reassessment, student exiting, and appeals procedures for both entry and exit from gifted program services. |
| | 2.2.2. Educators select and use multiple assessments that measure diverse abilities, talents, and strengths that are based on current theories, models, and research. |
| | 2.2.3 Assessments provide qualitative and quantitative information from a variety of sources, including off-level testing, are nonbiased and equitable, and are technically adequate for the purpose. |
| | 2.2.4. Educators have knowledge of student exceptionalities and collect assessment data while adjusting curriculum and instruction to learn about each student's developmental level and aptitude for learning. |
| | 2.2.5. Educators interpret multiple assessments in different domains and understand the uses and limitations of the assessments in identifying the needs of students with gifts and talents. |
| | 2.2.6. Educators inform all parents/guardians about the identification process. Teachers obtain parental/guardian permission for assessments, use culturally sensitive checklists, and elicit evidence regarding the child's interests and potential outside of the classroom setting. |
| 2.3. *Identification*. Students with identified needs represent diverse backgrounds and reflect the total student population of the district. | 2.3.1. Educators select and use non-biased and equitable approaches for identifying students with gifts and talents, which may include using locally developed norms or assessment tools in the child's native language or in nonverbal formats. |
| | 2.3.2. Educators understand and implement district and state policies designed to foster equity in gifted programming and services. |
| | 2.3.3. Educators provide parents/guardians with information in their native language regarding diverse behaviors and characteristics that are associated with giftedness and with information that explains the nature and purpose of gifted programming options. |
| 2.4. *Learning Progress and Outcomes*. Students with gifts and talents demonstrate advanced and complex learning as a result of using multiple, appropriate, and ongoing assessments. | 2.4.1. Educators use differentiated pre- and post- performance-based assessments to measure the progress of students with gifts and talents. |
| | 2.4.2. Educators use differentiated product-based assessments to measure the progress of students with gifts and talents. |
| | 2.4.3. Educators use off-level standardized assessments to measure the progress of students with gifts and talents. |

*Reprinted with permission of the National Association for Gifted Children, Washington, DC, www.nagc.org

## GIFTED EDUCATION PROGRAMMING STANDARD 2: ASSESSMENT (CONT.)

| | |
|---|---|
| | 2.4.4. Educators use and interpret qualitative and quantitative assessment information to develop a profile of the strengths and weaknesses of each student with gifts and talents to plan appropriate intervention. |
| | 2.4.5. Educators communicate and interpret assessment information to students with gifts and talents and their parents/guardians. |
| 2.5. *Evaluation of Programming.* Students identified with gifts and talents demonstrate important learning progress as a result of programming and services. | 2.5.1. Educators ensure that the assessments used in the identification and evaluation processes are reliable and valid for each instrument's purpose, allow for above-grade-level performance, and allow for diverse perspectives. |
| | 2.5.2. Educators ensure that the assessment of the progress of students with gifts and talents uses multiple indicators that measure mastery of content, higher level thinking skills, achievement in specific program areas, and affective growth. |
| | 2.5.3. Educators assess the quantity, quality, and appropriateness of the programming and services provided for students with gifts and talents by disaggregating assessment data and yearly progress data and making the results public. |
| 2.6. *Evaluation of Programming.* Students identified with gifts and talents have increased access and they show significant learning progress as a result of improving components of gifted education programming. | 2.6.1. Administrators provide the necessary time and resources to implement an annual evaluation plan developed by persons with expertise in program evaluation and gifted education. |
| | 2.6.2. The evaluation plan is purposeful and evaluates how student-level outcomes are influenced by one or more of the following components of gifted education programming: (a) identification, (b) curriculum, (c) instructional programming and services, (d) ongoing assessment of student learning, (e) counseling and guidance programs, (f) teacher qualifications and professional development, (g) parent/guardian and community involvement, (h) programming resources, and (i) programming design, management, and delivery. |
| | 2.6.3. Educators disseminate the results of the evaluation, orally and in written form, and explain how they will use the results. |

*Reprinted with permission of the National Association for Gifted Children, Washington, DC, www.nagc.org

APPENDIX B

## RESEARCH SUPPORT FOR PRE-K-12 GIFTED EDUCATION PROGRAMMING STANDARDS: 2010 PRE-K–GRADE 12 GIFTED PROGRAMMING STANDARDS REFERENCES*

NATIONAL ASSOCIATION FOR GIFTED CHILDREN • 1331 H ST., NW, SUITE 1001 • WASHINGTON, DC 20005 •
202.785.4268 • WWW.NAGC.ORG

### STANDARD 2: ASSESSMENT

Assouline, S. G. (2003). Psychological and educational assessment of gifted children. In N. Colangelo and G. A. Davis (Eds.), *Handbook of gifted education* (3rd ed., pp. 124-145). Boston, MA: Allyn & Bacon.

Assouline, S. G., Nicpon, M. F., & Doobay, A. (2009). Profoundly gifted girls and autism spectrum disorder: A psychometric case study comparison. *Gifted Child Quarterly, 53*, 89-105.

Avery, L. D., Van Tassel-Baska, J., & O'Neill, B. (1997). Making evaluation work: One school district's experience. *Gifted Child Quarterly, 41*, 124-132.

Bain, S., Bourgeois, S., & Pappas, D. (2003). Linking theoretical models to actual practices: A survey of teachers in gifted education. *Roeper Review, 25*, 166-172.

Baker, E. L., & Schacter, J. (1996). Expert benchmarks for student academic performance: The case for gifted children. *Gifted Child Quarterly, 40*, 61-65.

Baldwin, A.Y. (2005). Identification concerns and promises for gifted students of diverse populations. *Theory into Practice, 44*(2), 105-114.

Bass, G. M., & Ries, R. (1995, April). *Scientific understanding in high ability high school students: Concepts and process skills*. Paper presented at the annual meeting of the American Educational Research Association, San Francisco, CA. (ERIC Document Reproduction Service No. ED387319).

Baum, S. M., Owen, S. V., & Oreck, B. A. (1996). Talent beyond words: Identification of potential talent in dance and music in elementary students. *Gifted Child Quarterly, 40*, 93-101.

Borland, J. II., & Wright, I. (1994). Identifying young, potentially gifted, economically disadvantaged students. *Gifted Child Quarterly, 38*, 164-171.

Briggs, C. J., Reis, S. M., & Sullivan, E. E. (2008). A national view of promising programs and practices for culturally, linguistically, and ethnically diverse gifted and talented students. *Gifted Child Quarterly, 52*, 131-145.

Brown, S. W., Renzulli, J. S., Gubbins, E. J., Siegle, D., Zhang, W., & Chen, C-H (2005). Assumptions underlying the identification of gifted and talented students. *Gifted Child Quarterly, 49*, 68-79.

Callahan, C. M. (2005). Making the grade or achieving the goal? Evaluating learner and program outcomes in gifted education. In F. A. Karnes & S. M. Bean (Eds.), *Methods and materials for teaching the gifted* (2nd ed., pp. 211-246). Waco, TX: Prufrock Press.

Callahan, C. M. (2004). *Program evaluation in gifted education*. In S. M. Reis (Series Ed.), *Essential readings in gifted educatio*. Thousand Oaks, CA: Corwin Press.

Castellano, J. A. (1998). *Identifying and assessing gifted and talented bilingual Hispanic students* (Report No. EDO-RC-97-9). Charleston, WV: ERIC Clearinghouse on Rural Education and Small Schools. (ERIC Document Reproduction Service No. ED 423104).

Coleman, M. R. (2003). *The identification of students who are gifted*. ERIC Digest #E644. Arlington, VA: ERIC Clearinghouse on Disabilities and Gifted Education.

Copenhaver, J. (2002). *Primer for maintaining accurate special education records and meeting confidentiality requirements when serving children with disabilities--Family Educational Rights and Privacy Act (FERPA)*. Logan: Utah State University, Mountain Plains Regional Resource Center.

Cunningham, C. M., Callahan, C. M., Plucker, J. A., Roberson, S. C., & Rapkin, A. (1998). Identifying Hispanic students of outstanding talent: Psychometric integrity of a peer nomination form. *Exceptional Children, 64*, 197-209.

Ferrell, B. G. (1992). Lesson plan analysis as a program evaluation tool. *Gifted Child Quarterly, 36*, 23-26.

Feng, A. X., VanTassel-Baska, J., Quek, C., Bai, W., & O'Neill, B. (2005). A longitudinal assessment of gifted students' learning using the Integrated Curriculum Model (ICM): Impacts and perceptions of the William and Mary language arts and science curriculum. *Roeper Review, 27*, 78-84.

*Reprinted with permission of the National Association for Gifted Children, Washington, DC, www.nagc.org

Fernández, A. T., Gay, L. R., Lucky, L F., Gavilan, M. R. (1998). Teacher perceptions of gifted Hispanic limited English proficient students. *Journal for the Education of the Gifted, 21*, 335-351.

Ford, D. Y. (2004). *Intelligence testing and cultural diversity: Concerns, cautions, and considerations* (RM04204). Storrs: University of Connecticut, National Research Center on the Gifted and Talented.

Ford, D. Y., & Trotman, M. F. (2000). The office for civil rights and non-discriminatory testing, policies, and procedures: Implications for gifted education. *Roeper Review, 23*, 109-112.

Gentry, M., & Owen, S. V. (1999). An investigation of the effects of total school flexible cluster grouping on identification, achievement, and classroom practices. *Gifted Child Quarterly, 43*, 224-243.

Grantham, T. C. (2003). Increasing Black student enrollment in gifted programs: An exploration of the Pulaski County special school district's advocacy efforts. *Gifted Child Quarterly, 47*, 46-65.

Harris, B., Plucker, J. A., Rapp, K. E., & Martinez, R. S. (2009). Identifying gifted and talented English language learners: A case study. *Journal for the Education of the Gifted, 32*, 368-393.

Hertzog, N. B. (2005). Equity and access: Creating general education classrooms responsive to potential giftedness. *Journal for the Education of the Gifted, 29*, 213-257.

House, E. R., & Lapan, S. (1994). Evaluation of programs for disadvantaged gifted students. *Journal for the Education of the Gifted, 17*, 441-466.

Huff, R. E., Houskamp, B. M., Watkins, A. V., Stanton, M., & Tavegia, B. (2005). The experiences of parents of gifted African American children: A phenomenological study. *Roeper Review, 27*, 215-221.

Hunsaker, S. L., & Callahan, C. M. (1993). Evaluation of gifted programs: Current practices. *Journal for the Education of the Gifted, 16*, 190-200.

Indiana Department of Education, Division of Exceptional Learners, High Ability (2007). *Indiana standards for high ability education.* Indianapolis: Author.

Johnsen, S. K. (1997). Assessment beyond definitions. *Peabody Journal of Education, 72*(3), 137-153.

Johnsen, S. K. (2000). What the research says about accountability and program evaluation. *Tempo, 20*(4), 23-30.

Johnsen, S. K. (2004a). Evaluating the effectiveness of the identification procedures. In S. K. Johnsen (Ed.), *Identifying gifted students: A practical guide* (pp. 133-139). Waco, TX: Prufrock Press.

Johnsen, S. K. (Ed.). (2004b). *Identifying gifted students: A practical guide.* Waco, TX: Prufrock Press.

Johnsen, S. K. (2004c). Making decisions about placement. In S. K. Johnsen (Ed.), *Identifying gifted students: A practical guide* (pp. 107-131). Waco, TX: Prufrock Press.

Johnsen, S. K. (2008). Using portfolios to assess gifted and talented students. In J. VanTassel-Baska (Ed.), *Alternative assessments with gifted and talented students* (pp. 227-257). Waco, TX: Prufrock Press.

Johnsen, S. K., & Ryser, G. (1994). Identification of young gifted children from lower income families. *Gifted and Talented International, 9*(2), 62-68.

Joseph, L., & Ford, D. Y. (2006). Nondiscriminatory assessment: Considerations for gifted education. *Gifted Child Quarterly, 50*, 42-51.

Kanevsky, L. (2000). Dynamic assessment of gifted learners. In K. A. Heller, F. J. Mönks, R. J. Sternberg, & R. F. Subotnik (Eds.), *International handbook of giftedness and talent* (2nd ed., pp. 283-295). New York, NY: Pergamon.

Kingore, B. (1995). Introducing parents to portfolio assessment: A collaborative effort toward authentic assessment. *Gifted Child Today, 18*(4), 12-13, 40.

Kirschenbaum, R. J. (1998). Dynamic assessment and its use with underserved gifted and talented populations. *Gifted Child Quarterly, 42*, 140-147.

Kitano, M., & DiJiosia, M. (2002). Are Asian and Pacific Americans overrepresented in programs for the gifted? *Roeper Review, 24*, 76-80.

Kitano, M. K., & Espinosa, R. (1995). Language diversity and giftedness: Working with gifted English language learners. *Journal for the Education of the Gifted, 18*, 234-254.

Kitano, M., Montgomery, D., VanTassel-Baska, J., & Johnsen, S. (2008). *Using the national gifted education standards for PreK-12 professional development.* Thousand Oaks, CA: Corwin Press.

Lee, S-Y, Olszewski-Kubilius, P., & Peternel, G. (2009). Follow-up with students after 6 years of participation in Project EXCITE. *Gifted Child Quarterly, 53*, 137-156.

Louis, B., & Lewis, M. (1992). Parental beliefs about giftedness in young children and their relation to actual ability level. *Gifted Child Quarterly, 36*, 27-31.

Lubinski, D., & Benbow, C. P. (1994). The study of mathematically precocious youth: The first three decades of a planned 50-year study of intellectual talent. In R. F. Subotnik and K. D. Arnold (Eds.), *Beyond Terman: Contemporary longitudinal studies of giftedness and talent* (pp. 255-281). Norwood, NJ: Ablex.

Lupkowski-Shoplik, A., & Assouline, S. G. (1993). Identifying mathematically talented elementary students: Using the lower level of the SSAT. *Gifted Child Quarterly, 37,* 118-123.

Lupkowski-Shoplik, A., & Swiatek, M. A. (1999). Elementary student talent searches: Establishing appropriate guidelines for qualifying test scores. *Gifted Child Quarterly, 43,* 265-272.

Matthews, D. J., & Foster, J. F. (2005). A dynamic scaffolding model of teacher development: The gifted education consultant as catalyst for change. *Gifted Child Quarterly, 49,* 222-230.

McKenna, M. A., Hollingsworth, P. L., & Barnes, L. L. B. (2005). Developing latent mathematics abilities in economically disadvantaged students. *Roeper Review, 27,* 222-227.

Mills, C. J., & Barnett, L. B. (1992). The use of the secondary school admission test (SSAT) to identify academically talented elementary school students. *Gifted Child Quarterly, 36,* 155-159.

Mills, C. J., Stork, E. J., & Krug, D. (1992). Recognition and development of academic talent in educationally disadvantaged students. *Exceptionality, 3,* 165-180.

Moon, S. M. (1996). Using the Purdue three-stage model to facilitate local program evaluation. *Gifted Child Quarterly, 40,* 121-128.

Moon, T. R., & Brighton, C. M. (2008). Primary teachers' conceptions of giftedness. *Journal for the Education of the Gifted, 31,* 447-480.

Moon, S. M., Swift, M., & Shallenberger, A. (2002). Perceptions of a self-contained class for fourth- and fifth-grade students with high to extreme levels of intellectual giftedness. *Gifted Child Quarterly 46,* 64-79.

Morrison, W. F., & Rizza, M. G. (2007). Creating a toolkit for identifying twice-exceptional students. *Journal for the Education of the Gifted, 31,* 57-76.

National Association for Gifted Children & The Council of State Directors of Programs for the Gifted (2009). *2008-2009 State of the states in gifted education: National policy and practice data.* Washington, DC: Author.

Neumeister, K. L. S., Adams, C. M., Pierce, R. L., Cassady, J. C., & Dixon, F. A. (2007). Fourth-grade teachers' perceptions of giftedness: Implications for identifying and serving diverse gifted students. *Journal for the Education of the Gifted, 30,* 479-499.

Olszewski-Kubilius, P., Lee, S-Y, Ngoi, M., & Ngoi, D. (2004). Addressing the achievement gap between minority and nonminority children by increasing access to gifted programs. *Journal for the Education of the Gifted, 28,* 127-158.

Pierce, R. L., Adams, C. M., Neumeister, K. L. S., Cassady, J. C., Dixon, F. A., & Cross, T. L. (2007). Development of an identification procedure for a large urban school corporation: Identifying culturally diverse and academically gifted elementary students. *Roeper Review, 29,* 113-118.

Pletan, M. D., Robinson, N. M., Berninger, V. W., & Abbot, R. D. (1995). Parents' observations of kindergartners who are advanced in mathematical reasoning. *Journal for the Education of the Gifted, 19,* 30-44.

Purcell, J. H. (1995). Gifted education at a crossroads: The program status study. *Gifted Child Quarterly, 39,* 57-65.

Purcell, J. H., Burns, D. E., Tomlinson C. A., Imbeau, M. B., & Martin, J. L. (2002). Bridging the gap: A tool and technique to analyze and evaluate gifted education curricular units. *Gifted Child Quarterly, 46,* 306-321.

Reis, S. M., Burns, D. E., & Renzulli, J. S. (1992). *Curriculum compacting: The complete guide to modifying the regular curriculum for high ability students.* Mansfield Center, CT: Creative Learning Press.

Rogers, K. (2002). *Re-forming gifted education: Matching the program to the child.* Scottsdale, AZ: Great Potential Press.

Reyes, E., Fletcher, R., & Paez, D. (1996). Developing local multidimensional screening procedures for identifying giftedness among Mexican American border population. *Roeper Review, 18,* 208-211.

Ryser, G. R. (2004). Culture-fair and nonbiased assessment. In S. K. Johnsen (Ed.), *Identifying gifted students: A practical guide* (pp. 51-106). Waco, TX: Prufrock Press.

Ryser, G. R., & Johnsen, S. K. (1996). Toward more research on effective practices with gifted students in general-education settings. *Journal for the Education of the Gifted, 19,* 481-496.

Silky, W., & Readling, J. (1992). REDSIL: A fourth generation evaluation model for gifted education programs. *Roeper Review, 15,* 67-69.

Scott, M. S., Deuel, L. S., Jean-Francois, B., & Urbano, R. C. (1996). Identifying cognitively gifted ethnic minority children. *Gifted Child Quarterly, 40,* 147-153.

Scroth, S. T., & Helfer, J. A. (2008). Identifying gifted students: Educator beliefs regarding various policies, processes, and procedures. *Journal for the Education of the Gifted, 32,* 155-179.

Simon, R., Penix, K., & Biggers, A. (1999). *Gifted and talented rules and regulations: Program approval.* Little Rock: Arkansas Department of Education.

Stephens, K. R. (1999). Parents of the gifted and talented: The forgotten partner. *Gifted Child Today, 22*(5), 38-43, 52.

Swanson, J. D. (2007). Policy and practice: A case study of gifted education policy implementation. *Journal for the Education of the Gifted, 31,* 131-164.

Swiatek, M. A., & Lupkowski-Shoplik, A. (2005). An evaluation of the elementary student talent search by families and schools. *Gifted Child Quarterly, 49,* 247-259.

Texas Education Agency, Division of Advanced Academic Services (2000). Texas state plan for the education of gifted/talented students. Austin, TX: Author.

Tomlinson, C., Bland, L., & Moon, T. (1993). Evaluation utilization: A review of the literature with implications for gifted education. *Journal for the Education of the Gifted, 16,* 171-189.

Tomlinson, C. A., Brighton, C., Hertberg, H., Callahan, C. M., Moon, T. R., Brimijoin, K., Conover, L., & Reynolds, T. (2003). Differentiating instruction in response to student readiness, interest, and learning profile in academically diverse classrooms: A review of the literature. *Journal for the Education of the Gifted, 27,* (2/3), 119-145.

VanTassel-Baska, J. (2006). A content analysis of evaluation findings across 20 gifted programs: A clarion call for enhanced gifted program development. *Gifted Child Quarterly, 50,* 199-215.

VanTassel-Baska, J. (Ed.). (2008). *Alternative assessments with gifted and talented* student. Waco, TX: Prufrock Press.

VanTassel-Baska, J., Feng, A. X., & de Brux, E. (2007). A study of identification and achievement profiles of performance task-identified gifted students over 6 years. *Journal for the Education of the Gifted, 31,* 7-34.

VanTassel-Baska, J., Johnson, C. E., & Boyce, L. N. (1996). A study of language arts curriculum effectiveness with gifted learners. *Journal for the Education of the Gifted, 19,* 461-480.

VanTassel-Baska, J., Johnson, D., & Avery, L. D. (2002). Using performance tasks in the identification of economically disadvantaged and minority gifted learners: Findings from Project STAR. *Gifted Child Quarterly, 46,* 110-123.

Westberg, K. L., & Archambault, F. X. (1997). A multi-site case study of successful classroom practices for high ability students. *Gifted Child Quarterly, 41,* 42-51.

Yoon, S. Y., & Gentry, M. (2009). Racial and ethnic representation in gifted programs: Current status of and implications for gifted Asian American students. *Gifted Child Quarterly, 53,* 121-136.

**NAGC – CEC TEACHER KNOWLEDGE & SKILL STANDARDS**

**FOR GIFTED AND TALENTED EDUCATION**

## Standard 8: Assessment

Assessment is integral to the decision-making and teaching of educators of the gifted as multiple types of assessment information are required for both identification and learning progress decisions. Educators of the gifted use the results of such assessments to adjust instruction and to enhance ongoing learning progress. Educators of the gifted understand the process of identification, legal policies, and ethical principles of measurement and assessment related to referral, eligibility, program planning, instruction, and placement for individuals with gifts and talents, including those from culturally and linguistically diverse backgrounds. They understand measurement theory and practices for addressing the interpretation of assessment results. In addition, educators of the gifted understand the appropriate use and limitations of various types of assessments. To ensure the use of nonbiased and equitable identification and learning progress models, educators of the gifted employ alternative assessments such as performance-based assessment, portfolios, and computer simulations.

| K1 | Processes and procedures for the identification of individuals with gifts and talents. |
|----|----|
| K2 | Uses, limitations, and interpretation of multiple assessments in different domains for identifying individuals with exceptional learning needs, including those from diverse backgrounds. |
| K3 | Uses and limitations of assessments documenting academic growth of individuals with gifts and talents. |
| S1 | Use non-biased and equitable approaches for identifying individuals with gifts and talents, including those from diverse backgrounds. |
| S2 | Use technically adequate qualitative and quantitative assessments for identifying and placing individuals with gifts and talents. |
| S3 | Develop differentiated curriculum-based assessments for use in instructional planning and delivery for individuals with gifts and talents. |
| S4 | Use alternative assessments and technologies to evaluate learning of individuals with gifts and talents. |

Reprinted with permission of the National Association for Gifted Children, Washington, DC, www.nagc.org

## Chapter 8 Study Guide

**Prompt 1** *Knowledge*

According to the programming standards, what is the teacher's initial instructional responsibility to support identification of students as gifted and talented?

**Prompt 2** *Opinion*

Slade argues that perhaps the best way to assure the integrity of the student identification process is to base practice on the highest standards used by a knowledgeable and skillful staff. This statement implies that both implementing the highest standards and having a knowledgeable and skilled staff are necessary conditions for a quality gifted identification system. Do you agree that both are necessary? Why or why not? Given all the standards discussed in this chapter, are the two conditions together sufficient for quality gifted identification? Why or why not?

**Prompt 3** *Affect*

Slade states that, ultimately, it is the use by education professionals of instruments in student identification that matters most to the success of a good fit of gifted education programming to individual gifted students. Explain any pressures such a statement causes you or your colleagues.

**Prompt 4** *Experience*

Select any one set of Questions for effective practice or Recommended best practices from the chapter section on teacher preparation standards and describe any experience you or a colleague have had in responding to the questions or implementing the practices in a gifted identification system in your school, district, or state.

**Prompt 5** *Preconception/Misconception*

Discuss why it may have been important, especially for purposes of identification, to align the programming standards with the teacher preparation standards.

# SECTION III.

# IDENTIFICATION PRACTICE

# STAGES OF GIFTED IDENTIFICATION

SCOTT L. HUNSAKER, UTAH STATE UNIVERSITY
REBECCA H. ODOARDI, DAVIS SCHOOL DISTRICT, FARMINGTON, UT
ELLEN VIRGINIA SMITH, PROVO SCHOOL DISTRICT, PROVO, UT

Identification in gifted education can be defined as the process of gathering data or information on a particular student to guide decision making by professionals as to the optimal match between that student's profile of learning strengths, needs, interests, and styles and the available or needed educational services or interventions in a school setting. This definition is consistent with the purpose of identification as articulated by Richert (2003) who insists that "the identification process should be a *needs assessment* whose primary purpose is the placement of students into educational programs designed to develop their intellectual, emotional, and social potential" (p. 148, emphasis in the original). This purpose must supersede all other purposes that others might have for an identification process, including, according to Richert, the prediction of adult giftedness, the confirmation of the value of school conformity, or the ego extension of parents.

The actual stages for accomplishing the purpose of identification have been expressed in various ways by different scholars. Feldhusen and Jarwan (2000), for example, list application, screening, data synthesis, identifying specific talents, and selection-placement as the stages. Johnsen (2004), on the other hand, lists nomination, screening, and selection as the steps, with added discussion about an appeals process. Tannenbaum (2009) suggests the identification phases of screening, selection, and differentiation.

In this chapter, we will attempt a synthesis of points from these and other perspectives into the configuration of stages of identification illustrated in Figure 1. In this figure, a stage refers specifically to the action taken by the professionals who are conducting the identification process. The orientation column contrasts different perspectives that could influence the way the actions are taken. These perspectives might be seen as opposing one another, but careful professionals may find ways to actually blend the perspectives. The final column of the figure contrasts the outcomes of the action depending on the orientation taken. Each of the stages, with its attended orientations and outcomes, will be explained further in the remainder of the chapter.

As each stage is presented, the reader should consider what is being presented in light of standards for best practice in identification.

| OVERVIEW OF THE GIFTED IDENTIFICATION PROCESS | | |
|---|---|---|
| **Stage** | **Orientation** | **Outcome** |
| Observation | Needs | Referral |
| | Rewards | Nomination/Screening |
| Evaluation | Clinical | Assessment |
| | Psychometric | Testing |
| Decision-Making | Professional | Planning |
| | Criterial | Verification |
| Service | Child | Development |
| | Program | Placement |

**Figure 1.** Stages of identification.

Discrepancies between standards and actual practice may be a reflection of the theory-practice gap recognized in the field of gifted education for many years (Yarborough & Johnson, 1983). The standards might include the programming standards from national organizations (see Chapter 7, for example), but might also include standards issued by government bodies such as the following, as listed in the *National Excellence* report (U. S. Department of Education, 1993): (a) seeks variety, (b) uses many assessment measures, (c) is free of bias, (d) is fluid, (e) identifies potential, and (f) assesses motivation. A decade earlier, another national report (cited in Richert, 2003) posited the following as guiding principles for identification:

- Defensibility—basing procedures on current research and recommendations
- Advocacy—keeping the best interests of students in mind
- Equity—protecting equal access to programs and opportunities
- Pluralism—using the broadest definitions of giftedness

- Comprehensiveness—identifying as many learners, including those with gifted level potential, as possible
- Pragmatism—using available instruments and personnel as much as possible

### OBSERVATION STAGE

The first stage in the gifted identification process is called *observation*. The stage gives educators an opportunity to gather preliminary information on a student in the general classroom environment, as well as other environments within and outside the school, to determine the need for further evaluation. Usually the student is displaying some well-accepted characteristics of giftedness that lead observers to believe that further attention is needed. This stage might be thought of as a prompt to action—a stage for discovering clues that closer attention should be paid to a particular child.

## ORIENTATIONS AND OUTCOMES OF THE OBSERVATION STAGE

When a *rewards* orientation is taken at this stage, the focus is on the student's classroom behavior and accomplishment. For example, Goldberg (1986) has charged that teachers tend to recommend students for further consideration who are highly motivated, work hard, and are compliant in the school setting. Richert (2003) refers to this phenomenon as reaffirming "the values of conformity inherent in the school system" (p. 148). Hunsaker, Finley, and Frank (1997) found a focus on high academic accomplishment in teacher ratings of students as part of an identification procedure. While they conjecture that this might be due to the teachers' knowledge of the highly academic nature of the programs themselves, it does not rule out the possibility of a rewards orientation also. However, Seigle and Powell (2004) found that while teachers generally rated students who completed school work higher than those who did not, other factors could override this characteristic; but even in their study, classroom teachers had a greater tendency to focus on student weaknesses rather than strengths when considering students for further evaluation. The focus on weakness is apparently more pronounced among teachers whose classes contain a high percentage of minority and economically disadvantaged students (Speirs Neumeister, Adams, Pierce, Cassady, & Dixon, 2007). Further, in a study comparing the attitudes of administrators, gifted education specialists, and regular classroom teachers on various tools for identification, Schroth and Helfer (2008) found possible confusion, particularly among regular classroom

teachers, of the "relative importance of general or specific aptitude and good effort and study habits" (p. 168). Siegle, Moore, Mann, and Wilson (2010) also found a tendency in teachers to nominate older students who were willing to tutor struggling peers. The reward orientation in this practice is self-evident. However, teachers who have received specific training in the characteristics of gifted children are more likely to recognize characteristics of giftedness in children than teachers who have not had the training (Siegle et al., 2010). Another factor that seems to improve teachers' ability to recognize giftedness in students who need to be referred is the teachers' experience in teaching gifted students previously. Such personal experience "results in more precise and realistic concepts of giftedness" (Endepohls-Ulpe & Ruf, 2005, p. 227).

One result of the observation stage is known in the field of gifted education as a *nomination*. The very use of this word tends to support a rewards orientation. One is nominated for an honor or an office of some sort. It implies that something is deserved because of what one has done up to that time. For example, Seigle et al. (2010) found that teachers are more likely to recognize positive descriptors (e.g, natural leader, highly sensitive) of gifted students than they are negative descriptors (e.g., bossy, emotional) and that the students who were voracious readers were particularly more likely to be nominated. However, Powell and Siegle (2000) also reported a tendency of teachers to be more likely to nominate boys who showed negative behaviors over girls who showed the same behaviors. We might do well as a field to consider the implications of the use of the term *nomination* as we continue to be faced with charges of elitism, particularly in light of evidence that stereotypical thinking, at least regarding gender, may influence some nominations.

Nominations or referrals are usually sought through the use of a teacher rating scale or checklist. Students whose scores on the rating scales or checklists are sufficiently high are generally considered eligible for further consideration in the identification process. (For more information on teacher rating scales, see Chapter 14.)

Nominations or referrals are also sometimes solicited from members of the community, especially from parents or students, usually from the students themselves or from peers. Research has indicated that peer nomination forms can be particularly useful for three reasons:

1. The number of judges is large, normally over 20;

2. They produce talent scores based on the number of choices received and their rank, and these scores may be much more stable than those obtained from individual teachers or parents, even taking into account the lesser maturity of the judges; and

3. Peers are in a position to observe abilities or talents that are not obvious in the classroom setting.

(Massé & Gagné, 1996, p. 24)

This research also shows that if self-nominations are permitted, these have no detrimental effect on talent ratings and, therefore, could serve as another source of information, particularly in the older grades when students become more aware and accurate in assessing their own abilities as well as those of others.

Nominations or referrals are not the only path to further consideration within a rewards perspective. A practice known as *screening* is also regularly employed. Screening can best be employed where census testing on norm-referenced achievement tests has been conducted across a school district. In this practice, a cut score is generally established (for example, the 85th percentile) on the composite score or subtest scores such as total reading, total language, or total math. Some districts require a student to meet the cut-off on one specified score (usually the composite), while other districts may check all scores, any one of which may be above the cut-off to make the student eligible for further consideration. This practice will often lead to the inclusion of students who would not be nominated by their teachers. However, districts using this procedure often fall prey to rigid use of the cut-off or to cosmetic application of this score as evidence that multiple criteria are being used, when in fact the screening is only a gateway to taking an aptitude test that is the real arbiter in the decision about gifted education services (Borland, 2009; Callahan, 1982, 2009; Friedman-Nimz, 2009; Jenkins-Friedman, 1982).

Another perspective to be taken at this stage is the *needs* perspective. For the most part, this perspective seems to dominate the field. Research has shown that teachers who are provided with training in the characteristics of gifted children are able to attend to these characteristics quite accurately (Buchanan, 1987; Siegle & Powell, 2004). Interestingly, Siegle and Powell have noted a tendency by teachers to attend to unusual behaviors of students as a key factor in recommending them for further consideration. They caution that being different in and of itself is not a characteristic of giftedness and that teachers should be taught to observe for a more comprehensive set of characteristics.

The outcome of a needs perspective is a *referral* of a student for further consideration in the gifted identification process. The term *referral* is borrowed from special education and is the term used in Standard 8: Assessment of the professional teacher preparation standards developed jointly by the National Association for Gifted Children and the Council for Exceptional Children (Johnsen, VanTassel-Baska, & Robinson, 2008). The term *nomination* is markedly missing from these standards.

### MECHANICS OF THE OBSERVATION STAGE

Classroom observation is the key professional skill employed during this stage. An old charge against teachers is that they rarely keep systematic records of their observations (Hagen, 1980). Yet others have found teachers who use a variety of approaches for recording their observations and using them in making nominations or referrals within gifted identification systems (Hunsaker, 1991). A typical strategy is the use of *jot-downs* during class instructional time.

To conduct a jot-down, a teacher needs a piece of paper (8½" x 11" would work just fine) that can be posted on a lectern, desk, or clipboard. The teacher then needs to note on the paper (usually across the top) which characteristics of giftedness she or he is watching for. During class time, when the teacher sees a student respond in a way that gives evidence of a certain characteristic, she or he jots the student's initials and a word or two that can remind the teacher later of what she or he saw. At the end of the day, a number of these jot downs will have been placed on the form (see Figure 2). In the example provided, the initials of JK and AH are already beginning to appear frequently, prompting the teacher to pay particularly close attention to these two students in the coming days. Jot-downs are usually most effective if they have been conducted for two weeks. This time-frame generally results in sufficient data to justify the rating a teacher might be asked to give on a rating scale.

It can, of course, seem overwhelming to try to observe all students on every characteristic. Some teachers have simplified the task by focusing on one characteristic per day (as shown in Figure 2), while others have focused on a few students each day, listing their names down the left side of the form, with the characteristics listed across the top.

| LARGE STOREHOUSE OF INFORMATION | ADVANCED VOCABULARY | UNUSUAL APPROACH TO PROBLEM-SOLVING | INTENSE INTERESTS | INQUISITIVENESS |
|---|---|---|---|---|
| JK-presidents JK-state flowers | AH-predicament JK-flora and fauna | AH-long division PS-pencil drawing JK-memory hooks | JK-presidents JK-flowers JK-brain | JK-"I've got to figure out how my brain works?" AH-alternative division algorithms |

Figure 2. Completed jot-down form for day 1 of observation.

As has already been implied, the information on the jot-downs can be used to assist teachers in making more systematic and defensible ratings on whatever rating scales, checklists, or referral forms they are asked to complete at the conclusion of this stage. Referrals or nominations that follow from such an approach can give the referring or nominating teacher and the gifted education specialist or identification committee greater confidence in the names they receive for further consideration.

When parents are asked to nominate or refer a student, they are typically asked to complete a rating scale similar to that completed by teachers. When students are asked for nominations or referrals, they are asked to respond to a series of questions such as "Who would be the best partner for a science project?" or "Who is really good at math in your class?" Tallies of the number of mentions a student receives are then calculated. A specified number of mentions is usually established as a guide for further consideration of a student.

## SCHOOL DISTRICT EXAMPLE

As an example of each of the broad stages, specific steps taken by the director of gifted education in a real school district follow. This school district is in one of the fastest growing counties in Utah, with nearly 300,000 people. At the elementary level, the district offers a continuum of services with the Schoolwide Enrichment Model (SEM) being offered at every school and full-time gifted magnet classes offered at selected sites in grades three through six. The identification procedures presented are those used for the magnet program. The identification activities for this district are not being shown because they necessarily represent recommended practice, but because they illustrate the range of activities that must be carried out to successfully conduct identification.

Table 1 displays fifteen specific actions taken by the director to obtain applications for the testing required to enter the magnet program. As can be seen from the table, this district makes considerable effort to obtain nominations from a wide constituency of parents, with a screening of test scores providing one basis for obtaining the nominations. The results of these two specific efforts are characterized as nominations because they are not based on formally gathered observation data. However, referrals were also gathered from teachers based on their observations of ten specific behaviors identified within the full-time program as being essential for success in the program. It should be noted, also, that such data are gathered from teachers for the school-based SEM program options. Thus this district follows both perspectives—reward and need—for the observations stage

## EVALUATION STAGE

The second stage in the gifted identification process is referred to as *evaluation*. At this stage, the information that has already been gathered on a student is collated and a determination is made as to what additional information is needed. Remembering the purpose of identification as gathering data to provide information about decision making for a specific student, educators will need to keep in mind what the decisions are that need to be made and what data or information will best support those decisions.

**Table 1.** Stage One: Observation—Activities of Example School District

1. Teacher/principal/secretary packets sent to schools. (September)
2. Email regarding the testing information packets sent to principal/secretaries. (September)
3. Poster advertising information sent to schools to be hung on all outside doors during Parent-Teacher conferences. (September)
4. Email reminders sent to secretaries/principals. (September-December)
5. Information shared with local school newsletter persons (PTA/Secretaries) with packet suggesting news article, etc. (September/October)
6. Information shared with Community Relations staff to be distributed in newspapers, tv spots, radio broadcasts, etc. Material is translated into Spanish.
7. Information shared with Full-Time Spectrum Committee. (November-May)
8. Approximately 3,000 personal letters are mailed to parents whose students scored in the top 10% on the State of Utah End of Level tests grades 2-5 in math and or reading.
9. Approximately 1,000 personal letters are mailed to parents of ESL students who scored in the top 10% of that group on the State of Utah End of Level tests grades 2-5 in math and or reading.
10. Parent information meeting held to discuss program with interested parents. (December) Information about this meeting is shared via email with principals/secretaries at local schools. Information is also given as part of personal letter mailing and is on the bottom of all application forms filled out by parents.
11. Applications are collected from all schools. (December/January)
12. Applicants are entered into the student system. (December)
13. Letters are mailed to homes of all applicants providing them with critical testing information. (first week in January)
14. SIT (Student Identification Team) information forms are labeled, collated, and sent to all 2-5 grade teachers and principals to gather school information about each applicant. SIT form is completed by Teacher Team at the school. (February)
15. SIT information is collected from schools. (February/March)

## ORIENTATIONS AND OUTCOMES OF THE EVALUATION STAGE

One possible orientation at this stage is a *psychometric* point of view. Schools usually follow this orientation when a more formal approach to identification is taken and labeling is important as a gateway for receiving services. Information is gathered with an awareness of the criteria to be met to qualify a student as gifted. The outcome of a psychometric perspective is usually gathering more assessment data through additional *testing*. The purpose of gathering more information might be construed as an effort to assemble evidence to prove that a learner is gifted. For example, a teacher may have completed a rating scale as part of the observation stage, and the student's cumulative file may contain scores from a recent norm-referenced achievement test, but the student lacks aptitude testing. An identification committee or gifted identification coordinator may then request that the aptitude testing be done. Depending on the prevailing practice and budget as well as the definition of giftedness in the district, the school may choose an individual or group IQ test or a creativity test or both.

Another orientation is the *clinical* orientation. In this point of view, the focus is more on articulating interventions for the child rather than on labeling. A committee would again look at already available data and determine what additional data is needed to make the best decision about what to do for a child. However, there is not necessarily an attempt to have the same data on every child. The intended outcome is an *assessment* of the interventions that will be most helpful to the growth of the child. Both quantitative (including rating scales, checklists, and tests) and qualitative (including interviews, observations, and artifacts) information are sought to inform a decision.

## MECHANICS OF THE EVALUATION STAGE

When it is decided to gather additional information on a student, a file is assembled containing all information required for identification. Demographic information on the student is recorded, including contact information on parents, guardians, or caregivers. It is usually at this stage that parents are first informed that their child is being considered more fully for identification and that permission is sought, as required by law, for additional evaluation. If a psychometric approach to evaluation is taken, the file is considered complete when all necessary elements (e.g., permission form, demographic information, teacher rating

scale score, achievement test scores, aptitude test scores, creativity test scores) are present in the file. If a clinical approach is taken, the file is considered complete when the person or persons required to make a decision believe that the information present in the file is sufficient to support the decision to be made. When a committee is asked to review the data in a file, summaries of the contents of the file are usually prepared by a gifted education coordinator from the school or district so that all committee members have an overview of the information available.

## SCHOOL DISTRICT EXAMPLE

In the example school district, fourteen specific activities are undertaken by the district leadership to identify students for the magnet gifted program. These activities are listed in Table 2. Given the emphasis on testing (i.e., specifically the *Naglieri Nonverbal Ability Test* [NNAT] and the *Iowa Test of Basic Skills* [ITBS]), this district clearly takes a psychometric approach to identifying students for its magnet program. However, it should be noted that information is also garnered from an SEM identification team, suggesting that information between the schoolwide program and districtwide program is shared so that the best decision for a child's placement can be made.

## DECISION-MAKING STAGE

The third stage of the gifted identification process is the decision-making stage. At this stage a committee is usually brought together to review the data obtained and to determine a course of action.

**Table 2.** Stage Two: Evaluation—Activities of Example School District

1. Student scan sheets are preslugged. (Data Processing Department and Research and Assessment Department) (January)
2. Testing materials are organized and collated and folders are created for each student applicant. (December-January)
3. Testing meeting is held to finalize each Full-Time Spectrum School's site plan for testing. (December and January)
4. Teacher Testing Coordinators are contacted weekly before testing to make sure plans are being implemented and to problem solve any issues that may arise. (January-until testing)
5. Teacher testing packets are organized by grade level. (January-February)
6. Teacher testers are trained regarding testing protocol before actual testing occurs.
7. Testing materials are divided into classes, organized for testing, and delivered to the schools. (Three days before testing occurs)
8. Class lists, volunteer sheets, name badges, extra scan sheets, pencils, and recording information is given to Testing Coordinator (three days before testing occurs) and to Teacher Testers. (Day before testing occurs)
9. District security is alerted regarding testing process and protocols for emergencies are discussed and planned for.
10. Testing is facilitated (four sites, two weekends). District Director and Assistant are available to facilitate testing at each site. Regular contact is made between the two district-level staff to make sure things run smoothly. (January/February)
11. Parent Information Packet is distributed to parents during testing. (January/February)
12. Testing materials and scan sheets are collected and returned to District where they are secured for the weekend (All testing materials are always kept in locked files at the District Office except when being used). (January/February)
13. NNAT, ITBS, Schoolwide Identification Team, and Parent Information Form Scan sheets are doubled checked for any errors and then scanned at Research and Assessment. (February/March)
14. All data is again checked for accuracy and completion. Unusual occurrences are noted. Problems remediated. (March)

## DECISION-MAKING ORIENTATIONS AND OUTCOMES

One orientation that can be taken at the decision-making stage is a *criterial* orientation. From this point of view, the committee usually likes to see information gathered during the evaluation stage synthesized to a more succinct form. The concern of the committee is typically to determine eligibility for a specific program or service, thus leading to an outcome of *verification* that criteria have been met. There is a major focus in this orientation on the defensibility of any decisions made.

An alternative orientation is the *professional* orientation. From this point of view, the role of the educator as a professional who has the knowledge and skills to analyze complex data sets and make decisions based on that analysis is acknowledged.

Decisions are typically based on an understanding of the total school program and how different aspects of that program address learner needs. Some criticize this orientation as relying too much on subjective judgment. If the educators who are cast in a decision-making role make their decisions based on personal whim, this would certainly be a fair assertion. However, if the educators act in a professional manner, applying a systematic approach to the analysis, the judgment is professional and not subjective, much in the same way a doctor's judgments include both quantitative and qualitative information and are based on a vast background knowledge of symptomology and treatments. The outcome of such an approach is *planning* a comprehensive intervention program for a student.

## DECISION-MAKING MECHANICS

Under the criterial orientation there are two similar and popular methods used to synthesize data for decision making. These are the matrix and multiple check-off systems. Each of these will be discussed in turn, with a presentation of their strengths and weaknesses. Under the professional orientation, the most typically used decision-making system is the case study system. This system will also be presented with its strengths and weaknesses.

### MATRIX IDENTIFICATION.

In order to synthesize the multiple sources of data available to a committee or district coordinator to determine eligibility for a gifted program, some districts organize the data into a matrix. The matrix consists of a listing of the multiple criteria along one side of the grid, with a scale of points to be awarded for different levels of performance along a perpendicular side of the grid. The cells created in the matrix indicate the performance ranges for which the different point levels will be awarded. An example is shown in Figure 3.

The number of criteria used is best determined by an analysis of the data needed to best represent a district's or school's definition of giftedness. Some districts have as many as eleven criteria; others limit them to three. Sometimes budgetary constraints limit the amount of information that can be used. The ranges of the scores for each criterion should also be based on an analysis of the definition of giftedness, but often they're set according to the number of students the different levels would produce based on the number of seats available in a specific program.

To use the matrix, a student's performances on the different criteria are circled and then the points are added up to determine a total score. Figure 4 presents the matrix for Amber, whose aptitude test score is at the 99th percentile, achievement total battery is at the 97th percentile, creativity rating scale raw score is 29, motivation rating scale raw score is 40, and gpa is 3.69. With these levels of performance, Amber earns 4, 4, 3, 4, and 2 points, respectively, for a total of 17. Because the cut-off for eligibility has been set at 16, and Amber scored 17 on the matrix, she is eligible for placement in the gifted program. Of course, a student who scores 15 is not eligible. A committee's function with such a system is to verify that the scores are accurate and that the form has been filled out correctly. Usually the circling of the eligibility result is left until a committee meeting has been held.

| Student Information: | | | | | |
|---|---|---|---|---|---|
| Scale | 4 | 3 | 2 | 1 | Score |
| Aptitude %ile | 99-96 | 95-92 | 91-88 | 87-84 | |
| Achievement %ile | 99-96 | 95-92 | 91-88 | 87-84 | |
| Creativity √-list Raw Score | 32-30 | 29-27 | 26-24 | 23-21 | |
| Motivation √-list Raw Score | 40-38 | 37-35 | 34-32 | 32-30 | |
| Grades: GPA | >4.00 | 4.00- 3.90 | 3.89-3.80 | 3.79-3.70 | |
| Totals | | | | | |
| Qualifying Total | 16 | Student Total | | | Eligibility Y    N |

**Figure 3.** Matrix identification example.

| Student Information: Amber | | | | | |
|---|---|---|---|---|---|
| Scale | 4 | 3 | 2 | 1 | Score |
| Aptitude %ile | (99-96) | 95-92 | 91-88 | 87-84 | 4 |
| Achievement %ile | (99-96) | 95-92 | 91-88 | 87-84 | 4 |
| Creativity √-list Raw Score | 32-30 | (29-27) | 26-24 | 23-21 | 3 |
| Motivation √-list Raw Score | (40-38) | 37-35 | 34-32 | 32-30 | 4 |
| Grades: GPA | >4.00 | 4.00- 3.90 | (3.89-3.80) | 3.79-3.70 | 2 |
| Totals | 12 | 3 | 2 | 0 | 17 |
| Qualifying Total | 16 | Student Total | | 17 | Eligibility (Y)    N |

**Figure 4.** Completed identification matrix for Amber.

This system has a couple of strengths. First, depending on a student's performance on other criteria, it is possible for a student to gain eligibility without earning any points on one criterion, so no one criterion can keep a student out of the program. Some see the clarity of the cut-off point as an additional strength, which makes the decision of eligibility easy for the committee.

There are, however, a number of weaknesses to this decision-making system. First, when matrices are built in the way Amber's is, which is not uncommon, the different kinds of scores that are not psychometrically equivalent are being compared as such. Higher weighting with such non-equivalent scores is automatically given to the criteria with the greatest variability. This usually means that tests carry greater weight (Ford, 2006). Second, the ranges of the scores for the various levels of performance are often set arbitrarily and fail to recognize important psychometric concepts such as standard error of measure. In a similar way, the eligibility cut-off is often set arbitrarily and is frequently adjusted from year to year depending on the number of seats available for a specific program. Administrators and teachers will sometimes claim that this system is easy to defend, yet, if they were ever faced with a psychometrically savvy parent, they would find it difficult to explain.

**MULTIPLE CHECK-OFF.**

The multiple check-off system is similar to the matrix system in that several criteria are generally listed along one side of a grid. The difference comes in the means by which a final score is generated. In the multiple-check-off system, a cut-off score is set for each criterion. Then a student's scores are

compared to those cut-offs, and if a minimum number of cut-offs have been met, the student is considered eligible for gifted services. An example is shown in Figures 5 and 6.

The criteria selected and the cut-offs set should be based on an analysis of the district's definition of giftedness. However, as with the matrix, practical considerations such as budget and seat availability often influence the levels at which cut-offs are set.

As an example of how this system would be used, imagine a student, Barry, whose scores are as follows: aptitude, 88th percentile; achievement, 92nd percentile; creativity rating, 30 points; motivation rating, 30 points; and gpa, 4.10. Placing these score on the form, we see that Barry does not qualify.

The strengths and weakness of this system are very much like those for the matrix. Data is synthesized for making decisions readily and clearly. Yet, again unlikes are again being compared and standard error of measure is being ignored.

Both of these systems also raise the question of the *near miss*. What does it mean to score a 15 on the matrix, or, as Barry did, to qualify on only two criteria. When this happens, it is a common practice to retest or rerate the student. In some districts, a provisional placement in the program may be tried if there is room. Pyschometrically, of course, because the scores generated by such systems really have no meaning, it is difficult to use a near miss score to generate ideas for potential differentiation or services outside the formal gifted program.

**CASE STUDY SYSTEM.**

In a case study system for gifted identification, data is usually not synthesized but is summarized on a form that presents both the quantitative and

| Gifted Identification Criteria | | | | |
|---|---|---|---|---|
| Student Name: | | Date: | | |
| Teacher Name: | | Grade: | | |
| Criterion Type | Name of Instrument | Score | Cut-off | ∞ |
| Aptitude | | | 96%ile | |
| Achievement | | | 96%ile | |
| Creativity Checklist | | | 30 | |
| Motivation Checklist | | | 38 | |
| GPA | | | 4.00 | |
| Required ∞ | | | 3 | |
| Student Performance | | | | |
| Committee Decision | | | Yes    No | |

**Figure 5.** Multiple cut-off system.

| Gifted Identification Criteria | | | | |
|---|---|---|---|---|
| Student Name: Barry | | Date: | | |
| Teacher Name: | | Grade: | | |
| Criterion Type | Name of Instrument | Score | Cut-off | ∞ |
| Aptitude | | 88 | 96%ile | |
| Achievement | | 92 | 96%ile | |
| Creativity Checklist | | 29 | 30 | |
| Motivation Checklist | | 40 | 38 | ∞ |
| GPA | | 4.10 | 4.00 | ∞ |
| Required ∞ | | | 3 | |
| Student Performance | | | 2 | |
| Committee Decision | | | Yes   (No) | |

**Figure 6.** Multiple cut-off system scores for Barry

the qualitative information that has been gathered on a student. Committee members are given access to the summary or to the entire file to review. They then determine through discussion any particular strengths or concerns shown by the data about the child. Based on the profile of strengths and concerns, specific or general recommendations may be made for specific gifted program placement, access to other school services, general education classroom differentiation, and community resources the parents might use.

One issue with this method is the ability of the committee members to move beyond subjective judgments to professional recommendations. Without appropriate professional development in how to analyze case data, educators are likely to fall back on familiar means for making decisions, such as those based on cut-off scores. The following is an actual illustrative case of an identification committee attempting to use a case study method without having been trained on how to use the information given.

The next name was read. Mrs. Callas [the gifted specialist] said, "The scores aren't as high." They were 94, 94, 95 [CogAT Verbal, Quantitative, Non-verbal, respectively]; but the teacher highly recommended. Mrs. Adam [the resource teacher] asked what the basic feeling was on scores. Mrs. Callas replied that for first and second graders they were looking at 96, 97. Mrs. Adam added a story about the child's problem in the spelling bee where the pronouncer said, "And" and the child spelled It "H-A-N-D." The father tried to talk them into giving the boy another chance, but it was determined that it was the boy's responsibility to clarify the word. Members of the committee discussed the 97 guideline. Mrs. Cherubini [the guidance counselor] said, "I'm kind of worried about that, too. It might open it up." They decided to bring the teacher in and ask her about the child. Mrs. Adam said, "Someone will say, 'Mine were one point off.'" Mrs. Cherubini, Mrs. Adam, and Mrs. Levine [the principal] discussed how the child is passive. Mrs. Levine said she was in favor of waiting. Mrs. Adam noted the parents were recently separated. . . . It was suggested that maybe they could discuss this child again at [a later time].

Mrs. Callas pointed out, however, that the mother knew they were meeting on the child today. Mrs. Cherubini went to find the teacher and the others waited. Mrs. Norman, the teacher, finally came in, having been taken away from her lunch period. She's a first grade teacher. She was asked to talk about the child. She said he is an excellent student, has very high academics, shows leadership, but is shy, and goes beyond expectations of 1st grade. Mrs. Callas asked about his answers to questions. Mrs. Norman said that his thinking is broader; he reads above level; his comprehension is excellent. He's an all-around excellent student. "He stands out as far as academics are concerned." "He challenges himself." He attempts things others don't, even though he is shy. Mrs. Cherubini explained they wanted to talk to the teacher because the child's scores were "borderline." Mrs. Callas explained they were "trying not to over-identify." The teacher indicated she was surprised by the CogAT scores. Students she thought would do well sometimes didn't; and students she didn't expect to do well did. Mrs. Callas said it sounded like to her the child needed to be identified. Mrs. Adam expressed concern that "if we let him in, we have to let others in." Mrs. Cherubini guessed that his achievement was high. "He's over achieving." His Metropolitan Readiness Test was high. Mrs. Levine mentioned the 97 cut-off, but stated, "We can deviate." Mrs. Cherubini said, "Once we start deviating, we have to let everyone in." Mrs. Norman said, "I can understand that." Then they all started discussing the family dynamics, which parent had which children. Mrs. Norman compared the boy to a brother who was nominated once but didn't make it. She said this boy would be better off than his brother. Mrs. Callas asked when more scores would be available. They come in spring (actually June) of second grade—more than a year away. Mrs. Callas asked about the possibility of getting additional testing done now because she saw things that indicated giftedness. Mrs. Adam dismissed Mrs. Norman so she could have more of her lunch. Mrs. Callas felt over a year was too long to wait, but Mrs. Levine and Mrs. Adam wanted more testing. Mrs. Adam cautioned that somehow information leaks out. Mrs. Levine commented that they didn't want to have egg on their face next spring when the testing was done. Mrs. Cherubini said, "I don't see him in the same ball park as 99." Mrs. Levine asked if they would be doing him an injustice by putting him in the program. Mrs. Callas said they would give the option to the parent to have additional testing done now or to wait until spring of second grade. Mrs. Levine assigned Mrs. Callas to talk to the parent. (Hunsaker, 1991, pp. 165–168)

This type of floundering does not have to occur in the case study method. For example, another school district gathered a variety of information on students, including teacher rating scales, nationally normed achievement tests, a non-verbal ability test, a criterion referenced reading, and a parent input form. A committee was then formed to review the data. Committee members included a school level administrator with significant background in gifted education, the district gifted program coordinator, and a school level gifted coordinator.

The committee began the process for each grade level by reviewing the data packets for the students who had participated in the ability testing. Committee members sorted the initial pool into three piles: students whose data provided no evidence of giftedness, students whose data revealed at least one compelling piece of evidence of giftedness, and students whose data was incomplete or questionable. The packets for students who had at least one piece of compelling evidence were divided between the three committee members for further review. A committee member served as an advocate for each child under further consideration. The advocate would speak for the student in the identification process to present the student's data in the most favorable light. At a designated meeting, each committee member took turns presenting his or her students to each other, highlighting the assessment and input data that supported the strengths of the child and "hints and clues of giftedness" (Council for Exceptional Children, 2001). After discussing each child's information, student files were again sorted into three groups—those whose information obviously demonstrated a need for the particular services that would be offered in the full-time gifted program, those who showed some evidence of giftedness but did not appear to require full-time gifted services, and those who needed a closer look to determine their need. The committee spent a great deal of time poring through the data of the third group. There was substantial evidence in the case of many of these students that indicated asynchronous development, social struggles with their age peers, and a mismatch between them and their regular classroom learning experiences. It was apparent that they needed some kind of intervention. The critical question was whether or not this particular full-time program, with its focus on math and science, would be the best fit for them.

As the committee deliberated, it became apparent that the students who were not invited to participate in the program needed to have specific recommendations made for services they would benefit from, whether or not they had been available in the past at neighborhood schools. For students with obvious gifts and needs in particular academic or creative domains, that information was indicated on a note attached to their packet. The committee then prioritized students (with a *high priority* or *moderate priority* designation) to provide neighborhood school gifted specialists and principals, many of whom have limited experience in identification, with good information to guide them as they planned for services at their site. It was important that the time and effort the committee spent would benefit all of the students

considered, not just those who were selected to attend the full-time program. The stakeholders needed to come to understand that identification is not about creating a set of *winners* and *losers*. It is about meeting students' needs wherever they are.

## SCHOOL DISTRICT EXAMPLE

As can be seen in Table 3, there are four specific activities that constitute the decision-making stage in the example school district. This school district does not use any of the decision-making strategies described in this section of this chapter. Rather, personnel of the Research and Assessment staff have developed a formula that rank orders all students who have completed the evaluation stage. Decisions are made by a districtwide committee that uses rank-order information, as well as information about space availability in the program. Predetermined cut-offs are not used to make the decision. Instead cut-offs are set once the data for that particular year are available. Decisions then are primarily criterial for top ranked students. Even then, the committee examines the scores carefully. If there is inconsistency in the data, particularly a discrepancy between what the teacher has shared and what the tests show, the committee communicates with the teacher to discuss the student. Often, the teacher has not implemented observation and assessment procedures properly.

Table 3. Stage 3: Decision-Making—Activities of Example School District

1. All data is complied and analyzed. (Research and Assessment and Spectrum Staff)
2. Reapplication procedures are begun for students currently in the program. (March)
3. Feedback report is given back to District. (First week in April)
4. Information is carefully reviewed by District Team and cut-off areas are delineated.

In these cases, because the committee wants to be as fair as possible, a piece of the data set may be disregarded. Clearly, as the committee continues its work through the rank-order list, it must begin relying more completely on professional judgments as more students are often similarly qualified for the last few positions available. Information on students not selected for the magnet program is made available to SEM personnel at the appropriate schools so they can use it in planning at the local site.

## SERVICES STAGE

The final stage of the identification process is the services stage. It is imperative that this stage be part of the identification process so that there is a logical connection between the measures and assessments used in the process and the services the student will receive. At this stage, appropriate services, based on previous information gathered and analyzed, are provided to the learner.

### SERVICES ORIENTATIONS AND OUTCOMES

Services oriented to the *child* take into account the unique profile of strengths, interests, needs, and learning styles of the child when determining programs. Specific programs may already be in place that address the profile, or modifications may need to be made to fit extant programs to the child's profile. In some cases, new programs may be initiated if a critical mass of children is found who have strengths, interests, needs, or styles not already addressed by the schools programs. The child orientation requires responsive instruction and differentiated curriculum resulting in the outcome of *development* of the child's unique abilities.

A *program* orientation starts with a specifically defined service to be provided, such as a magnet classroom or an accelerated math program, and uses identification information to find the students who will be most likely to succeed in that program. The outcome of such an orientation is, obviously, *placement* in the program. These programs usually have established curriculum and performance standards. Districts that provide programs across a continuum of services generally need to employ both the child and program orientations to optimize opportunities for learners.

### SERVICES MECHANICS

Specific services that a child is to receive are usually communicated to parents through a letter. The letter should contain four pieces of information: (1) the specific decisions relative to the services a child will or will not receive, (2) a listing of the assessments used to make the decision, (3) a description of how the assessments were used to make the decision, and (4) an indication of who the parents/guardians/caregivers can contact if they want to discuss the decision further. The following quotes an actual letter used by a district that includes the requisite information:

> During the month of October, your son or daughter was assessed using the Matrix Analogies Nonverbal Abilities Test, the Woodcock Johnson III Achievement Test (in reading comprehension and math reasoning), and a creative writing sample. The district's gifted program selection committee, comprised of parents, teachers, and administrators, has reviewed the data and determined that your child **does**

[or, **does not**] **qualify** to be in the gifted program. This determination was made based on a minimum weighted average of 90% on the Matrix Analogies, and either reading comprehension or math reasoning (depending on individual student's strength), with the writing sample used as additional information. [Emphasis in the original.]

The letter then provides differing statements depending on the determination made. The *does qualify* letter states, "You will be contacted to set up a conference to go over placement options and student programming with [the] teacher of the gifted program. Your child's classroom teacher will also be involved in the conference." The *does not qualify* letter states, "Your child's teacher will be informed of areas of strength so that differentiated accommodations can be made by his/her classroom teacher."

Such a letter raises a few issues. It's uncertain, for example, if the educators using the data

indicated really understand what the data means and how to correctly use the data, given the referrals to percentages rather than percentile ranks. (For more on this issue, see Chapter 12). The letter seems dominated primarily by a placement orientation but seems to imply a desire to use a services orientation.

**SCHOOL DISTRICT EXAMPLE**

The services stage in the example school district is clearly about placement in the magnet program. The five activities overseen by the director are shown in Table 4. While it is certainly not desirable that students who would otherwise qualify for a program should be wait-listed, gifted education leaders in this district have made their best effort to accommodate as many qualified learners as possible, given the limitations on resources provided through state and district funding. In fairness, it should be noted that the director includes alternative path of entry procedures that can be

Table 4. Stage 4: Services—Activities of the Example School District

1. Placement letters (In Program, Waiting List, Not Appropriate Placement) and feedback reports are sent to the families.
2. Phone calls are taken regarding acceptance of or decline of offer for placement into next year's Full-Time Spectrum Program. (April)
3. Schools are given information regarding students who will be entering the program or returning to program. (April/May)
4. Waiting list is created for each school (May-December) and once a school's waiting list has been depleted, students on the waiting list at another school are offered placement (out of their target school) in that program.
5. Adjustments are made as people change their mind, move, or for some reason decide not to accept placement (August-December) and students are placed in the program from the waiting list until December 1st).

completed by families that did not participate in the testing for a variety of reasons.

## CONCLUSION

A number of realities affect the differing orientations that a school district will foster as it establishes the procedures used through the stages described. On the face, it would seem that a rewards orientation at the observation stage would be followed by a psychometric orientation at the evaluation stage, with a criterial orientation for decision making that places a child in a specific program. On the other hand is a needs orientation at the observation stage, followed by a clinical approach at the evaluation stage, with professional decision-making focusing on a developmental approach to the child's learning needs. However, as has been illustrated with the specific school district example, such a clean division is not really possible and is, perhaps, not even desirable. In the end, we must believe that school personnel will do what they believe is best given their understanding of the research and standards for best practice in the context of the political realities of their specific school situations and the needs of the children in their locale.

## REFERENCES

Borland, J. H. (2009). Myth 2. The gifted constitute 3% to 5% of the population. Moreover, giftedness equals high IQ, which is a stable measure of aptitude: Spinal tap psychometrics in gifted education. *Gifted Child Quarterly, 53*, 236–238.

Buchanan, N. K. (1987). Evaluating the identification process of a program for the gifted: A case study. *Roeper Review, 9*, 231–235

Callahan, C. M. (1982). Myth: There must be "winners" and "losers" in identification and programming! *Gifted Child Quarterly, 26*, 17–19.

Callahan, C. M. (2009). Myth 3. A family of identification myths: Your sample must be the same as the population. There is a "silver bullet" in identification. There must be "winners" and "losers" in identification and programming. *Gifted Child Quarterly, 53*, 239–241.

Council for Exceptional Children. The Association for the Gifted. (2001), April). *Diversity and developing gifts and talents: A national action plan.* Reston, VA: Council for Exceptional Children.

Endepohls-Ulpe, M., & Ruf, H. (2005). Primary teachers' criteria for the identification of gifted pupils. *High Ability Studies, 16*, 219–228.

Feldhusen, J. F., & Jarwan, F. A. (2000). Identification of gifted and talented youth for educational programs. In K. A. Heller, F. J. Mönks, R. J. Sternberg, & R. F. Subotnik (Eds.), *International handbook of giftedness and talent* (2nd ed., pp. 271–282). Oxford, UK: Elsevier Science.

Ford, D. Y. (2006, Fall). Creating culturally responsive classrooms for gifted students. *Understanding Our Gifted*, pp. 10–14.

Friedman-Nimz, R. (2009). Myth 6: Cosmetic use of multiple selection criteria. *Gifted Child Quarterly, 53*, 248–250.

Goldberg, M. L. (1986). Issues in the education of gifted and talented student. Part I. *Roeper Review, 8*, 226–233.

Hagen, E. (1980). *Identification of the gifted.* New York: Teachers College Press.

Hunsaker, S. L. (1991). *Teacher roles in multiple selection criteria systems for identifying gifted students.* Unpublished doctoral dissertation, University of Virginia, Charlottesville, VA.

Hunsaker, S. L., Finley, V. S., & Frank, E. L. (1997). An analysis of teacher nominations and student performance in gifted programs. *Gifted Child Quarterly, 41*, 19–24.

Jenkins-Friedman, R. (1982). Myth: Cosmetic use of multiple selection criteria! *Gifted Child Quarterly, 26*, 24–26.

Johnsen, S. K. (2004). Making decisions about placement. In S. K. Johnsen (Ed.), *Identifying gifted students: A practical guide.* Waco, TX: Prufrock.

Johnsen, S. K., VanTassel-Baska, J., & Robinson, A. (2008). *Using the national gifted education standards for university teacher preparation programs.* Thousand Oaks, CA: Corwin.

Massé, L., & Gagné, F. (1996). Should self-nomination be allowed in peer nomination forms? *Gifted Child Quarterly, 40*, 24–30.

Powell, T., & Siegle, D. (2000, Spring). Teacher bias in identifying gifted and talented students. *The National Research Center on the gifted and Talented Newsletter*, pp. 13–15.

Richert, E. S. (2003). Excellence with justice in identification and programming. In N. Colangelo, & G. A. Davis (Eds.), *Handbook of gifted education* (3rd ed., pp. 146–158). Boston: Allyn & Bacon.

Schroth, S. T., & Helfer, J. A. (2008). Identifying gifted students: Educators beliefs regarding various policies, processes, and procedures. *Journal for the Education of the Gifted, 32*, 155–179.

Siegle, D., Moore, M., Mann, R. L., & Wilson, H. E. (2010). Factors that influence in-service and preservice teachers' nominations of students for gifted and talented programs. *Journal for the Education of the Gifted, 33*, 337–360.

Siegle, D., & Powell, T. (2004). Exploring teacher biases when nominating students for gifted programs. *Gifted Child Quarterly, 48*, 21–29.

Speirs Neumeister, K. L., Adams, C. M., Pierce, R. L., Cassady, J. C., & Dixon, F. A. (2007). Fourth grade teachers' perceptions of giftedness: Implications for identifying and serving diverse gifted students. *Journal for the Education of the Gifted, 30*, 479–499.

Tannenbaum, A. J. (2009). Defining, determining, discovering, and developing excellence. In J. S. Renzulli, E. J. Gubbins, K. S. Mc-Millen, R. D. Eckert, & C. A. Little (Eds.), *Systems and models for developing programs for the gifted and talented* (2nd ed., pp. 503–569). Mansfield Center, CT: Creative Learning.

Yarborough, B. H., & Johnson, R. A. (1983). Identifying the gifted: A theory-practice gap. *Gifted Child Quarterly, 27*, 135–138.

U. S. Department of Education. (1993). *National excellence: A case for developing America's talent*. Washington, DC: Author.

## CHAPTER 9 STUDY GUIDE

**Prompt 1 Knowledge**

Describe in your own words one of the outcomes at each stage of identification.

**Prompt 2** *Opinion*

Decide, if possible, at each stage of identification which orientation is more desirable than the other. If it is possible, defend your choice. If it is not possible, explain why not.

**Prompt 3 Affect**

At each stage of identification, the following has been provided: (1) an explanation of the orientations and outcomes, (2) a description of the mechanics of the stage, and (3) a specific school district example. Describe the degree to which and reasons for which this presentation structure was helpful in understanding the stage or not.

**Prompt 4 Experience**

Select any one strategy suggested in the mechanic part of any step and describe your experience or the experience of a colleague in employing that strategy.

**Prompt 5 Preconception/Misconception**

As is apparent in this chapter's descriptions of the stages and an actual school district's reality, some compromises must be made between the ideal and the actual. Upon what bases should these compromises be made? Who should decide when and what compromises are necessary?

# CHAPTER 10

# DECISION STRATEGIES

David F. Lohman, The University of Iowa

## TALENT IDENTIFICATION AS AN ILL-STRUCTURED PROBLEM

Identifying gifted students was once as simple as administering the Stanford-Binet Intelligence Test. If the IQ score was 130 or higher, then the child was deemed gifted. Although some would gladly return to such policies (Delisle, 2010), most would not. And even if we wanted such simplicity, it is no longer possible. The emergence of other intelligence tests—first the Wechsler Scales and then many other tests—complicated the picture. IQ scores on these other tests often differed from those obtained on the Stanford-Binet. To further complicate matters, most tests provided more than one score. For example, the Wechsler test reported a Verbal IQ and a Performance IQ. What was once a well-structured problem was starting to become much more ill-structured.

Models of abilities also became more differentiated. Procedures for identifying talent that were developed by Terman emphasized the measurement of a cognitive potential that was thought to forecast successful learning in any cognitively

challenging domain or learning context. But some children excel in mathematics, some in music, some in creative writing, some in graphic arts, and so on. Very few excel in all of these domains. Thus, while not dismissing the importance of general intellectual ability, most psychologists now view talent as a more variegated concept and the development of excellence as dependent on much more than superior general cognitive ability.

### BEYOND COMPOSITE SCORES

Traditionally-structured programs for the gifted have continued to cater to a very small and homogenous segment of the population, often in spite of efforts to move beyond IQ as the sole criterion for admission. In some schools, children are admitted to the gifted program only if they obtain high full-scale or composite scores on multi-factor ability tests. Limiting admission to those with high full scale IQ scores eliminates students who show significant discrepancies among the different abilities measured by the intelligence test. For example, a student who excels on the Verbal Comprehension Index of the WISC-IV but not

219

on the Perceptual Reasoning Index would not be as likely to be admitted as the student who obtained somewhat lower but similar scores on both WISC Indexes. Adding the Working Memory and Processing Speed indexes further complicates the picture.[1]

Requiring high composite scores on achievement tests has the same effect. The student who scores at the 99th percentile on the *Iowa Test of Basic Skills* (ITBS) Math Total but obtains a lower score on the Reading Total would not be admitted to a gifted and talented program whose admission criteria only considered those students with high scores on the overall Composite achievement score. It is difficult to obtain a high overall Composite score if Reading scores are significantly lower than Mathematics scores, no matter how high the scores on the mathematics portion of the test might be. Similarly, admitting only students who excel on both an ability test and an achievement test eliminates both those whose academic achievement failed to meet expectations set by the ability test and those whose academic achievement exceeded expectations. Finally, adding points for teacher ratings to the mix favors those who have impressed their teacher and works against those who might need different teachers or instructional environments. By requiring high scores on a series of measures, most of which in turn measure multiple abilities or achievements, one ensures that only those students who excel or at least have moderately high scores on everything—including pleasing their teachers—are included in the program.

Such students are usually a joy to teach, even though they constitute only a small percentage of the academically talented children in the school. Programs that have attempted to serve a broader population of students inevitably find that more adaptations to the abilities, achievements, personalities, and learning styles of students are needed.

## SELECTION VERSUS CLASSIFICATION

Talents that schools are ostensibly prepared to develop in children require that the school do more than simply name or identify the talent. Educational resources must be allocated for the development of the students' abilities. However, resources are often scarce and not all children will benefit equally from receiving them. The task, then, is to select those students most likely to profit from a particular kind of educational intervention or, when possible, to create new programs that better meet the needs of these students. Sometimes selection is for a well-defined program such as taking Algebra I.[2] At other times, it is defined broadly, as when children are selected to participate in an educational enrichment program that has many different options.

If the context is well defined, selection is most likely to be successful if the personal characteristics that predict success in that context can be measured efficiently and accurately. Well-structured academic programs such as learning algebra, how to speak another language, or how to develop web pages fall in this category. In such cases, the talent identification process is best understood as a selection for a

---

1. Note that NAGC (2010) recommends that users of the WISC-IV use the General Ability Index (GAI) when testing for giftedness. The GAI excludes the Working Memory and Processing Speed indices.

2. The Iowa Algebra Aptitude Test (Schoen & Ansley, 2005) is an excellent example of this kind of test.

particular kind and level of instruction or enrichment (see Box 2 in Chapter 12).

If more than one intervention is possible, the selection morphs into *classification,* that is, making the most appropriate placement for each student. A global assessment that is useful for selection into several different kinds of programs will generally be less useful for classification of individuals to different programming options (Cronbach, 1990). For example, suppose (contrary to recommendations!) students are admitted to the program on the basis of a Full Scale score on the WISC-IV. Since WISC-IV Full Scale scores show approximately equal correlations with success in mathematics courses and with success in literature courses, WISC Full Scale scores provide no basis for assigning the student to one or the other course of study. For that decision, one would need a test that showed much higher correlations with success in one domain than with success in the other domain. To continue the example, scores on the WISC-IV Verbal Comprehension Index will show higher correlations with performance in literature whereas the Perceptual Reasoning Index will show somewhat higher correlations with performance in mathematics. Using information on the discrepancy between the Verbal Comprehension and Perceptual Reasoning scores would help one make better classification decisions into one area of study or the other. Tests that even more directly measured the specific aptitudes required for success in each program would do an even better job. A score that averages across the several aptitudes for these domains obscures information about the student's relative strengths and weaknesses in each domain.

## SELECTION DECISIONS

The accuracy with which students are selected for a program depends on both predictive validity of the selection test and the proportion of students selected. The expected performance of the selected group on the outcome measure increases in direct proportion to the validity coefficient. For example, a test with validity coefficient of $r = .8$ is 33% more effective than a test with a validity coefficient of $r = .6$. It is useful to keep this in mind when making decisions about the relative utility of different tests for talent identification. For example, in the Project Bright Horizon study (Lohman, Korb, & Lakin, 2008), the correlations with Reading Achievement at grade 3 were $r = .35$ and $r = .76$ for the Naglieri Nonverbal Ability Test (NNAT) and Cognitive Abilities Test (CogAT) Verbal, respectively. This means that the verbal reasoning test was more than twice as effective as the nonverbal test in identifying the best readers. The corresponding correlations for English language leaner (ELL) children were .38 and .68, indicating that even for these children the verbal reasoning tests was about 80% more effective.[3]

The value of the selection test also increases as the admission criteria become increasingly stringent. Increases in the expected performance level of the admitted group accelerate when less than 10% of the population is admitted.

---

3. Note, however, that the verbal reasoning scores of ELL students must be compared to the verbal reasoning scores of other ELL students in order to make these selections. Using only national norms would select very few, if any, of these students (see Chapter 12).

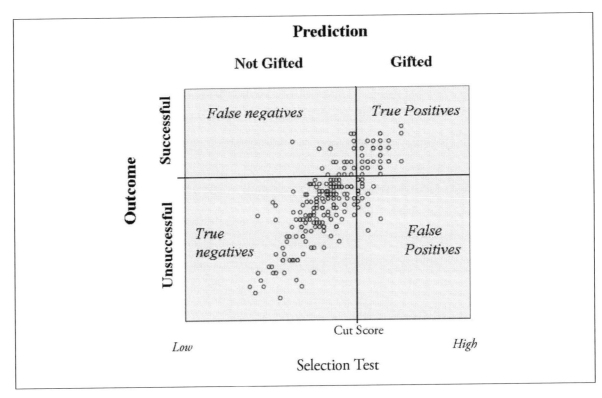

**Figure 1.** Four outcomes of a selection decision.

### CLASSIFICATION DECISIONS

The four types of classification decisions are illustrated in Figure 1. In this example, scores on the selection test are on the horizontal axis. Low scores are on the left, high scores on the right. Students who score above the cut score on the selection test would be admitted. These students fall to the right of the vertical line that is perpendicular to the cut score. We predict that these students will succeed in the program. The outcome measure (some measure of academic learning) is represented on the vertical axis. Once again, a cut score is established to distinguish between those students who were successful (above the horizontal line) and those who were unsuccessful (below the horizontal line) in the gifted program.

The four possible outcomes of a selection decision may be called true positives, false positives,

true negatives, and false negatives. When identifying gifted students, true positives and true negatives are students who were correctly placed either in gifted programs or mainstream classrooms. False positives are students who were placed in gifted programs but subsequently did not succeed. False negatives are students who were placed in mainstream classrooms but who could have been successful in a gifted program.

Both false negatives and false positives have troubling consequences. On the one hand, false negatives, where potentially successful students are denied access to gifted programs, are detrimental to individual students and to society as the talents of these students may not be developed appropriately. On the other hand, false positives are a problem because resources are misused when students are placed in instructional contexts that were not beneficial to them. If there are a limited number of slots in a gifted program, every false positive keeps one potentially successful student out of the program (i.e., causes more false negatives). Further, if the outcomes are sufficiently unsatisfactory, then the student may need to be exited from the program which is difficult and, in some programs, explicitly disallowed.

## CAUTIONS.

Although the classification scheme in Figure 1 seems straightforward, there are several cautions that must be kept in mind.

*First*, the common penchant for classifying children as "gifted" (and, by implication as "not gifted") presumes a fixed or at least highly stable categorical variable. Although the variable used to make the decision (e.g., IQ, other assessments) varies continuously, establishing a fixed cut score and using categorical labels (as in Figure 1) encourages the unwary to treat it as a fixed category with sharp boundaries. This is an intellectual fiction that we use only because it simplifies communication.

*Second*, there is no one criterion measure. Different ways of estimating academic success would classify somewhat different groups of children as succeeding or as not succeeding. Teacher marks or grades, end-of-course exams, performance assessments, subsequent attainment of excellence in a domain, creative contributions to a domain as a student or adult professional, and many other measures could be defended as important indicators of success. Many educational systems use measures of achievement to estimate learning. Although such tests have many desirable properties, even in the best of cases, they capture only some of the many

possible outcomes of education that one might hope to predict. For some students—especially high-potential students who have had fewer opportunities to attain academic excellence—success might be defined as graduating from high-school or college. For others, it might be the attainment of national or international awards for their work. It is critical that the limitations of the criterion measures be kept in mind when developing a selection system. For example, seemingly more authentic outcome measures are usually much less reliable and sample from a much smaller portion of a domain than more objective tests. Hard-won knowledge about the importance of reliability and validity of an assessment cannot be ignored even when a measure is considered more authentic or desirable in other ways. Keeping track of multiple outcome measures can help programs avoid the trap of placing too much emphasis on any one criterion.

*Third*, even with highly reliable selection tests, there is much movement into and out of the top scoring group over time. As discussed in the section on regression to the mean in Chapter 12, changes in rank order are captured by the correlation between test scores at Time 1 and at Time 2. Anything that reduces the correlation between scores at Time 1 and Time 2 increases the number of classification mistakes at Time 2. Tests or combinations of tests that do not measure some of the aptitudes needed to succeed in the program or that do not measure these aptitudes reliably will increase the number of selection and classification errors. The abilities needed to excel in early reading, mathematics, or playing the piano are not the same as those needed to excel in critical reading, more complex mathematics, or sight reading music. Further, even when the aptitudes are the same at both times, students vary in the quality of instruction that they receive, their motivation for learning, and a long list of other personal and environmental factors that impact the competencies that they develop over time. Thus, it is unsurprising that the number of students correctly classified at Time 1 but who are no longer correctly classified at Time 2 increases as the interval between Time 1 and Time 2 increases. Reducing the number of students incorrectly admitted or excluded is especially important when policies mandate that children cannot be exited from a program. This argues for leniency in the initial selection criterion,[4] for an ongoing process of identifying new children to participate in the program, and for periodically reassigning students to other educational programs if they do not need or seem to be profiting from the level of challenge provided by the gifted program (Lakin & Lohman, 2011; Renzulli, 2005).

*Fourth*, because it uses information on the success of students currently served by the program, selection works to preserve the existing program. Prior to the development of the SAT, admission to prestigious private colleges and universities was based primarily on the recommendations of the headmasters of a limited set of private schools (Lemann, 1999). At first only tentatively but then in a grand way, the SAT opened the doors of these colleges to a much broader segment of the high-school population. Indeed, when combined with

high school GPA, the test did such a good job of predicting success in college that there is now little variation in ability among the entering students at the most selective colleges (Hernstein & Murray, 1994). Although some decried this homogenization of the student population, the issue went unchallenged until advocates for underrepresented minority students brought claims of unfair selection practices against the College Board (see Zwick, 2004). Paradoxically, the test that had been lauded for opening doors to higher education for some was now criticized for closing them for others. The debate about the SAT that ensued foreshadowed a similar debate in gifted education.

For better or worse, selecting those individuals most likely to succeed in any system contributes to the preservation of that system. Pressure to preserve the system is strongest when the training system is elaborate and the cost of failure is high. For example, the military must exercise great care when selecting individuals for training as pilots. The training is not only long and expensive, but failure can result in the death of the pilot (and others) or the destruction of a multimillion dollar aircraft. That some applicants are screened out of training who might have succeeded is considered acceptable if failures can be avoided. In this case, the needs of the system (or society at large) outweigh those of the individual.

Sometimes, however, the system needs to be changed or at least adapted to better meet the needs of individuals who could succeed in a differently structured training or performance environment. In many of these cases, the needs of society to ensure fairness for all of its citizens are often given priority over the desire of the keepers of the system

---

4. A lenient cut score for admission does not mean using unreliable selection measures. It merely recognizes the inherently probabilistic nature of the prediction that is being made about future success in the program. As always, more valid and reliable measures will reduce the error in selection and classification.

to preserve their training procedures and selection criteria. Pilots need not be male; students need not be sighted to succeed in college; all students with a talent for writing need not exhibit the same competence in the English language nor need they all be placed in the same writing class. Categorical thinking about the talent development program is as unnecessary and unhelpful as categorical thinking about the nature of talent.

Most cases are less clear cut than the example of pilot selection. For example, all theories of human abilities recognize the importance of spatial abilities. However, students who excel in spatial ability often have considerable difficulty in elementary school as well as in programs for the gifted that presume high levels of competence in academic learning. Should special programs be developed for these students? Although there are many factors that should be considered in making such decisions, one critical piece of information is whether it can be shown that such children can succeed in a differently-structured program or in the existing program when different but equally valued outcome measures are used. Further, the new program must be one that the institution could reasonably be expected to offer given its resources. In the case of spatial ability, the critical factor in predicting success in academically-oriented programs is whether the student also excels in verbal or (more commonly) quantitative reasoning abilities. When coupled with one or both of these abilities, high spatial ability says more about *how* students learn than *whether* they can learn. In such cases, a modification of the existing program to accommodate the students learning style is all that is needed. Alternatively, if the child excels only

in spatial visualization abilities and not in verbal or quantitative reasoning, then different kinds of programs are needed that may not even have a traditionally academic focus.[5]

## USING MULTIPLE ASSESSMENTS

All good talent identification programs rely on multiple sources of evidence when deciding whether a student needs special educational programming. Some programs admit only those students who score above a certain level on two or more consecutively administered tests. For example, all students may be administered a screening test. Students who score at or above a given level on the screening test are invited to take a second test. Other programs have a more differentiated curriculum and admit students if they achieve high scores on tests that predict success in any one of the programs that they offer. For example, admission to the literary arts program may require high scores on reading achievement and verbal reasoning tests whereas admission to the mathematics programs may require high scores in mathematics achievement and on a quantitative reasoning test. Sometimes other information is gathered (school

---

5. It is commonly, but erroneously assumed that nonverbal ability tests (such as the Raven Progressive Matrices or the Nonverbal Battery of CogAT) are good measures of spatial ability. They are not. Good measures of spatial ability require a kind of analog cognition that shows large mean differences between the sexes. Three-dimensional rotation tests are a good example. Nonverbal reasoning tests typically require very little of this kind of thinking and, when they do (as on the Paper Folding subtest of CogAT), are typically amenable to more analytic solution strategies that rely on reasoning rather than spatial visualization. Consequently, nonverbal reasoning tests typically show small or no sex differences (at least near the mean). See Lohman (1994) and Lohman & Lakin (2009).

grades, teacher and parent rating scales, creativity tests, etc.). The information is then arrayed in a matrix, and scores on each assessment are assigned point values that are then summed or averaged to make a decision about admission.

Three different ways of combining assessment information are embedded in these examples. For the simplest case of two assessments, these rules are (a) requiring a high score on both Test 1 *and* Test 2, (b) requiring a high score on either Test 1 *or* Test 2, and (c) require a high score on the *average* of Test score 1 and Test score 2. Figure 2 illustrates these three rules. Each panel in the figure shows a scatter plot of students' scores on the two tests. The left panel shows the students who would be identified by the *"and"* rule, the center panel those who would be identified by the *"or"* rule, and the right panel those who would be identified by the *"average"* rule.

### THE *"AND"* RULE.

Requiring students to score above a particular cut score on both Tests 1 *and* 2 is the most restrictive rule. This is the effect of a two-stage screening process in which students must achieve a high score on the first test (e.g., a norm referenced achievement test) and then a high score on a second test (e.g., an individually administered ability test). Consider the case in which the cut score is set at the top 5% on both tests and the correlation between them is quite high, say $r = .80$. Only about 50% of the students in the population who meet this criterion on the first test will also meet it on the second test (see Figure 3). This means that 50% of the 5% who met the criterion on Test 1, or 2.5% of the total student population, will be admitted. The effects of making the cut score more stringent or more lenient is shown in Figure 3. Note that very few students will be admitted

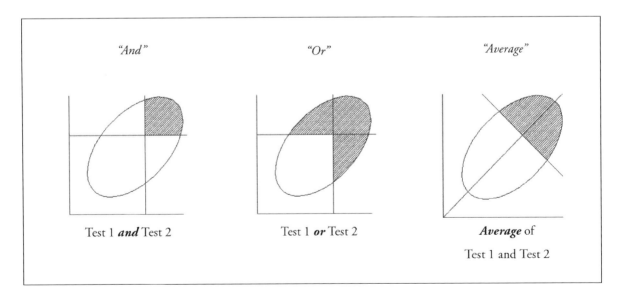

"And"          "Or"          "Average"

Test 1 *and* Test 2          Test 1 *or* Test 2          ***Average*** of
Test 1 and Test 2

**Figure 2.** Plots of the effects of three selection rules: (a) high scores on Test 1 *and* Test 2; (b) high scores on Test 1 *or* Test 2; and (c) high scores on the *average* of Test 1 and Test 2. The darkened portion of each ellipse identifies selected students.

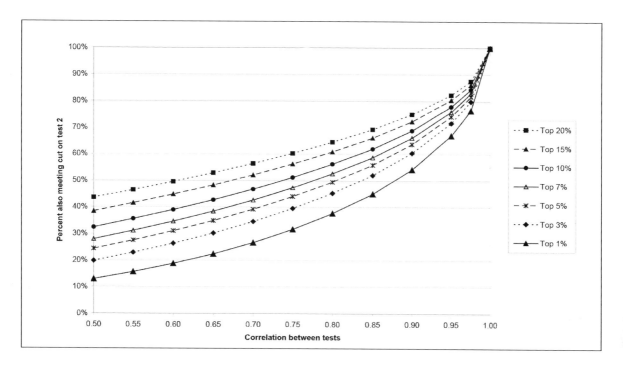

**Figure 3.** Percent of students whose scores exceed given cut score on Test 1 whose scores will exceed the same cut on Test 2, by the correlation between the two tests. To use the figure, first locate the approximate correlation between the two tests on the abscissa. Draw a line perpendicular to this value. Find the point where the line intersects the curve that identifies the cut score for admission. Finally, locate the value on the vertical axis that corresponds with this point.

when stringent cut scores are used on both tests, even when the two tests are highly correlated (see Lohman & Korb, 2006, for details and other examples).

The primary advantage of the *"and"* rule is administrative convenience; the primary disadvantage is that it is very unforgiving. It makes no difference how high the score was (or might have been) on Test 2 if the score on Test 1 was even one point below the established cut score. Unfortunately, this commonly occurs, even when the two tests are highly correlated. In the language of Figure 1, there will be many false negatives—that is, there will be many students who were rejected but who would have succeeded admirably in the program.

**THE *"OR"* RULE.**

The *"or" rule* has quite different effects. Again, the percentage of students admitted is easily estimated from Figure 3. Once again assume a correlation of $r = .8$ between the tests. Test 1 admits 5% of the population. Test 2 also admits 5%, but, as was shown above, half of these students were already admitted by the first test. Therefore, in all, 7.5% of the student population would be admitted. In this case, changing the rule from *"and"* to *"or"* triples the number of students admitted from 2.5 to 7.5% of the population.

Whether this is a good thing or a bad thing depends on the constructs that the tests measure. The disjunctive *"or"* rule is most defensible if the two tests measure different constructs such as language

arts and mathematics. One should seek to identify students who excel in either domain, not just
those who excel in both domains. However, when
applied to tests that presumably measure the same
construct, the result is an increase in the number
of false positives. For example, some programs admit students who present a sufficiently high score
on any one of several different ability tests. The erroneous assumption is that ability is best indicated
by a student's highest score. However, the highest
score in a set of presumably parallel measurements
is actually one of the most error-laden scores,
which means that it will show the most regression
to the mean. Considering the highest scores as the
best estimate of ability is like the child who thinks
that his skill in playing basketball is best given by
the most difficult shot that he once made rather
than by the most difficult shot that he can make
with some consistency.[6]

### THE "AVERAGE" RULE.

If both tests measure the same construct, however, the statistically optimal rule is neither "or" nor
"and" but rather "average." For a given set of cut
scores, the "average" rule will admit more students

---

6. Score gains upon retesting for ability tests that present
items in novel formats (e.g., Matrices) or are timed can be
quite large, especially for the most able students. Therefore,
repeated administrations of the same test advantage those
children whose parents lobby for them. Schools should avoid
policies that allow retesting unless there is good evidence
that something was amiss in the original test administration.
On CogAT, score warnings signal such difficulties (e.g., performing inconsistently on subtests within a battery, adopting
a very slow but accurate test-taking strategy, etc.). Even in
these cases, a better strategy is to omit the invalid test battery
and rely instead on the scores for the other two test batteries.
Both problems—practice effects and misunderstandings in
test directions or procedures—can be substantially reduced
by providing all students with informative practice exercises
prior to taking the test.

than the restrictive "and" rule and fewer than the
liberal "or" rule. Essentially, students are admitted
on the basis of where they fall on the 45-degree
diagonal in Figure 2 rather than on either the $x$
axis or the $y$ axis. A very high score on one test
will compensate for a somewhat lower score on the
other test. The averaged score also will be more
reliable than separate scores. Improvements in reliability are especially important when scores are
extremely high since these scores typically have
much larger errors of measurement than scores
near the mean of the distribution (see discussion
of conditional standard errors in Chapter 12).

Although averaging scores is generally the best
way to combine information from two or more assessments that measure the same construct, there
are several complications. First, the scores should
be on the same scale. The variability of the scores
needs to be similar or else the final ranks will be
more heavily determined by the score with the
greater variance. Unequal variances can even occur when scores on several dimensions are converted to point values, typically 0 to 5, and then
the point values summed or averaged. This means
that, other things being equal, the score with the
greatest variability will have the greatest impact on
the final rank orders, which may not be the score
that one wishes to emphasize.

### POINTS, PRs, AND SCALE SCORES

Many programs simplify the task of combining measures by assigning points to different score
ranges. Although such schemes can be convenient,
it is best not to discard information by assigning one number (e.g., a point value) to an entire
range of scores. However if such a conversion is

attempted, *then the mapping should try to preserve information in the scale scores* (such as USS or SAS scores on CogAT) *rather than in percentile ranks* (PRs). If available, scale scores allow the average number of points across different measures to reflect better the true range of ability among the students. PRs discard information in scale scores for high-scoring students (see Box 1 and also Figure 3 in Chapter 12). Table 1 shows an example of a scheme for converting PRs to points that preserves some of the information in the original scale scores. Notice that one additional point is added for each increment of 3 SAS points, thus preserving information on the SAS scale (at least up to an SAS score of 140). This particular scheme is used in the Lohman-Renzulli plan for combining ability test scores, achievement test scores, and teacher ratings that is summarized in Box 2.

Percentile ranks are not on an equal interval scale and thus generally should not be averaged. The PR of the average of two or more scores is often not the same as the average of the corresponding PRs. Creating standard or z scores from the

**Table 1.** Table to Convert PR from Any Test or CogAT SAS Scores to Points

| POINTS | PR | SAS |
|---|---|---|
| 1 | 80-83 | 113-115 |
| 2 | 84-88 | 116-119 |
| 3 | 89-92 | 120-123 |
| 4 | 93-95 | 124-127 |
| 5 | 96-97 | 128-131 |
| 6 | 98 | 132-135 |
| 7 | 99 | 136-139 |
| 8 | 99+ | 140+ |

original scale scores is one of the best ways to put scores from different tests on the same scale and to equate variances so that they can be averaged. Normal Curve Equivalent (NCE) scores work well if student scores are not above the 98th PR. Most testing companies provide NCE scores (or tables that show how to convert PRs to NCEs) but do not allow the NCE scores to exceed 99. This artificial ceiling curtails discriminations among students who score more than 2.33 standard deviations above the mean (e.g., an IQ of 135 or above). As is so often the case, statistical procedures that work flawlessly for most students can break down when used with highly gifted students.[7]

Once scores are on the same scale and have similar variances (e.g., by converting them to z-scores or NCE scores), then simply averaging them is not necessarily the best way to proceed. Averaging assumes that both assessments are of equal quality and make approximately equal contributions to success in the program. If one assessment is much less reliable or valid than the other assessment, then the more reliable or valid measure should be weighted more heavily. For example, teacher ratings, creativity tests, and classroom grades are generally much less reliable and/or less valid than well-constructed ability and achievement tests. *An unreliable score can easily add more noise than useful information to the final rankings.* One solution is to

7. Beginning with regression to the mean (which is non-existent at the mean), there is a list of statistical and measurement issues that plague extreme scores. Errors of measurement for IQ scores are often much larger for extreme scores than for less extreme scores; assumptions about the shape of the ability distribution (normal? skewed?) can dramatically alter what IQ score is associated with extremely high scores (as the discussion of scaling issues for the SB-LM in Chapter 12 shows).

## Box 1

### RELATIONSHIPS BETWEEN PERCENTILE RANKS, STANDARD AGE SCORES, AND THE ARBITRARY EIGHT-POINT GROUPING SCHEME SHOWN IN TABLE B1

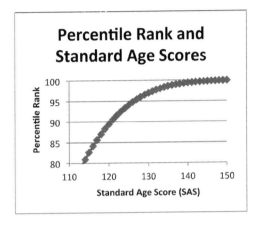

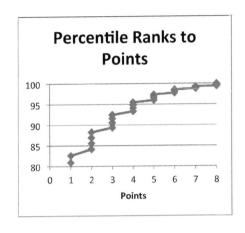

TABLE B1

| SAS | PR | POINTS |
|-----|-----|--------|
| 150 | 99 | 8 |
| 149 | 99 | 8 |
| 148 | 99 | 8 |
| 147 | 99 | 8 |
| 146 | 99 | 8 |
| 145 | 99 | 8 |
| 144 | 99 | 8 |
| 143 | 99 | 8 |
| 142 | 99 | 8 |
| 141 | 99 | 8 |
| 140 | 99 | 8 |
| 139 | 99 | 7 |
| 138 | 99 | 7 |
| 137 | 99 | 7 |
| 136 | 99 | 7 |
| 135 | 99 | 6 |
| 134 | 98 | 6 |
| 133 | 98 | 6 |
| 132 | 98 | 6 |
| 131 | 97 | 5 |
| 130 | 97 | 5 |

Plot in the upper left shows relationships between Percentile Ranks (PRs) and Standard Age Scores (SAS) for PRs of 80 through 99. (SAS scores have a mean of 100 and SD of 16.) Note that the relationship is reasonably linear until the 95th PR. Thereafter increases in SAS are associated with ever smaller increases in PR. This is also shown in the table at the left. All SAS scores of 135 or higher have the same PR of 99.

The point scheme (see Table B1) arbitrarily uses a scale of 1 to 8. Since the scheme is based on SAS scores, it is able to make rough distinctions between SAS scores up through 140. However, as is shown in the plot on the upper right, the point scheme discards information between SAS scores within each category.

weight separate assessments by a combined estimate of their reliability and validity. Another, much easier, solution is to use the Lohman-Renzulli scheme outlined in Box 2 (later in the chapter).

## AN EXAMPLE OF A SCREENING PROGRAM

The following case study shows how these general principles can be applied in an operational setting. Those responsible for implementing a selection system often want a recipe that they can follow. Although the examples given here sometimes make specific recommendations, intelligent application of the general principles requires understanding the consequences of combining information in different ways or adopting different cut scores. *Every decision required to build a working identification system involves tradeoffs.* It is helpful to understand how altering these decisions can affect the outcomes. For this reason, I provide tables and graphs that show the consequences of using other cut scores or tests that have stronger or weaker relationships with the outcomes.

The accuracy of any screening program depends critically on the correlation between the screening test and the test used for placement (or on the criterion measures, if a second test is not used). The lowest correlations will be observed when the screening test measures somewhat different abilities than the placement or criterion measure. The most common example of this is when a short nonverbal reasoning test is used for screening (e.g., NNAT) and the second test is a short, individually administered ability test (e.g., *Kaufman Brief Intelligence Test* [K-BIT]). The correlation between NNAT and K-BIT are typically in the range of $r = .5 - .6$ for the

K-BIT Nonverbal score but only $r = .4 - .5$ for the K-BIT Verbal score. Much higher correlations will be observed if both the screening test and the placement test are longer and multidimensional (i.e., assess more than nonverbal abilities). For example, screening with CogAT Form 7 and placement with ITBS Form E would give correlations of approximately $r = .8$ within the verbal/reading and quant/math domains. This is an improvement of in prediction accuracy of 60–100% over the NNAT/K-BIT scenario.

An interesting, somewhat different case occurs when the CogAT Form 7 Screening Form (Lohman, 2011) is first administered to all students and only a subset are then administered the complete CogAT Form 7. The district in this case mandated a two-step testing program. First, all grade 2 students were to be administered the CogAT Screening Form. This Screening Form consists of matrix (or analogy) subtests in each of three content areas: verbal concepts, quantitative concepts, and nonverbal/figural concepts. These three subtests are taken directly from the complete CogAT Form 7 test. Examples of the item formats are shown in Figure 1 of Chapter 12. At level 8 (which is typically used in Grade 2), each of the three subtests in the Screening Form present 18 pictorial items (Picture Analogies, Number Analogies, and Figure Matrices), which ensures fairness to ELL children.[8] Children who

8. Each matrix/analogy test is actually the first subtest in the corresponding batteries of the complete CogAT Form 7 test. For example, the first 18 items come from the Picture Analogies test of the Verbal Battery. The complete Verbal Battery contains two other subtests: Picture Classification and an orally administered English/Spanish Sentence Completion test. Students who take the complete CogAT after the Screening Form can skip the three matrix/analogy subtests that they have already taken. Or, the Screening Form can be considered a practice test, in which case the

Footnote continues on the next page.

scored well on the Screening Form would then be administered the remaining six subtests of the complete CogAT Form 7 test. It was expected that some students would take these subtests online; others would be administered paper and pencil tests individually or in small groups.

The CogAT scores used for eventual placement in the gifted program incorporate the scores students obtained on the Screening Form.[9] For example, a child's score on the Picture Analogies subtest in the Screening Form is one of three subtests that make up the Verbal Battery. This statistical dependency increases the correlations between scores on the Screening Form and each of the three batteries of the full CogAT. However, this dependency is entirely acceptable if the goal is to exclude as few students as possible who would have been admitted had they taken the complete CogAT. Using the Screening Form in this way would allow the district to administer a relatively short screening test to all students, but then also have confidence that placement decisions would be made using the profile of the child's Verbal, Quantitative, and Nonverbal reasoning abilities rather than the single score on the Screening Form.[10]

---

student would take all subtests on the CogAT. Although practice on one subtest in each battery would be expected to raise scores slightly, the expected gain would be the same for all students. However, students who were initially unfamiliar with the matrix format would be expected to gain more, thereby increasing the validity of their scores.

9. Alternatively, students can be re-administered the three subtests in the Screening Form when they take the full CogAT. This gives students a practice opportunity to attempt the common items on the two tests. See footnote 8.

10. A disadvantage of this procedure, however, is that teachers and parents receive only the child's Screening Form score

The selection questions to be addressed are:

1.  *Which scores on the tests should be used?* The Screening Form reports only one ability score, and so there is no decision to be made. However, the full CogAT reports separate scores for each battery: Verbal (V), Quantitative (Q), and Nonverbal (N) and a three-battery composite (VQN) score. In addition, one or more of the two-battery partial composites (VQ, VN, and QN) are reported if requested. Which of the scores/composites on CogAT7 should be used? The three battery scores? The overall composite? Or one partial composite and one battery-level score?

2.  *Which norms should be used?* Should the CogAT cut score(s) be based on National norms, on Local (i.e., school) norms, subgroup norms (ELL or low SES), or some combination of this set?

3.  *Which rules should be used to combine information from the two tests?* Should test scores on the Screening Form and CogAT7 be combined with an *"and"* rule (the student's scores must exceed a fixed cut score on the Screening Form and CogAT7) or with an *"average"* rule (the average of the student's scores on the two tests must exceed a fixed cut score).

4.  *Where should the cut score be set on the Screening Form? On the complete CogAT?* Specifically, how lenient must one be on the Screening Form to insure that few academically talented students will be excluded?

---

rather than the CogAT ability profile and the suggestions for helping the child learn that are linked to the profile.

Our recommendation for Question 1 *(Which scores?)* applies only to the complete CogAT. As discussed above, it makes little sense to use an overall composite score to assign students to differentiated learning programs. Specifically, the CogAT Verbal (V) score is the best predictor of success in verbally demanding domains, whereas the Quantitative-Nonverbal (QN) partial composite is the best predictor of success in mathematical, engineering, and similar domains. Using the overall VQN composite score would screen out children who excel in only one domain. Thus, we use the Verbal and the Quantitative-Nonverbal scores from CogAT.

For Question 2 *(Which norms?),* we use local norms because our goal is to serve the most able students in the local school population. How students in this district rank when compared with students elsewhere in the country (or the world, for that matter) is interesting, but secondary to how they rank compared with each other. In any local population, the students who are most mismatched with the instruction they are receiving will be those whose academic and cognitive development is well above that of their classmates.[11]

Question 3 *(Which rules?)* usually poses a difficult choice between the convenient *"and"* rule and the more desirable *"average"* rule. Since only

a subset of the children who are administered the Screening Form will also take the remaining subtests on the full CogAT, it appears that we must use the convenient but less desirable *"and"* rule. However, scores on the complete CogAT will include scores from the Screening Form. For example, children's scores on the Picture Analogy items on the Screening Form are combined with their scores on Picture Classification and Sentence Completion subtests to obtain the total score on the CogAT Verbal Battery. Scores from the Number Analogies and Figure Matrices subtests of the Screening Form are similarly combined with the remaining two tests in the Quantitative and Nonverbal batteries (see Figure 1 in Chapter 12). In this way, scores from the two test sessions are combined in a weighted average. Thus, the procedure combines the convenience of the *"and"* rule with the statistical power of the *"average"* rule.

Question 4 *(What should the cutoff score be?)* requires decisions for both Screening Form and the final CogAT scores. In the section that follows, we explore the consequences of using different cut scores on the Screening Form. Cut scores on the complete CogAT, however, will be set using information on the types of programs available and the number of students who can be served. Since the district has acceleration/enrichment programs in mathematics and in literature/writing, children will be offered special programming if they achieve sufficiently high scores on *either* CogAT Verbal *or* the CogAT Quant-Nonverbal composite. Since we are using local norms, the cut score will be determined by the number of students that the school can serve. In this case, students who score in the top 3% will be considered strong candidates

---

11. When attempting to identify the talents of students who have had markedly different opportunities to develop the knowledge and skills measured by the test, one should also compare students' test scores to others of the same age or grade who have had roughly similar opportunities to learn (OTL). The simplest procedure is to sort test scores within OTL groups (e.g., students receiving free/reduced price lunch versus other students.) Importantly, educational programming must take into account the student's level of achievement within the talent domain. A one-size-fits-all program will often not be able to accommodate the needs of these students and their more advantaged peers at the same time.

for whole-grade acceleration in mathematics or literacy studies, whereas those who score in the top 10% (but not top 3%) will be considered strong candidates for enrichment.

## SETTING CUT SCORES ON THE SCREENING FORM

The goal is to select a cut score on the Screening Form that identifies children who are likely to obtain high scores on CogAT, to administer the remaining CogAT subtests to these students, and then to consider placement in the gifted program for those students who obtain high scores on either CogAT Verbal or CogAT QN.

### PICKING CUT SCORES.

The likelihood that a particular cut score identifies children who probably will succeed on the second test while, at the same time, excludes children who probably would not succeed depends on the correlation between the tests (see Figure 3). Correlations between the Screening Form and the two major CogAT scores (Verbal and Quant-Non-

verbal) are very high: both correlations are about $r = .8$. Using this correlation, we computed the probability that a student who exceeded a given cut score on the Screening Form would exceed a more stringent cut score on the CogAT. The results are shown in Table 3. For comparison, we have also included a table that shows the corresponding probabilities for the case in which the correlation was $r = .6$ (see Table 4). This is closer to the level of correlation that would be observed in the more typical scenario in which non-overlapping screening and placement tests are used.

The probabilities given in Tables 3 and 4 assume that the two tests were normed on the same population, which is clearly the case for the Screening Form and the CogAT. When using tests normed on different samples, it is likely that one set of norms will be easier or older than the other set of norms. This could substantially alter the entries in the table. *The easiest way to ensure that the assumption of equivalent norming samples holds is to use local norms.*

**Table 3.** Proportion of Students in Top X Percent of Screening Test Who Exceed the Same or a More Stringent Cut Score on Follow-up Test. Correlation $r = .8$

|  | Top X% | FOLLOW-UP TEST 2 | | | | | | | | |
|---|---|---|---|---|---|---|---|---|---|---|
|  |  | 30% | 25% | 20% | 15% | 10% | 7% | 5% | 3% | 1% |
| SCREENING TEST | 30% | 0.70 | 0.75 | 0.80 | 0.85 | 0.90 | 0.94 | **0.96** | 0.98 | 0.99 |
|  | 25% | 0.63 | 0.68 | 0.73 | 0.79 | 0.86 | 0.90 | 0.93 | 0.96 | 0.99 |
|  | 20% | 0.53 | 0.59 | 0.65 | 0.71 | 0.79 | 0.85 | 0.89 | 0.93 | 0.98 |
|  | 15% | 0.43 | 0.48 | 0.54 | 0.61 | 0.70 | 0.77 | **0.82** | 0.88 | 0.96 |
|  | 10% | 0.30 | 0.34 | 0.40 | 0.47 | 0.56 | 0.64 | 0.71 | 0.79 | 0.91 |
|  | 5% | 0.16 | 0.19 | 0.22 | 0.27 | 0.35 | 0.43 | 0.50 | 0.60 | 0.77 |
|  | 3% | 0.10 | 0.12 | 0.14 | 0.18 | 0.24 | 0.30 | 0.36 | 0.45 | 0.65 |

**Table 4.** Proportion of Students in Top X Percent of Screening Test who Exceed the Same or a More Stringent Cut Score on Follow-up Test. Correlation *r* = .6

|  | **FOLLOW-UP TEST 2** | | | | | | | | |
|---|---|---|---|---|---|---|---|---|---|
| Top X % | 30% | 25% | 20% | 15% | 10% | 7% | 5% | 3% | 1% |
| 30% | 0.58 | 0.61 | 0.64 | 0.68 | 0.74 | 0.77 | **0.80** | 0.84 | 0.91 |
| 25% | 0.51 | 0.54 | 0.57 | 0.62 | 0.67 | 0.72 | 0.75 | 0.80 | 0.87 |
| 20% | 0.43 | 0.46 | 0.50 | 0.54 | 0.60 | 0.64 | 0.68 | 0.73 | 0.82 |
| 15% | 0.34 | 0.37 | 0.41 | 0.45 | 0.51 | 0.55 | **0.59** | 0.65 | 0.75 |
| 10% | 0.25 | 0.27 | 0.30 | 0.34 | 0.39 | 0.44 | 0.48 | 0.54 | 0.65 |
| 5% | 0.13 | 0.15 | 0.17 | 0.20 | 0.24 | 0.28 | 0.31 | 0.36 | 0.48 |
| 3% | 0.08 | 0.10 | 0.11 | 0.13 | 0.16 | 0.19 | 0.22 | 0.26 | 0.36 |

(SCREENING TEST — row labels)

The first row in Table 3 (30%) shows what happens when we select the 30% of students who obtain the highest scores on the screening test. These students score at or above the 70th Local PR on the screening test. For example, setting the cut score at the 70th PR will get us 96% of those who score in the top 5% (Local PR) on the placement test (underlined entry). If we retested only the top 15%, we will still get 82% of these students (doubly underlined entry). Examined by columns, one can pick the final criterion on the placement test (top 5%, top 3%, etc.) and then work backwards to see the effect of different cut scores on the screening test. The main point here is that there is a tradeoff: the larger the fraction of the sample that is administered the second test, the more confident one can be that one will not miss students who might make the cut on the actual admissions test.

The high correlation between the Screening Form and the CogAT is a critical factor. What would happen if the correlation between the screening test and placement test were lower? This

is shown in Table 4. Here, the correlation is *r* = .6. Now, if we retest the top 30% on the screening test, we get only 80% of those who would have been admitted if all had been administered the admissions test. If we retest 15%, this drops to 59%. Stated the other way, we would miss 41% of the students who would have been admitted had they been given the chance to take the second test. *As Table 4 shows, unless the screening test and placement test are highly correlated, one must set a lenient cut score on the screening test to be assured of not excluding many students who might qualify on the basis of the second test.*

**USING AN ACHIEVEMENT TEST INSTEAD OF TWO ABILITY TESTS.**

If a large fraction of the students must be administered the second test, it may be more convenient to eliminate the screening test and administer the placement test to all of the children. An even better option is to administer both an ability test and an achievement test to all children. For example, instead of administering the CogAT Screening Form and then the complete CogAT, one could administer the CogAT and an achievement test to all children. This strategy is most defensible when both tests provide instructionally useful information for all students. The profile of scores on CogAT is linked to instructional strategies that teachers and parents can use to help children learn. The CogAT Screening Form and other brief ability tests cannot do this. Such tests can be resented by teachers who must take up precious class time to administer tests that provide little or no useful information for most of their students.

Administering both a multidimensional ability test (i.e., one that measures more than one ability) and a multidimensional achievement test is in many ways the preferred strategy. Why?

- First, short screening tests are much less reliable than a group achievement test such as the ITBS or a group ability test such as CogAT. Because of the greater reliability of the ITBS, the correlations are commonly about $r = .8$ between CogAT batteries (or partial composites) and ITBS Reading and Math Total scores. As a comparison of Table 3 and Table 4 shows, higher correlations make quite a difference in the proportion of the population that must be administered the second test to achieve a given level of accuracy of identification.

- Second, if all students are administered both tests, then there is no need to set a cut score on whichever test is administered first. More importantly, scores on the two tests can be averaged. This can be

easily done using software that the publisher provides. For example, Riverside Publishing gives test users access to its Interactive Results Manager (iRM). This system allows test users to combine, sort, and report scores on CogAT and the ITBS in many different ways. Importantly, because the averaged CogAT-ITBS scores are so reliable, they show little regression to the mean across years. Put differently, children who would be identified as needing special services in Grade 2 would be likely to qualify for those same services in Grade 3. This is often not the case when only a short screening test is administered.

- Third, readiness for more advanced *academic challenge* is best estimated by combining measures of reasoning abilities (CogAT) with measures of academic achievement (ITBS). For example, by combining the CogAT Quantitative-Nonverbal score with a measure of mathematics achievement, one is much more likely to identify children who show talent for mathematics than by using either score alone. This applies both to ELL and to non-ELL children. Note, however, that accounting for opportunity to learn would require separating the CogAT Verbal and ITBS Reading scores of ELL students from those on non-ELL students. (See Chapter 12.)

- Fourth, the achievement test can directly inform teachers about what level of instruction is probably needed. This can be particularly helpful either if the children have not been administered an achievement test or if the state achievement test scores are insufficiently challenging for many students.

- Fifth, census testing allows one to use local norms in addition to national norms.

When averaging scores on the ability test (here CogAT Verbal) and the achievement test (here ITBS Reading), one once again selects those students in the upper right corner of the scatter plot that is defined by the two tests. But when we use the average of the two test scores, students are ranked by the projection of their scores on the dashed diagonal line, as seen in Figure 4. Here, students indicated by an x in the plot would be admitted using the average score. Look at the point where the circles end and the x's begin. The students at this meeting point fall on the line that is perpendicular to the dashed diagonal line. These students have the same *average* score on the two tests. For students above the dashed diagonal, the ITBS reading score was greater than the CogAT verbal reasoning score; for students with scores below the line, the verbal reasoning score was greater. But the average score was the same for all of these students. Note too that some of those who would be admitted using the average score would be excluded by fixed cut scores on either test.

For example, consider the case in which the cut scores on both tests are set at the 95th PR. As Figure 4 shows, the wedge of x's to the left of a CogAT SAS score of 125 would be excluded. Similarly, the wedge of x's below the ITBS Reading score of 200 would also be excluded. Some of these students have very high scores on one test and surely should be considered for special pro-

gramming. Using the *"and"* rule excludes them unless both cut scores are set at a lower value (e.g, the 90th PR). However, lowering the cut scores increases the number of students who must be administered both tests and also the number who are unlikely to succeed in the program. Importantly, the differences between the *"and"* rule and the *"average"* rule are small when the correlation between the two tests is very high ($r = .8$ or greater). This is why the example of the CogAT Screening Form followed by the full CogAT is unusual.

## SUMMARY.

Although it is administratively convenient, the *"and"* rule is generally less effective than the *"average"* rule when combining information across tests. If the more convenient rule is used, then one must be satisfied with a system that excludes many students who could have been admitted had they been given the chance to take the second test. The example in which the CogAT Screening Form was followed by the complete CogAT Form 7 was a noteworthy exception to this rule. Finally, although one can estimate the effects of different cut scores using the tables and figures in this chapter, the best way to establish effective cut scores on a newly implemented selection system is to administer both tests to all students or a representative sample of the student population and plot the results.

## INCLUDING RATINGS IN A SELECTION SYSTEM

### WHY RATINGS CAN BE HELPFUL

Schools should endeavor to identify students who exhibit unusual talent in any domain that

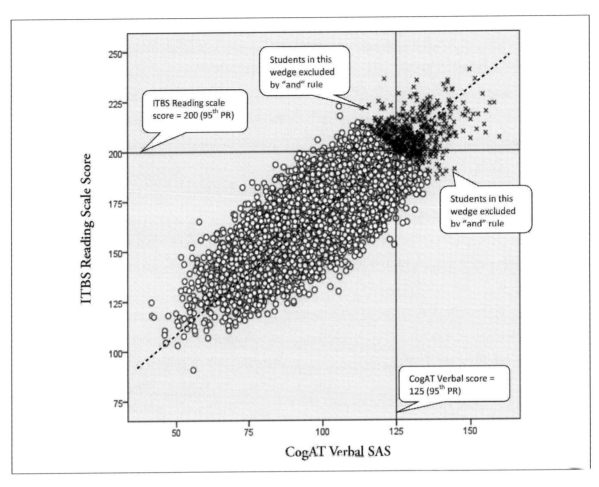

**Figure 4.** Scatter plot of SAS scores on CogAT Verbal and scale scores on ITBS Reading Total. Students are selected by the average of their scores on the two tests. Any line drawn perpendicular to the dashed line identifies students with the same average score. Those who fall on the diagonal have exactly the same score on the two tests.

the school can help develop, either through its own programs or through collaboration with other agencies in the community. This is a broader charge than identifying the sorts of academic talent that are required by the standard school curriculum. The objective assessments of ability and achievement that we have emphasized clearly focus on this important but narrower conception of talent. However, even within the domains of academic talent, it is important to assess a student's motivation and perseverance in the pursuit of excellence within the available training systems. Many theories of giftedness also

emphasize the critical importance of creativity. Rating scales provide one way to gather this sort of information.

## CAUTIONS WHEN USING RATING SCALES

Rating scales can add important information to the selection or classification decision, or they can add noise. There is a saying among personnel psychologists: If you want to add noise to a hiring decision, conduct interviews. Personal interviews often do not increase the accuracy of the selection decision. Because they are significantly less reliable and valid than other measures, adding points for the interview often adds more noise than information to the decision.

The goal of any good assessment is to transform subjective impressions into objective information. Gathering this information requires more than soliciting teachers' intuitive impressions of children. Rather, well-constructed rating scales aim to make the teacher's subjective impressions more objective by anchoring them to specific behaviors. Similarly, judgments of the quality of a complex performance (e.g., dance, essay, debate, or painting) are rendered more objective by the quality of the scoring rubric that is used to assign points to different aspects of the performance and how well raters are trained in using the rubric. Therefore, although it is important to try to capture aspects of performances that are poorly sampled by traditional assessments, proper use of these measures requires considerable professional judgment and training.

Ratings from teachers who are unfamiliar with the characteristics of gifted children or untrained in using the rating scale often add more noise than useful information. This noise often comes in the form of halo effects (i.e., giving consistently high or low ratings to a student across different items or dimensions). Halo effects occur because the rating that is given reflects the psychology of the rater as well the events that the rater observed. What one teacher interprets as disruption, another may interpret as creativity. Attempts to gather ratings on multiple dimensions are prone to halo effects (Cronbach, 1990), especially when the dimensions are known to be highly correlated. For example, the *Gifted Rating Scales (GRS)* (Pfeiffer &

Jarosewich, 2003) ask teachers to rate students on several dimensions, including ability and achievement. The ratings for these two scales (ability and achievement) correlated $r = .95$ in the standardization sample. A correlation of this magnitude means that teachers did not distinguish between the two constructs.

Halo effects should also be suspected if measures of internal consistency (e.g., coefficient alpha) for individual scales are extremely high (i.e., greater than .80). For example, it is well-known that creativity is at best only moderately correlated across different domains. If the creativity scale asks for ratings of students in different domains, then a high coefficient alpha for the scale indicates that raters gave students similar ratings across all domains. This invalidates the ratings. Indeed, the proper measure of reliability for rating scales is given by the correlations between the ratings made by independent observers on different occasions. On the *GRS*, for example, coefficient alpha for each of the five scales (ability, achievement, creativity, artistic talent, leadership, and motivation) ranged from .97 to .99. However, inter-rater reliabilities ranged from .64 to .79. The latter values better estimate the reliability of the ratings; the former tell us that teachers did not vary much in the ratings that they gave to children across items within each scale.

Some of the better rating scales emphasize specific behaviors in context ("is often the last student to stop working on a test when there are no time limits") rather than general traits ("perseveres"). However, unless the contexts covered in the statements effectively sample all of the contexts of interest, contextualizing the ratings with more elaborate statements may not be helpful. Unlike reasoning abilities, traits such as creativity, motivation, and perseverance are much more situation specific. The boy who exhibits remarkable perseverance in conquering video games may show precious little perseverance in academic domains.

## PROBLEMS IN COMBINING RATINGS WITH OTHER MEASURES

Most schools that gather ratings assign them a point value and then combine the ratings with test scores and other assessment data. This can be effective if the ratings are as reliable and as valid as the other measures. If not, then even assigning ratings a lesser weight (or point value) can be problematic. For example, although one could certainly justify providing enrichment opportunities to a child whom a teacher rates as highly creative, it would be difficult to defend a decision to deny the opportunity for advanced instruction to a child who received lower ratings on creativity but obtained high ability and achievement test scores. Yet this can easily happen when points are summed across diverse measures. *For every child who gains admission because of high ratings or scores on the creativity test, another with equally high test scores is denied admission because of lower ratings or test scores.* An effective way to overcome this dilemma is to use ratings (and other measures that are potentially less reliable and valid) to provide opportunity but never to remove it.

## A PARADIGM FOR INCORPORATING RATINGS WITH ABILITY AND ACHIEVEMENT TEST SCORES

Box 2 shows an identification procedure that uses teacher ratings to provide enrichment oppor-

tunities (Lohman & Renzulli, 2007). Although the example uses both ability and achievement test scores, ability test scores could be used alone. Similarly, although the example uses three scales from the *Scales for Rating the Behavioral Characteristics of Superior Students* (SRBCSS; Renzulli et al., 2004), other teacher rating scales or measures (e.g., a creativity test) could be used. The vertical dimension distinguishes children who exhibit superior abilities from those who exhibit above-average abilities. We have arbitrarily set the cut points as scoring at or above the 97th local PR or at or above the 80th local PR on either a verbal-reading or a quantitative-nonverbal-mathematics composite. The first criterion is commonly used in gifted programs; the second is recommended when casting a broader talent net (Renzulli, 2005). The horizontal dimension distinguishes between children who, when compared to other children *nominated* for the program, obtain above-average teacher ratings on any one of the three SRBCSS main scales (Learning Motivation, and Creativity) and students who obtain average or below-average teacher ratings.[12] Note that, for ratings, the average is computed only on the subset of the student population who are nominated for inclusion in the program. Asking teachers to provide ratings for all students is usually neither practical nor possible. Combining these two criteria gives four categories of assessment results shown in Figure 5.

---

12. Because one is using an *"or"* rule, considerably more than half of the students will be in Categories I or III than in II or IV. If the correlations among the scales are known, one could estimate this proportion from Figure 3. If a smaller fraction of the population is desired, then the selection rule could be changed to, say, top quartile versus all others on any one of the three rating scales.

**Box 2**

**A Procedure for Combining Test scores and Teacher Ratings** (Lohman & Renzulli, 2007)

Here are steps for implementing this procedure.

1. Enter percentile ranks (PRs) from the three CogAT batteries (Verbal, Quantitative, and Nonverbal) in the first column of the worksheet.
2. Convert Percentile Ranks (PRs) to points using Table 1. Enter these points in the worksheet below.
3. Average the points for the Quantitative and Nonverbal batteries. Enter this value on the worksheet.
4. Sum the points for CogAT Verbal and Reading Total.
5. Sum the points for the CogAT Quant-Nonverbal Composite (from step 3) and Mathematics Total.
6. Enter ratings for the three SRBCSS scales.
7. Compute the average teacher rating on each of the three SRBCSS scale for the group of students who were nominated for the program.

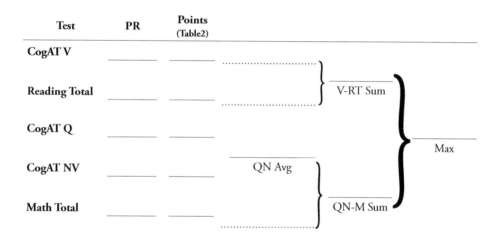

The point totals for the composite verbal/reading total and the composite quant/nonverbal/mathematics total can now be used to identify students. Figure 5 assumes that cut points are set at the 80th and 96th PRs.

- Children in *Category I* exhibit superior reasoning and achievement in either the Verbal-Reading or Math-Quant-Nonverbal domains. These children are also rated as highly capable, motivated, or creative by their teachers.

- Children in *Category II* also exhibit superior reasoning and achievement but, when compared to other children who were nominated, are not rated as highly by their teachers on any one of the three major scales of the SRBCSS. Programs that follow a traditional identification scheme (e.g., self-contained classrooms or schools) would accept children in Category I. Most would also accept children in Category II, especially if it is difficult to defend rejection on the basis of a low teacher rating. Either way, the progress of children in Category II should be monitored more closely.

- Children in *Category III* exhibit somewhat lower but strong reasoning abilities (between 80th and 96th PR) on one of the ability-achievement composites and are rated as highly capable, motivated, or creative by their teachers. These children would be included in school-wide enrichment programs that aim to serve a broader range of children (Renzulli, 2005). Schools with highly diverse student populations would find that many of their best students from underrepresented groups would fall in this category. Combining test scores and ratings in this way would enable these schools to identify the students most likely to benefit from curriculum compacting or enrichment

programs, including instruction at a higher level than that received by most other students in the school.

- Finally, children in *Category IV* exhibit good but not exceptional abilities (between 80th and 96th PR) but are not rated as unusually capable, motivated, or creative by their teachers. Although good students, these children would not be provided with special programming on the basis of either their ability-achievement scores or teacher ratings. However, if the needs of students for special services are routinely re-evaluated, then these students would be considered anew at each evaluation. [13]

## OTHER SOURCES OF INFORMATION

Many sources of information other than the formal procedures discussed in this chapter can help professionals make better decisions about which children to assist and how to assist them. For example, unbeknownst to their teachers, children often develop substantial levels of competence in particular domains. A good talent identification system will try to discover children's interests and build on their developing expertise in the domain. Interests that the child has maintained for several years are particularly important. Science fairs, music recitals, art exhibitions, and similar events can be especially helpful in this regard. Formal interest inventories can also be quite helpful. For example, the Renzulli Learning System (www.renzullilearning.com) uses an interest inventory to help direct

---

13. One could combine this procedure with the multiple norm group procedure, especially for identifying ELL students who show promise in the verbal-reading domain.

| | | TEACHER RATING ON LEARNING, MOTIVATION, OR CREATIVITY | |
|---|---|---|---|
| | | BELOW AVERAGE TEACHER RATINGS | ABOVE AVERAGE TEACHER RATINGS |
| **COGAT VERBAL + READING T. OR COGAT QN + MATH T.** | **8 OR MORE POINTS (≥96TH PR)** | II | I |
| | **2 – 7 POINTS (80TH – 95TH PR)** | IV | III |

**Figure 5.** Using CogAT, achievement test scores, and teacher ratings.

the child toward web sites that describe projects that might engage the child.

There is no easy way to quantify this sort of information, nor is there usually a need to do so. Understanding a child's interests and particular competencies is most useful when deciding how best to engage the child rather than whether to admit the child to a program. The sorts of information that we have emphasized—measures of general reasoning abilities in different symbol systems; academic achievement in reading, mathematics, and particular content domains; and the ratings of trained observers—should always form the bedrock for selection decisions.

## DECISION MAKING: SOME GENERAL PRINCIPLES FOR IDENTIFICATION

The general principles summarized in this section necessarily combine topics discussed in this chapter and elsewhere in this book, especially Chapter 12.

## PRINCIPLE #1: CONGRUENCE BETWEEN IDENTIFICATION MEASURES AND PROGRAM ACTIVITIES

"There must be congruence between the criteria used in the identification process and the goals and types of services that constitute the day-to-day activities that students will pursue" (Renzulli, 2005, p. 11). The best prediction of success in any situation will be given by a properly weighted combination of measures of those personal characteristics that are required for successful learning or performance in that situation. Some of these traits will predict success in many other situations. Other traits will be unique to that situation. The goal in developing an identification system is to achieve a balance between the extremes of measuring general traits that only moderately predict success in many activities and situations and measuring a larger set of unique traits that are tuned to success in particular situations.

A reliable measure of general ability predicts success across a wide variety of cognitively demanding tasks. But one can improve the prediction by understanding the cognitive and affective demands of the educational activities that the students will pursue. If instruction is in creative writing, then the identification criteria should aim to find students who bring the requisite verbal abilities, writing skills, and interests to the table. A high score on a nonverbal intelligence test would not be the most effective measure. If the program emphasized mathematical problem solving, then scores on the nonverbal ability test would be more appropriate since nonverbal tests better predict success in mathematics than in more verbally-demanding domains. One would do even better in predicting success in future mathematics courses by also measuring students' quantitative reasoning abilities, their current achievement in mathematics, their general interest in mathematics, and their interest in participating in the particular instructional opportunities at hand.

Measures of the specific aptitudes required by a learning situation better predict success in that learning situation and thus better identify those students who are more likely to succeed in the talent-development program. This applies to students from all ethnic and cultural backgrounds. More distal measures, such as tests of general ability or overall academic achievement, would be preferred only in those circumstances in which the learning is similarly undifferentiated. In this respect, the prediction of cognitive skills mirrors the prediction of physical skills. A measure of general physical fitness provides a moderate prediction of success across a wide range of physically demanding activities. But if the goal is to identify athletes most likely to benefit from advanced training in basketball, then measures of the physical attributes and skills required for success in basketball will

dramatically reduce the errors in identification. Even with these more proximal measures, though, a measure of general physical fitness will often add to the prediction of success. Similarly, when it is available, the best measure of future success in mathematics, science, creative writing, art, or any other domain is evidence of prior success in that domain. But a measure of general reasoning ability will often improve the prediction of success, especially over the long haul. Even then, prediction will be superior if the test measures reasoning abilities in the symbol systems) most required for future learning in the domain. For example, a measure of verbal reasoning will better predict success in verbally demanding domains than a measure of general reasoning ability that averages across verbal and nonverbal domains.

## PRINCIPLE #2: IDENTIFICATION AS AN ONGOING TASK

Studies of the development of cognitive and academic abilities show a consistent pattern. Correlations among test scores are highest for assessments closest in time and decline systematically with increases in the interval between assessments (Lohman & Korb, 2006). This pattern (called a simplex) means that many who excel on the earliest assessment do not excel on later assessments. For tests of general intelligence administered to elementary-age children, the drop-off after one year is about 50% of those children who scored in the top 3% on the first year. The drop-off increases with the interval between test and retest. Further, for every child who drops out of the top group, another moves into it. Changes are particularly great in the early elementary years. Although there are other reasons to encourage an ongoing identification and placement process, these data cry out for an ongoing identification process. They are also blatantly inconsistent with policies that assume "once gifted, always gifted."

## PRINCIPLE #3: USE MULTIPLE MEASURES

Talent is best identified by a combination of measures that sample current accomplishments in a domain and the promise of future excellence. Invariably, this is best done using measures that focus on the domain in question. For example, talent in mathematics is indicated by evidence of unusual achievement in mathematics; strong quantitative and spatial reasoning abilities; interest in mathematical puzzles, games, and occupations; and evidence of persistence in acquiring competence in a mathematics or a related discipline. Similarly, domain-focused measures can be used to identify talent in creative writing, science, music, art, and any other area in which the program has, or could develop, educational programs.

## PRINCIPLE #4: COMBINE MEASURES APPROPRIATELY

When using scores on a multi-aptitude ability or achievement test battery, use the *"or"* rule to identify children who have talents in different domains. When focusing on a particular domain, avoid multiple hurdles (the *"and"* rule), unless the correlation between the measures is very high ($r$ = .8 or greater.). Instead, average scale scores that have similar variabilities. Avoid throwing away information by converting scale scores to PRs and, again, by converting ranges of PRs to points that are summed. Use less reliable

and valid measures (e.g., teacher ratings, measures of creativity) to provide opportunities but not to remove them. Do not simply add points for such measures to points earned on ability and achievement tests. Rather, use something like the Lohman-Renzulli procedure when using such information.

## PRINCIPLE #5: USE MULTIPLE PERSPECTIVES: NATIONAL, LOCAL, AND OPPORTUNITY TO LEARN

The need for special programming depends primarily on the discrepancy between a child's levels of cognitive and academic development and that of her immediate peers. How other children in the nation (or world) are performing is interesting but not of primary import when instruction is to be delivered locally. Those who find this odd should consider how athletes are chosen for varsity teams. The inference of talent (or aptitude) is only justified when one has controlled for significant variations in opportunity to learn. This is generally a much more palatable idea if the goal is to identify talent rather than giftedness. Few would argue with the goal of identifying the most talented writers in particular segments of the population and assisting them in the development of their writing talent. Labeling children as "gifted" simply invites controversy and implies that one "is" or "is not" a member of a fixed and exclusive category.

## PRINCIPLE #6: USE THE MOST RELIABLE (AND VALID) MEASURES POSSIBLE

Errors of measurement are the primary cause of instability (especially regression to the mean) for the highest scores in a group. These errors are much larger than most people realize, even on tests that have acceptable levels of reliability for those scoring near the mean. In Chapter 12 (see Table 1 in that chapter), we showed that some widely-used screening tests have standard errors of 6 or more IQ-like points. This translates to a 67% confidence interval of over 12 points and a 95% confidence interval of 24 points for scores near the mean. For extreme scores, the confidence intervals would be several times wider and skewed toward the mean. Such large errors mean that many students who should have been admitted will not be admitted, and many who are admitted should not have been admitted. This helps no one. In addition to using the most reliable tests available, one can dramatically reduce regression effects by combining scores across similar measures. Thus, when it is appropriate, one can combine scores on a measure of ability and achievement. Or, one can combine scores on different ability tests (e.g., the Quantitative and Nonverbal batteries of CogAT).

## PRINCIPLE #7: THE HIGHER THE STAKES, THE COSTLIER THE ERRORS

There are two sides to this issue. On the one hand, if one is attempting to decide whether a child is sufficiently precocious to be admitted to a special school for the gifted, then errors in selection or placement can have deleterious consequences for the child and the system. On the other hand, if the program is deliberately formulated to minimize the need for high selectivity and long term decisions, then errors (although always troublesome) have less draconian consequences. School-based programs should aspire to this ideal rather than attempt to perpetuate a model that assumes that the only "truly gifted children" are those who achieve

Full Scale scores well in excess of 130 on an individually administered intelligence test and whose educational needs exceed what any but the largest schools or school systems might be equipped to offer.

## PRINCIPLE #8: EMPHASIZE TALENT IDENTIFICATION AND DEVELOPMENT, NOT GIFTEDNESS

A talent identification and development perspective (see Chapter 12) leads to different beliefs about the purpose of identification than traditional beliefs about giftedness. A giftedness perspective encourages program administrators to make qualitative distinctions between gifted and nongifted children. It encourages one-time identification early in primary school and, if possible, permanent separation into special classes or schools. Returns to a "nongifted" status are discouraged or explicitly disallowed. It encourages the use of identification methods that favor only those children who show promise of excellence in all domains. Programs tend to be exclusive, even elitist. Admission requirements emphasize IQ scores or the use of national norms on ability and/or achievement tests. Parents often covet the label of "gifted" for their child and will go to great lengths to obtain it. At the same time, program administrators often must go to great lengths to achieve better racial and ethnic balance in their programs, often switching among tests or using inferior assessment practices in order to achieve these goals. On the positive side, the children who are identified are a relatively rarefied group who, although different in many other respects, tend to achieve at high levels in most all academic domains.

A talent identification and development perspective encourages an ongoing identification process. It is expected that children will cycle in and out of the program as they mature and the level of support and academic challenge that they need changes. It encourages a multidimensional rather than unidimensional identification model; it is expected that many children will excel in one or two domains and not in others. It encourages direct links between identification practices and development activities. This discourages the use of poorly validated thinking skills programs and other generic activities that make little if any contribution to the development of specific talents in mathematics, science, creative writing, and other disciplines.

It encourages the use of local and even subgroup norms in addition to national norms. This eliminates or greatly reduces the need to make ad hoc modifications to the identification process in order to serve more poor, minority, and ELL children. Further, because educational programming is guided by current levels of talent development, there is no need to worry about using different criteria for identification of talent in students who have had different educational, linguistic, and cultural opportunities. It is an inclusive model that will propel gifted education programs well into the 21st century by providing diverse students the ability to excel in their talent domains.

## REFERENCES

Cronbach, L. J. (1990). *Essentials of psychological testing* (5th ed.). New York: Harper & Row.

Delisle, J. (2010, March 31). What educators can learn from Sarah Palin. *Education Week, 29* (27), p. 25.

Hernstein, R. & Murray, C. (1994). *The bell curve.* NY: Free Press.

Lakin, J. M., & Lohman, D. F. (2011). The predictive accuracy of verbal, quantitative, and nonverbal reasoning tests: Consequences for talent identification and program diversity. *Journal for the Education of the Gifted, 34,* 595–623.

Lemann, N. (1999). *The big test. The secret history of the American meritocracy.* New York: Farrar, Straus and Giroux

Lohman, D. F. (1994). Spatial ability. In R. J. Sternberg (Ed.), *Encyclopedia of human intelligence* (pp. 1000–1007). New York: Macmillan.

Lohman, D. F. (2011). *Cognitive Abilities Test (Form 7).* Rolling Meadows, IL: Riverside Publishing Company.

Lohman, D. F., & Korb, K. A. (2006). Gifted today but not tomorrow? Longitudinal changes in *ITBS* and *CogAT* scores during elementary school. *Journal for the Education of the Gifted, 29,* 451–484.

Lohman, D. F., Korb, K., & Lakin, J. (2008). Identifying academically gifted English language learners using nonverbal tests: A comparison of the Raven, NNAT, and CogAT. *Gifted Child Quarterly, 52,* 275–296.

Lohman, D. F., & Lakin, J. M. (2009). Consistencies in sex differences on the Cognitive Abilities Test across countries, grades, and cohorts. *British Journal of Educational Psychology, 79,* 389–40.

Lohman, D. F., & Renzulli, J. S. (2007). *A simple procedure for combining ability test scores, achievement test scores, and teacher ratings to identify academically talented children.* Retrieved from http://faculty.education.uiowa.edu/dlohman

National Association for Gifted Children (2010). *Use of the WISC-IV for gifted identification.* Retrieved from http://www.nagc.org/uploadedFiles/Information_and_Resources/Position_Papers/WISC-IV.pdf

Pfeiffer, S., & Jarosewich, T. (2003). *Gifted Rating Scales.* San Antonio, TX: The Psychological Corporation.

Renzulli, J. S. (2005). *Equity, excellence, and economy in a system for identifying students in gifted education: A guidebook* (RM05208). Storrs, CT: The National Research Center on the Gifted and Talented, University of Connecticut.

Renzulli, J. S., Smith, L. H., White, A. J., Callahan, C. M., Hartman, R. K., Westberg, M., Gavin, K., Reis, S. M., Siegle, D., & Sytsma, R. E. (2004). *Scales for Rating the Behavioral Characteristics of Superior Students.* Mansfield Center, CT: Creative Learning Press.

Schoen, H. L. & Ansley, T. N. (2005). *Iowa Algebra Aptitude Test* (5th edition). Rolling Meadows, IL: Riverside Publishing Company.

Zwick, R. (2004). *Rethinking the SAT: The future of standardized testing in university admissions.* New York: RoutledgeFalmer

## CHAPTER 10. DECISION STRATEGIES

**Prompt 1** *Knowledge*

Explain the distinctions among the *"and"* rule, the *"or"* rule, and the *"average"* rule.

**Prompt 2** *Opinion*

Explain which of the cautions given for classification decisions is most serious if ignored. Why do you believe this to be the case?

**Prompt 3 Affect**

The author indicates that because of limited resources, schools must choose those students most likely to benefit from certain activities to participate in those activities. When are such limitations helpful to you? When are they hurtful?

**Prompt 4** *Experience*

Explain the degree to which any two of the principles articulated in this chapter have been followed or ignored in your school setting.

**Prompt 5** *Preconception/Misconception*

Explain why the use of composite scores from ability tests or achievement tests is not recommended by the authors of this chapter.

# CHAPTER 11

# EXPERIENCE WITH IDEALIZED IDENTIFICATION PROCEDURES

SCOTT L. HUNSAKER, UTAH STATE UNIVERSITY

From time to time in working with school districts, a consultant is given permission to implement what he or she would consider to be an ideal in an area of expertise. This opportunity has been given to me on at least three occasions during which I was asked to assist in formulating identification procedures. This chapter presents three systems—pyramid identification, careful consideration, and cluster identification—that were developed for rather specific purposes, but that can provide some sense of what identification might be if some traditional barriers, such as over-reliance on testing or use of rigid cut-offs, were removed. The systems are drawn (1) in the case of pyramid identification from a program that predated much of the current popularity of the *response-to-intervention* models now employed in special education, but which is built on a similar idea, (2) in the case of careful consideration, from a federally funded program focused on advanced readers, and (3) in the case of cluster identification from a program in a school district that was implementing *professional learning communities* as a means for teachers to study and respond to student learning needs. A focus in all these systems is the use of professional decision making as key to matching gifted education services (or otherwise) with student needs.

## SYSTEM 1: PYRAMID IDENTIFICATION

The first identification procedure, pyramid identification, borrows from the practice of *response-to-intervention* (RTI) now employed in special education. According to Vanderheyden (2011),

> When properly implemented RTI generates a dataset that allows educators to respond to students' learning needs and determine when their needs for instructional support outpace the capacity of general education. RTI can facilitate coherent and continuous support for student learning that transcends the eligibility decision and could create a more logical and transparent system of service delivery for students, parents, and families. (p. 335)

Identification models similar to RTI have been employed in gifted education previously and have often been referred to as pyramid models (Cox, Daniel, & Boston, 1985). Such a pyramid is shown in Figure 1. In this model, interventions to address student learning needs are provided at different levels. Interventions at Tier 1 are those available to all students. If it appears that these interventions are insufficient to meet a student's needs, information is gathered to determine if the next level of interventions, Tier 2, would be more appropriate. When Tier 2 interventions appear not to be sufficient to meet student needs, then further information is gathered to determine if Tier 3 intervention might better address them, and so on to Tier 4. As Tier 1 interventions are available to all students, Tier 2 interventions are available to most students, Tier 3 interventions are available to some students, and Tier 4 interventions are available to few students. It is the student's response to the specific level of intervention that triggers the need to gather additional data. This chapter focuses on a systematic means of making appropriate identifications at the Tier 1 level only.

A four-level pyramid model was used to articulate the comprehensive gifted program design for the school district in which this first system was used. For the first level, Tier 1, activities that were available to enrich the lives of all students included Spelling Bee, History Day, Geography Bee, Future Problem Solving, Science Fair, Junior Great Books, and Community Youth Orchestra. The identification activities at this level were called pre-screening. More formalized procedures such as those described in other chapters in this text were used for the remaining tiers, which lead to placement in language arts cluster classrooms, pull-out programs, full-time magnet classrooms, and the like. School district personnel believed that the most fundamental decisions concerning the development of gifts and talents belong to the parents and students. Thus, pre-screening represents a determination by parents and students to commit personal resources and to use their school and community resources for a particular talent development opportunity. Following from this belief, pre-screening has three components that occur on a continuing basis throughout the students' academic experience (see Figure 2):

(a) parent/student assessment of abilities, interests, motivations;

(b) discussion of abilities, interests, and motivations with appropriate educators; and

(c) meeting enrollment requirements of specific talent development opportunities.

The graphic in Figure 2 implies no particular time sequence to the components. Each would occur naturally as the student develops new interests, educators notice emerging abilities, or talent development opportunities become available. The shaded area represents the space in which actual involvement in a talent development program might occur.

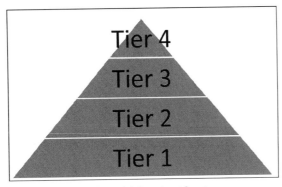

**Figure 1.** Pyramid model for identification

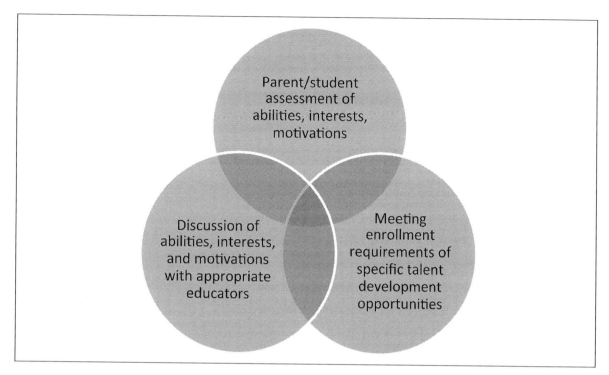

**Figure 2.** Components of pre-screening.

Parent and student assessment of interests and motivations should begin as early as possible in a student's academic career. Parents should share their personal academic passions with students early in life. Students should be encouraged to explore a wide variety of experiences. As the student shows greater interest in any particular area, opportunities to explore that area in-depth should be provided. Continuous discussion between parents and students about what the student enjoys doing, what the student does well, and why certain activities are chosen for the student is the hallmark of this component of pre-screening.

Discussion of interests and motivations with appropriate educators provides an opportunity for outside input into the development of a student's gifts and talents. Parents and students may learn about new interests to explore from a child's teachers, coaches, counselors, or advisors. The educator may

be aware of programs and resources not known to the family or may be able to identify curricular areas in which the student has shown particular promise.

Meeting the enrollment requirements of specific talent development opportunities is often necessary based on the goals of program and any resource constraints they may have. Some may be offered by the school district; others may be available within the community through local government entities, churches, service organizations, or businesses. Information about these programs is often communicated to students and parents through school newsletters, newspaper articles, posters, parent-teacher conferences, announcements at school meetings, and the like. It is the responsibility of parents and students to inquire about these opportunities and to meet enrollment requirements. What is key here for school personnel to understand are the aims of programs such as Future Problem Solving, Junior Great Books, or science fairs. In some school districts, such programs are reserved for identified gifted and talented students and, in some cases, serve as the gifted and talented program. While there is certainly some overlap between the goals of these talent development programs and services for gifted-level learners, such exclusive participation practices are likely not justified in most cases, especially if these special programs are conducted after school or by community volunteers, which they often are in many school settings.

Again, it should be emphasized that this more open identification procedure was employed for Tier 1 activities only. Access to Tier 2 through 4 services was obtained through more traditional identification processes. However, a strong message is delivered through this type of identification procedure at this level—that the gifted and talented program in the school district takes a keen interest in the development of abilities of all students in the district.

## SYSTEM 2: CAREFUL CONSIDERATION

The second system—careful consideration—was developed by a cooperative group of school districts and an institution of higher education in Utah, which successfully competed for and implemented a project under the federal Javits program focused on the needs of advanced readers. The project included components of identification, professional development, classroom implementation, and program evaluation. The project was called Advanced Readers at Risk (ARAR), and *advanced readers* were defined as students who read well

above grade level and who require instruction beyond that normally provided at grade level to continuously improve as a reader, as determined by a professional educator trained in the characteristics and needs of advanced readers. (More information on the project in its entirety can be obtained from Bartlett and Hunsaker [2009], Hunsaker, Nielsen, and Bartlett [2010], and Odoardi [2010].)

The phrase *careful consideration* was drawn initially from the philosophy of Dr. Mary Frasier (Frasier & Passow, 1994) that educators need to be careful, in both senses of the term—the affective and the procedural—as the carry out the processes of identification. In one sense of the word, educators need to be full of care as they make decisions about students. That is, educators need to remember that decisions are being made about living, breathing human beings who can be greatly affected by the outcomes of those decisions. Secondly, educators need to take full care as they make decisions about students. That is, educators need to be vigilant that processes are followed faithfully, the assessment data are understood completely, and that decisions recognize the "the identification of talent potential and the cultivation of that potential as integrated processes" (Frasier & Passow, 1994, p. 7).

In like manner, the word *consideration* has a dual connotation—both cognitive and affective. In the cognitive sense, the word consideration implies that thorough and thoughtful examination of data and processes has been conducted while making decisions about individual students. In the affective sense, the word consideration implies that the professionals making the decisions have done so in a way that is considerate of the learner, that treats the student in a respectful, courteous manner—having the students' best interests at heart and giving the benefit of the doubt where possible.

With this philosophy in mind, leaders of the Advanced Readers at Risk Project (ARAR) articulated three bases upon which identification of advanced readers would be founded:

- Classroom Basis—Teachers explore or generate data on students in their own classrooms as a primary basis for identification of advanced readers.

- Multiple Pathways—A variety of criteria are used for identification, including standardized aptitude tests, normed achievement tests, criterion referenced tests, and teacher rating scales, any of which can qualify a student as an advanced reader.

- Inclusiveness—Students not identified as advanced readers benefit from the im-

provement in the teacher's instructional skill as the teacher is not limited to implementing principles and strategies with advanced readers only.

From this foundation, the ARAR Steering Committee (which included individuals from higher education, local school districts, and an outside consulting agency and, within that group, individuals with expertise in gifted education, literacy education, and program evaluation) developed a standard for identification of advanced readers that all participating teachers were expected to meet. The standard is provided in Table 1.

The careful consideration system established to assist teachers to meet this standard consisted of four stages, each applying a different type of consideration. Stage 1, labeled *general consideration*, required the educator to describe the general classroom environment in which consideration occurred, including an instructional description

Table 1. Identification of Advanced Readers Standard

| COMPONENT #1: IDENTIFICATION OF ADVANCED READERS | | | |
|---|---|---|---|
| 1 | 2 | 3 | 4 |
| Giving careful consideration to all relevant data, the teacher applies established criteria for standardized tests, criterion-referenced tests, informal reading inventories, and research-based teacher rating scales to identify a student as an advanced reader. | The teacher applies established criteria for standardized tests, criterion-referenced tests, informal reading inventories, and research-based teacher rating scales to identify a student as an advanced reader, but ignores other relevant data that may help better understand student performance. | The teacher applies only one of the established criteria to identify a student as an advanced reader. | The teacher makes no consideration of who is an advanced reader. |

of content and strategies used that are conducive to advanced readers displaying their characteristics and needs, as well as the timeframe over which instruction and observation of students as readers occurred. Stage 2, labeled *specific consideration*, required the educator to describe her or his particular awareness of student strengths, interests, needs, and learning styles, including descriptions of school-based strengths, interests, needs, and styles based on observed behaviors, choices, and performance during reading instruction, sustained silent reading, read-aloud, and the like, and outside-of-school strengths, interests, needs, and styles based on reading habits, preferences, and so forth reported by parents, child care professionals, community librarians, or others who would have this information concerning the child. These two stages emphasize the idea that "whether or how a particular trait or characteristic will be manifested depends on the context in which it exists or is exercised" (Frasier & Passow, 1994, p. 6).

Stage 3 of the careful consideration system, labeled *criterial consideration*, leans more completely on a traditional view of identification, but with an inclusive twist. In this stage the educator assembles and analyzes at least three psychometric data points to determine performance levels, any one of which qualifies a student as an advanced reader. Specific criteria are as follows:

- A score at least at the 75th percentile on a relevant subsection of a standardized test (e.g., verbal aptitude or total reading achievement); or

- An assessed reading level two years or more ahead of current grade level on an informal reading inventory; or

- A three-year pattern of performance at the highest level on a state-developed criterion-referenced test (e.g., end-of-level test); or

- A raw score higher than 35 on the Reading Scale of the *Scales for Rating the Behavior of Superior Students* (Renzulli et al., 2010).

Table 2 displays the results of the criterial stage from the first year of the ARAR project. Teachers involved in the project were drawn from Title 1 and non-Title 1 schools. The chart categorizes the students according to their placement with the teacher who identified them for participation as an advanced reader in the ARAR project. Thus, at first glance, it appears that non-Title 1 teachers are identifying students as advanced readers at a higher rate than Title 1 teachers. However, the data in this chart miss two important parts of the story. First, some of the teachers from Title 1 schools, upon first entering the project, made claims that they had no advanced readers in their classes. The fact that these teachers ended up finding, on average, about 14 students they could identify as advanced readers indicates a significant shift in attitude. Second, teachers for the ARAR project were drawn from regular classrooms and gifted magnet classrooms. All gifted magnet classrooms in this project happened to be housed at non-Title 1 schools. This means that advanced readers placed in these classrooms from Title 1 schools have been counted in the non-Title 1 school row. When project leaders realized this, it was too late to go back to the data and determine how many magnet school students identified as advanced readers originated from Title 1 schools (because of the

**Table 2.** ARAR Identification Totals by School Type

| | ADVANCED READER IDENTIFICATION TOTALS | | | | |
|---|---|---|---|---|---|
| | STUDENTS | | TEACHERS | | |
| | **N** | **%** | **N** | **%** | **S:T RATIO** |
| **T1** | 283 | 59.5 | 20 | 64.5 | 14.15 |
| **NT1** | 193 | 40.5 | 11 | 36.5 | 17.55 |
| **TOTAL** | 476 | 100 | 31 | 100 | 15.35 |
| TI: Title 1 School | | | | | |
| NTI: Non-Title 1 School | | | | | |

use of code numbers rather than names to protect student identity). Thus the discrepancy between the rates of identification is not as pronounced as shown in the table.

Stage 4 of the careful consideration system is labeled *additional consideration*. In this stage, the educator is invited to apply additional considerations if she or he believes that psychometric data points are not accurate. The educators then provides descriptions of the justification for additional considerations, detailing why psychometric data points are not accurate due to specific, known testing conditions or student environmental conditions (e.g., cultural, language, economic, or family factors), as well as other evidence such as performance on demanding reading tasks or other outstanding reading accomplishments. Teachers are encouraged to maintain an assessment journal when they are proctoring standardized assessments to note any unusual conditions that can then be documented as described. Through this means, a strong case can be made for disregarding quantitative data points that otherwise would indicate that the student is not an advanced reader. This stage can also be used when other data points do not exist. For example, in one case in this project, a student transferred to a participating school district because of an evacuation due to hurricane damage in his home school. Because the school and its records no longer existed and other quantitative data points could not be produced in a timely fashion, other observed reading activities inside and outside the classroom were used to document the student's eligibility for the program.

In analyzing the procedures used in the careful consideration system, it is apparent that a great deal of trust is placed in teachers as professionals who are uniquely trained to make decisions about appropriate instructional interventions for their students. The professional development aspect of this project in which teachers learned the characteristics of advanced readers, the use of criteria, the skills of observation, and the possibilities of advanced reading instruction was important to the successful implementation of the identification process.

## SYSTEM 3: CLUSTER IDENTIFICATION

The focus of any identification system, of course, should be on the students who are to receive services. A secondary focus ought to be on the teachers who are very often called upon to make initial referrals for services and are expected to carry out the service recommendations. The identification system described in this section re-lies strongly on educators, particularly teachers, as professionals who are capable of making critical decisions about the services a student may need to optimize his or her learning experience. The system is known as *cluster identification*. This name is not derived from the popular model of serving gifted students known as cluster classrooms (in which the identified gifted students at any particular grade level are clustered together, full-time in the same classroom with a teacher who has specialized training in differentiating for gifted and talented learners), but rather refers to how the data are used in the identification procedure.

Cluster identification uses an eight-page form called the *D-Scribe* (see Appendix A). The *D-Scribe* is a tool that assists professional educators in moving through each of the stages of the cluster identification process. The first stages of the identification process do not address the characteristics or needs of a specific child, but rather ask education professionals to investigate the context in which decision making will occur relative to the school's philosophy or conception of giftedness. It is very important, at least at the school level, that those who make decisions about the services a student will receive have reached a consensus on what they mean institutionally when they use the word *gifted*. If this consensus is achieved at the conceptual level, rather than at the operational level, the opportunity presents itself to offer richer, more varied, and more defensible service options. Two excellent resources for this investigation are *Conceptions of Giftedness* by Sternberg and Davidson (2005) and *Handbook of Gifted Education (Handbook)* by Colangelo and Davis (2002).

The district interested in this system was a large, rapidly growing school district in a community that had been recently discovered by retirees. Despite this, a school funding vote was passed in the district, giving the district an opportunity to explore new possibilities for serving its students. Investigation and implementation of this identification procedure was one of the initiatives started. To conduct this investigation, one school in the district studied the appropriate chapters in the *Handbook* and then completed Advantages-Limitation-Unique Opportunities (ALU) charts, as suggested in the creative problem solving process (Treffinger, Isaksen, & Stead-Dorval, 2006). ALU charts serve as a graphic organizer for a decision-maker to explore the advantages, limitations, and unique opportunities provided by alternatives being considered. An example of an ALU chart like those completed by the school is provided in Table 3.

Following such a discussion, a school or district would complete the second page of the *D-Scribe*, as shown in Appendix B. In the illustration, the school district adopted the theory of successful intelligence. However, the district in this example must also meet the administrative law requirements as adopted by the state of Utah as follows:

> Children and youth whose superior performance or potential for accomplishment require a differentiated and challenging education program to meet their needs in any one or more of the following areas:
>
> 1. *General Intellectual*—students who demonstrate a high aptitude for abstract reasoning and conceptualization, who master skills and concepts

**Table 3.** ALU Chart for Investigating a Theoretical Definition of Giftedness

| THEORETICAL DEFINITION: TRIARCHIC THEORY OF INTELLIGENCE (STERNBERG, 2002) | | |
|---|---|---|
| **ADVANTAGES** | **LIMITATIONS** | **UNIQUE OPPORTUNITIES** |
| • Goes beyond traditional IQ<br><br>• Includes practical and creative aptitudes<br><br>• Is also compatible with a three ring conception, so programming could be similar to SEM | IWWMW . . . *<br><br>• Locate assessments for each component of intelligence in the theory?<br><br>• Develop learning opportunities that are responsive to an individual learner's profile across the three components?<br><br>• Gain general acceptance for the theory beyond the members of the committee who have been working on this project? | • Enhance the conception of intelligence held by educators in the district<br><br>• Establish an exemplary model for the entire district to serve gifted students in a way that honors a child's profile rather than overly focusing on labeling an placement |
| * IWWMW . . . signifies "In what ways might we . . .", encouraging the individual completing the chart to think of limitations as challenges or problems to be solved rather than as barriers. | | |

quickly, and who are exceptionally alert and observant;

2.  *Specific Academic*—students who evidence extraordinary learning ability in one or more specific disciplines;

3.  *Visual and Performing Arts*—students who are consistently superior in the development of a product or performance in any of the visual and performing arts;

4.  *Leadership*—students who emerge as leaders, and who demonstrate high ability to accomplish group goals by working with and through others;

5.  *Creative, Critical, or Productive Thinking*—Students who are highly

insightful, imaginative, and innovative, and who consistently assimilate and synthesize seemingly unrelated information to create new and novel solutions for conventional tasks.

(Utah Administrative Code R277-211-1)

In collaboration with university personnel, the district determined that this definition, while mandated by the Utah State Board of Education, is conceptually weak. Thus, the district correlated the official definition with the theory of successful intelligence as a means to guide the program conceptually. The three components of successful intelligence—analytical, synthetic, and practical— were seen by the district as being associated with three components of ability for which the schools are uniquely organized to serve as follows:

*Academic Expression*—Associated with Specific Academic opportunities,

*Artistic Expression*—Associated with Visual and Performing Arts opportunities, and

*Affective Expression*—Associated with Leadership opportunities.

These ideas would then be recorded on the third page of the *D-Scribe* as shown in Appendix B.

The district believed that a broad spectrum of services, including district-wide magnet classrooms for identified gifted students, ought to be available to serve a variety of gifts and talents. However, district leaders determined that, given the resources of the district, initial efforts at school-based services and classroom differentiation should focus on reading and math, particularly because these were the main discussion points on the agenda of the Professional Learning Communities that meet as grade level teams each week. These emphases, then, are noted on the third page of the *D-Scribe* (see Appendix B).

The materials on the Conception and Definition pages remain the same for all students being considered. The work on these two pages is not redone with each student. Within the recasting of the definition, the identification plan attempts to focus attention on individual children, rather than on a set program. It provides a means to assess program needs, as well as student needs.

The identification system consists of five stages: Referral, Data-Gathering, Clustering, Decision-Making, and Service Planning. Each of these stages is supported through information recorded on a specific page of the *D-Scribe*.

## REFERRAL

The referral page of the *D-Scribe* is provided on the back of the form. It requires three pieces of information: (a) the referral source, (b) the referral basis, and (c) the referral information.

The referral source is typically one of two types—a personal referral or a testing referral. A personal referral can come from anyone with an interest in a particular child, including, but not limited to, the child's regular classroom teacher, specialist teachers, media center specialist, parents, community leaders, or the child him or herself. The testing referral occurs when a building principal (or his or her designee) conducts a survey of the normed achievement tests given in the school. The principal (or designee) then lists the test name as the referral source.

For a personal referral, material provided in the referral basis section is similar to that which a person writing a letter of recommendation puts in the opening paragraph—how well, how long, and under what circumstances the referee has known the child. It need not be an extensive description. If testing is the referral source, then the referral basis is simply a listing of the testing period and year (e.g., Spring 2011) so that decision-makers can know how recent the scores are.

In the referral information area, the referee making a personal referral indicates the evidence he or she has seen that supports his or her belief that the child should be considered further in the identification process. This information should be based on sufficient observations of the child to determine that it meets at least a *preponderance of the evidence* standard. For a testing referral, the composite and subscores from the indicated test should be reported. The example form in Appendix B presents a personal referral from the regular classroom teacher.

When the referral is received by the person in charge of identification (e.g., a building administrator or school gifted coordinator), the date is noted on the front of the form. The person in charge then forms the Professional Decision Team (PDT). The PDT should consist of at least three individuals: (a) one who is familiar with gifted education—usually the school or district gifted coordinator, (b) one who is familiar with the district or school and its resources, and (c) one who is familiar with the child—usually a current teacher. The person representing the interests of the child can be the teacher who made the referral, but doesn't have to be. In some cases, it may be appropriate to invite a parent to represent the child's interests.

In the example school district, gifted education leaders determined to use Professional Learning Communities as the PDT. In this district, grade level teams meet together weekly as members of a Professional Learning Community. In addition to general curriculum planning for the grade level, the team is responsible for participating in agreed-upon professional development activities. Further, they are required to review data on student performance and make decisions about interventions for students not yet meeting standards (DuFour, DuFour, Eaker, & Karhanek, 2004). District personnel determined that discussions concerning high ability students would fit very naturally into these meetings. While the types of representation presented in the previous paragraph are missing from these Professional Learning Communities, all members had a clear understanding of the system and, particularly, how the cluster identification system differs from other identification systems. Names of the PDT are noted on the form.

Regardless of which approach is taken to form the PDT, there are critical reasons for using groups to make decisions. According to Hare (1996), small groups are preferred in decision making because they facilitate more efficient recall of information, more frequent correct or accurate responses, and fewer errors in judgment. They also provide opportunities for professional networking and modeling. To make these outcomes more likely, the small group should include individuals with common characteristics, such as general knowledge of gifted and talented students and their educational needs, motivation to do what is best for any individual child, and commitment to the group decision-making process. However, divergent characteristics are also needed, such as knowledge and access to varied resources or particular specializations in curriculum and instruction. This avoids over-conformity within the group.

With the referral now available, the PDT meets and reviews the referral information to determine if further evaluation is justified. The PDT should evaluate the strength of the argument made through a personal referral with an affirmative judgment perspective—in other words, the group should look for reasons *to do further assessment* rather than for reasons *not to*. If further evaluation is indicated, the PDT may ask the regular classroom teacher or a specialist teacher to conduct a formal observation of the child. In most cases the regular classroom teacher can complete the observation, however, observation by a specialist teacher may be appropriate in cases where it is believed that a particular student's abilities may be expressed in the content areas covered by the specialist teachers. Observations should be based on an appropriate observation instrument (see Chapters 4 and 14 of this volume for additional discussion). Observation should take place over an appropriate time period, perhaps a minimum of two weeks, to form a reliable basis for the teacher's judgments. Teachers may wish to use jot-down systems (see Chapter 9) to create a reliable record of student behaviors that support teacher judgments on the forms used. The example shown in Appendix B presents selected scales from the *Scales for Rating the Behavioral Characteristics of Superior Students* (Renzulli et al., 2010) were used.

When the observation is done, the teacher completes and returns the checklist or rating scale to the PDT. The PDT then determines whether the observation evidence supports a commitment to extensive evaluation of the child. This judgment may be based on two criteria: 1) the student consistently displays many of the characteristics on the form, or 2) the student intensely displays any of the characteristics on the form. Once the PDT makes this decision, they record the date on the front of the *D-Scribe* and the data-gathering process begins.

## DATA

When the PDT makes a recommendation for further evaluation, they send a Parental Letter of Evaluation Permission to the parents. If the PDT makes a recommendation for no further evaluation, they inform the regular classroom teacher, as well as anyone else who may have submitted a request for consideration. If parent permission is not re-ceived, these same people are so informed. When parental permission is granted, the next stage of identification, data gathering, begins.

The first step of this stage is a "data need" review. In this step, a member of the PDT inspects a student's cumulative file and other pertinent records to determine what information is already available on a student. Desired information on a student could include group aptitude tests, group normed achievement tests, group criterion achievement tests, content and skill area grades, individual aptitude and achievement tests, narrative information about school honors, extracurricular activities, outside achievements, interests, and hobbies. The team should determine what information they have about the student's abilities in each area articulated in the school's definition of giftedness. Based on this assessment, the team determines what additional information it needs. Information from at least one individual aptitude test should be available. In addition, the team may need to gather further ratings from teachers and parents. It is highly likely that the PDT will need to gather narrative information from teachers, parents, or the child through questionnaires or interviews. Once the PDT determines which information is available and what further information is needed, they oversee the gathering and recording of new information on the *D-Scribe*, as shown in Appendix B.

In the example provided in Appendix B, the third grade student has no standardized test scores available because criterion referenced end-of-level tests do not begin in this state until the end of third grade. What is available in the cumulative file are checklists of student achievement of objectives in math and reading for Grades K-2. It isn't much to go on, so the PDT determines that the student will take the *Cognitive Abilities Test* (CogAT) so that at least one set of standardized scores are available for the student. Other PDTs may make this same determination for students referred to them so that all the CogAT testing can be done on a scheduled date for all students at the school.

### CLUSTERS

The next step requires the team to identify clusters. Clusters are similar to the concept of *hot spots* used in the creative problem solving process (Treffinger, D. J., Isaksen, S. G., & Stead-Dorval, K. B. (2006). The PDT should identify pieces of data that can be grouped together because they address an important dimension of the conception and definition of giftedness articulated previously on the conception and definition pages of the *D-Scribe*. Using the relevant data from all that

is available on a student, team members begin to identify specific clusters of traits exhibited by the student. It is important in this step and the two that follow to refocus on the decision-making rules that the PDT will follow. Table 4 shows the various decision rules that can be applied and the way these would be expressed if the membership of the PDT were constructed as suggested earlier in the chapter—with one representative for the program, one representative for the school, and one representative for the child. Hare (1996) believes that it is imperative that the consensus rule be followed so that no one voice in the decision is given too much or too little weight and the focus can remain on the child. Hare further suggests that to reach consensus, group members must seek differences of opinion from all, avoid arguing their own position, address all remarks to the whole group, show concern for individual opinion, avoid confrontation or criticism, explore the bases for agree-

**Table 4.** Decision-Making Rules.

| RULE | FORCE | MAJORITY | COMPROMISE | CONSENSUS |
|---|---|---|---|---|
| FOCUS | STATUS | DEMOCRACY | SOLUTIONS | GOALS |
| DESCRIPTION | Decision made by ceding to the most powerful person in the group | Decision made by vote, leading to potential winners/losers attitudes | Decision made by each giving in to others on some point so that there are no winners/losers | Decision made by shared understanding of group goal and working till that is achieved |
| APPLICATION | District gifted coordinator's opinion takes precedence over any other person's | Representative for child (classroom teacher) is outvoted on all decisions | District coordinator sees that principal and teacher don't like a suggestion so gives up trying to adapt it to something they might agree to | Group agrees that meeting needs of child is most important consideration and continues working until they feel they have achieved that for each child considered |

ment, avoid changing their minds only to reach agreement, accept responsibility for the decisions made as a group, and postpone decisions if more time is needed.

In the example in Appendix B, the team identified three different types of clusters: 1) those data that cluster together indicating the presence of the three components of intelligence—analytic, creative, and practical; 2) those data that cluster together indicating accomplishment in the specific fields of focus from the correlation of the theoretical conception and the official definition—in this case, math and reading; and 3) those data that cluster together around other parts of the definition that have not been chosen for specific focus. The PDT records all clusters and supporting data on the *D-scribe*. As shown in the example in Appendix B, any one piece of data may be used in more than one cluster.

## DECISIONS

In the next step, the PDT decides, by examining the data placed in the specific clusters, which clusters indicate excellent, outstanding, or extraordinary levels of potential or accomplishment depending upon broader and broader comparisons. A decision of *excellent* might be based on a comparison to other children of the same age or grade within the school. A decision of outstanding might be based on a comparison to children of the same age or grade across the district. A decision of extraordinary might be based on a comparison to children of the same age or grade state-wide or nationally. Consideration of the child's background experience or environment might also be basis for a decision. The basic question that guides

the PDT's decision is this: "Given this cluster of data, what is our judgment of how this child compares to other children of the same age, grade, experience, and background?" The PDT records decisions about clusters on the appropriate pages of the *D-scribe*, with the date of decisions recorded on the back page. Refer to Appendix B for the example form.

## SERVICES

The final stage of the identification process is planning for service to be provided for the child, given the decisions the PDT made. The PDT records these services on the appropriate page of the *D-scribe*. At this stage, the composition of the PDT (i.e., a representative for the gifted program, a representative for the school, and a representative for the child) can be most useful, as individuals with such diverse rolls will be more knowledgeable about the resources available beyond the school setting. The task here is to match available resources to a student's decision profile, attempting to address both strengths and concerns. Where district-wide services, such as a gifted magnet program, are provided, district leaders should articulate the student profile (i.e., in terms of the specific cluster areas and levels) that best predicts students' potential success in the program, given the academic rigors of the program. For example, if the example school district were to offer a gifted magnet program that focused on the application of reading and mathematics as tool skills for deeper learning in the integrated content areas of language, mathematics, science, and social studies, then they may require for entry into that specific program a decision of at least "outstanding" in mathematics and reading and in at least one of the components of intelligence mentioned in the conception and definition of giftedness. However, the PDT does not have to be limited to such district-wide programs for its service plan. Resources derived from the school, community, and family should also be considered. In the example school district in which the PDT was constituted by the grade level PLC, teachers would have had to seek information on community and district resources themselves or through the local school administrator.

A key piece of the service plan is the identification of areas in which the child needs services but for which there are currently no resources available at the school, district, or community levels. This information is duly noted on the form. When a critical mass (say, five or six students) are identified with a similar unfulfilled need, it would serve as a needs assessment to school or district personnel to investigate the possibility of implementing a new service that would address the newly identified need.

Following the planning stage, the PDT informs teachers of the service decisions, and teachers implement the decisions. When the child's current teacher has been a member of the PDT representing the interests of the child, he or she already knows the decision and can move forward. The PDT also informs the parents, and, where appropriate, parents should implement those portions of the plan for which they are responsible. There is no need, when decisions have been based on this system, to inform parents that their child has been identified as gifted or not. The PDT primarily communicates what information they used to make decisions and what plan resulted from the

analysis of that information. A sample plan appears on the *D-Scribe* in Appendix B.

## PROFESSIONAL DECISION MAKING

Perhaps each of the systems explained in this chapter are too idealistic or specific to the situations in which they were used to have broad application in other contexts, but they do have one over-riding commonality that is important to consider—the role of the professional educator in the decision-making process. Smylie (1992) has suggested that teachers are selective in the types of decisions they like to be involved in when group decision making is used. If teachers sense that they have the knowledge and skills to make good decisions, they are willing participants. Thus, teachers involved in any of the systems described in this chapter need knowledge about gifted learners and their educational needs, in addition to knowledge about classroom, school, and community resources. Second, teachers are willing to participate in group decision making if they perceive that the decision will help them fulfill their teaching responsibilities, especially as they relate to classroom instruction. When teachers see "the prospect of enhancing success with students as a primary benefit" (p. 55) of group decision making, they will participate. The three systems described in this chapter attempt to maximize this prospect.

The idealism expressed in the systems described in this chapter represents efforts to honor education as, using a term coined by Bogue (1991), a "servant profession" (p. 71). According to Bogue, professions are often charged with "a narrowness of interest and perspective, a contempt for political concerns" (p. 71), and a tendency to let "professional confidence [become] professional arrogance" (p. 71). Bogue suggests that a servant profession would have five characteristics that would guard against these charges becoming true for education. These characteristics are

1. nobility of purpose—service to improvement of society and humankind,

2. systematic knowledge foundation—a body of ideas and concepts to guide decision making,

3. rigorous selection and education—a process attending to the intellectual, clinical, and ethical development of persons,

4. governance of s—the authority and means to deal with standards of practice and questions of incompetent professional behavior, and

5. linkage to laity—the active involvement of laypersons on policy issues related to professional preparation, licensure, and practice, including cost effectiveness and effectiveness of practice.

(pp. 71–72)

Flowing from this characterization of the servant profession, the three identification systems described in this chapter are focused on the developmental potential of human beings and thoughtful, knowledgeable educators as the key public resource for optimizing that potential.

## REFERENCES

Bartlett, B., & Hunsaker, S. L. (2009, Winter). Reading to serve: Service learning for gifted readers. *Teaching for High Potential*, pp. 1, 10–12.

Bogue, E. G. (1991). *A journey of the heart: The call to teaching*. Bloomington, IN: Phi Delta Kappa Educational Foundation.

Colangelo, N., & Davis, G. A. (2002). *Handbook of gifted education* (3rd ed.). Boston, MA: Allyn & Bacon.

Cox, J., Daniel, N., & Boston, B. O. (1985). *Educating able learners: Programs and promising practices*. Austin, TX: University of Texas Press.

DuFour, R., DuFour, R., Eaker, R., & Karhanek, G. (2004). Whatever it takes: How professional learning communities respond when kids don't learn. Bloomington, IN: National Education Service.

Frasier, M. M., & Passow, A. H. (1994). *Toward a new paradigm for identifying talent potential*. Storrs, CT: University of Connecticut, National Research Center on the Gifted and Talented. [RM 94112]

Hare, P. (1996). *Small groups: An introduction*. West Port, CT: Praeger.

Hunsaker, S. L., Nielsen, A., Bartlett, B. (2010). Correlates of Teacher Practices Influencing Student Outcomes in Reading Instruction for Advanced Readers. *Gifted Child Quarterly, 54*, 273–282.

Odoardi, R. H. (2010, February). Gifted readers and libraries: A natural fit. *Teacher/Librarian, 37*(3), 32–36.

Renzulli, J. S., Smith, L. H., White, A. J., Callahan, C. M., Hartman, R. K., Westberg, K. L., Gavin, M. K., Reis, S. M., Siegle, D., & Sytsma Reed, R. E. (2010). *Scales for rating the behavioral characteristics of superior students: Technical and administration manual* (3rd ed.). Mansfield Center, CT: Creative Learning Press.

Smylie, M. A. (1992). Teacher participation in school decision making: Assessing willingness to participate. *Educational Evaluation and Policy Analysis, 14*, 53–67.

Sternberg, R. J. (2002). Giftedness According to the Theory of Successful Intelligence. In N. Colangelo, & G. A. Davis (Eds.). *Handbook of gifted education* (3rd ed., pp. 88–99). Boston, MA: Allyn & Bacon.

Sternberg, R. J., & Davidson, J. E. (2005). *Conceptions of giftedness* (2nd ed.). New York: Cambridge University Press.

Treffinger, D. J., Isaksen, S. G., Stead-Dorval, K. B. (2006). *Creative problem solving: An introduction* (4th ed.). Waco, TX: Prufrock Press.

Vanderheyden, A. M. (2011). Technical adequacy of response to intervention decisions. *Exceptional Children, 77*, 335–350.

## A Professional Tool to Assist in Making Decisions About Students' Gifts and Talents

| Demographics | | |
|---|---|---|
| Student Name: | | Date: |
| Parent/Guardian/Caretaker Name(s): | | |
| Parent/Guardian/Caretaker Contact Information (Address; Phones; E-Mail): | | |
| School: | Grade: | Teacher: |

### Process Checklist

Referral Source (name/position of person or name of screening instrument):

(See back page for further information on Referral.)

| Professional Decision Team | | |
|---|---|---|
| For the School: | For the Program: | For the Child: |
| | | |

| Activity | Date |
|---|---|
| Referral Received | |
| Professional Decision Team (PDT) Formed | |
| Further Consideration Approved (PDT) | |
| Teacher Observation | |
| Observation Review (PDT) | |
| Extended Evaluation Recommendations (PDT) | |
| Parent/Guardian/Caretaker Permission | |
| Data Need Review (PDT) | |
| Data Gathering Completed | |
| Cluster Formation (PDT) | |
| Cluster Evaluation (PDT) | |
| Service Planning | |
| Parent/Guardian/Caretaker Notification | |
| Teacher/Counselor Notification | |

Note: A designation of (PDT) following an activity indicates a meeting of the members of the Professional Decision Team is required. Multiple activities that require a PDT meeting may be addressed in a single meeting.

| Conception |
|---|
| Theoretical Basis for Conception: |
| Reference: |
| Statement of Conception: |

| Definition |
| --- |
| Legal Definition (from State or District Legislation or Policy): |
| Correlation of Theoretical Conception and Legal Definition: |

| Data | | |
|---|---|---|
| Quantitative Data | | |
| Test/Instrument:<br><br>Scores: | Test/Instrument:<br><br>Scores: | Test/Instrument:<br><br>Scores: |
| Test/Instrument:<br><br>Scores: | Test/Instrument:<br><br>Scores: | Test/Instrument:<br><br>Scores: |
| Narrative Data | | |
| Accomplishments: | Hobbies: | Interests: |
| Extra-curricular School Activities: | Community Involvement: | Awards: |
| Family: | Behavior: | Dispositions: |

| Clusters | | |
|---|---|---|
| Cluster | Cluster | Cluster |
| | | |
| Supporting Data | Supporting Data | Supporting Data |
| | | |
| Cluster | Cluster | Cluster |
| | | |
| Supporting Data | Supporting Data | Supporting Data |
| | | |

| Decisions | |
|---|---|
| Areas of Strength | Areas of Concern |
| Area:<br><br>Level: | Area:<br><br>Level: |
| Area:<br><br>Level: | Area:<br><br>Level: |
| Area:<br><br>Level: | Area:<br><br>Level: |
| Area:<br><br>Level: | Area:<br><br>Level: |
| Area:<br><br>Level: | Area:<br><br>Level: |
| Area of Strength Evaluation Options | Area of Concern Evaluation Options |
| Excellent (in comparison to others of similar age and opportunity in school setting) | Basic (in comparison to others of similar age and opportunity in school setting) |
| Outstanding (in comparison to others of similar age and opportunity in community setting) | Urgent (in comparison to others of similar age and opportunity in community setting) |
| Extraordinary (in comparison to others of similar age and opportunity in settings beyond community) | Critical (in comparison to others of similar age and opportunity in settings beyond community) |

| Services | |
|---|---|
| Placement in District/School Programs | Accommodations by Classroom Teacher |
|  |  |
| Counseling and Guidance Needs | Recommendations to Parents |
|  |  |
| Recommended Community Resources | Need Not to be Addressed Currently |
|  |  |

| Referral |
|---|
| Student Name: |
| Referral Source:<br>Enter name/position of person making the referral, OR name of screening instrument used in making referral. |
| Referral Basis:<br>Describe the basis upon which you (i.e., the referral source) know the student, including the role(s) you have played in the student's life and the length of time in that/those role(s); OR list the date of testing. |
| Referral Information:<br>Provide information you have about the student that you believe necessitates consideration for differentiated services, including observed characteristics of giftedness you believe the child possesses and the evidence that he or she does indeed exhibit those characteristics, OR provide the screen scores upon which a testing referral is based. |

A Professional Tool to Assist in Making Decisions About Students' Gifts and Talents

| Demographics | | |
|---|---|---|
| Student Name: Sydney Jefferson | | Date: 9/30/2011 |
| Parent/Guardian/Caretaker Name(s): Karma Madrid | | |
| Parent/Guardian/Caretaker Contact Information<br>(Address; Phones; E-Mail):     4333 Higher Road, Sandstone, UT  84999<br>435-555-5555<br>karma@xyz.com | | |
| School: Sandstone Elementary | Grade: 3 | Teacher: Washington |

| Process Checklist | | |
|---|---|---|
| Referral Source (name/position of person or name of screening instrument):<br>Eunice Washington, 3rd Grade Teacher<br>(See back page for further information on Referral.) | | |

| Professional Decision Team | | |
|---|---|---|
| For the School: | For the Program: | For the Child: |
| Dr. Lake | Ms. Victoria | Mrs. Washington |

| Activity | Date |
|---|---|
| Referral Received | 10/4/2011 |
| Professional Decision Team (PDT) Formed | 10/4/2011 |
| Further Consideration Approved (PDT) | 10/4/2011 |
| Teacher Observation | 10/18/2011 |
| Observation Review (PDT) | 10/18/2011 |
| Extended Evaluation Recommendations (PDT) | 10/18/2011 |
| Parent/Guardian/Caretaker Permission | 10/21/2011 |
| Data Need Review (PDT) | 10/25/2011 |
| Data Gathering Completed | 11/11/2011 |
| Cluster Formation (PDT) | 11/15/2011 |
| Cluster Evaluation (PDT) | 11/15/2011 |
| Service Planning | 11/22/2011 |
| Parent/Guardian/Caretaker Notification | 11/22/2011 |
| Teacher/Counselor Notification | 11/22/2011 |
| Note: A designation of (PDT) following an activity indicates a meeting of the members of the Professional Decision Team is required.  Multiple activities that require a PDT meeting may be addressed in a single meeting. | |

| Conception |
|---|
| Theoretical Basis for Definition: Theory of Successful Intelligence |
| Reference: Sternberg, R. J. (2003). Giftedness According to the Theory of Successful Intelligence. In N. Colangelo, & G. A. Davis (Eds.). *Handbook of gifted education* (3rd ed., pp. 88-99). Boston, MA: Allyn & Bacon. |
| Statement of Definition:<br><br>• Intelligence is defined in terms of the ability to achieve success in life in terms of one's personal standards, within one's sociocultural context. (p. 88)<br><br>• One's ability to achieve success depends on capitalizing on one's strengths and correcting or compensating for one's weaknesses. (p. 89)<br><br>• One is successfully intelligent by virtue of how one adapts to, shapes, and selects environments. (p. 89)<br><br>• Success is attained through a balance of analytic, [synthetic], and practical abilities. (p. 89)<br><br>    ○ Giftedness in analytic skills involves being able to dissect a problem and understand its parts. (p. 89)<br><br>    ○ Synthetic giftedness is seen in people who are insightful, intuitive, creative, or simply adept at coping with novel situations. (p. 89)<br><br>    ○ Practical giftedness … involves applying whatever analytic or synthetic ability one may have to everyday, pragmatic situations. (p. 90)<br><br>    ○ Giftedness is as much a well-managed balance of the three abilities as it is a high sore in any one or more of them. (p. 90) |

| Definition |
|---|
| Legal Definition (from State or District Legislation or Policy):<br><br>Children and youth whose superior performance or potential for accomplishment requires a differentiated and challenging education program to meet their needs in anyone or more of the following areas:<br><br>    (1)    *General Intellectual*--students who demonstrate a high aptitude for abstract reasoning and conceptualization, who master skills and concepts quickly, and who are exceptionally alert and observant;<br><br>    (2)    *Specific Academic*--students who evidence extraordinary learning ability in one or more specific disciplines;<br><br>    (3)    *Visual and Performing Arts*--students who are consistently 'superior in the development of a product or performance in any of the visual and performing arts;<br><br>    (4)    *Leadership*--students who emerge as leaders, and who demonstrate high ability to accomplish group goals by working with and through others;<br><br>    (5)    *Creative, Critical, or Productive Thinking*--Students who are highly insightful, imaginative, and innovative, and who consistently assimilate and synthesize seemingly unrelated information to create new and novel solutions for conventional tasks. (Utah Administrative Code R277-211-1.) |
| Correlation of Theoretical Conception and Legal Definition:<br><br>High degrees of general intellectual and critical thinking abilities (i.e., analytic intelligence), creative and productive thinking abilities (i.e., synthetic intelligence), and relational skills expressed through leadership (i.e., practical intelligence), as well as the well-managed combination of these abilities (i.e., successful intelligence) are expressed in Specific Academics, Visual and Performing Arts, and Leadership.<br><br>Given current resources and other initiatives occurring in the district, we are particularly well prepared to address the needs of those students who require services in the areas of literacy and mathematics. |

| Data | | |
|---|---|---|
| Quantitative Data | | |
| Test/Instrument:<br>CogAT Verbal<br>Scores:<br>90%ile | Test/Instrument:<br>CogAT Quantitative<br>Scores:<br>95%ile | Test/Instrument:<br>CogAT Non-Verbal<br>Scores:<br>99%ile |
| Test/Instrument: SRBCSS<br>Learning  Creativity  Motivation<br>Scores:<br>97%      98%      95% | Test/Instrument: SRBCSS<br>Leadership  Reading   Math<br>Scores:<br>71%      92%      100% | Test/Instrument: SRBCSS<br>Technology<br>Scores:<br>100% |
| Narrative Data | | |
| Accomplishments:<br>100% of Literacy objectives achieved for Grades 1 and 2; 93% for Grade K<br>100% of Math objectives achieved for Grades K-2 | Hobbies:<br>Drawing<br>Chess<br>Video Games | Interests:<br>*Tree House* Mysteries<br>Chess books |
| Extra-curricular School Activities:<br>Chess Club (2nd Grade) | Community Involvement:<br>Boys/Girls Club of Basil County | Awards:<br>2nd Grade Reflections Art—School, 2nd place; District, 3rd place |
| Family:<br>Mother owns and runs a photography business out of her home. | Behavior:<br>Cooperative, quiet in class, doesn't interact much with other children at recess; spends lots of time with tangrams during free time in class | Dispositions:<br>Seems a little withdrawn, internally reflective, creative (see tessellation created in 3rd grade) |

| Clusters | | |
|---|---|---|
| Cluster | Cluster | Cluster |
| Mathematics | Reading | Analytic |
| Supporting Data | Supporting Data | Supporting Data |
| CogAT Quantitative 95%ile<br>CogAT Non-Verbal 99%ile<br>SRBCSS Mathematics 100%<br>100% of Math objectives<br>achieved for Grades K-2<br>Chess<br>Chess books<br>Chess Club (2nd Grade)<br>Spends lots of time with<br>tangrams during free time in<br>class<br>Creative (see tessellation created<br>in 3rd grade) | CogAT Verbal 90%ile<br>SRBCSS Reading 92%<br>100% of Literacy objectives<br>achieved for Grades 1 and 2;<br>93% for Grade K<br>*Tree House* Mysteries<br>Chess books | CogAT Verbal 90%ile<br>CogAT Quantitative 95%ile<br>CogAT Non-Verbal 99%ile<br>SRBCSS Learning 97%<br>100% of Literacy objectives<br>achieved for Grades 1 and 2;<br>93% for Grade K<br>100% of Math objectives<br>achieved for Grades K-2<br>100% of Literacy objectives<br>achieved for Grades 1 and 2;<br>93% for Grade K<br>Chess<br>Video Games<br>Chess Club (2nd Grade)<br>Spends lots of time with<br>tangrams during free time in<br>class<br>Internally reflective |
| Cluster | Cluster | Cluster |
| Synthetic (Creative) | Practical | Visual/Spatial/Artistic |
| Supporting Data | Supporting Data | Supporting Data |
| SRBCSS Creativity 98%<br>Drawing<br>2nd Grade Reflections Art—<br>School, 2nd place; District, 3rd<br>place<br>Spends lots of time with<br>tangrams during free time in<br>class<br>Seems a little withdrawn,<br>internally reflective, creative<br>(see tessellation created in 3rd<br>grade) | SRBCSS Motivation 95%<br>SRBCSS Leadership 71%<br>SRBCSS Technology 100%<br>Cooperative, quiet in class,<br>doesn't interact much with other<br>children at recess<br>Seems a little withdrawn,<br>internally reflective | CoGAT Non-verbal 99%ile<br>Drawing<br>Chess<br>Video Games<br>Chess books<br>Chess Club (2nd Grade)<br>2nd Grade Reflections Art—<br>School, 2nd place; District, 3rd<br>place<br>Spends lots of time with<br>tangrams during free time in<br>class<br>Creative (see tessellation created<br>in 3rd grade) |

| Decisions | |
|---|---|
| Areas of Strength | Areas of Concern |
| Area: Mathematics<br><br>Level: Outstanding | Area: Practical<br><br>Level: Basic |
| Area: Reading<br><br>Level: Excellent | Area:<br><br>Level: |
| Area: Analytic<br><br>Level: Outstanding | Area:<br><br>Level: |
| Area: Synthetic (Creative)<br><br>Level: Outstanding | Area:<br><br>Level: |
| Area: Visual/Spatial/Artistic<br><br>Level: Outstanding | Area:<br><br>Level: |
| Area of Strength Evaluation Options | Area of Concern Evaluation Options |
| Excellent (in comparison to others of similar age and opportunity in school setting) | Basic (in comparison to others of similar age and opportunity in school setting) |
| Outstanding (in comparison to others of similar age and opportunity in community setting) | Urgent (in comparison to others of similar age and opportunity in community setting) |
| Extraordinary (in comparison to others of similar age and opportunity in settings beyond community) | Critical (in comparison to others of similar age and opportunity in settings beyond community) |

| Services | |
| --- | --- |
| Placement in District/School Programs | Accommodations by Classroom Teacher |
| Provide placement with 4th grade during geometry lessons or units. Continue participation with Chess Club. Encourage participation in this year's PTA Reflections contest. Continue observation during school year for possible placement in GT Magnet that begins next year in 4th grade, particularly watching for stronger evidence in reading. | Continue using anchor activities that involve visual spatial abilities. Begin use of MDF for all math units. Introduce to mysteries at a more challenging reading level. Provide resources for 3 dimensional visualization such as origami, modular origami, and construction kits. |
| Counseling and Guidance Needs | Recommendations to Parents |
| Seek permission from mother for assessment of Sydney to determine the degree to which seeming withdrawal is problematic academically and socially (e.g., aloneness v. loneliness). | Monitor amount of video game playing. Consider play dates with others, particularly 4th graders from the class Sydney will attend for geometry, who participate in Chess Club. |
| Recommended Community Resources | Need Not to be Addressed Currently |
| Locate a possible Chess Mentor who could meet with Sydney and others during his time at County Boys/Girls Club. | Discuss with mother possibility of offering an after-school photography class. |

| Referral |
|---|
| Student Name:  Sydney Jefferson |
| Referral Source:<br>Enter name/position of person making the referral, OR name of screening instrument used in making referral.<br><br>Eunice Washington, 3<sup>rd</sup> Grade Teacher |
| Referral Basis:<br>Describe the basis upon which you (i.e., the referral source) know the student, including the role(s) you have played in the student's life and the length of time in that/those role(s), OR list the date of testing.<br><br>Sydney has been in my 3<sup>rd</sup> grade class for the past 6 weeks.  In addition, he was a participant in the after school chess club that I ran last year during the last 3 months of school. |
| Referral Information:<br>Provide information you have about the student that you believe necessitates consideration for differentiated services, including observed characteristics of giftedness you believe the child possesses and the evidence that he or she does indeed exhibit those characteristics, OR provide the screen scores upon which a testing referral is based.<br><br>Sydney caught on very quickly to chess last year, and while he participated in only recreational matches last year (since there is no competitive program for 2<sup>nd</sup> graders), he regularly beat the 3<sup>rd</sup> graders, and could occasionally pull off a victory against the 4<sup>th</sup> grade girl from our club who eventually took 3<sup>rd</sup> place in the district competition last year. He is very quick to recognize patterns.  I also made the observation that of all the members of the club, he was the most likely to peruse the chess books I had on hand when I wasn't teaching a specific skill or he wasn't playing a game.<br><br>This year already in math and art, I've noted a strong tendency toward visual-spatial abilities.  He has really latched on to tessellations and tangrams, which are offered as an anchor activity in my classroom. He usually has no trouble figuring out the tangram patterns.  I'm looking for a more advanced book of tangrams for him now.  In art, I've noticed that his projects show a preliminary sense of perspective that is unusual in a 3<sup>rd</sup> grader. |

## CHAPTER 11 STUDY GUIDE

**Prompt 1** *Knowledge*

Explain the dual nature of each word used in the phrase *careful consideration* and how this applies to gifted identification.

**Prompt 2** *Opinion*

Explain why or why not, in your opinion, teachers are worthy of the trust placed in them by identification systems such as those described in this chapter.

**Prompt 3** *Affect*

Explore how thinking of yourself as a servant professional influences the affect with which you would approach the demands made on you for gifted identification.

**Prompt 4** *Experience*

Explain how the use of a pyramid system, such as Response To Intervention (RTI), has been helpful to you or a colleague in addressing the individual needs of your students, either for their strengths or their weaknesses.

**Prompt 5** *Preconception/Misconception*

Labeling is often seen as a gateway to services beyond those provided by the general education program. Yet the author of this chapter suggests that, in many ways, this may not be necessary. What is the role of labeling in education in your opinion, and is it necessary to continue its use? Why or why not?

# SECTION IV.

# INSTRUMENTATION

# CHAPTER 12

# ABILITY TESTING & TALENT IDENTIFICATION

DAVID F. LOHMAN & MEGAN FOLEY NICPON, THE UNIVERSITY OF IOWA

## BACKGROUND AND THEORETICAL FOUNDATION: DEFINING GIFTEDNESS

Identifying something presupposes understanding what that something might be. Giftedness is no exception. Unfortunately, the term *gifted* has as many definitions as there are theories of giftedness (Kaufman & Sternberg, 2007). For some, giftedness means high general ability (*g*). For others, it means the promise of excellence in a domain in which achievements are valued by a society. For yet others, real giftedness means making extraordinary contributions to a field as an adult. Some include creativity in the definition, either as an aspect of giftedness that all gifted students would be expected to display or as a unique form of giftedness. Others include constructs such as leadership, practical intelligence, music, art, and athleticism.

When people define a word differently, their conversations are prone to miscommunication and conflict. Even if the staff of a talent identification and development program share a well-articulated definition of the term gifted, other teachers in the

school, the school administrators, and parents will surely have different understandings. Often, these beliefs will be inconsistent with much that experts know about giftedness (Lohman, 2006a). Most non-experts would define giftedness as innate, general cognitive ability. This is no longer the view of experts in the field. For this reason, some of these experts suggest replacing the word "gifted" with a less value-laden and misunderstood term (Borland, 2004; Renzulli, 2005). For example, instead of a gifted program, one might speak of a talent identification and development program.

Too often, students are first labeled "gifted" and only then do program administrators worry about what to do with them. A talent identification and development perspective avoids this problem because it more clearly binds the identification process to educational programming. If a child is said to have mathematical talent or musical talent, or both, then the only question is how best to develop those talents. A creative writing program would not be the most appropriate match. Talents of greatest interest to school personnel are those needed to develop the forms of expertise sanctioned by society through the formal training systems made available in its schools.

A talent perspective also makes it easier to identify the particular interest, motivation, perseverance, and other personal characteristics that will be needed for talent development. Efforts to assist a child in developing her musical abilities are unlikely to succeed if the child is uninterested in learning music or unable to persist in the study of it. By focusing on specific talents, one also makes it more likely that schools will value a broader range of outcome measures that can index talent development, such as above-level test scores, individual performances, and regional competitions. In this way school personnel are more likely to recognize behaviors and accomplishments that indicate unusual creativity in the specific talent domain.

## Talent Development and Expertise

Talent development can be understood as the process of acquiring expertise in a domain. At some point, the most talented and dedicated individuals attain levels of competence that are exhibited by only a handful of other people. But getting there requires many years of sustained effort on the part of the learner and a parallel commitment by teachers and coaches. Understanding the magnitude of the task helps clarify the importance of engaging the child in learning activities that directly assist in developing that expertise. For example, helping students develop mathematical talent or musical talent means providing advanced instruction in mathematics or music rather than exercises in thinking skills. It means choosing projects and other enrichment activities that are not only interesting and enjoyable, but also contribute to the attainment of competence in the domain. This is especially important for school-based programs that serve students whose parents cannot afford summer classes or other focused talent-development activities. These students must rely almost exclusively on the school to assist in the development of their talents.

Identifying academically talented children thus depends not only on a clear definition of giftedness, but also on the range of educational programs that will be made available to children who are selected to participate in them. Programs range from highly selective schools for profoundly gifted children to enrichment activities for all children in a school who show interest in a particular activity and the ability to engage meaningfully and productively in it. Clearly, the procedures that one would use to identify those children who might succeed in a highly selective school for the gifted would not be appropriate for a program that follows a Schoolwide Enrichment Model (Renzulli, 2005). Nevertheless, the same principles govern each. It is these principles that are the focus of this chapter.

## Talents Schools Should Develop

At the most general level, identifying talent means discovering or recognizing an individual's predisposition to acquire competence in some domain. Deep learning in that domain proceeds at a more rapid pace for the talented individual than in otherwise similar individuals. Potentially, then, there are as many different talents as domains of human competence. Some domains are broader than others. For example, mathematics is a much broader domain than calculation. To show remarkable abilities in mental calculation does not mean that one has great potential for mathematics. Similarly, some domains are more highly valued by society: remarkable penmanship is less valued in schools today than creative writing skills; this was not always the case. Some talents have instrumental value to society whereas others are deemed to be of inherent value and are often pursued as an avocation. For example, surgical skills have instrumental value; people usually do not learn to be surgeons just for their personal enrichment or edification. Musical skills however, are often developed for their own sake.

Given the diversity of talents, it is useful to distinguish among talents that schools are (or should be) prepared to develop, talents that schools can encourage through their connections with external organizations, and talents that are outside of the schools' purview. Each category is described in Box 1.

A broad focus on talent identification and development both liberates and complicates. We move from a single clearly defined and well-measured talent (general academic aptitude) to a much larger set of talents, some of which are poorly defined and difficult to measure. Although the diversity of talents

---

**BOX 1**

**A TALENT CLASSIFICATION SCHEME FOR SCHOOLS**

1. Talents that schools can (or should) develop. This category includes academic subjects that, by custom or mandate, schools already strive to develop. All elementary schools have well-developed educational programs in literature, writing, mathematics, social studies, and science; most also have at least rudimentary programs in music and the arts. In many of these domains, the level of instruction needed for academically or artistically precocious children may only be offered at more advanced grades. In other cases, the school may not have programs in the domain (e.g., art or music) but could well be lobbied to develop such programs. Access to such programs is thus a different issue than whether schools aim to develop a particular kind of talent.

2. Talents that schools cannot themselves develop but should encourage though involvement with external organizations. Teachers observe a wide range of other talents that children and their parents can be encouraged to develop with the assistance of organizations outside of the school. Musical and athletic talents can sometimes be developed in school-based programs. But schools may not have the resources to provide more than an elementary development. Many of the summer and extracurricular programs offered by talent search programs such as John Hopkins University, Northwestern, and the Belin-Blank Center at The University of Iowa provide such enrichment opportunities for academically precocious youth. Increasingly, administrators of these programs have endeavored to make them available to all children, not just those children whose parents can afford them.

3. Talents that are outside of the school's purview. Everything from sports clubs to political action groups fall in this category. Talent development in these specific domains certainly should be encouraged when a student exhibits motivation and interest, but they are not directly supported by school resources. In these cases, school support personnel, such as counselors, can assist students with discovering extracurricular activities that can develop and foster their unique interests and talents.

that schools recognize and develop should, by no means, be limited by current practices, at the very least, schools should be able to recognize and develop talents in those domains in which they already have programs, some of which are extensive and well-funded. Van Tassel-Baska and Brown (2007) suggest starting with the range of offerings in the local high school curriculum, such as honors and Advanced Placement classes, dual-enrollment, International Baccalaureate programs, art, music, theater, and the like. (If post-secondary schooling is available, then the range of options could be expanded to include these offerings as well.) This broad range of curricular options can be narrowed to the curricula at the middle-school level that would prepare students for or directly feed into these programs at the high-school level. Stepping back to the elementary level, schools can focus on talent development in those domains that feed into the middle school curriculum. Thus, the process starts with the diversity of talent development programs that are currently or potentially available at the high-school level and works backwards through the middle school and elementary years, at each step emphasizing development of those competencies that most directly serve as preparation for attainment at the next level. Good talent development programs offer multiple routes to engage and develop students' interests, creativity, and competence. The programs also have well-articulated links between curricula at different educational levels that help insure that students are not only having fun, but are also being prepared for further talent development (Van Tassel-Baska & Brown, 2007).

## MOVING FROM TALENT TO APTITUDE

Although the term talent is ordinarily the preferred way to talk about giftedness with the public, an in-depth understanding of how best to develop talent requires more than simply identifying it. One must consider a much broader range of personal and environmental factors that can impact the process of turning talents into competencies (see, e.g., Gagné, 2009). Aptitude theory offers one approach. Aptitude is a word much like talent, but more inclusive. Aptitude includes the cognitive (or physical) characteristics that typically define the term "talent," but it also includes any other personal characteristics that are required for successful learning (or performance) in a particular environment. Although usually grounded in biological predispositions, those characteristics that function as aptitudes are invariably developed though the child's interactions with the environment. Some of these interactions are common to most children in a particular culture. Others are unique to the child's family and its circumstances. And some are explicitly developed through schools and other social systems. For example, school achievements commonly function as aptitudes for future learning. Basic skills in reading, writing, and mathematics are required for the acquisition of expertise in all academic domains. Existing content knowledge in a domain provides the foundation for new learning, and thus current achievement in a domain functions as an important aptitude for new learning in that domain.

The word aptitude encompasses much more than cognitive constructs such as ability or achievement. Attaining competence in any domain of nontrivial complexity requires years of learning.

Interest, motivation, and persistence are thus critical aptitudes for the developing expertise.

Finally, and most importantly, the term aptitude is not a descriptor of a person that is somehow independent of context or circumstance. Aptitude is inextricably linked to context. Indeed, defining the situation or context is part of defining the aptitude. Changing the context can subtly or substantially alter the personal characteristics that influence success.

Consider what transpires when students confront a new learning task. Every student comes to that situation with a repertoire of knowledge, skills, attitudes, values, motivations, and other propensities that they have developed and refined through life experiences to date. Situations sometimes demand, sometimes evoke, or sometimes merely afford the use of particular subsets of these characteristics. Of the many characteristics that might influence a person's behavior in a particular situation, only a small set aides one in achieving his or her learning or performance goals. These characteristics function as aptitudes for that person in that situation. Formally, then, aptitude refers to the degree of readiness to learn and to perform well in a particular situation or domain (Corno et al., 2002). Examples of characteristics that commonly function as academic aptitudes include the ability to understand and follow directions, to use previously acquired knowledge appropriately, to make good inferences and generalizations, to resist distractions, and to persist in the pursuit of excellence.

Not all of the characteristics that a person brings to a situation are helpful. Those characteristics that impede learning or performance function as inaptitudes. Common examples of characteristics that function as inaptitudes include impulsivity, high levels of anxiety, or prior learning that interferes with the acquisition of new concepts and skills. Even characteristics that we would generally value might not be helpful in a particular context. For example, a teacher who values routine over innovation might interpret creativity as disruption. Many bright adults recall times when teachers valued being right more than encouraging students whose questions threatened their own feelings of competence. However, changing the context can replace rejection with acceptance and thereby transform the outcomes. Therefore, characteristics that functioned as inaptitudes in one context can be irrelevant or even function as aptitudes in a different context.

An aptitude theory of talent development thus helps dispel the common myth that superior general intellectual ability should be sufficient for the attainment of excellence. Many years ago, Thorndike (1963) pointed out that the concepts of over- and underachievement were grounded in this fallacy. The typical interpretation of underachievement, for example, assumes that the child has requisite aptitude for success, but for some reason fails to use that aptitude. A more reasonable interpretation, Thorndike argued, is not underachievement, but rather that our model of what is required for learning is under-complicated. It is like assuming that all tall people should excel in basketball and calling those who do not excel "basketball underachievers." Rather, the attainment of high levels of skill in basketball requires many other characteristics, both physical (strength, coordination) and psychological (interest in the game, competitiveness). Further, the context in which these skills must be developed defines the importance of some of these characteristics. Learning basketball on playgrounds in the inner city requires different personal characteristics than learning the game in the gyms of private schools.

## EFFECTS OF CONTEXT

The same situation that assists one student can thwart goal-attainment in another. For example, discovery-oriented or constructivist teaching methods generally succeed better with more able learners, while more didactic methods may work better with less able learners (Cronbach & Snow, 1977; Snow & Yalow, 1982). Less-structured learning situations allow more able students to use their superior reasoning abilities, which function as aptitudes. However, anxious students often perform poorly in relatively unstructured situations (Peterson, 1977). Thus, the same situation that affords the use of reasoning abilities can also evoke anxiety. Recent efforts to understand how individuals behave in academic contexts have emphasized the importance of interest, personality, and ability traits that commonly work together to produce the outcomes that we observe. For example, Ackerman (2003) found that high scores on measures of interest in developing social relationships had negative associations with knowledge acquisition, even in samples of talented individuals. This last finding reinforces the admonition that gifted students will vary as much from each other on those dimensions least correlated with $g$ as students in the general population (Lubinski & Benbow, 2000).

Understanding which characteristics of individuals are likely to function as aptitudes begins with a careful examination of the demands and affordances of target tasks and the contexts in which they must be learned or performed. This is what we mean when we say that defining the situation is part of defining the aptitude (Snow & Lohman, 1984). The affordances of an environment are what it offers or makes likely or useful. Discovery learning often affords the use of reasoning abilities; direct instruction often does not.

Aptitude is linked to context. Unless we define the context clearly, we are left with distal measures that capture only some of the aptitudes needed for success. Because they lack context, $g$-like measures of ability correlate imperfectly with success in any particular school task, especially when students are allowed a choice over what they study and how they might go about it. Averaging performance measures across learning situations and outcome measures often obscures the impact of the particular abilities and magnifies the relative importance of $g$ (Lubinski, 2004; see Box 2). Domain-specific abilities add importantly to predicting school achievements in particular domains, even after controlling for the relationship between general ability and general school achievement (Gustafsson & Balke, 1993). Therefore, identifying talent must go beyond measures of general ability or academic competence to consider other personal and social skills that are required to succeed in the educational programs that are available—or that could be developed.

## MEASURING APTITUDES
### GENERAL PRINCIPLES

#### TWO METHODS FOR INFERRING APTITUDE

Aptitude is commonly inferred in two ways. In the first way, aptitude for learning in a domain is

---

**Box 2**

**THE EFFECTS OF AVERAGING** (FROM LUBINSKI, 2004)

The figure below illustrates what happens when a test with three score scales that are moderately correlated (say quantitative, spatial, verbal) are summed (or averaged). All three test scales ($X_1$, $X_2$, and $X_3$), have .90 reliabilities (or 10% random error). For each, the preponderance of their variance measures a specific construct (55%), namely, quantitative, spatial, or verbal ability, but each also has an appreciable general factor component (35%). Aggregation of these three scales results in a composite score that primarily reflects the general factor running through all three indicators (61%). The remaining components of unique variance associated with each indicator shrink to tiny slivers of content homogeneity (11% each) and random error (2% each).

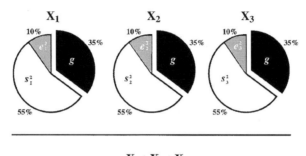

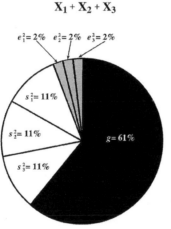

---

estimated from the ease or speed with which the individual acquires competence in that domain. Aptitude is then inferred retrospectively, when the individual learns concepts or skills after a few exposures that others learn only after much practice. When available, this information provides the most unambiguous evidence of aptitude. Indeed, the concept of aptitude was initially introduced to help explain the enormous variation in learning rates exhibited by individuals who seemed similar in other respects (Bingham, 1937). However, people differ

in their learning opportunities on the task itself or on other tasks that allow transfer to the target task, and so inferences about aptitude are defensible only when learning opportunities for the group being compared do not differ markedly. Tests include finely-differentiated age and grade norms because of the difference even a few months can make in the child's rank in cognitive or academic development. But such adjustments for opportunity to learn are effective only when the child has had learning experiences that are typical of others in the norm group. When a child has not had typical learning experiences, then even the most carefully developed national norms will over- or underestimate the student's aptitude. There are simple ways around this problem, but they require a rethinking of how to interpret scores on assessments.

In the second way, aptitude is inferred from performance on tasks outside of the domain of interest that require cognitive or affective processes similar to those required for learning in the domain (Carroll, 1974). Because these measures only predict success in the domain, they will more often err in identifying those students who will later excel than inferences based on performance to date in the domain itself. For example, dance instructors screen potential students by evaluating their body proportions, ability to turn their feet outwards, and ability to emulate physical movements (Subotnik & Jarvin, 2005). Although none of these characteristics require the performance of a dance routine, all are considered important aptitudes for acquiring dance skills. In the cognitive domain, measures of general ability are used because they measure thinking skills that are required for academic learning. For both dance and academic learning, these inferences are valid only if the students have had similar opportunities to develop the abilities required by the outside assessments.

Predictions about future learning based on current estimates of aptitude presume that the person, the content of the domain, and the learning environment will remain constant for future learning as for learning to date. In most cases, such a situation is only approximately true, especially as the time lag increases. Children develop

new abilities, the learning demands change as children acquire expertise in a domain, and the learning environments themselves change as children change instructors, grades, and schools. If the child has had unusually strong or weak preparation for a particular school task, such as reading, then rank orders can change dramatically as other children catch up and sometimes surpass those who had early preparation. Status scores, such as percentile ranks (PRs) and IQs, reflect the consequences of these changes, but not the differential development that produced the changes in rank order. For these and other reasons, the identification of aptitude (or talent) must be an ongoing or at least regularly-repeated activity, not a one-time affair.

The primary aptitudes for academic learning are current academic knowledge and skills, reasoning abilities, interests, and persistence (Corno et al, 2002). All of these are best understood as tied to particular domains of learning and methods of instruction. For example, success in a verbally demanding domain, such as creative writing, requires verbal reasoning skills, knowledge of the conventions of the language and skill in applying them, interest in writing, and the ability to persist in the development of creative writing skills. Learning in other domains is similarly contextualized. Other chapters in the book discuss ratings scales, interest inventories, performance assessments, and other measures of aptitude In this chapter, we focus on the measurement of reasoning abilities using individual and group intelligence tests. Chapter 10 illustrates procedures for integrating some of these other measures into a talent identification system.

## HIGH-ACCOMPLISHMENT VERSUS HIGH-POTENTIAL STUDENTS

Two groups of children should be considered when designing programs for the academically gifted (Robinson, 2008). Although most students fall somewhere between the poles that these groups define, naming the endpoints of the continuum helps clarify the children the programs should be serving.

The first group consists of those students who currently display academic excellence in a particular domain. We refer to these students as belonging to the high-accomplishment group. Although the measurement of accomplishment in any domain is not a trivial matter, these students are generally easier to identify than those in the second group. Students in the second group do not currently display excellence in the target academic domain, but are likely to do so if they are willing to put forth the effort required to achieve excellence and are given the proper educational assistance. We refer to these students as belonging to the high-potential group. Students commonly fall in the high-potential group because, through age, circumstance, or choice, they have not developed expertise in a particular domain. Because of their necessarily limited experience, young children most commonly fall in this group. Even the measures of accomplishment that we assess for young children, such as reading skills, are best seen as aptitudes that will later be needed for the acquisition of significant subject-matter expertise. Indeed, if one defines scholarly productivity or artistry in a domain as something beyond expertise (Subotnik & Jarvin, 2005), then even the most accomplished students will at best exhibit high potential. If, on the other hand, expertise is defined in terms of academic achievement well in advance of age or grade peers (e.g., Gagne, 2008), then many more children will exhibit high accomplishment. However, some students who do not display high accomplishment might also currently do so had they had the opportunities to develop these skills. Put differently, high-potential students display the aptitude to develop high levels of accomplishment offered by a particular class of instructional treatments.

High-accomplishment students typically need different educational programs than high-potential students. An undifferentiated label such as "gifted" does not usefully guide educational programming for a group that contains a mix of both high-accomplishment and high-potential students. Both groups need instruction that is geared to their current levels of accomplishment. Because their levels of accomplishment differ, instruction aimed at one group will often be inappropriate for the other group. (For example, high-accomplishment students often can best be served by academic acceleration within the domains in which they excel.)

The distinction between high-potential and high-accomplishment students is especially important in the identification of academically talented minority students. Many of the most talented minority students will not have had opportunities to develop high levels of accomplishment in the skills valued in formal schooling. Therefore, identifying such students depends on a clear understanding of how one can make inferences about academic aptitude using measures of both learning-to-date and potential for future learning. Providing advanced learning opportunities that meet the needs of both groups of students often requires differentiating the curriculum so that students are exposed to materials and opportunities specific to their individual needs.

## GATHERING DATA ON STUDENTS

### MEASURING DOMAIN KNOWLEDGE AND SKILLS

Academic learning at all levels builds on what the student already knows and can do (Glaser, 1992). Measures of current knowledge and skill are therefore usually the best predictors of future success in similar academic environments, especially when new learning depends heavily on old learning. The more closely measures of accomplishment sample critical aspects of emerging expertise in the domain, the better they will capture aptitude for learning in that domain. Measures of current knowledge and skill include on-grade-level and above-grade-level achievement tests, end-of-course examinations, and well-validated performance assessments such as rankings in debate contests, art exhibitions, and science fairs. Teacher grades and a host of other measures of academic learning are sometimes useful, but often have serious limitations because of their subjectivity or the limited sample of behavior that they represent. For example, even though trained raters can give highly reliable ratings of a particular essay, performance on one essay shows only modest correlations with performance on another essay.

Although useful as a measure of basic skills in reading and numeracy, most achievement tests—especially those designed for children in the elementary grades—contain relatively little content knowledge, particularly in domains such as history, social science, literature, and the physical sciences. An achievement test that is designed to be fair to all children can hardly be expected to reveal much about the specialized knowledge a student has acquired. But bright children assemble vast amounts of knowledge about specific topics that are, at best, represented only superficially on achievement tests. In this respect, the dilemma that confronts those who assess gifted children is the same dilemma that has stymied those who investigate adult intelligence. Adults develop substantial competencies in specialized domains. Any attempt to assess their functional intelligence by a test that can be administered to all adults misses much more than it captures. Hunt (2000) suggests that we might do a better job if the metaphor that guided assessment construction were to conduct an inventory rather than a survey. When designing educational interventions, this metaphor asks us to attend to what children know and can do in domains of their own choosing and the activities that fascinate them.

Out-of-level testing is a useful way to gather more information on the student's achievement than can be gleaned from an on-level-test that is too easy for the student. Tests such as PLAN and EXPLORE Global (published by ACT, Inc.) can give estimates of achievement, but because they are short, they include only a few items at each grade level. Above-level versions of longer, norm-referenced achievement tests, such as the Iowa Tests of Basic Skills (ITBS; Hoover, Dunbar, & Frisbie, 2005), offer more specific information on levels of competence within domains. As children mature, end-of-course exams and exams designed for high-school students that are modeled after the

Advanced Placement exams or the SAT II exams (published by the College Board) can provide useful information on the level of development within particular academic domains. The increasing availability of computer-based tests delivered over the internet should make it easier for school personnel to gather such information on students.

Whenever such tests are used to help make decisions about possible acceleration of a student within a domain, the test should be aligned with the local curriculum, and the student's performance on the test should be compared with the performance of students in the potential accelerated classroom. Norm-referenced achievement tests can be used in this way if the child is administered the same level of the test that is administered to students in the potential accelerated class. Sometimes other measures are available that offer even more focused estimates of readiness. For example, many schools in Iowa administer the Iowa Algebra Aptitude Test (IAAT; Schoen & Ansley, 2005) to all sixth-grade students. The performance of the child on this test can be compared with the performance of children in the school who will be enrolled in Algebra. A useful rule of thumb is that the child should score at about the 80th percentile (or higher) in distribution of scores for the target class before being accelerated into the class. Of course, many other factors should be considered before making such decisions as is discussed in the Iowa Acceleration Scale (IAS; Assouline, Colangelo, Lupkowski-Shoplik, Lipscomb, & Forstadt, 2009).

## MEASURING REASONING ABILITIES

Although current knowledge and skill in a domain are often the most important aptitudes for new learning in that domain, other aptitudes enter the picture with each step into the future. For example, given the same type of instruction, continued improvement in a domain requires interest, or at least persistence. More commonly, continued success requires a new mix of abilities: Algebra requires important thinking skills not needed in arithmetic; critical reading requires thinking skills not needed in beginning reading. Teachers, teaching methods, and classroom dynamics also change over time, each requiring, eliciting, or affording the use of somewhat different personal characteristics. Indeed, in most disciplines, developing expertise requires mastering new and, in some cases, qualitatively different types of tasks at different stages. Sometimes the critical factor is not only what is required for success, but also what is allowed or elicited by the new context that might create a stumbling block for the student. For example, in moving from a more structured to a less structured environment, a student may flounder because he is anxious or is unable to schedule his time.

It should be no surprise, then, that the second most important set of personal characteristics for academic learning is the ability to go beyond the information given, to make inferences and deductions, and to see patterns, rules, and instances of the familiar in the unfamiliar. The ability to reason well in the symbol system(s) used to communicate new knowledge in that domain is critical for success in learning. Academic learning relies heavily on reasoning (a) with words and about the concepts they signify and (b) with quantitative symbols and the concepts they signify. Thus, the critical reasoning abilities for all students (minority and majority, monolingual and multilingual) are verbal reasoning and quantitative reasoning. Nonverbal reasoning abilities are less important and show lower correlations with school achievement, especially in verbally demanding domains (Anastasi & Urbina, 1997; Gohm, Humphreys, & Yao, 1998; Lohman, 2005b; Thorndike & Hagen, 1987; 1995).

Good reasoning tests will present a broad sample of different reasoning tasks. Performance on a set of items that follow the same format provides only limited information about individual differences in broad ability constructs such as "reasoning." The term ability implies consistency in performance across a class of tasks that vary widely in their surface features. Psychological tests are simply organized collections of such tasks. However, typically less than half of the variation on well constructed, reliable tests is shared with other tests that measure the same construct using somewhat different kinds of tasks. An early, but still reasonable rule in psychological measurement is that when measuring any ability, one should combine performance across at least three different measures that use different formats to reduce the specific effects of individual tasks (Mulaik, 1972). This fundamental principle of psychological measurement is sometimes violated on individually administered ability tests that attempt to estimate many different abilities in a single testing session with fewer than three subtests and on group-administered tests in which all items follow the same format.

## INDIVIDUALLY-ADMINISTERED INTELLIGENCE TESTS

Individually-administered intelligence tests are often used in the identification of academic talent and, in some cases, function as the primary criterion for admission to programs. Indeed, for many years, an IQ score of 130 on an individually-administered intelligence test was the standard requirement. Individually administered tests are now used much less frequently, primarily because of the cost and inconvenience of arranging for each child to be tested by a professional psychologist. However the requirement of an IQ of 130 is still widely used, albeit often disguised as a national percentile rank of 97 or higher.

### EQUITY AND FAIRNESS ISSUES.

Individualized assessments for the purpose of identifying giftedness almost always must be paid for out of pocket, which raises issues of equity (Renzulli, 2005). Parents who have the financial resources to pay for testing are more likely to secure outside testing for their child than are parents without these advantages. Furthermore, scores from outside examiners may not be comparable with scores on group-administered tests that are administered to other children. For example, scores on the individually-administered test can be inflated because the child has been tested several times or because the examiner used a test with out-of-date norms. Or, scores on the individual test can be depressed because the examiner reports Full Scale scores rather than scores that exclude subtests that have lower $g$ loadings. Therefore, if individual tests are required or accepted, policies should be developed that explicitly name which tests and test scores will be accepted and that inform parents of their rights to obtain such testing if they cannot afford it.

Inferences about ability or talent require comparison of a child's performance on a test with the performance of other children who have had similar opportunities to develop the knowledge and skills required by the test. The assumption of similarity is often indefensible when national norms are used to interpret the performance of poor, minority, and ELL children, even on nonverbal tests. Subgroup norms that compare a student's performance on the test to the performance of other children who have had similar learning opportunities make the assumption more defensible. With the notable exception of the WISC-IV Spanish, such norms are not available for individually administered tests. However, unless all students are administered the test, even the WISC-IV Spanish cannot provide the local norms that are recommended for school-based talent development programs. Furthermore typically only children who are nominated for the program are tested individually, which can exclude children who do not conform to the teacher's conception of a gifted child. For these and other reasons, individually administered tests should not be the primary tool for screening admission to school-based programs.

## Some appropriate uses.

Individually administered tests do have important uses for gifted identification and placement (Robinson, 2008). Admission to special programs for the exceptionally or profoundly gifted offers a clear example. When administered in conjunction with a battery of other assessments, individually administered ability tests also can assist in the identification of twice-exceptional students (i.e., students with a disability as well as a

talent; Assouline, Foley Nicpon, & Bramer, 2006; Kaufman & Harrison, 1986; Newman, Sparrow, & Pfeiffer, 2005). Individual testing provides the opportunity for a professional psychologist to observe behavioral and neurological factors that could impair performance. For example, a child may perseverate unnecessarily on difficult problems, display high levels of anxiety, or exhibit other behaviors that impact performance on the test or in the classroom.

## Interpreting score discrepancies.

Even when scores on individual ability tests are available and the norms are appropriate, interpretation of those scores is not straightforward. Gifted students show larger discrepancies between subtests than average-ability students (Saccuzzo, Johnson, & Russell, 1992; Sweetland, Reina, & Tatti, 2006; Wilkinson, 1993). Composite or full scale scores poorly summarize the abilities of examinees when the score profile has marked peaks and valleys. Areas of exceptional ability are masked by lower scores when the composite is computed.

Large discrepancies among subtests for highly able students also cannot be interpreted the same way similar discrepancies for average-ability students are interpreted. For example, a superior score on a verbal comprehension index coupled with a high average score on a working memory index does not necessarily mean anything clinically important (Newman, et al., 2008). Or, when verbal skills are significantly higher than nonverbal skills in a high-ability student, a clinician would need to gather corroborative evidence before considering a nonverbal learning disability diagnosis (Assouline, Foley Nicpon, & Whiteman, 2010).

## USING COMPOSITE SCORES FROM MODERN ABILITY TESTS.

There also has been much discussion about whether the composite or full scale scores on modern ability tests should be used for making inferences about giftedness. Modern intelligence tests sample a much broader range of abilities than older intelligence tests. The number of scores on the *Stanford-Binet* increased from the single IQ score on the first edition to the five separate scores on the fifth edition of the test (Roid, 2003). Similarly, the two scores on the initial Wechsler tests doubled to four separate scores on the fourth edition of the test. The *Woodcock-Johnson III Tests of Cognitive Abilities* (WJ III COG) offers even more scores (see Box 3).

The multiple abilities measured by modern intelligence tests are helpful for making diagnoses of learning problems. They can be less helpful for making inferences about academic giftedness. Students classified as gifted by other methods obtain much higher scores on tests that require reasoning than on the tests that emphasize working memory,

---

**Box 3**

**WIDELY USED INDIVIDUALLY-ADMINISTERED ABILITY TESTS**

*Wechsler Intelligence Scale for Children, Fourth Edition (WISC-IV)*
- Ages 6.0 – 17.11
- Contains 10 core and 5 supplemental subtests. Core subtests are summed to a full scale IQ and four indices: Verbal Comprehension Index (VCI), Perceptual Reasoning Index (PRI), Working Memory Index (WMI), and Processing Speed Index (PSI).
- General-Ability Index (GAI) recommended in many assessment situations, such as when a significant and unusual (base rate of less than 10 - 15%) discrepancy exists between the VCI and WMI, the PRI and PSI, and/or WMI and PSI; or when unusual scatter exists among WMI and/or PSI subtests.
- Extended norms to 210 for composites, and 28 points for subtests; new and requires additional clinical validation; very rarely will be used.

*Stanford-Binet Intelligence Scale, 5th Edition (SB-5)*
- Ages 2 – 85+
- Contains 10 subtests which are combined into a full scale IQ, two domain scores (Verbal IQ and Nonverbal IQ), and five indices (Fluid Reasoning, Knowledge, Quantitative Reasoning, Visual-Spatial Processing, and Working Memory)
- An experimental Gifted index has been proposed that sums 3 nonverbal and 4 verbal tests. This excludes the NV Visual-Spatial Processing and Working Memory subtests.
- Extended norms to 160 for composites; experimental and supplemental; very rarely will be used.

*Woodcock-Johnson III Tests of Cognitive Abilities (WJ III COG)*
- Ages 2 – 90+
- Contains 10 standard and 10 supplemental tests. These are summed to give multiple indices: General Intellectual Ability (based on 7 standard tests), General Intellectual Ability (based on 7 standard and 7 supplemental tests), and Brief intellectual Ability (based on 3 standard tests). Other scores are reported for Cognitive Categories (6 indices), CHC Factors (7 indices), and Clinical Clusters (7 indices).
- Range of Standard Scores for total test composite: 0 – 200.

perceptual speed, and other more specific abilities. For example, academically gifted students often obtain much higher scores on the Verbal Comprehension and Perceptual Reasoning indexes of the *Wechsler Intelligence Scale for Children* (WISC-IV) than on the Working Memory and Processing Speed indexes (Williams, Weiss, and Rolfhus, 2003; Newman et al., 2008; Rimm, Gilman, & Silverman, 2008). Since all four of the WISC-IV indices contribute to the Full Scale IQ score, gifted students sometimes obtain lower than expected Full Scale IQ scores. In an effort to circumvent this problem, as well as minimize misinterpretation of the Full Scale IQ when the four factor indices are discrepant, a composite called the General Ability Index (GAI) was introduced. Only the Verbal Comprehension and Perceptual Reasoning indexes contribute to the GAI score. Therefore, examiners are encouraged to rely on the GAI rather than the Full Scale IQ when making inferences about giftedness (NAGC, 2008).

The admonition not to use the WISC-IV Full Scale score can be confusing to those who equate intelligence with *g* and thus define giftedness as a high level of *g*. An aptitude perspective on talent helps explain why narrower measures of ability, such as the old *Stanford-Binet* LM or the WISC-IV GAI, may better predict academic success in some domains than the full WISC-IV battery. As discussed, an aptitude perspective requires that one specify the psychological processes that are needed to learn and perform well in a particular class of situations. An undifferentiated construct such as *g* is not nearly as helpful for talent identification as a list of more specific constructs that capture the ability to reason in the symbol systems used

for developing expertise and communicating new knowledge in a particular domain. When stated in this way, it is clear that the sort of abstract, verbal reasoning abilities measured by the older forms of the *Stanford-Binet* will always be critical for many forms of academic learning. But this formulation also makes it clear that reasoning abilities in other symbol systems (e.g., quantitative, spatial, musical) will be even more important than verbal reasoning for talent development in quantitative, spatial, and musical domains.

## SCALING ISSUES.

Another debate about individual tests is whether the procedures used for scaling modern intelligence tests give scores that properly reflect the abilities of profoundly gifted individuals. For many years, degrees of giftedness followed the classification scheme based on IQ scores on the 1960 revision of the *Stanford-Binet*.

Moderately Gifted 125+

Highly Gifted 145+

Exceptionally Gifted 160+

Profoundly Gifted 180+

Modern tests do not produce such high scores, in spite of heroic efforts to provide extended norms for both the *Stanford-Binet*, Fifth Edition (SB-5) and the WISC-IV (Roid, 2003; Zhu, Clayton, Weiss, & Gabel, 2008). For this reason, some have argued that the old *Stanford-Binet* LM (SB-LM) is a better test for distinguishing among exceptionally and profoundly gifted children (Silverman, 2009). That newer tests give fewer extremely high scores is not a consequence of including subtests for specific abilities such as working memory and perceptual speed. If that were the case, then the new tests would identify the same number of high-scoring students as the old SB-LM identified when its norms were current. Rather, the old and new tests would simply identify somewhat different groups of students. It is important to understand why this is not the case.

The standardization sample for most ability tests includes only about 100 individuals in each age group. Thus, on average, there will be only one examinee that scores in the 99th percentile of the distribution in each age group. Even if the sample included 1000 individuals at each age, there would be only 10 individuals with IQs of 135 or greater. Given this paucity of individuals at the tails of the score distributions, normative standards for extreme scores either implicitly or explicitly rely on some model for how scores are distributed in the population. The most common assumption is that scores should follow a normal distribution just as is observed for many other characteristics that we can measure with great confidence. The assumption that the distribution of ability for the non-clinical population is approximately normal is probably more defensible than that it is not normal. It is surely more convenient. The debate could be resolved if we had objective scales for ability and then could empirically determine if the observed score distributions were in fact normal. Modern ability tests (like the SB-5 and WJIII COG) that are constructed using only those items that fit an Item Response Theory (IRT) model come closer to the ideal of an objective score scale than older tests. Empirical distributions of IRT-based scale scores for the very large CogAT standardization samples do in fact appear to be normal (see Lohman, 2010, for a non-technical summary

of the norming process), which strengthens the assumption of normality. Unlike CogAT Standard Age Scores, however, deviation IQ-like scores on modern tests are based on much smaller samples and thus are constructed by assuming that the scale scores are distributed normally within all age groups.

IQ scores on the SB-LM were computed by forming the ratio of the scale score or Mental Age (MA) on the test by their chronological age (CA). The assumption that the IQ distribution is not normal is inherent in the computation of ratio IQs, even the modified ratio IQs used in the SB-LM. Growth in MA is largest at the early years and gets smaller until leveling off at about age 16. The leveling off of MA was handled by fixing the maximum CA at 16. However, the variability of the distributions of ratio IQ's differed across ages. When Form LM was standardized, these variations in standard deviation across age were removed by multiplying the observed standard deviation of scores at each age by whatever constant that made the standard deviation equal to 16. However, adjusting or modifying IQs in this way did not remove skewness in the score distributions.

IQ distribution gets skewed to the right when the denominator (i.e., CA) has a much smaller range than the numerator (i.e., MA). In such cases, small differences in mental age translate into very large differences in the corresponding ratio IQ score. For example, consider the 6-year-old child who has a mental age of 9, or three years in advance of age-mates. The corresponding ratio IQ is 150. Now consider the same child with a chronological age of 9. If she is still mentally three years in advance of peers, her MA will be 12 and

302

the ratio IQ only 133. In order to preserve the 150 IQ, her mental age would have to be 13.5, or 4.5 years in advance of her peers. This is why exceedingly high ratio IQ's become increasingly unlikely as the denominator (CA) gets larger. It is also why "very few clinicians have been able to make practical use of the [*Stanford-Binet*-LM] for bright children over the age of 10" (Ruf, 2003, p. 5).

The spreading out of scores for young children at the extremes of the ratio IQ scale is viewed as a positive attribute of the SB-LM by clinicians who want to distinguish among the highly and profoundly gifted (Silverman, 2009). Although spreading out the test scores in this way may be helpful, the corresponding normative scores (i.e., IQs) cannot be trusted both because they are based on out-of-date norms and because the spread of IQ scores is a necessary consequence of the way ratio IQs are constructed, not a fact of nature.

### Short forms.

Short forms of individually-administered ability tests are popular among those who either cannot or do not wish to administer a complete test battery. Examples include the *Kaufman Brief Intelligence Test II* (K-BIT-II) and the *Screening Assessment for Gifted Elementary and Middle School Students, 2nd edition* (SAGES-2). In addition to brevity, such tests have the advantage of placing the examiner in direct contact with the student.

There are several problems with these tests and similar brief ability estimates on other tests, such as the WISC-IV GAI score or the Brief Ability Index on the WJIII. First, because they are short, these tests (and indices) sample only a limited portion of a much larger domain. Broad constructs

(such as fluid reasoning ability) are often underrepresented. For example, the Reasoning subtest of the SAGES-2 uses only about 30 pictorial/figural analogy items. Similarly, the K-BIT-II requires only 15-30 minutes to administer both the Verbal (Riddles and Verbal Knowledge) and Nonverbal (Matrices) subtests. Second, because of the limited sampling of abilities, these tests cannot support inferences about ability profiles, which are needed for placement into programs that emphasize the development of different talents, such as mathematics versus literacy. Third, scores on short tests are less reliable than scores on otherwise similar tests that present more items and use a broader selection of item formats. Longer tests are critical for identifying giftedness. As discussed below, errors of measurement are much larger for extreme scores than for scores near the mean. Short tests only compound this problem. Life-altering decisions about a child should be based on the best evidence that can be obtained. The few minutes saved by using short tests and indices come at a considerable cost to the children and the program.

Sometimes using a short test can be defended if it can successfully reduce the number of students who must be administered a more comprehensive assessment battery. But this practice must be done without screening out students who would have been admitted had they been administered the more comprehensive assessment. Unfortunately, this is not easy to do. It helps if the screening test is highly reliable, if items on the screening test sample from several different domains rather than a single domain (e.g., only figural reasoning), and if the cut score on the screening test is set quite low. More specific recommendations on how to implement a two-stage testing program that starts with a screening test are provided in Chapter 10.

## GROUP-ADMINISTERED ABILITY TEST

Group ability tests are commonly viewed as rough screening tools that will at best give a global and somewhat labile estimate of a child's abilities. Individually administered ability tests are generally considered the gold standard. Although such skepticism about group ability tests is amply warranted, as with most stereotypes, it is not always the case. The generalization is most likely to hold when the group-administered test is relatively short, samples only a portion of the cognitive domain, or has out-of-date or poorly developed norms. However, a group-administered test will sometimes give the better estimate of the student's academic aptitude than the individually administered test. This will happen if the group administered test samples more comprehensively from the domain of abstract reasoning abilities than the individually administered test.

Although many different tasks have been used to measure reasoning on group-administered tests, a few are used much more common than others: analogies, matrix problems, series completions, and classification tasks. Some test batteries also measure verbal reasoning through sentence-completion tests, sentence-comprehension tests, and even vocabulary. Others include more specific spatial tasks, such as form boards or paper-folding tests. And others use quantitative tests that require examinees to make relational judgments (such as greater than or less than) between quantitative concepts or to determine how numbers

and mathematical operators can be combined to generate a product.

Some of the major group-administered ability tests are summarized in Box 4. The tests vary in the number and type of abilities they measure, the quality and recency of their norms, the support materials for teachers and parents, and their reliability.

Examples of the nine reasoning tasks used in the most recent version of Thorndike and Hagen's Cognitive Abilities Test (Form 7 of CogAT, Lohman, 2011) are shown in Figure 1. The left column shows an example of one of the language-reduced item formats that are used with younger children. The right column shows an example of the standard item formats used with older children. Each reasoning ability is estimated by three subtests that require somewhat different processing. Although each of the three batteries can be administered and interpreted independently, most users administer all three batteries. Those who need a shorter test can administer the Screening Test that contains only the first subtest in each battery. The three reasoning abilities measured by the complete test correspond with the three aspects of fluid reasoning ability identified in Carroll's (1993) compendium.

Because they measure a much broader sample of different abilities, individually administered ability tests developed in recent years actually have fewer and shorter reasoning subtests (Frazier & Youngstrom, 2007). Thus, the CogAT scores are generally more reliable (see Table 1), a better measure of $g$ (Lohman, 2003a, b), and an equally good or better predictor of success in school.

| | Scores | Grades | Items per Battery | Total Items | Testing Time (min) | Score Warnings | Conditional Errors of Measurement | Most recent norms |
|---|---|---|---|---|---|---|---|---|
| **Cognitive Abilities Test (CogAT) (Form 7)** | Verbal, Quantitative, & Nonverbal | K - 12 | 38 to 62 | 118 to 176 | 90 | 9 | yes - for scale scores | 2010 |
| **INVIEW** | Verbal, Quantitative, & Nonverbal | 2 - 12 | 20 to 40 | 100 | 95 | 0 | yes- for raw scores | 2000 |
| **Naglieri Nonverbal Ability Test (NNAT-2)** | Nonverbal | | 30 | 30 | 30 | 0 | no | 2007 |
| **Otis-Lennon School Ability Test (OLSAT) (Form 8)** | Verbal & Nonverbal | K - 12 | 30 to 36 | 60 to 72 | 60 | 0 | no | 2002 |
| **Standard Progressive Matrices (Raven)** | Nonverbal | 3 - 12 | 60 | 60 | un-timed | 0 | no | 1970s user norms |

**Box 4 — Commonly Used Group Ability Tests**

## The Importance of Ability Profiles in Talent Identification

Although many have advocated for multidimensional theories of giftedness (Feldhusen & Jarwan, 2000; Gagné, 2009; Sternberg, 2003), children often are admitted to programs for the gifted and talented using group or individually administered measures of general ability (Assouline, 2003). Some programs require an IQ score of at least 130 (or national PR of 97). Other programs follow the recommended practice of collecting multiple sources of information, but unwittingly collapse it into a measure of general ability. For example, schools collect scores from different tests, classroom grades, and teacher ratings, assign points to each (often using somewhat arbitrary rules), and then add them together. Admission is based on the total number of points, which estimates the general factor common to all of the measures.

A single, omnibus score—whether from an intelligence test, an achievement test, or a more complex collection of ratings and assessments—will identify only that fraction of children who

305

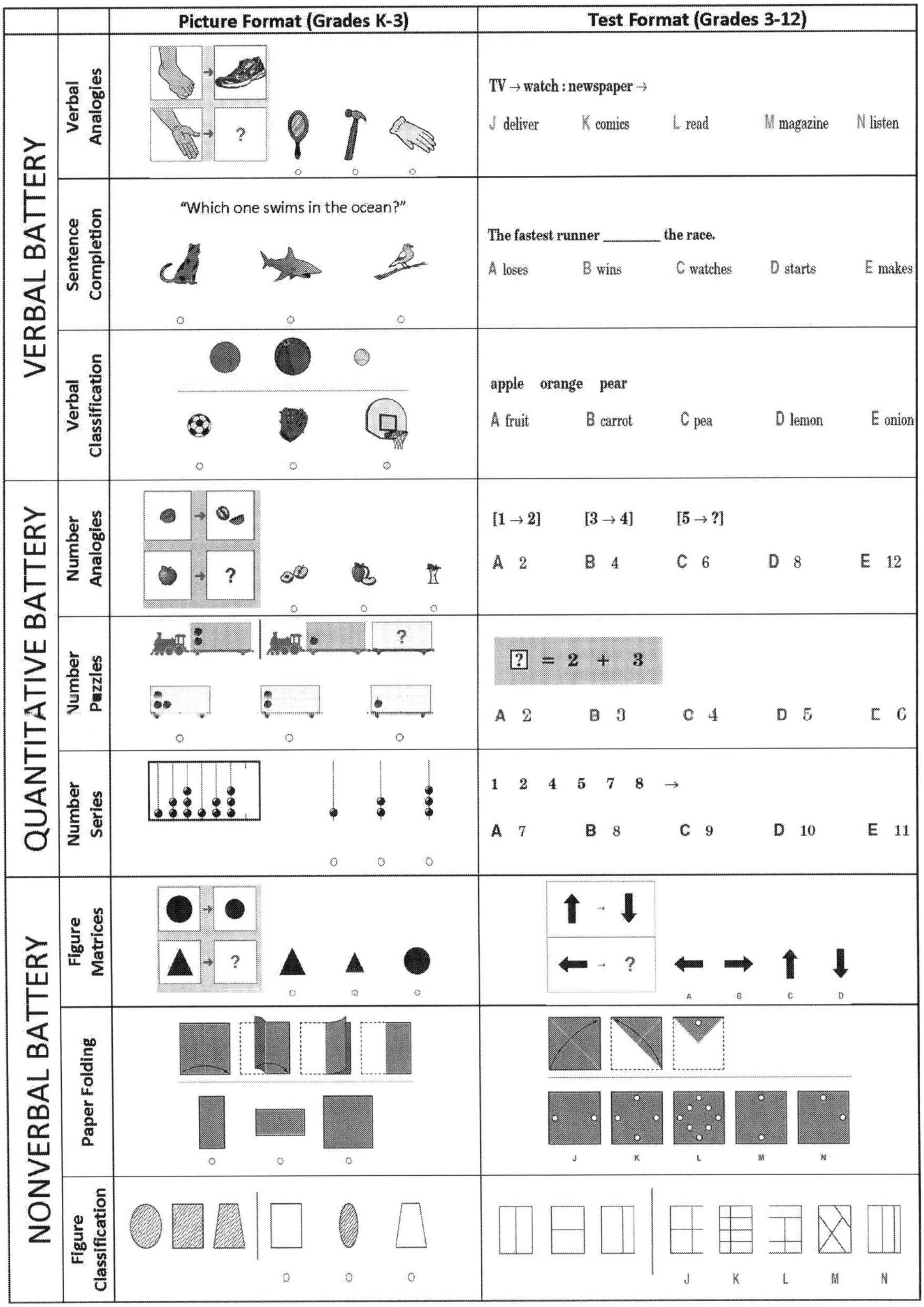

| | | Picture Format (Grades K-3) | Test Format (Grades 3-12) |
|---|---|---|---|

The table shows reasoning subtests organized by battery type. The content is primarily figural/pictorial examples paired with text-format items.

**VERBAL BATTERY**

*Verbal Analogies* (Test Format):
TV → watch : newspaper →
J deliver  K comics  L read  M magazine  N listen

*Sentence Completion* (Picture Format): "Which one swims in the ocean?"
(Test Format): The fastest runner _____ the race.
A loses  B wins  C watches  D starts  E makes

*Verbal Classification* (Test Format):
apple   orange   pear
A fruit  B carrot  C pea  D lemon  E onion

**QUANTITATIVE BATTERY**

*Number Analogies* (Test Format):
[1 → 2]   [3 → 4]   [5 → ?]
A 2  B 4  C 6  D 8  E 12

*Number Puzzles* (Test Format):
$? = 2 + 3$
A 2  B 3  C 4  D 5  E 6

*Number Series* (Test Format):
1  2  4  5  7  8  →
A 7  B 8  C 9  D 10  E 11

**NONVERBAL BATTERY**

*Figure Matrices*
*Paper Folding*
*Figure Classification*

Figure 1. Reasoning subtests on Form 7 of the Cognitive Abilities Test (Lohman, 2011) showing examples of item formats for grades K–3 (Col 1) and grades 3–12 (Col 2).

excel across all of the abilities measured by the tests and rating scales. The score profile for such students shows no unusual peaks or valleys. Only a minority of gifted students show this sort of flat score profile (Achter, Benbow, & Lubinski, 1997; Lohman, Gambrell, & Lakin, 2008). Indeed, as we will show below, the probability that a student has a flat score profile decreases as the students' scores depart from the mean. Furthermore, these differences in abilities have important long-term consequences. For example, profiles on ability tests administered at age 13 help predict the undergraduate majors students choose and the advanced degrees that they obtain (Lubinski, Webb, Morelock, & Benbow, 2001; Park, Lubinski, & Benbow, 2007).

Although some researchers have demonstrated that ability profiles have utility for both research and guidance counseling with gifted students, others have questioned both their reliability and usefulness. The criticisms have been especially strong for subtest scores on individually administered ability tests (Watkins, Gluting, & Youngstrom, 2005). Any effort to move beyond IQ's or similar omnibus scores assumes that the variations in scores captured by the profile reflect more than noise.

## Why Profiles Are Often Unreliable

Although some researchers have demonstrated that ability profiles have utility for both research and guidance counseling with gifted students, others have questioned both their reliability and usefulness. The criticisms have been especially strong for subtest scores on individually administered ability tests (Watkins, Gluting, & Youngstrom, 2005). Any effort to move beyond IQ's or similar omnibus scores assumes that the variations

in scores captured by the profile reflect more than noise.

The simplest profile consists of scores from two tests. Even if the two scores are moderately reliable, difference between them can be quite unreliable. The difference score retains the measurement errors in both tests, thereby doubling the measurement error in the difference score from what it was in either of the original test scores. To make matters worse, the difference score discards any systematic variability that the tests share. The shared variance is reflected in the correlation between the two tests. For example, suppose that the profile consists of scores on two, twenty-item tests. Because they are short, each test has only moderate reliability (say $r_{xx'} = .75$ for both). Further, as usually is the case in ability testing, the tests correlate $r = .6$ with each other. In this case, the reliability of the difference score (d) will be only $r_{dd'} = .37$.

The interpretation of a profile depends on which scores differ and by how much. The unreliability of these difference scores is what renders suspect most score profiles. Large differences between scores may not replicate and, conversely, seemingly similar scores may mask true differences. Thus, even if a student has equal abilities on several tests, it is likely that her scores will differ across the tests if the tests are short and therefore unreliable.

Although many factors influence the reliability of the difference scores that provide the unique information in the score profile, most important are the magnitude of the correlations among the separate scores and the reliability of each. Therefore, the first way to increase the reliability of the profile is to measure traits that are uncorrelated.

Unfortunately, one cannot increase reliability in this way when measuring abilities, especially abilities that require reasoning or problem-solving. Such abilities are strongly correlated.

The second way to increase the reliability of the profile is to increase the reliability of the separate test scores used in the profile. Reliability of test scores can be improved by increasing the number of items on the test. For example, if the lengths of two tests in the previous example were increased from 20 to 60 items, then reliability of each test would increase to $r_{xx'} = .90$ and the reliability of the difference score would increase to $r_{dd'} = .75$ (which was the reliability of the original, 20-item tests.) Longer tests make a big difference. As a rule of thumb, each test score in a profile should be based on at least 50 items in order to obtain adequate reliability to compare them. Unfortunately, administering tests with at least 50 items in each of several ability domains conflicts with most teachers' and school administrators' desire to spend no more than a few minutes on ability testing. Unless those responsible for identification understand the problems created when using short tests, convenience will win the day and life-altering decisions will be made about children on the basis of inadequate and unreliable information.

Obtaining highly reliable subtest scores is difficult not only because the test battery often must be administered in a relatively short time, but also because it must measure the ever-growing list of abilities that characterize modern theories of intelligence (Frazier & Youngstrom, 2007). The number of scores on ability tests has increased from the single IQ score on the original *Stanford-Binet* to four or five separate scores on the test's fifth edition

(Roid, 2003). One cannot obtain reliable measures of four or five dimensions in approximately the same time that it took to measure one dimension.

One way to avoid this problem is to measure only those abilities that directly inform the identification process and to measure each as reliably as possible with several different subtests. Thorndike and Hagen (1971) followed this strategy when developing the CogAT. Rather than measure many different abilities, they measured only those reasoning abilities with predictive validity for educational achievement: verbal reasoning, quantitative reasoning, and nonverbal/spatial reasoning. Importantly, each of the three batteries of reasoning tests contained 60 to 65 items. Thus, although the correlations between scores on the batteries are high ($r \approx .73$), the reliabilities of the batteries are considerably higher ($r_{xx'} \approx .94$). From one-third to one half of the reliable variance on each battery is not shared with one of the other two test batteries, thus allowing meaningful interpretation of the information that is embedded in the test profiles.

## CAPTURING THE UNIQUE INFORMATION IN SCORE PROFILES

Every score profile contains three kinds of information: altitude, scatter, and shape (Cronbach & Gleser, 1953). Altitude refers to the overall height or level of the score profile. It reflects the influence of the general factor common to the scores in the profile. It is estimated by the average of the separate scores. Scatter refers to the variability of subtest scores. Finally, shape refers to the particular pattern of elevations and depressions in the profile. Profiles with the same amount of scatter can have quite different shapes.

The shape of the profile can be indexed by comparing the similarity of the score profile with some standard. A logical standard can be established by enumerating the patterns that could logically be observed. This option is reasonable when the number of test scores in the profile is relatively small and the correlations among them are fairly uniform. For example, for the three CogAT scores [Verbal (V), Quantitative (Q), and Nonverbal (N)], there are three profiles that show a strength on one battery (V+, Q+, or N+), three that show a weakness (V-, Q-, or N-), and six more that show both a strength and a weakness (V+Q-, V+N-, Q+N-, Q+V-, N+V-, and N+Q-). All non-flat score profiles can be classified into one of these 12 categories.

## FREQUENCY OF OCCURRENCE OF DIFFERENT SCORE PROFILES

Are some profiles more common than other profiles for the most or least able students? Figure 2 shows the percentage of students in the 2000 CogAT US standardization sample who had different score profiles on the CogAT multilevel battery. Scores for the Verbal, Quantitative, and Nonverbal Reasoning batteries are highly correlated, indicating a strong general factor that is virtually coincident with the general factor on the WISC-III (Lohman, 2003a). A strong general factor suggests that score profiles would not be dependable. As it turns out, this is not the case.

Figure 2 shows that about 40% of the students showed an approximately flat profile for Verbal, Quantitative, and Nonverbal reasoning. The performance of these students is well summarized

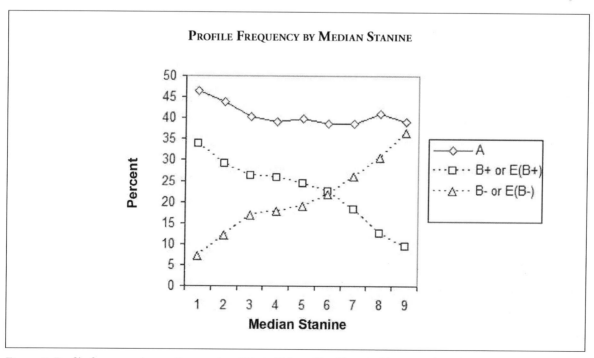

**Figure 2.** Profile frequency by median stanine. Flat or "A" profiles (diamonds); a significant strength (B+) or extreme strength [E(B+)] (squares); a significant weakness (B-) or extreme weakness [E(B)] (triangles)

in a single composite or average score. However, the majority of students (60%) showed a profile in which scores differed significantly. A significant or extreme strength [a score that was 20 or more Standard Age Score (SAS) points higher than the other two scores] was most common among students with a median stanine score of 1 and least common for students with a median stanine score of 9. A significant or extreme weakness (20 or more SAS points lower) shows the opposite pattern. The most able students were much more likely to show this profile than other students. Importantly, although only 3.4% of the population had profiles that showed an extreme weakness, 15.4% of the most able students showed this profile. Thus, profiles that show extreme differences between scores are much more common for the most and least able students than for average ability students. Consequently, one should never use the composite score on a diverse collection of tests when screening for giftedness. In addition, screening students on only nonverbal reasoning is also not advised. Most of the gifted students who obtain higher scores in quantitative reasoning or verbal reasoning than in nonverbal reasoning will not be identified if only those with high scores on the nonverbal test are given further consideration.

A moment's reflection shows why the frequency of extreme profiles varies by ability. For low-scoring students, an even lower score on the third battery is much less likely than a somewhat higher score. There is little room to move down and much room to move up. Conversely, high scoring students are much more likely to show a relative weakness than to show a relative strength

on the third battery. This is what is meant, but not explained, by "regression to the mean."

## REGRESSION TO THE MEAN

Any presentation of ability testing and giftedness would be incomplete without a discussion of "regression to the mean." Many in the field of special education ignore and some even deny the existence of regression to the mean. It is particularly odd that people trained in gifted education would do this. Regression to the mean, which was first observed by Galton when he plotted the heights of fathers and their sons, is one of the oldest empirical phenomena in the study of individual differences. It should be on page one of every text on gifted children. Regression is not acknowledged because many hold entity beliefs about abilities. Such beliefs are encouraged by the use of labels such as "gifted," by the use of status scores such as IQ or percentile rank that mask growth and other changes in ability over time, and by the human tendency to attend to information that confirms our expectations and to ignore information that challenges our beliefs (Lohman & Korb, 2006).

Regression to the mean will be observed whenever the correlation between two variables is less than perfect (r =1.0). Anything that reduces the correlation between two sets of observations increases the amount of regression that will be observed. Some of this regression reflects errors of measurement. Measurement errors include not only the random fluctuations in attention or memory that impact thinking on individual items on a particular occasion, but also the selection of items on the test and format of the test itself. To make an inference about a child's level of reasoning ability, one must go beyond the child's performance on a particular set of test items that were administered on a particular day. The best estimates of error include changes in performance across time, forms of the test, and even test formats. Internal consistency estimates of reliability do not capture any of these sources of error. Estimating reliability by administering parallel forms of the same test on different occasions comes closer. Administering a different test on each occasion is best. For example, internal consistency estimates of reliability for the WISC-IV Full Scale scores are about .97. However, the correlations between WISC-IV Full Scale scores and total scores on other ability tests (administered within a one month period) are in the .6 to .8 range (Daniel, 2000; Wechsler, 2003).

### ESTIMATING EXPECTED REGRESSION.

The expected regression in scores is easily estimated from the correlation. The predicted score on test 2 is simply

$$\hat{z}_2 = z_1 \times r_{12}$$

where $\hat{z}_2$ is the predicted standard score on test 2, $z_1$ is the standard score on test 1, and $r_{12}$ is the correlation between the tests 1 and 2.

The expected score at time 2 will equal the score at time 1 only if the correlation is 1.0 or if the standard score at time 1 is zero (i.e., the mean). The lower the correlation is, the greater the expected regression. Indeed, when the correlation between two tests is zero, the expected test score at time 2 is the mean (i.e., 0) for all test takers. Although there is no regression at the mean (i.e., $z_1 = z_2 = 0$), the amount of regression increases as scores depart from the mean. Students who receive

extremely high scores on test 1 are unlikely to receive similarly high scores on test 2. Box 5 gives some examples.

Regression will also be observed when two tests measure different constructs. Consider the three CogAT batteries. The reliabilities of scores on the three batteries are much higher than their correlations with each other (see Lohman, Gambrell, & Lakin, 2008). Therefore, the largest contributor to regression in the scores obtained on two different batteries is not error of measurement, but the fact that each test battery measures somewhat different abilities. The probability of obtaining an extremely high score on all three test batteries is much less than the probability of obtaining a high score on one battery. On CogAT, four out of every 100 students in grades 3 – 12 obtain a stanine score of 9 on each battery. However, only 2.4 out of every hundred obtain a stanine score of 9 on any two batteries. And only 4 out of every 1000 obtain a stanine score of 9 on all three batteries. Selection rules that admit only those who obtain high scores on multiple tests admit only a very small and unusual set of students (see chapter 10).

The greater frequency of one extremely low score for high-altitude profiles is not unique to CogAT. Indeed, the lower the correlation among scores in the profile (for reasons including multi-dimensionality as well as measurement error), the more common it will be. As a result, the CogAT authors have advised test users not to use the three-battery composite score to screen children for admission to programs for the gifted (Lohman & Hagen, 2001b; Thorndike & Hagen, 1986; 1994). Many quite capable students are likely to have one battery score that is low enough to bring down

---

**BOX 5**

**ESTIMATING EXPECTED REGRESSION IN TEST SCORES**

Equation 1 can be used to estimate the expected regression in status scores such as IQs. Note that regression effects for gifted students can be offset by practice effects, which can be substantial for tests that use novel formats or are speeded. Studies that report no regression in the average score for a group usually do not account for general improvements due to practice.

The first step is to convert the IQ to a z score by subtracting the mean IQ and dividing by the population SD for the test. For example, if the mean is 100 and the SD is 15, then an IQ of 130 converts to a z score of = 2.0.

If the correlation between scores at time 1 and time 2 is r = .8, then the expected z score at time 2 is 2.0 x .8 = 1.6.

This converts to an IQ of (1.6 x 15) + 100 = 124. The expected regression is 6 IQ points.

If the IQ were 145, then the expected regression would be 9 IQ points. This does account for the effects of practice, which can be just as large but in the opposite direction.

---

their averaged composite score. Rather than using only an estimate of *g*, the better procedure is to match the selection criteria with the demands of the educational program (Lohman, 2005a; Renzulli, 2005). At the very least, schools should distinguish between verbal and quantitative/spatial abilities when identifying academic talent.

### CAUTIONS AND CLARIFICATIONS.

Regression is sometimes not observed (especially in the average scores of a group of students) because it is counteracted by practice or training effects, which can be substantial (Kaufman, 1994). Such effects are especially likely for students who are unfamiliar with the test formats and on tests that are most susceptible to practice effects, such as Block Design from the WISC-IV, matrix items on nonverbal tests, or any test that is speeded.

Although errors of measurement (broadly construed) are the largest contributor to regression for tests measuring the same construct, even error-free measures show regression, especially as the time lag between the two assessments increases. Cognitive abilities develop at different rates in children and the sources of individual differences change as one moves up the developmental scale. (See Lohman & Korb, 2006 for discussion). Regression to the mean is about change in rank order, not about the change in absolute score levels. Even if all of the students in an educational program improve, regression will be observed if all do not improve equally. The critical mistake is to assume that the score on an ability test reflects a fixed characteristic rather than relative status on a fallible estimate of a constantly growing (and changing) set of mental characteristics. Indeed, in order to maintain a particular rank across time, a child must not only get better each year but must improve at the same rate as others who had the same initial rank.

## ERRORS OF MEASUREMENT

Of the many things that one might want to know about the scores on a test, group or individually administered, one of the most important is the dependability of those scores. Measurement experts have long advocated that test users rely on the Standard Error of Measurement (SEM) rather than the reliability coefficient when making inferences about the dependability of test scores. The SEM makes it much easier to estimate the magnitude of score changes one is likely to see upon retest, at least for students who do not have extreme scores. For example, consider three ability tests (M= 100, SD = 16) that have reliabilities of

.80, .90, and .95. The corresponding SEM's are 3.2, 1.6, and .8 IQ points. Put differently, changing the reliability from .8 to .9 cuts the expected error in half. Going from .90 to .95 halves it again. What are the consequences for a 95 percent confidence interval around the observed IQ score? The respective intervals have widths of 25, 12.4, and 3.1 IQ points. The confidence interval for the test with a reliability of $r_{xx^1} = .8$ is 8 times larger than the confidence interval for the test with a reliability of $r_{xx^1} = 95$.

Table 1 shows how errors of measurement vary across several widely used individually- and group- administered ability tests. For ease of comparison, all scores are reported on a scale with mean 100 and standard deviation 16.(See also Chapter 10.)

**Table 1**. Standard Errors of Measurement for a 10-Year-Old Child Scoring Near the Mean on Several Ability Tests

|  | WISC-IV[a] | SB-V | OLSAT-8 | Inview[c] | Raven[d] SPM | NNAT | CogAT 6 |
|---|---|---|---|---|---|---|---|
| Verbal | 3.9 | 3.6 | 5.7 | 5.3 |  |  | 3.4 |
| Nonverbal/ Perceptual | 4.2 | 3.9 | 5.8[b] | 4.5[b] | 3.0 | 6.1 | 3.7 |
| Quantitative | 4.5 | 5.3 |  |  |  |  | 3.3 |
| Composite/ Full Scale | 2.8 | 2.8 | 5.7 | 3.5 |  |  | 2.2 |

Note: All SEMs on a scale with mean=100, SD=16

[a] Working Memory Composite used to estimate Quantitative for WISC IV.

[b] On OLSAT and Inview, the quantitative subtests are included in the nonverbal score. The proper comparison with CogAT is therefore with the CogAT QN partial composite. The SEM for the QN Composite is 2.7.

[c] Inview only reports SEMs for the individual subtests, not the three composite scores that are reported. SEM's for composite scores were estimated by $(\sum e^2/k^2)^{.5}$ (Feldt & Brennan, 1989). These were then converted to CSI scores (M 100, SD 16) using the norms tables.

[d] Estimated from Table RS3 147 and RS3 148 in Raven et al. (2000). Table RS3 147 shows approximate 67 percent confidence intervals for PR scores by age. These were then converted to a scale with M 100, SD 16 using Table RS3 148.

SEMs vary widely, both within a test (e.g., 3.6 for the Verbal Fluid Reasoning and 5.3 for the Quantitative factor index on the SB-V) and between tests. In general, reliability increases with the number of items. For example, each level of the *Naglieri Nonverbal Ability Test* (NNAT; Naglieri, 1997) has 38 items. Students are allowed 30 minutes to attempt as many as they can. It has the largest SEM of any test in Table 1. On the Raven, however, students are given as long as they need (typically an hour or more) to attempt 60 items. Its SEM is less than half as large. But do the differences in SEM shown in the table matter? The 90 percent confidence interval for a student who receives a score of 100 on the NNAT is 88 to112 – a range of 24 points. For the CogAT Composite score it is 95.6 to 104.4 – a range of 8.8 points.

### CONDITIONAL SEMS.

The concerns associated with SEMs are actually substantially worse for scores at the extremes of the distribution, especially when scores approach the maximum possible on a test, such as when, on a group test, students answer most of the items correctly. In these cases, errors of measurement for scale scores will increase substantially at the extremes of the distribution. Commonly the SEM is from two to four times larger for very high scores than for scores near the mean (Lord, 1980). This increase in errors of measurement for scale scores (but not for number correct scores) is shown in Figure 3 for Level A of the Verbal Battery of CogAT– Form 6. The errors increase for Universal Scale Scores (USS) because transforming raw scores into scale scores stretches the score scale at the extremes of the distributions. This increase in error for scale scores can have disastrous consequences for efforts to identify gifted students, especially when scores are reported on an IQ-like scale rather than on the percentile-rank (PR) scale because PRs are compressed at the tails of the distribution, whereas scale scores are spread out. For

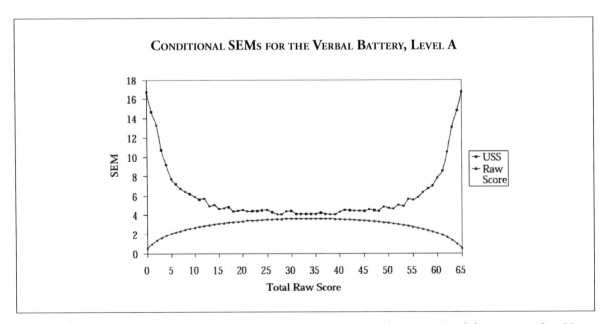

**Figure 3.** A comparison of errors of measurement for total raw scores (number correct) and the corresponding Universal Scale Scores (USS) for the Verbal Reasoning Battery of CogAT-Form 6 (from Lohman & Hagen, 2002, p. 58).

example, for tests such as CogAT and OLSAT that have a mean of 100 and standard deviation of 16, every Standard Age Score (SAS) above 134 receives the same PR of 99.

These relationships are shown in Figure 4. Notice that we have extended the upper scale so that the maximum SAS score is 150. Then, immediately below the figure, we have shown the raw scores that correspond to this SAS score for a 10-year-old child taking the CogAT Verbal Battery. Notice that once we get above 130 every additional item adds 10 SAS points. As a result, the error of measurement is much larger for high scores than for scores at, or, in this case, below the mean.

### OUT-OF-LEVEL TESTING.

The best way to reduce these errors of measurement is to test out of level. Put differently, one administers a level of the test that better matches

the abilities of the student to make it less likely that the student will be unfairly penalized (or credited) for missing (or solving) a single item. Indeed the higher level of the test includes more difficult items, which allows the student a better opportunity to demonstrate his or her abilities. On CogAT for example, users who need dependable scores for students in grades 3 and above who score above the 95th percentile are advised to move up two test levels (Lohman & Hagen, 2002), which is easy to do because all tests at these grades have the same directions and time limits.

People who balk at the need for this sort of adjustment must realize that it is precisely what happens when the child is tested individually. The examiner presents items until the student makes several mistakes in a row. Group tests also contain a single, long set of items for each subtest. However, for the convenience of administering

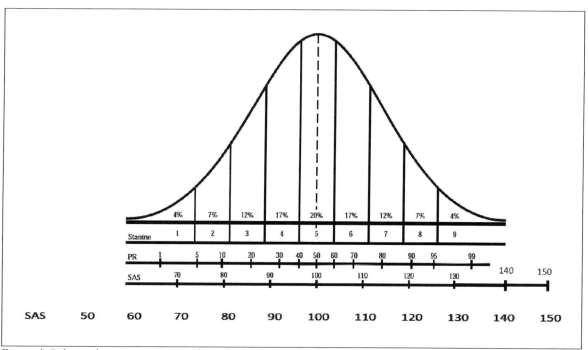

**Figure 4.** Relationships among Percentile ranks (PRs), Standard Age Scores (SAS), and raw scores for Level B of the CogAT (Form 6) Verbal Battery.

the same test to an entire class, only a portion of the items are included in the common test booklet for each test level. The test constructor divides the long set of items into overlapping sets of items that progressively increase in difficulty. However, only those items that can be administered to the typical class will be included in the test. Children who are 3 to 4 standard deviations above the mean need items that are appropriate for children several years older than the typical student of the same age. It is helpful to remember that these will be the same children who will be earning SAT scores of 500 or above when they are 12 or 13 years old.

Because they are more easily adapted to the ability of the student, scores on individually administered tests do not show such large increase in SEM for high-scoring children. Nonetheless, even on these tests, true scores (i.e., the scores that would be obtained if the students could be tested many times without any memory of the previous test) are on average always closer to the mean than observed scores. The higher the score, the more likely it is to regress. Therefore, confidence intervals for extreme scores are always skewed toward the mean. The higher the score, the more substantial the skew (Stanley, 1971).

## CONTROVERSIES ABOUT NONVERBAL REASONING TESTS

Nonverbal tasks like the CogAT Figure Matrices and Figure Classification tests shown in Figure 1 have long formed an important part of both individual intelligence tests and group ability tests. Scores on the nonverbal batteries of these tests provided one indicator of ability for native speakers of

the language, but often served as the only measure of ability for examinees who were not fluent speakers of the language. However, measurement experts have long cautioned that nonverbal reasoning tests do not capture the same ability construct that is measured by tests that use language (Anastasi, 1937) and therefore should not be used alone to make decisions about academic giftedness (Terman, 1930) or general intellectual competence (J. Raven, Raven, & Court, 1998; McCallum, Bracken, & Wasserman, 2001;see Box 6). Language, mathematics, music, and art are not contaminants grafted onto a fixed, innate intelligence, but rather critical vehicles for the development and expression of intelligence in particular symbol systems. Paring the world down to the small set of geometric forms used on a nonverbal reasoning test carves off much that any reasonable person would call intelligent thought.

Even though most nonverbal reasoning tests such as Raven's Progressive Matrices Test (Raven et al., 2000) and the Nonverbal Battery of the CogAT are reasonably good measures of g, they do not measure the verbal and symbolic reasoning abilities that are required for academic success for students from all ethnic backgrounds (Gustafsson & Balke, 1993; Keith, 1999; Lohman, 2005b). Even on the longest and most reliable nonverbal tests, only about half of the variance in test scores can be explained by g. The remaining variance is explained by other abilities, task-specific factors, and errors of measurement, which means that individual differences in the scores that students actually obtain on these tests are as likely to reflect factors other than g as they are to reflect g. Somewhat surprisingly, spatial abilities are only a small

316

---

**Box 6**

**NONVERBAL TESTS**

"When general intelligence is the targeted construct, the heavy verbal-demands of most language-loaded tests can create unfair construct-irrelevant influences on the examinees' performance." (McCallum, Bracken, & Wasserman, 2001, p. 4)

"Tests (such as the Progressive Matrices or Naglieri Nonverbal Ability test) should not be used interchangeably with traditional intelligence tests in situations in which decisions about eligibility are made." (McCallum, Bracken, & Wasserman, 2001, p. 9.)

"Non-verbal tests are often misleadingly described as tests of intelligence when, in fact, they sample only certain aspects of intellectual functioning. " (Raven, Court, & Raven, 1998, p. G70).

"For . . . items . . . such as those on the Raven Progressive Matrices Test, understanding the task is more than half the battle. In one study, many of the ethnic minority children in the sample did not understand the instructions to the 'game' and thus could not solve the problem." (Scarr, 1994, p.XX)

"[A] growing body of evidence suggests that nonlanguage tests may be more culturally loaded than language tests." (Anastasi & Urbina, 1997, p. 343).

"There is an aspect of problem solving that is clearly rooted in culture, namely the habit of translating pictorial events into sentences and talking about them. Although children may all recognize ovals, triangles, and trapezoids, and may all know about making things bigger or shading them with horizontal rather than vertical lines, the habit of labeling and talking aloud about such things varies across cultures (Heath, 1983). Children who do not actively label objects and transformations are more likely to resort to a purely perceptual strategy on nonverbal tests. Such strategies often work well on the easiest items that require the completion of a visual pattern or a perceptually salient series, but fail miserably on more difficult items that require the identification and application of multiple transformations on multiple stimuli." (Lohman, 2005b, p.115).

---

part of this non-*g* variance. Other tests that specifically measure spatial ability are needed to identify students who excel in visual thinking (Lohman, 1994).

## IDENTIFYING ACADEMICALLY TALENTED ELL CHILDREN.

The main reason that schools use nonverbal tests, however, is not because they hope to identify visual-spatial learners or even because they believe that nonverbal tests are a good way to measure academic giftedness. Rather, the overriding reason

is that differences between native and non-native speakers of English are substantially smaller on these tests than on tests that use English. For example, Lohman, Korb, and Lakin (2008) found that differences between the mean scores of ELL and non-ELL students were half as large on the CogAT Nonverbal Battery as on the CogAT Verbal Battery. There is thus a tradeoff in using nonverbal tests. On the one hand, nonverbal reasoning tests can reduce the amount of construct-irrelevant variance in test scores for nonnative speakers by reducing the impact of language. But by not measuring the ability to reason using verbal or quantitative symbol systems, nonverbal tests seriously under-represent the construct of academic aptitude (Braden, 2000; Lohman, 2005b; Mills & Tissot, 1995).

This loss in validity is shown not in the mean or average scores of groups, but in the correlations between test scores and various criteria of academic success. Unlike the means, the magnitude of these correlations does not differ across ethnic groups. Correlations between nonverbal, figural reasoning abilities and reading achievement typically range from $r = .3$ to $r = .5$; correlations with mathematics achievement typically range from $r = .4$ to. $r = .6$ (Lohman & Hagen, 2002; Naglieri & Ronning, 2000b; Powers, Barkan. & Jones, 1986). Although significant, these correlations are considerably smaller than the correlation of $r = .8$ between verbal reasoning and reading achievement or between quantitative reasoning and mathematics achievement (Lohman & Hagen, 2002; Thorndike & Hagen, 1995). Lower predictive validity substantially impairs the ability of the test to identify academically talented students, regardless of ethnicity or language background. Put another way, using the nonverbal test will admit more ELL students, but will miss many of the most academically talented ELL students.

## THE IMPORTANCE OF ACCOUNTING FOR OPPORTUNITY TO LEARN

The fact that the predictors of academic success are the same for all ethnic groups means that the identification of academic talent requires measurement of the same aptitude variables for all children. What it does not mean is that the test scores of all children should be compared to a common norm group. Rather, inferences about talent (or aptitude) require the simple step of comparing a child's performance to that of other children who have had roughly similarly opportunities to develop the abilities measured by the test. This is not an option, as it is when making inferences about achievement. The statement that a 7-year-old child is reading English-language texts at the third grade level is meaningful regardless of the child's familiarity with the English language. However, making an inference about ability or talent from these same test scores requires first controlling for the child's opportunity to learn the English language. That this is not commonly done says more about naïve beliefs about what ability tests measure and, historically, of the difficulty of controlling for anything beyond age (in years and months) or grade (also in years or months). Norms tables for ability tests that make careful adjustments in estimated ability from small changes in age assume that the number of years and months since the child's birth provide a reasonable estimate of opportunity to learn. But this is not the case whenever the child's experiences differ markedly from those of other children in the norming sample. Simply including some of these children in the norming sample does not fix the problem. With the advent of personal computers, however, the task of separating test scores for all ELL and all non-ELL children is no more difficult than separating the scores for boys and girls or for third graders and fourth graders. The tradeoff is between obtaining precise estimates of talent using the wrong norm group or less precise estimates using a much better norm group.

We demonstrate procedures for obtaining within-group comparisons in Chapter 10.

ELL students who might someday excel as writers, mathematicians, or artists will generally show rapid learning when given the opportunity to learn concepts and skills in those domains. These students will also obtain higher scores on the verbal, quantitative, or spatial tests that measure the specific aptitudes required to develop competence in each domain than other ELL students (Corno et al., 2002). Measuring only nonverbal reasoning and not these more proximal aptitudes actually excludes most minority children who are likely to excel in domains that require more than nonverbal reasoning. But the development of these children will not be considered unusual unless their test scores are compared to the test scores of other children who have had roughly similar opportunities to develop the abilities that are measured (Lohman & Lakin, 2007). This applies to all abilities—even those abilities measured by nonverbal reasoning tests.

## Do Nonverbal Tests Level the Playing Field for ELL Children?

It is commonly assumed and sometimes asserted that nonverbal tests level the playing field for ELL children (Naglieri, Booth, & Winsler, 2004). That this is not the case was shown in a large study in which approximately 2000 children (approximately 40% ELL) in grades K-6 were administered the Standard Progressive Matrices, the NNAT, and the CogAT by trained examiners. Directions were given in English or Spanish as appropriate. Large differences between the mean scores of all ELL and non-ELL children were reduced only slightly when the researchers controlled for ethnicity by comparing only Hispanic ELL and non-ELL students, all of whom were receiving free or reduced-price lunch at school. Non-ELL Hispanic students outperformed their ELL Hispanic classmates by 7.5, 7.3, and 9.5 IQ-like points on the Raven, CogAT, and NNAT, respectively. The data also showed that the norms on the Raven were about 10 IQ-like points too easy and that the norms on the NNAT were incorrectly computed, vastly over-identifying the number of high-scoring children.

Finally, as in several other studies (e.g., Carmen & Taylor, 2010) there was no support for Naglieri and Ford's (2003) claim that the NNAT identified equal proportions of White, Hispanic, and Black children. Indeed, ELL children were much more likely to receive very low scores on NNAT than on the other two nonverbal tests. Some of these findings are summarized in Figure 5.

Both naïve theories about what ability tests measure (Lohman, 2006a) and exaggerated claims for the efficacy of improperly normed nonverbal tests (see Carman, 2010; Lohman, Korb, & Lakin, 2008) have misled many well-meaning educators. Nonverbal tests need not fulfill a utopian vision as measures of innate ability unencumbered by culture, education, or experience in order to play a useful role in the identification of academically gifted children. Nonverbal reasoning tests can help identify bright children, especially those who are poor or who are not fluent in the language of the dominant culture. When combined with measures of quantitative reasoning and spatial ability, nonverbal reasoning tests are particularly helpful in identifying students who will excel in engineering,

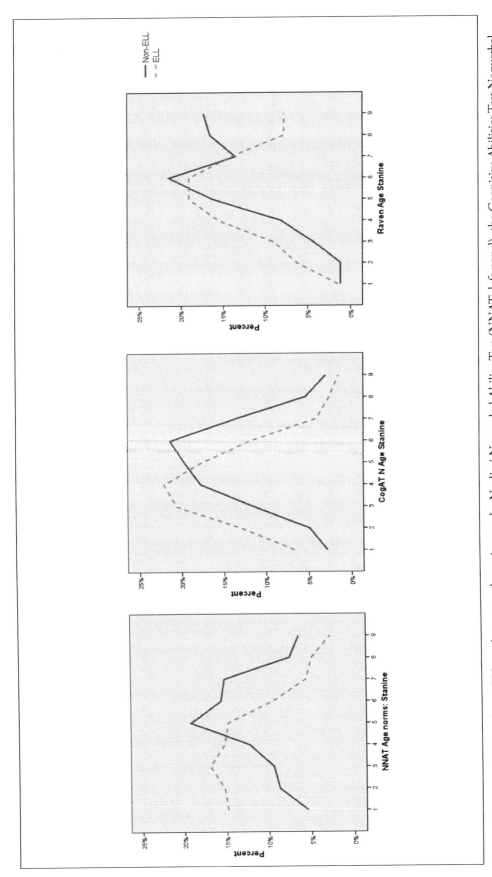

**Figure 5.** Percent of ELL and non-ELL students at each stanine on the Naglieri Nonverbal Ability Test (NNAT; left panel), the Cognitive Abilities Test Nonverbal Battery (CogAT N; center panel), and the Standard Progressive Matrices (Raven; right panel). The dashed green line is for ELL students and the solid blue line for non-ELL students. Note the large number of low-scoring ELL children in Panel 1 and the large number of high-scoring non-ELL children in Panel 3. Both lines should approximate a normal or bell-shaped curve. Curves would overlap if scores for ELL students did not differ from the scores of non-ELL students.

mathematics, and related fields (Shea, Lubinski, & Benbow, 2001). But the development of these children will not be considered unusual unless their test scores are compared to the test scores of other children who have had roughly similar opportunities to develop the abilities that are measured by the test – even if it is a nonverbal reasoning test (Lohman & Lakin, 2007).

## "Nonverbal" Measures of Verbal and Quantitative Reasoning

In their book on nonverbal testing, McCallum, Bracken, & Wasserman (2001) distinguish between unidimensional and comprehensive nonverbal tests. A unidimensional test is composed of items that all come for a common domain—typically the sort of figural-spatial reasoning required on the Progressive Matrices (Raven et. al., 2000), the NNAT (Naglieri,1997), and the Nonverbal Battery of CogAT (Lohman & Hagen, 2001a). Alternatively, comprehensive nonverbal tests sample from a broader domain of test content. Examples include the Leiter International Performance scale (Roid & Miller, 1997), the Universal Nonverbal Intelligence Test (Bracken & McCallum, 1998), and the primary-level tests of Form 7 of CogAT (Lohman, 2011) shown in Figure 1.

Form 7 of CogAT differs from earlier editions of CogAT, most importantly in ways that make the primary-level tests more accessible to ELL children.

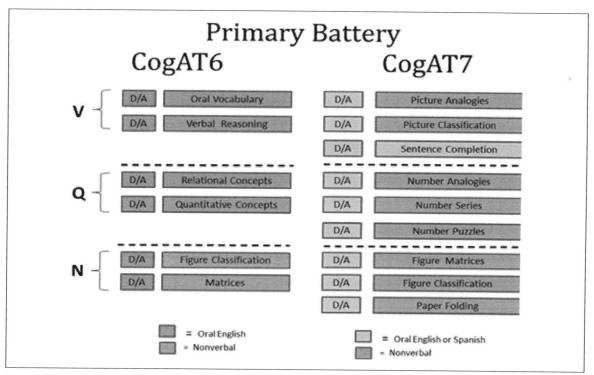

Figure 6. Comparison of subtests on the Primary-level tests (Grades K, 1, and 2) of Forms 6 and 7 of CogAT. Both have Verbal (V), Quantitative Q), and Nonverbal (N) batteries, each of which has two subtests on Form 6 and three subtests on Form 7. Total testing time is slightly less for Form 7. Both English and Spanish Directions for Administration (D/A) fare provided for the paper-and-pencil version of CogAT7. Several other widely used languages are also provided as audio files on the computer-administered version of Form 7.

These differences are summarized in Figure 6. On previous editions of CogAT, all four subtests on the primary-level verbal and quantitative and batteries required that students listen to a question that was presented orally by the test administrator and then select a picture that best answered that question. (The two subtests on the nonverbal battery did not use items that required language.) On Form 7, however, only one of the nine subtests on the primary battery (i.e., Sentence Completion) requires comprehension of oral language. This test can be administered in English or Spanish or omitted altogether. Figure 1 showed sample items from the three verbal subtests on Form 7 that demonstrate how a pictorial format can be used instead of a text-based format with young children. Eight of the nine CogAT subtests at grades K-2 measure reasoning without the use of verbal prompts or responses: three subtests use figural spatial content (Figure Matrices, Figure Classification, and Paper Folding), three use quantitative content (Number Analogies, Number Series, Number Puzzles), and two use verbal content (Picture Analogies & Picture Classification). These subtests allow one to estimate the child's ability to reason "nonverbally" in three content domains: spatial, numerical, and verbal. Importantly, ELL, low SES, and minority students perform as well or better on these picture-verbal and picture-quantitative tests than on figural reasoning tests (Lohman & Gambrell, in press). Three content domains on the Form 7 primary-level CogAT tests (picture-verbal, picture-quantitative, and spatial/figural) provide a much broader measure of ability than earlier editions of CogAT (in which only the Figure Matrices and Figure Classification subtests were presented non-verbally) and other nonverbal tests that use only figure matrices (e.g., Raven or NNAT).

## MISUSES OF GROUP TESTS

The difference between individually administered ability tests and group administered ability tests is like the difference between prescription and over-the-counter drugs. On the one hand, while non-experts are likely to be misled in their beliefs about the efficacy of drugs obtained from either source, there is at least some semblance of control over the claims about and usage of prescription drugs. On the other hand, claims made by the purveyors of over-the-counter drugs often exaggerate their efficacy, ignore their negative side effects, and sometimes purposely mislead. Likewise, the restraints on the marketing and use of group-administered ability tests that do not require professional certification to administer are few and rarely enforced. The only real restraints are those that are self-imposed by the integrity of the test author and the company that markets the test.

Misuses of scores on group-administered ability tests abound. Some are errors of commission, others of omission. Since such tests enter prominently into decisions about academic talent that educators must make, we discuss several of the most egregious claims made for these tests.

### ¶ *Does the test purport to be a panacea?*

Most people believe that ability tests measure (or ought to measure) innate ability unfettered by contaminants such as education, culture, and language. Such an ancient belief is more akin to theories held by novices in physics and other scientific domains (Lohman, 2006). Although the vast majority of experts in measurement do not subscribe to this view, the handful that do gather much attention. Unfortunately, most educators have little training in educational and psychological measurement, and thus have little preparation to dispute such claims. In fact, because they have little training in measurement, most find these beliefs congenial with their own beliefs about ability. Some of the more exaggerated claims about ability tests include:

1. that a test is culture fair, culture free, or, more recently, culture neutral;

2. that it will identify equally proportions of minority and non-minority, poor and rich, or ELL and non-ELL children;

3. that it can give tests scores that are sufficiently reliable for gifted identification with approximately 30 minutes of testing; and

4. that pantomime or pictorial directions can adequately prepare students to do their best on these tests.

### ¶ *Does the test provide instructionally useful information for all students?*

Administrators of talent development programs often encourage their schools to administer an ability test to all children so that talent identification is not contingent on teacher or parent nomination. Census testing also enables the program to obtain local norms. Scores from the screening test serve an obvious purpose for those students who are subsequently offered enriched or more challenging instruction. But what about the other 95% of the children? Does the test give these children, their parents, or their teachers educationally useful information? If not, is it any wonder that teachers might oppose taking precious class time to administer the ability test? Misinterpreting test scores for low-scoring students can be even more problematic if the test is thought to provide a culture-fair measure of innate ability.

### ¶ *Does the test report errors of measurement that apply to gifted students?*

Some tests report only reliability coefficients and do not present standard errors of measurement (SEM). Test users commonly over-estimate the dependability of scores when given only reliability coefficients. Others report SEMs, but not on the score scale that test users will need. For example, InView reports SEMs for number correct scores rather than for the IQ-like scores used for talent identification, which is not helpful. Furthermore, errors of measurement for IQ-like scores are typically many times larger at the extremes of the distribution than at the mean. Thus, the average or typical SEM substantially overestimates the precision of extreme scores, which has obvious implications for using the test to identify gifted students.

### ¶ *Do score reports warn the user when scores for an examinee may be undependable?*

Given the likelihood that scores on ability tests will be misinterpreted—if not by the user then by someone else reading the student's file—aberrant scores either should not be reported or should be marked as possibly erroneous. Although there are a few cases in which the mistake could result in an over-estimate of ability (e.g., coding a lower age or grade than was appropriate), most testing aberrations reduce test scores. There are many more ways to get something wrong than to get it right. For these reasons examiners or test administrators should report behavioral observations that could negatively influence performance. Although some group administered tests (e.g., NNAT-2 and CogAT) will not report a score if the age score seems unusual, only CogAT cautions scores if the student responded inconsistently to items or subtests that measure the same ability, appeared to have adopted a very slow and cautious response style, or exhibited other obvious problems. Warnings caution users not to make high-stakes decisions about the child using that test score. All computer-scored, group-administered tests should provide these sorts of warnings.

### ¶ Are the test norms recent?

The scores on ability tests have risen dramatically over the past 70 years. Performance on IQ tests has been improving ever since ability tests were first introduced. Flynn (2007) estimated an increase of about three IQ points per decade between 1948 and 2002, with the largest increase occurring on figural reasoning tests such as the Progressive Matrices Test (Raven, Court, & Raven, 1996). The mean IQ score remains 100 only because intelligence tests are re-normed every few years; therefore, old norms are invariably too lenient. For example, the 2000 edition of the Progressive Matrices test uses normative data collected in the 1970s and 1980s . A comparison of these normative scores with two more recently normed tests showed that scores on the Raven were approximately 10 IQ-like points (.67 SD) too high (Lohman, Korb, & Lakin, 2008). Normative

scores on the Culture-Fair Intelligence test (Cattell & Cattell, 1965), which has not been normed since the 1960s, are even more out of date. One study found that its normative scores were about 17 IQ-like points too lenient (Shaunessy, Karnes, & Cobb, 2004).

### ¶ Are the norms dependable?

On other tests, the problem is not the recency of the norms, but their dependability. Norms can be undependable if the norming sample is not representative of the population. Several studies now suggest that the normative sample for the SB-V may have over-represented exceptional children. If this is true, then normative scores on the test would be too high for low-scoring children and too low for high-scoring children. This phenomenon was first suggested in the SB-V technical manual (Roid, 2003). Standard deviations for the SB-V were smaller than standard deviations on the SB-IV, the WIPPSI-R, the WISC-III, the WAIS-III, and the WJIII COG. Although some of the differences were small, others were not. Test users noted a similar restriction in the range of scores on the SB-V, with fewer students obtaining very high scores (Minton & Pratt, 2006). This situation is troubling because, in all other respects, test construction exemplified best practices in psychometrics.

Norms derived retrospectively from user data, rather than purposefully obtained through a sampling plan, are always suspect, even if based on very large samples. Those who choose to purchase and administer a particular test are not a random sample of all potential test users. The normative data for the Progressive Matrices test were obtained in this way. Even when a national sampling plan is used, many of the schools or individuals who are contacted refuse to participate. When test users refuse to participate, replacements are sought or data for other participants who were in the same cell of the sampling design are given greater weight. This tactic can bias the norms that are obtained. Such refusals are increasingly common in an educational system overburdened with testing, even when schools are offered substantial financial incentives for participation. As a result, trustworthy national norms on ability tests are increasingly difficult to obtain.

Norms can also be undependable if the procedures used to develop them were either suboptimal or incorrect. The 1997 norms for the NNAT exhibited both problems. The norming procedures were suboptimal in that the within-age score distributions were not smoothed. Smoothing ensures that IQ-like scores do not change erratically as one moves across age groups. The NNAT norming procedures were incorrect in that the standard deviation of the IQ-like score (called the nonverbal ability index or NAI) was substantially greater than 15 at all but one test level. Inferences about giftedness depend critically on the standard deviation of scores. Excessive variability of NAI scores means than the test over-identified the number of students receiving high scores. For example, the number of students who received NAI scores of 130 or higher on Level A of the NNAT was over three times greater than it should have been. Although one would hope that these problems were corrected in the norming of the NNAT-2, they exemplify the sort of problems that test users should not have to worry about when they purchase a

recently-normed test from a major publishing company.

## ¶ Does the test provide practice materials?

Since the early days of testing, psychologists have endeavored to measure intelligence by seeing how well the examinee adapted to the demands of novel problems. To this day, ability tests rely heavily on item types and formats that are unfamiliar to most students. The problem is that not all students are equally unfamiliar with the item formats used on the test. In some cases, unfamiliarity leads to serious misconceptions about how to solve items. In other cases, it leads to sub-optimal performance, especially when the test is speeded. Alternatively, performance is enhanced for those who have practiced using the item formats. How large are these practice and training effects? Practicing unfamiliar item formats commonly results in improvements of 8 or more IQ points. Effects are largest for nonverbal tests and smallest for verbal tests.

There are several ways to reduce these effects. First, those who have custody of tests need to treat the responsibility seriously. Lax security of test booklets increases the likelihood that booklets will be stolen or copied. Copying tests is not only unfair, but illegal. Second, whenever possible, students should be retested with an alternate form of the test. Some tests have alternate forms; most do not. Even when more than one form of the test is available (e.g., Otis-Lennon forms 7 and 8 or NNAT and NNAT-2), tables are not provided that show how scores on the old form map on to the scores on the new form, so that one can use the most recent norms tables for interpreting both sets of scores. Some widely used tests (e.g. the Progressive Matrices Test) have used the same items since they were first developed. Others (e.g., the Otis-Lennon) replace some items and repeat others. When forms use the same items, lax security on one form compromises other forms. Third, students should receive practice in solving items that use the item formats that they will see on the tests. Savvy parents can now buy practice test materials on the internet. The availability of these materials has significantly enhanced the likelihood that children who have access to practice materials will obtain high scores on the tests. Practice for all children is necessary to level the playing field. Good practice should do more than rehearse a few items; it should help students learn how to think about the items, not merely how to respond to them. For example, learning to use language to label stimuli and rules that connect them can be critical for performance on nonverbal tests.

## SUMMARY

Ability testing is a critical component of any academic talent identification system. It is most important for those who, though age, experience, circumstance, or choice have not developed high levels of competence in some academic or cognitive domain. This is commonly true for young children, for poor and minority students whose circumstances have limited their opportunities to acquire academic skills, and for twice-exceptional children, whose disability may have negatively affected their classroom performance. Although ability data is critical, it should never be expected to stand alone. Furthermore, the abilities that should be measured cannot adequately be assessed in a

few minutes by administering two or three subtests from a larger assessment battery, or worse, a single kind of test-task. Decision makers who use brief, unidimensional tests are often misled by seemingly high reliabilities. High internal consistency reliabilities mean only that the items on the test measure the same thing, not that they generalize to anything else. Tests need multiple formats and contents for greater generalizabilty. Further, instead of reliability coefficients, information about standard errors of measurement and how they vary depending on ability level are more useful.

Test interpreters must move beyond overall composite scores and other measures of g in order to understanding how well students reason in different symbol systems commonly required for academic learning: verbal, spatial, and quantitative. This is particularly true for high ability students who are more likely to have uneven ability profiles than students who score closer to the mean. When selecting ability tests that will most fairly and accurately assess student's abilities, it is important to go beyond simple differences in the mean scores between groups and attend to issues of predictive validity, or the extent to which the test measures those aptitudes that are necessary for and thus predictive of success in the talent domain. In other words, the assessment tools must measure skills that will be needed in the talent development program. Although concerns about equity can in part be addressed by using comprehensive non-verbal reasoning tests, no test can measure innate ability in a way that is independent of education, culture, and experience. Developing talent identification systems that allow ability test scores to be interpreted using different norm groups—local,

326

and opportunity-to-learn—usually offers a better way to achieve equity without compromising excellence.

There are individual as well as group administered ability tests, and each has its own set of advantages and disadvantages. Individually administered tests have the advantage of allowing for observations of behaviors that influence scores, generally well-developed normative data, better understanding of twice-exceptional students, and well-trained examiners to interpret test data. At the same time, the use of individually-administered tests as a part of an identification program for gifted students raises questions about equity, cost-effectiveness, and efficiency. Group ability tests address these limitations because they can be administered quickly to large groups of students, and local norms can be easily developed for comparisons that better account for differences in opportunity to learn. However, many group-administered tests are poorly developed, have inadequate norms, or are advertised in misleading ways. Frank discussions with current users of a test who have looked carefully at their test data and how well it has lived up to expectations can be helpful in selecting a test to administer.

Misconceptions about ability abound. Parents, teachers, and even professionals not explicitly trained in assessment have naïve beliefs about what these tests measure, which makes it imperative that those who administer ability tests not use them in ways that reinforce these misconceptions.

REFERENCES

Achter, J. A, Benbow, C. P., & Lubinski, D. (1997). Rethinking multipotentiality among the intellectually gifted: A critical review and recommendations. *Gifted Child Quarterly. 41*, 5–5.

Ackerman, P. L. (2003). Aptitude complexes and trait complexes. *Educational Psychologist, 38*, 85–94.

Anastasi, A. (1937). *Differential psychology*. New York: Macmillan.

Anastasi, A., & Urbina, S. (1997). *Psychological testing* (7th ed.). Upper Saddle River, NJ: Prentice Hall.

Assouline, S. G. (2003). Psychological and educational assessment of gifted children. In N. Colangelo & G. A. Davis (Eds.), *Handbook of gifted education* (3rd ed., pp. 124–145). Boston: Allyn & Bacon.

Assouline, S. G., Colangelo, N., Lupkowski-Shoplik, A., Lipscomb, J., & Forstadt, L. (2009). *Iowa acceleration scale*, third edition. Scottsdale, AZ: Great Potential Press.

Assouline, S. G., Foley Nicpon, M., & Bramer, D. M. (2006). The impact of vulnerabilities and strengths on the academic experiences of twice-exceptional students: A message to school counselors. *Professional School Counseling, 10* (1), 14–25.

Assouline, S. G., Foley Nicpon, M., & Whiteman, C. S. (2010). Cognitive and psychosocial characteristics of gifted students with written language disability. *Gifted Child Quarterly, 54*, 102–115. doi: 10.1177/0016986209355974.

Bingham, W. V. (1937). Aptitudes and aptitude testing. New York: Harper & Brother.

Borland, J. H. (2004). Issues and practices in the identification and education of gifted students from under-represented groups RM04186). Storrs, CT: The National Research Center on the Gifted and Talented, University of Connecticut.

Bracken, B. A., & McCallum, S. (1998). *Universal Nonverbal Intelligence Test—UNIT*. Itasca, IL: Riverside Publishing.

Braden, J. P. (2000). Perspectives on the nonverbal assessment of intelligence. Journal of *Psychoeducational Assessment, 18*, 204–210.

Carmen, C. A, & Taylor, D. K. (2010). Socioeconomic status effects on using the Naglieri Nonverbal Ability Test (NNAT) to identify the gifted/talented. *Gifted Child Quarterly, 54, 75–84*.

Carroll, J. B. (1974). The aptitude-achievement distinction: The case of foreign language aptitude and proficiency. In D. R. Green (Ed.), *The aptitude-achievement distinction* (pp. 286–303). Monterey, CA: CTB/McGraw-Hill.

Carroll, J. B. (1993). *Human cognitive abilities: A survey of factor-analytic studies*. Cambridge, UK: Cambridge University Press.

Cattell, R. B., & Cattell, K. S. (1965). *Manual for the Culture-Fair Intelligence Test, Scale 2*. Champaign, IL: Institute for Personality and Ability Testing.

Corno, L., Cronbach, L. J., Kupermintz, H., Lohman, D. F., Mandinach, E. B., Porteus, A. W., & Talbert, J. E. (2002). *Remaking the concept of aptitude: Extending the legacy of*

*Richard E. Snow.* Hillsdale, NJ: Lawrence Erlbaum.

Cronbach, L. J. & Gleser, G. C. (1953). Assessing similarity between profiles. *Psychological Bulletin, 50,* 456–473.

Cronbach, L. J., & Snow, R. E. (1977). *Aptitudes and instructional methods: A handbook for research on interactions.* New York: Irvington.

Daniel, M. H. (2000). Interpretation of intelligence test scores. In R. Sternberg (Ed.), *Handbook of intelligence* (pp. 477–491). New York: Cambridge.

Feldhusen, J. F. & Jarwan, F. A. (2000). Identification of gifted and talented youth for educational programs. In K. A. Heller, F. J. Monks, R. Subotnik, & R. J. Sternberg (Eds.) *International handbook of giftedness and talent* (pp. 271–282). Oxford, UK: Elsevier

Feldt, L. S., & Brennan, R. L. (1989). Reliability. In R. L. Linn (Ed.), *Educational measurement* (3rd ed., pp. 105–146). New York: Macmillan.

Flynn, J. (2007). *What is intelligence: Beyond the Flynn effect.* NY: Cambridge University Press.

Frazier, T. W. & Youngstrom, E. A. (2007). Historical increase in the number of factors measured by commercial tests of cognitive ability: Are we overfactoring? *Intelligence, 35*(2), 169–182.

Gagné, F. (2009). Talent development as seen through the differentiated model of giftedness and talent. The Routledge international companion to gifted education. In T. Balchin, B. Hymer, & D. J. Matthews (Eds). *The Routledge international companion to*

*gifted education.* (pp. 32–41). New York, NY, US: Routledge/Taylor & Francis Group.

Glaser, R. (1992). Expert knowledge and processes of thinking. In D. F. Halpern (Ed.), *Enhancing thinking skills in the sciences and mathematics* (pp. 63–75). Hillsdale, NJ: Lawrence Erlbaum.

Gohm, C. L., Humphreys, L. G., & Yao, G. (1998). Underachievement among spatially gifted students. *American Educational Research Journal, 35,* 515–531.

Gustafsson, J. E., & Balke, G. (1993). General and specific abilities as predictors of school achievement. *Multivariate Behavioral Research, 28,* 407–434.

Heath, S. B. (1983). *Ways with words: Language, life, and work in communities and classrooms.* New York: Cambridge University Press.

Hoover, H. D., Dunbar, S. B., & Frisbie, D. A., (2005). Iowa Tests of Basic Skills (Forms A, B, and C). Itasca, IL: Riverside.

Hunt, E. (2000). Let's hear it for crystallized intelligence. *Learning and Individual Differences, 12,* 123–130.

Kaufman, A. S. (1994). *Intelligent testing with the WISC-III.* Wiley New York.

Kaufman, A. S., & Harrison, P. L., (1986). Intelligence tests and gifted assessment: What are the positives? Roeper Review, *8*(3), 154–159.

Kaufman, A. S., & Sternberg, R. J. (2007). Giftedness in Euro-American culture. In S. N. Phillipson & M. McCann (Eds.), *Conceptions of giftedness: Socio-cultural perspectives.* Mahwah, NJ: Erlbaum.

Keith, T. Z. (1999). Effects of general and specific abilities on student achievement: Similarities and differences across ethnic groups. *School Psychology Quarterly, 14*, 239-262.

Lohman, D. F. (1994). Spatial ability. In R. J. Sternberg (Ed.), *Encyclopedia of human intelligence* (pp. 1000–1007). New York: Macmillan.

Lohman, D. F. (2003a). The Wechsler Intelligence Scale for Children III and the Cognitive Abilities Test (Form 6): Are the general factors the same? http://faculty.education.uiowa.edu/dlohman/pdf/CogAT-WISC_final_2col2r.pdf

Lohman, D. F. (2003b). The Woodcock-Johnson III and the Cognitive Abilities Test (Form 6): A concurrent validity study. http://faculty.education.uiowa.edu/dlohman/pdf/CogAT_WJIII_final_2col%202r.pdf

Lohman, D. F. (2005a). An aptitude perspective on talent identification: Implications for the identification of academically gifted minority students. *Journal for the Education of the Gifted, 28*, 333–359.

Lohman, D. F. (2005b). The role of nonverbal ability tests in the identification of academically gifted students: An aptitude perspective. *Gifted Child Quarterly, 49*, 111–138.

Lohman, D. F. (2006). Beliefs about differences between ability and accomplishment: From folk theories to cognitive science. *Roeper Review, 29*, 32–40.

Lohman, D. F. (2011). *Cognitive Abilities Test (Form 7)*. Rolling Meadows, IL: Riverside.

Lohman, D. F., & Gambrell, J. L. (in press). Use of nonverbal tests in gifted identification. Journal of Psychoeducational Assessment.

Lohman, D. F., Gambrell, J., & Lakin, J. (2008). The commonality of extreme discrepancies in the ability profiles of academically gifted students. *Psychology Science Quarterly, 50*, 269–282.

Lohman, D. F., & Hagen, E. P. (2001a). *Cognitive Abilities Test (Form 6)*. Itasca, IL: Riverside.

Lohman, D. F., & Hagen, E. P. (2001b). *Cognitive Abilities Test (Form 6): Interpretive guide for teachers and counselors*. Itasca, IL: Riverside.

Lohman, D. F., & Hagen, E. P. (2002). *Cognitive Abilities Test (Form 6): Research handbook*. Itasca, IL: Riverside.

Lohman, D. F., & Korb, K. A. (2006). Gifted today but not tomorrow? Longitudinal changes in ITBS and CogAT scores during elementary school. *Journal for the Education of the Gifted, 29*, 451–484.

Lohman, D. F., Korb, K., & Lakin, J. (2008). Identifying academically gifted English language learners using nonverbal tests: A comparison of the Raven, NNAT, and CogAT. *Gifted Child Quarterly, 52*, 275–296.

Lohman, D. F., & Lakin, J. (2007). Nonverbal test scores as one component of an identification system: Integrating ability, achievement, and teacher ratings. In J. VanTassel-Baska (Ed.). *Alternative assessments for identifying gifted and talented students* (p. 41–66). Austin, TX: Prufrock Press.

Lord, F. M. (1980). *Applications of item response theory to practical testing problems*. Hillsdale, N.J. : Erlbaum Associates.

Lubinski, D. (2004). Introduction to the Special Section on Cognitive Abilities: 100 years after Spearman's (1904) "General Intelligence, Objectively Determined and Measured." *Journal of Personality and Social Psychology, 86*(1), 96–111.

Lubinski, D., & Benbow, C. P. (2000). States of excellence. *The American Psychologist, 55*(1), 137–150.

Lubinski, D., Webb, R. M., Morelock, M. J., & Benbow, C. P. (2001). Top 1 in 10,000: A 10-year follow-up of the profoundly gifted. *Journal of Applied Psychology, 86*(4), 718–129.

McCallum, S., Bracken, B., & Wasserman, J. (2001). *Essentials of Nonverbal Assessment.* Hoboken, NY: Wiley.

Mills, C., & Tissot, S. L. (1995). Identifying academic potential in students from underrepresented populations: Is using the Ravens Progressive Matrices a good idea? *Gifted Child Quarterly, 39*, 209–217.

Minton, B. A., & Pratt, S. (2006). Gifted and highly gifted students: How to they score on the SB5? *Roeper Review, 28*, 232–236.

Mulaik, S. A. (1972). *The foundations of factor analysis.* New York, NY: McGraw-Hill.

National Association for Gifted Children (2008). Use of the WISC-IV for gifted identification. Retrieved from http://www.nagc.org/uploadedFiles/Information_and_Resources/Position_Papers/WISC-IV.pdf

Naglieri, J. A. (1997). *Naglieri Nonverbal Ability Test: Multilevel technical manual.* San Antonio, TX: Harcourt Brace.

Naglieri, J. A., & Ford, D. Y. (2003). Addressing underrepresentation of gifted minority children using the Naglieri Nonverbal Ability Test (NNAT). *Gifted Child Quarterly, 47,* 155–160.

Naglieri, J. A., & Ronning, M. E. (2000). The relationship between general ability using the Naglieri Nonverbal Ability Test (NNAT) and the Stanford Achievement Test (SAT) reading achievement. *Journal of Psychoeducational Assessment, 18,* 230–239.

Naglieri, J. A., Booth, A. L., & Winsler, A. (2004). Comparison of Hispanic children with and without limited English proficiency on the Naglieri Nonverbal Ability Test. *Psychological Assessment, 16,* 81–84.

Newman, T. M., Sparrow, S. S., & Pfeiffer, S. I. (2008). The use of the WISC-IV in assessment and intervention planning for children who are gifted. In A. Prifitera, D. H. Saklofske, & L. G., Weiss (Eds.), *WISC-IV clinical assessment and intervention.* San Diego, CA: Academic Press.

Park, G., Lubinski, D., & Benbow, C. P. (2007). Contrasting intellectual patterns predict creativity in the arts and sciences: Tracking intellectually precocious youth over 25 years. *Psychological Science, 18,* 948–952.

Petersen, P. (1977). Interactive effects of student anxiety, achievement orientation, and teacher behavior on student achievement and attitude. *Journal of Educational Psychology, 69,* 779–792.

Powers, S., Barkan, J. H., & Jones, P. B. (1986). Reliability of the Standard Progressive Matrices Test for Hispanic and White-American children. *Perceptual and Motor Skills, 62,* 348–350.

Raven, J. C., Court, J. H., & Raven, J. (1983). *Manual for Raven's Progressive Matrices and vocabulary scales, section 4: Advanced Progressive Matrices, sets I and II.* London: H. K. Lewis.

Raven, J., Raven, J. C., & Court, J. H. (1998). *Manual for Raven's Progressive Matrices and Vocabulary Scales: Section 1. General overview.* Oxford, UK: Oxford Psychologists Press Ltd.

Raven et al. (2000). *Manual for Raven Progressive Matrices and Vocabulary Scales: Research Supplement No. 3.* San Antonio: Harcourt Assessment.

Renzulli, J. S. (2005). Equity, excellence, and economy in a system for identifying students in gifted education: A guidebook (RM05208). Storrs, CT: The National Research Center on the Gifted and Talented, University of Connecticut.

Rimm, S., Gilman, B., & Silverman, L. (2008). Nontraditional applications of traditional testing. In J. L. VanTassel-Baska (Ed.), *Alternative assessments with gifted and talented students.* Wako, TX: Prufrock Press.

Robinson, N. M. (2008). The value of traditional assessments as approaches to identifying academically gifted students. In J. L. VanTassel-Baska (Ed.), *Alternative assessments with gifted and talented students.* Wako, TX: Prufrock Press.

Ruf, D. L. (2003). *Use of the SB5 in the assessment of high abilities (Stanford-Binet Intelligence Scales, Fifth Edition, Assessment Service Bulletin No. 3).* Itasca, IL: Riverside.

Roid, G. (2003). *Stanford Binet Intelligence Scales, technical manual (5th ed.).* Itasca, IL: Riverside.

Roid, G. H., & Miller, L. J. (1997). *Leiter International Performance Scale-Revised.* Wood Dale, IL: Stoelting Co.

Saccuzzo, D. P., Johnson, N. E., & Russell, G. (1992). Verbal versus performance IQs for gifted African-American, Caucasian, Filipino, & Hispanic children. *Psychological Assessment, 4,* 239–244.

Scarr, S. (1994). Culture-fair and culture-free tests. In R. J. Sternberg (Ed.), *Encyclopedia of human intelligence* (pp. 322–328). New York: Macmillan.

Shaunessy, E., Karnes, F. A., & Cobb, Y. (2004). Assessing potentially gifted students from lower socioeconomic status with nonverbal measures of intelligence. *Perceptual and Motor Skills, 98,* 1129–1138.

Schoen, H. L., & Ansley, T. N. (2005). *Iowa Algebra Aptitude Test, (5th ed.).* Itasca, IL: Riverside.

Shea, D. L., Lubinski, D., & Benbow, C. P. (2001). Importance of assessing spatial ability in intellectually talented young adolescents: A 20-year longitudinal study. *Journal of Educational Psychology, 93,* 604–614.

Silverman, L. K. (2009). The measurement of giftedness. In L. V. Shavinina (Ed.), *International handbook on giftedness.* New York, NY: Springer Science + Business Media.

Snow, R. E., & Lohman, D. F. (1984). Toward a theory of aptitude for learning from instruction. *Journal of Educational Psychology, 76,* 347–376.

Snow, R. E., & Yalow, E. (1982). Education and intelligence. In R .J. Sternberg (Ed.), *Handbook of human intelligence* (pp. 493-585). Cambridge, England: Cambridge University Press.

Stanley, J. (1971). Reliability. In R. L. Thorndike (Ed.), *Educational Measurement* (2nd ed.). Washington, DC: American Council on Education.

Sternberg, R. J. (2003). Giftedness according to the theory of successful intelligence. N. Colangelo & G. A. Davis (Eds.), *Handbook of gifted education* (3rd ed., pp. 88-99). Boston: Allyn & Bacon.

Subotnik, R., & Jarvin, L. (2005). Beyond expertise: Conceptions of giftedness as great performance. In R. J. Sternberg & J. Davidson (Eds.), *Conceptions of giftedness* (2nd ed., pp. 343-57). New York: Cambridge University Press.

Sweetland, J. D., Reina, J. M., & Tatti, A. F. (2006). WISC-III verbal/performance discrepancies among a sample of gifted children. *Gifted Child Quarterly, 50*(1), 7–10.

Terman, L. M. (1930). Autobiography of Lewis M. Terman. In Murchison, C. (Ed.), *History of psychology in autobiography* (Vol. 2, pp. 297–331). Worcester, MA: Clark University Press.

Thorndike, R. L. (1963). *The concepts of over- and under-achievement.* New York, Bureau of Publications, Teachers College, Columbia University.

Thorndike, R. L., & Hagen, E. (1971). *Cognitive Abilities Test.* New York: Houghton Mifflin.

Thorndike, R. L., & Hagen, E. (1978). *Cognitive Abilities Test (Form 3).* New York: Houghton Mifflin.

Thorndike, R. L., & Hagen, E. (1986). *Cognitive Abilities Test (Form 4): Examiner's manual.* Chicago: Riverside.

Thorndike & Hagen, 1987). *Cognitive Abilities Test (Form 4): Research handbook* .Chicago: Riverside.

Thorndike, R. L., & Hagen, E. (1994). *Cognitive Abilities Test (Form 5): Interpretive guide for teachers and counselors.* Chicago: Riverside

Thorndike, R. L., & Hagen, E. (1995). *Cognitive Abilities Test (Form 5): Research handbook.* Chicago: Riverside.

VanTassel-Baska, J., & Brown, E. F. (2007). Toward best practice: An analysis of the efficacy of curriculum models in gifted education. *Gifted Child Quarterly, 51*(4), 342-358.

Watkins, M. W., Gluting, J. J., & Youngstrom, E. A. (2005) Issues in subtest profile analysis. In D. P. Flanagan & P. L. Harrison (Eds.) *Contemporary intellectual assessment* (2nd ed., pp. 251-268). New York: The Guilford Press.

Wechsler, D. (2003). *Wechsler Intelligence Scale for Children* (4th ed.). San Antonio, TX: The Psychological Corporation.

Williams, P. E., Weiss, L. G., & Rolfhus, E. L. (2003). *Wechsler Intelligence Scale for Children – Fourth Edition Clinical Validity. Technical Report #3.* San Antonio, TX: Pearson Education Inc.

Wilkinson, S. C. (1993). WISC-R profiles of children with superior intellectual ability. *Gifted Child Quarterly, 37,* 84–91.

Zhu, J., Clayton, T., Weiss, L., & Gabel, A. (2008). *WISC-IV Extended norms. Technical Report No. 7.* San Antonio, TX: Pearson Education, Inc.

## Chapter 12 Study Guide

**Prompt 1** *Knowledge*

Explain in your own terms the distinction between the talents schools are best suited to develop and those they are not, as distinguished by the authors.

**Prompt 2** *Opinion*

Provide a rationale for whether or not out-of-level testing should be used in gifted identification.

**Prompt 3** *Affect*

The authors of this chapter give some vindication for the use of group administered tests as part of a gifted identification system. At an emotional level, is this vindication justified or not? Should emotion be part of this discussion? Why or why not?

**Prompt 4** *Experience*

Describe any experience you or someone you know has had with an individual ability test. Do you or they consider the experience worthwhile? Why or why not?

**Prompt 5** *Preconception/Misconception*

Select any concept from this chapter with which you are not familiar (e.g., discrepancies of subscale scores, use of composite scores, scaling issues at the extremes of the normal curve, use of short forms, use of profiles, regression toward the mean, errors of measurement, use of nonverbal tests) and prepare yourself to explain it to a colleague.

# THE AUDACITY OF CREATIVITY ASSESSMENT

BONNIE CRAMOND & LU WANG, THE UNIVERSITY OF GEORGIA

What a bold and grand idea—to measure creativity!! How is it possible? Who could think to do it? How can we believe in it? What kind of instrument could be used?

Let's think about some everyday experiences. A friend returns from a vacation and has some snapshots to show you. Your friend has been on a tour of Europe and has pictures of the major capitals. He feels like he has "done Europe" and you feel like you have seen it. But both of you have only sampled a very small portion of Europe—a sample that is narrowed by his choices of where to go and what to photograph as well as your attention to the pictures. There are things that he experienced, such as smells, tastes, feelings, and impressions that he was not able to photograph. However, you both have some ideas about Europe based upon your experiences and things you have read and heard, and these ideas, though not complete, may be accurate, though limited.

How can anyone think he has an accurate conceptualization of Europe based on a few weeks of travel? Or, from looking at pictures and reading books and articles? Europe is massive, diverse, and dynamic . However, we take a sample of the experience, limited in time, scope, and area, and feel that we have some understanding of it.

Psychological assessment is similar. Psychological constructs, which are concepts that cannot be directly observed but are theorized to exist (such as intelligence, creativity, motivation, or personality), are massive, multifaceted, and dynamic. However, we have found that we can take small samples of behaviors that can give us pretty accurate pictures of these constructs. As long as we remember that there are many things that are not in the pictures, that have changed since the pictures were shot, or are not able to be photographed, we may use the pictures to give us a good idea of the construct.

So, it is audacious and ambitious to attempt to measure a construct such as creativity, but it is the nature of human understanding to base our conceptions on samplings of information. We do it everyday. As long as we stay open to changing our ideas when new information is added and don't overestimate the degree of our understanding based on little data, we are usually able to operate effectively that way. So, it is with the identification of students for a gifted program. We must make decisions about placement in a gifted program based on samplings of data, but as long as we are open to new information and continually assess students' educational needs, we should be able to adjust students' placements accordingly.

## CAVEATS AND CONSIDERATIONS IN THE ASSESSMENT OF PSYCHOLOGICAL CONSTRUCTS: INTELLIGENCE AND CREATIVITY

The discussion of the relationships between intelligence and creativity is too extensive to include here, but a brief discussion of the relationship between measuring intelligence and measuring creativity is warranted. Creativity, like intelligence, is a psychological construct, which means that it cannot be directly observed or measured. Therefore, the measurement of creativity and intelligence are beset by the problems common to the measurement of all psychological constructs: no single approach to the measurement is universally accepted; measurement is based on limited samples of behaviors; it is subject to errors; there is a lack of well-defined units of measurement; the construct cannot be defined only in terms of operational definitions; and finally, the measurement must also demonstrate a mathematical relationship with other related psychological constructs or observable behaviors (Crocker & Algina, 2006). For these reasons, the measurement of any psychological construct is an audacious enterprise. Yet, we continue to use such measurements because we have found that measurements of creativity, intelligence, and other constructs can provide us with valuable information.

Many people argue that we certainly cannot attempt to measure something that we can't define. Yet, physicists have made a science of measuring phenomena that they have not yet defined or, in some cases, even named . Moreover, the issue is not that there are no definitions of intelligence or creativity; it is that there is no agreement on the definitions. In fact, one of the standards for the quality of a measure of a psychological construct is *construct validity*. This is a gauge of the degree to which an assessment measures the construct as defined. So, it is important to understand the theoretical basis, or construct, upon which any measure was based when choosing one (Hunsaker & Callahan, 1995).

With so much uncertainty, intelligence and creativity measures are still used because they are good predictors of intelligent or creative behaviors, respectively. Measures of intelligence tend to be good predictors of school success (Gottfredson, 1997; Sternberg, Grigorenko, & Bundy, 2001). This is logical because they are based upon school type activities (Binet, Simon, & Kite, 1916). Likewise, creativity measures, such as divergent thinking test scores and creativity inventory scores, are generally predictive of creative activities, interests, and accomplishments later in life (Cline, Richards, & Needham, 1963; Kogan & Pankove, 1974; Rimm & Davis, 1983; Russ, Robins, & Christiano, 1999; Torrance, 2002).

So, another standard of assessment is *predictive validity*, which is an indication of how well an assessment given at one time is correlated with another measure of the construct at a later time. It is important to consider predictive validity if one is choosing an instrument to foresee performance in the future, which is what identification for gifted programs is supposed to do. For example, the Torrance Tests given to children were correlated forty years later with a measure of their adult creative performance. The creativity index, a calculated combined score from three years of creativity testing in childhood, correlated with a quality of creative achievements score, expert judges' mean ratings on the creativeness and importance of participants' creative products (r = .43, $p \leq .01$). In addition, a structural equation model showed that although IQ was a significant predictor of TTCT scores, it explained very little of the variance in these scores ($R^2$ = .085). However, the combination of TTCT and intelligence explained 54% of the variance in creative achievement (Cramond, Matthews-Morgan, Bandalos, & Zuo, 2005).

According to research such as that cited above, both intelligence and creativity test scores are good predictors of gifts and talents, and, ultimately success in academic or creative endeavors, respectively. Yet, neither is perfect. They do not measure motivation, opportunity, or any of the other personality or environmental factors that can promote or impede success. Extending the example from the previous paragraph, although children from a housing project scored comparably to the other students on the Torrance Tests in Torrance's longitudinal study, they did not have the adult success that their scores would predict because they didn't have the same opportunities for creative accomplishments that some of the other students did (Millar, 2002). Likewise, the tests were less predictive for the girls in the cohort, who grew up in the late 50s and early 60s (Cramond, 1994).

So, in choosing any measure, we should be purposeful about choosing one that is valid for the use for which it is intended. Test validity is situational; tests are valid to measure certain qualities, in particular populations, in specified ways. A test that has excellent construct or predictive validity can be rendered invalid if used with an inappropriate group, for an unsuitable purpose, and/or administered improperly. This is a caution that should always be remembered in choosing instruments to identify students for a gifted program: instruments that are effective and appropriate in one setting may be invalid in another.

In addition, we must remember our snapshot metaphor. A creativity or intelligence test is a sample of some behaviors on particular tasks, on a particular day, and in a particular way. So much is not in the picture or not clear. Therefore, another similarity between creativity and intelligence measures is that they should be interpreted in light of what they are and what they do or do not do. Some of the things that individuals who use such measures should remember follow:

1. There are false negatives. There are intelligent and creative individuals who do not get high scores on intelligence and creativity measures for many reasons related to the person, the test, their expression of their abilities, and the conditions of testing . Therefore, the identification process should include behavioral observations that are ongoing, in addition to tests.

2. There are not likely to be false positives. Given valid measures, it is not likely that a student will get a high score on an intelligence test and not be intelligent, or

a high score on a creativity test without creative thinking. So, educators should look carefully at a student whose scores on tests are much higher than his/her performance. It is unlikely the test score is a false positive; it is more likely that the student is underachieving or has some type of learning disability.

3. All tests are not equal. So, one could get very different scores on two different measures of the same construct if the tests are based on different conceptions of the construct. (Of course, differences in the validity and reliability of tests can cause score differences, too.) Therefore, educators should carefully consider the abilities that different tests measure in choosing one for the identification of a gifted student. For example, some tests are very verbal and others are visual- or performance-based. If the child's strengths are known, a test that is most likely to demonstrate the child's strengths (or minimize weaknesses) should be chosen.

4. Assessments have a short shelf life. The content and form of the tests, as well as the norms, should be updated periodically to ensure that they are still relevant and representative of current populations. For example, the pictures on some IQ tests have been updated so that children of color are included and old-fashioned lace-up shoes were deleted. The Torrance Tests are re-normed every 10 years. Using a test with outmoded items or obsolete norms will produce invalid results.

5. Assessment results have a short shelf life, too. Constructs such as intelligence and creativity are now largely considered to be dynamic and developmental rather than fixed amounts at birth. Therefore, students may get different results on measures as they grow and develop. That is one reason that identification for the gifted program should be ongoing, and not considered the sole responsibility of the elementary school.

6. No assessments have pinpoint accuracy. They all have standard errors of measurement. In other words, they all have ranges of error that can occur randomly. So, one should never require a pinpoint score for admission to a gifted program; the standard error of measurement for the test should be considered.

With those caveats and considerations addressed, we can turn our attention to the methods and instruments used to assess creativity.

## METHODS AND INSTRUMENTS FOR ASSESSING CREATIVITY

Since Guilford's groundbreaking speech to the American Psychological Association audience at the 1950 Convention, great efforts have been made to define and theorize creativity. Throughout the years, the study of creativity has gradually become the battlefield of theorists/researchers coming into the field with different schools of thoughts or disciplinary training. Some of the tensions in the field are reflected in the choices of how to assess creativity.

## COGNITIVE OR PERSONALITY

In attempting to measure creativity, we should first have a theoretical model or definition to guide our decision making about what types of instruments to use and how to interpret the data we get. Many school districts choose instruments for gifted identification without considering the definition or theory upon which they were developed and, thus, what they are really measuring.

One way to conceptualize the different views of creativity is the degree to which creativity is seen as a cognitive ability versus a personality trait. Guilford's (1956) structure of intellect model is an example of the cognitive view. Although Guilford recognized the importance and existence of the creative personality, the emphasis of his tests and research was on the creative thinking skills that he theorized were part of the intellect. As he justifiably pointed out in the 1956 article, "Psychology and psychologists since Binet have taken a much too restricted view of human intelligence . . . In attempting to fathom the nature of intellect, more attention should be given to the human adult, particularly the superior human adult" (p. 267).

The other extreme views creativity as a personality trait that is either directly or indirectly reflected in scales on instruments such as the Minnesota Multiphasic Personality Inventory-2 (Graham, 1993), specifically the "psychoticism" or "schizotypy" scales, or, on the Neo Personality Inventory (Costa & McCrae, 1992), or Gough's Creative Personality Scale for the Adjective Checklist (1979). This view may indicate both negative and/or positive personality traits.

A middle position views creativity as having both a cognitive and a personality component, and

to some extent, as a result of the social milieu that individual creators find themselves in. Researchers such as Gardner (1997), Simonton (1984), and Csikszentmihalyi (1991) have endeavored to study the most unambiguous manifestations of human creativity from the perspective of a "persons-in-systems" approach, which embodies such a theoretical conceptualization.

In fact, even before Guilford proposed to the APA the necessity and, perhaps, the urgency to study human creativity, Cox (1926) had already embarked on an odyssey of exploring the eminent minds in history by looking at biographical data on those eminent creative achievers in the past centuries. These researchers' approach can be roughly categorized as biographical or historiometric.

If educators consider the philosophy of the gifted program and the definition of creativity that is being used, then they will have a better idea of whether to choose an identification instrument that emphasizes creative thought, the creative personality, or both. The more modern, complex view of creativity is of a multi-faceted construct that incorporates such diverse components as genetic influences, cognitive processes, temperament, neuroanatomy, the field, and the domain in an all-encompassing dynamic, or system (c.f. Csikszentmihalyi, 1988; Feldman, 1988; Gardner, 1997; Gruber & Davis, 1988; Simonton, 1988; Sternberg, 1988). So, a variety of measures should be used to identify creative students, including creative thinking tests, personality checklists, judgments of real products, and observations of creative behaviors in different situations. If schools want to truly identify and nurture creativity, they will ensure that students have opportunities to show their creativity in many situations, not just on tests. As Runco (2007) explained, "if schools care about creativity and give children exercises and tests of creative potential, but if those are given in a test-like academic atmosphere, the same children who always do well on tests will excel, and the children who do moderately or poorly on traditional tests will again do only moderately or poorly" (p. 3). Thus, it is important that the right atmosphere be fostered in the classroom to nurture creativity and students should be given many opportunities to develop and display their creative behaviors in school where these behaviors can be noticed, noted, and nurtured.

## EMINENT OR EVERYDAY

While some prefer to study the highest forms of human creativity, others have come to realize the shortcomings or pitfalls oftentimes associated with the biographical approach in studying deceased eminent creators. For instance, scarcity of data, false data, and the dramatic changes of the Zeitgeists across the epochs that eminent creators were born into are but a few confounding variables that we can name. These are serious limitations associated with the historiometric/biographical approach to studying creativity. Also, such investigations do not address the issues that prompted Guilford to admonish his peers in 1950, the identification and fostering of creative ability.

Hence, some contemporary psychologists have come to favor the empirical rigors of psychometric testing. But even among psychologists who have favored the psychometric approach in studying creativity (cf. Mednick—developer of the RAT, 1967; Wallach and Kogan—developers of several divergent thinking measures, 1966; Torrance—TTCT, 1966; 1998), opinions vary with regard to what creative thinking skills can and should be measured. Nor can they agree about whether creativity is best explained by divergent thinking ability, or to view creativity as the *blessed marriage* between convergent thinking and divergent thinking.

One way to measure everyday creativity has been developed by Richards, Kinney, Benet, and Merzel (1988) in the Lifetime Creativity Scales . These scales address two types of measures of creativity: quality, or *peak creativity* and quantity, or *extent of involvement in creative activity* (p. 476). Although concentrated on the creative products, there is consideration of the person and process. The scales were tested on three samples totaling 541 who were assessed on accomplishments at work and at leisure over the adult lifetime. The researchers were able to establish good content validity by comparing the results on the scales to vocational and avocational reports. Construct validity was investigated through factor analysis and correlation of the scales with various measures of creativity, predictors of creativity, interest inventories, and demographics such as work history, intelligence, appreciation for creativity, and socioeconomic status. Inter-rater reliability coefficients range from .76 – .91. Such scales hold promise for identifying creative students by considering the person, process, and product, but the scales would have to be adapted to students who don't have a lifetime of accomplishments.

## APTITUDE OR ACHIEVEMENT

Some believe that the best way to measure creativity is through products. This view maintains that individuals' achievements are the best predictors of future achievements. However, many children do not have the experiences, training, and resources to produce at an excellent level, even if they have raw talent. Therefore, others believe that in identifying creativity in children, the measurement of aptitude is fairer.

Some who ascribe to the achievement view, such as Baer (December 1993/January 1994) and Amabile (1983) (in discussing the Consensual Assessment Technique) and Piirto (2004), have asserted that the only real way to measure creativity is through a person's products. Similarly, Okuda, Runco, and Berger (1991) asserted that real world problem solving tasks were as effective as divergent thinking tests in predicting creative achievements. That does seem to be very logical, especially if one assumes that creativity is content specific, expressed through tangible products, and the products can be judged reliably. However, there is the issue of evaluating production (or achievement) versus potential (or aptitude). Individuals who are producing artifacts that can be judged as creative often have had experiences and specialized training that allows them to produce at a high level of excellence as compared with others who have not had such training or experiences. The child who has had private art lessons and possesses a myriad art supplies is more likely to produce a drawing that demonstrates the skills of adult representation than is the child who has not had lessons and is using crayons.

If the alternative is to provide children with the opportunities to create products and be trained to do so, such as with Maker's Project Discover (1992, 2009), then the problem of differences in training may be addressed; however, there is still the issue of the efficiency of obtaining judges and appropriate activities. Those who prefer to assess creativity via cognitive tests often do so for their efficiency, but there is also often the intent of finding creative potential. Torrance (1966) listed one of the main purposes for his creativity tests as, "to point out potentialities that might otherwise go unnoticed—especially in children from culturally diverse and lower socioeconomic backgrounds" (p. 6). In fact, Cropley (2000) argued that creativity tests must be considered as measures of potential because creative achievement requires additional factors such as motivation, mental health, technical skill, and field knowledge.

Although tests of cognitive thinking skills certainly open up the door of empirical testing of creativity, they are not without their problems, too. As Runco (1994, pp. 271) observed about the nebulous creativity assessment industry, "There is little agreement about possible influences on problem finding and problem solving, and only limited agreement concerning methodologies." Nevertheless, the idea of psychometric testing should be applauded for its bold attempt to predict creative potential—future creativity, rather than merely explaining this phenomenon retrospectively. Certainly, as used to identify creative children for special services in a gifted program, a predictive perspective is much more useful than a retrospective one.

## HOLISTIC, SUBJECTIVE JUDGMENTS OR SPECIFIC, OBJECTIVE CRITERIA

In describing the Consensual Assessment Technique, Amabile (1982) emphasized the importance of using a product-oriented measure that does not depend on objective criteria. She maintained that such objective criteria are impossible to develop. Rather, the consensual method depends upon the judgment of a product as creative by appropriate judges, "those familiar with the domain in which the product was created or the response articulated" (p. 1001). The judges use their inherent knowledge of the domain and their implicit standards for creativity and quality to rate the products in terms of each other rather than against some ideal. Thus, the Consensual Assessment Technique could be considered as involving holistic, subjective judgment.

In a number of trials with different individuals and different products, Amabile was satisfied with the interjudge reliabilities obtained, although they varied greatly by the type of judge and the number of judges in the group (anywhere from six to 21 judges). Of course, Amabile acknowledged that the number of judges used could increase the likelihood of obtaining a statistically significant reliability rating and even advised that more judges be used if the task is difficult or if the interjudge correlation is low (p. 7).

This is certainly the method by which most creative work is really judged. Whether it be academic writing, art, scientific discoveries, or any other product, the judgment of the product is usually conducted by a group of individuals who are considered experts in the field. However, Amabile, herself, acknowledged the impracticality of this method. It should be clear that it would be impractical to garner the services of a cadre of qualified judges in many situations, for example, in rural schools. Thus, this method would be very difficult to use in identifying creatively gifted students in most schools.

Also, the issue of reliability and validity pertain here. If there is high agreement among the judges (reliability), does that mean that what they are judging is really creativity (validity)? Amabile (1982) addressed this by what may be called circular reasoning—creativity is defined as that which judges agree is creative. She stated that, "By definition, interjudge reliability in this method is equivalent to construct validity; if appropriate judges independently agree that a given product is highly creative, then it can and must be accepted as such" (p. 1002). Also, to address this issue, she obtained separate ratings from the judges on other dimensions of the products, such as technical goodness and liking the product. The results of investigations of the independence of these judgments were mixed, which led her to conclude that, "although it may be possible for some types of creative products to obtain creativity judgments that are uncontaminated by assessments of liking, creativity judgments for other types of products may be tightly bound up with assessments of aesthetic appeal" (p. 1009).

On the other hand, there are those who maintain that the best way to get valid and reliable judgments of the creativity of products is to use specified criteria that are clearly linked to theories of creativity as well as real-world assessments of products. Pioneering work on this was done by Besemer and Treffinger (1981) and developed further by Besemer (1998) and with her colleague O'Quin (1999). They addressed the problem of evaluating products in a domain as one of combining the wisdom of domain knowledge with the sensitivity to and appreciation of innovation, and they developed a guide, the Creative Product Semantic Scale (CPSS, O'Quinn & Besemer, 1989; Runco, 2004) to do this. The CPSS has been demonstrated to measure three factors (Besemer & O'Quinn, 1999) that can be formed into a Creative Product Analysis Matrix (CPAM, Besemer, 1998) and used to successfully evaluate products in various domains (O'Quinn & Besemer, 2006). The three primary factors are: (a) novelty, (b) resolution, and (c) elaboration and synthesis. By rating a product on each of the descriptors under each factor, judges have been able to agree with each other on the quality and innovativeness of a product, though not necessarily with the creator.

Another criterion-based system has been developed by Cropley and Cropley (2009). It is similar to the CPAM by Besemer and O'Quin (2006), but differs in being more explanatory of the levels for each descriptor. The Cropleys report promising results with inter-rater reliability after a short training session.

Educators who want to use creative products as part of an identification system for a gifted program would be well advised to use an instrument such as those developed by Besemer and O'Quin or the Cropleys to ensure that the qualities that they are evaluating are truly representative of creativity. Unless they are able to enlist the services of a group of expert judges who are also knowledgeable about children's abilities at different developmental levels, the use of criterion-based instruments will provide guidance in judging creative products.

## CHILD OR ADULT

A major consideration, which has strong implications for the choice of an instrument or assessment system is whether one will be assessing children or adults. Certainly, when used to identify students for a gifted program, the emphasis will be on assessments appropriate for children. However, assessments used to judge the creativity of adults can provide information that is useful for identifying and nurturing creativity in children. For example, the biographical studies of eminence that have been done with adults have provided information on the personality characteristics most likely to be exhibited by creative individuals. This information has informed us about personality traits indicative of creativity that may be manifested by children. For example, Dabrowski's (Piechowski, 2003) research on the characteristics of creative, productive adults has helped us gain a more accepting view of the manifestations of overexcitabilities in children.

Other types of assessments can be geared toward children or adults. Product assessments can be used to judge artifacts produced by individuals of all ages, as Amabile (1982) demonstrated with her Consensual Assessment Technique or has been done with the criterion rating sheets like the Creative Product Analysis Matrix (O'Quinn & Besemer, 2006). Most of the tests of creative thinking, such as The Torrance Tests, Guilford's tests, and those of Wallach and Kogan can be administered to a broad age range from children to adults.

Some of the personality inventories would necessarily be limited to administration to adults or older adolescents. Yet, given the caution that creativity assessment should be ongoing and regarded as developmental, instruments intended for adolescents or young adults may be appropriate for some high school students and, thus, useful in identifying them as creatively gifted.

## DIVERGENT OR CONVERGENT THINKING

Some have criticized divergent thinking tests as less than adequate in measuring creative ability, but convergent thinking tests such as the Remote Association Test (1967) and standardized IQ tests (i.e. Wechsler's) do not reliably predict adult-level creative achievements. For instance, Terman's longitudinal study on 1528 gifted individuals suggested that although most of them grew up to be contributing members of the society as defined by their educational attainment (most completed college degrees and many attended graduate schools) and vocational success (most held intellectually demanding jobs), none achieved the status of a genius or thrived on their creative achievements (Goleman, 1980). Yet, the lack of creative contributions among this gifted cohort studied by Terman may be attributed to the IQ range of this population not matching up to the geniuses in Cox (1926)'s study, or it could be due to factors other than general intelligence, "g."

If neither divergent nor convergent thinking ability by itself sufficiently captures the creative potential of an individual and a confluence of both types of thinking abilities accounts for a larger variance of creative achievement or potential over either type of thinking alone, it is logical to infer that a complete creativity assessment model should take both factors into consideration. Indeed, as reported in the 40 year longitudinal study (Cramond, Matthews-Morgan, Bandalos, & Zuo, 2005) of the Torrance Tests of Creative Thinking (TTCT), the TTCT scores and IQ test scores together accounted for 54% of variance of the test taker's adult-level creative achievement.

However, the nature of the relationship between convergent thinking and divergent thinking in a creativity model is less than transparent. The threshold theory (Getzels & Jackson, 1962; Guilford, 1967) was an attempt to shed light on the relationship between these two types of thinking and their respective contributions to creativity, albeit with limited success. As revealed by Kim's (2005) meta-analysis, little relationship exists between creativity and IQ scores even at the level below the proposed *critical threshold* (roughly IQ < 120). It is worth mentioning that one of the assumptions made by Kim (2005) was that a person's levels of creativity and intelligence could be assumed from test scores alone. Although this is the nature of much psychological research, it is a limitation to be considered. Nevertheless, the fact that many studies cited by Kim (2005) already questioned the threshold theory's explanatory power over creative achievements may be sufficient to render the theory's validity questionable.

Thus, Terman's study offered a compelling piece of evidence that high IQ does not necessarily translate into adult creative productivity. Some explain the missing piece as accounted for by divergent thinking ability, and others prefer to see creative productivity as involving a confluence of non-intellectual factors such as level of motivation, emotional maturity, the Zeitgeist, and even chance, and hence favor the view of creativity as embedded in a context. People holding a holistic view of creativity tend to favor assessing creativity from the perspective of *person-in-the-system* (Gardner, 1997).

People holding a holistic view of creativity tend to favor assessing creativity from the systems perspective (Csikszentmihalyi, 1999). According to Csikszentmihalyi (1999), creative behaviors are best conceived of as involving the interaction among individuals, domains, and fields. "Domains" offer individual creators "raw materials" (i.e. symbol systems) to manipulate and to exert their creative potentials on. In other words, variation is impossible "without reference to an existing pattern" (p. 314). Similarly, "fields," which are formulated by gatekeepers, are also vital to individual creators in that "fields" provide individual creators a standard based on which their creative products can be evaluated. Without such evaluation systems, it is difficult to tell apart truly creative works from deviant arts.

Still others prefer to look at the phenomenon at the neurobiological level, hence bypassing the fuzzy boundaries between divergent thinking and creative thinking abilities, although the actual assessment tools these researchers use on human subjects are still, by and large, psychometric. Researchers such as Lubow (1989), Eysenck (1995), and, more recently, Carson, Peterson, and Higgins (2003) have suggested that *low latent inhibition* is characteristic of the cognitive style associated with creative thinking and cite a well-studied animal model in support of its presence. This is certainly a promising area for continued research.

However, this research is too new, the relationships too tenuous, and the tools too imprecise for use in the identification of creative individuals at this time.

## IN CONTEXT OR DECONTEXTUALIZED

An area of debate for assessment in general is that of authentic assessment, which is measurement in a natural setting versus testing that is decontextualized (cf. Messick, 1994). There is much to be said for the legitimacy of authentic assessment. Certainly, Maker's Discover Method, Amabile's Consensual Assessment Technique, and other observational methods or product evaluations are more likely to be situated in a learning or life context more than a paper and pencil test. This issue is important both for motivation, especially with children, and with the task specificity of the product or performance. So, if one is interested in performance in a particular field, it is logical to assess performance in the field. This can be done through the evaluation of a product or performance or through one of the many content-specific measures, such as Measures of Creativity in Sound and Music (Wang, 1985; Baltzer, 1988), The Seashore Measures of Musical Talents (Seashore, Lewis, & Saetveit, 1939), The Barron-Welsh Art Scale (1987), The Meier Art Test (1940), The Horn Art Aptitude Inventory (1945), and The Graves Design Judgment Test (1948).

## GENERAL OR SPECIFIC

This leads to a question that is one of the major tensions in the study of creativity—is creativity a generalized ability or is it task specific? One's belief about this issue will certainly impact the type of assessment chosen. General tests of creative thinking, such as the Guilford Tests, Torrance Tests, and personality measures, assume that creativity can be measured as a way of thinking or being that is generalizable, as conceptualized by the Root-Bernsteins (1999) and others. It may only be expressed in a certain area or areas, but it is a general way of thinking, similar to the idea for *g* as a general intellectual ability (Gottfredson, 1997). Others contend that creativity is domain-specific (c.f. Gardner, 1997). Clearly, measures of aptitude in specific areas or assessment of specific products are more appropriate for such assessment.

This question of whether creativity should be assessed as a general or task specific ability is connected to issues of development and aptitude versus achievement, also. Young children and those who have had fewer opportunities to develop their talents may not have focused interests and abilities in particular areas. There is also the measurement concern of bandwidth versus fidelity raised by Cronbach (1970). Cronbach contended that the wider the area measured (bandwidth) the less precise the measurement (fidelity). One might think of a flashlight with a variable-width beam of light—the wider beam casts light so that more area can be seen, but the light is dim. Narrowing the beam allows a sharper view, but obscures things that are right outside of the light. So, a test of general creativity would have a wider bandwidth resulting in lower fidelity. A specific test will have greater fidelity, but less bandwidth.

Which should be used in the identification of creative students? Again, that depends upon the philosophy and goals of the program for which students are being identified. If the intent is to cast a wide net in order to avoid the error of omission, if the program has a goal of developing creativity in a variety of fields, or if the students are young, then a test of general creativity might be preferred. On the other hand, if the aim is to be very precise and selective for a program in a defined field (such as music or mathematics) and the students are old enough to have developed demonstrable skills in the area, then a test of specific creative ability may be preferable.

## SELF OR OTHER

Another concern is the source of information for the assessment. Tests and product evaluations involve an initial response by an individual that is then rated by one or more judges. Self-identification checklists, such as the *RIBS* described below, are completely dependent upon input by the individual. Other checklists, though dependent upon observations of an individual's behavior, emphasize the input of the person completing the checklist. The former have the problem of individuals' attempts to represent themselves in the best light, to the extent that they can figure out how to do that and are self-aware. The latter depend on accurate, unbiased, and generalizable observations by others.

Some of the checklists that are used to identify creativity include the creativity scale from the *Scales for Rating the Behavioral Characteristics of Superior Students* (SRBCSS, Renzulli et al., 2004), or the *Gifted And Talented Evaluation Scales* (GATES, Gilliam, Carpenter, & Christensen, 1996). There are also checklists specifically designed to measure creative ability in children, such as the *Group Inventory for Finding Talent* for grades k–6 (GIFT,

Rimm, 1976) or the *Group Inventory for Finding Interest* for grades 6–12 (GIFFI, Davis & Rimm, 1982). The psychometric qualities of the instruments are reasonable when they are used as screening instruments. However, as with any assessment, users should be clear about what the checklists measure and their strengths and weaknesses. For example, the SRBCSS were originally designed to guide educators in finding gifted students by listing the characteristics that students might display. Therefore, the design of the checklists, which have all of the Likert type stems as positive indicators of the behavior, can lead to a global response set (c.f. Barnette, 2000; Cronbach, 1970).

The *Runco Ideational Behavior Scale* (RIBS, Runco, Plucker, & Lin, 2000-2001) was developed as a self-report instrument to assess an individual's behavior reflective of the "use of, appreciation of, and skill with ideas" (p. 393). In order to address the concern about response set, one third of the items are reverse-coded. Reasonable psychometric properties were described with three university samples, but the authors indicated that the instrument is being modified to increase the validity and reliability.

## THE FOUR Ps

One system for studying creativity that honors its multidimensionality is called the four Ps (Rhodes 1961): Person, Process, Product, and Press. By investigating the traits of creative individuals, the processes that they use to create or remove blocks to creativity, the products that they make, and the pressures from their environments, we can hope to refine our understanding of creativity. Through understanding, we might hope to recognize and foster innovation as well as innovative people.

## PERSON

In studies of the creative person, several common traits are evident regardless of the domain in which the individuals operate. Tardif and Sternberg (1988) compiled a list of such characteristics from research studies and concluded that although there is no one personality trait that can differentiate creative people from those less creative, there are constellations of traits that are commonly mentioned in studies of the personality of creative individuals (p. 435). These personality traits include, in order of the most commonly mentioned to the least commonly mentioned in the studies, psychological risk taking; perseverance; curiosity; openness to experiences; driving absorption; self-discipline, commitment, and task focus; high intrinsic motivation; freedom of spirit that rejects limits; self-organization; and a need for self-efficacy and challenge (p. 435–436).

The seminal studies of creative personality were the Institute for Personality Assessment and Research (IPAR) studies conducted at UC Berkeley with highly creative and productive individuals in fields such as physical science (Gough & Woodworth, 1960), mathematics (Helson & Crutchfield, 1970; Helson, 1971), architecture (MacKinnon, 1961), and writing (Barron, 1968). In particular, Gough's work continued into designing instruments to measure personality traits, including those of the creative person. The Gough Creative Personality Scale (1979), an outgrowth of the work, has been used in several research studies, which have indicated it has good construct validity and temporal stability (Barron & Harrington, 1981). A study conducted by Simonton in 1986 with a subset of the Gough adjectives found the personality factors had respectable internal consistency reliabilities and correlated well with other compatible, independent measures (p. 152-153). A more recent study (Lee, Lee, & Kim, 2004) using Gough's (1979) Creative Personality Scale led the researchers to conclude that the adjectives were accurate measures of creative personality as indicated through correlation with other measures and that the Eastern perception of a creative personality is in accordance with the Western view.

Because most personality scales were developed based upon adult personalities, it would be unwise to use them, even ones that have been adapted for children, as a sole or primary means of identifying creatively gifted students. However, when used as part of an identification system, the scales can help educators find students who show creative personality traits. As an additional benefit, educators who become aware of the salient personality traits of creative individuals are less likely to negatively stereotype students who exhibit such traits.

## Process

However, personality studies can only view one component of the phenomenon of creativity, the person. The process by which individuals create has also received considerable attention. Although the detailed creative process for each individual is probably idiosyncratic, Wallas' (1926) four-stage process—preparation, incubation, illumination, and verification—provides an overarching model that has been found to apply to both the arts and

the sciences (Langley & Jones, 1988). Yet, it was the operational processes of fluency, flexibility, originality and elaboration, as described by Guilford (1956, 1962, 1977) that enabled psychologists to create assessments of creativity .

Torrance, whose eponymous tests have been used around the world and translated into more than 35 languages (Millar, 2002), refined and expanded the Guilford scoring system to include more indicators of creative thinking. In 1979, after studying creativity for over thirty years, Torrance released the Streamlined Scoring for the figural version of the Torrance Tests of Creative Thinking (TTCT). This new scoring method examines many other creative abilities that Torrance extracted from other branches of psychology and his own lengthy research on creativity to include five norm referenced scores and 13 criterion-referenced scores. For example, he included Resistance to Premature Closure from Gestält psychology and the occurrence of Movement and Action as a measure of inventiveness from the Rorschach Test. In the over forty years of research on the Torrance Tests of Creative Thinking, these tests have become the most widely used in education and are even used in the corporate world (Davis, 1997; Kim, 2006). In addition, the Torrance Tests of Creative Thinking are the most referenced of all creativity tests (Lissitz & Willhoft, 1985).

The reliability estimates of the creative index from the KR-21, using 99th percentile scores as the estimates of the number of items, ranged between .89 and .94, which are good (Kim, 2006). The most important type of validity for this type of test, predictive validity, was established through Torrance's longitudinal studies begun in 1958 with the last data collection point in 1998 (Cramond, 1994; Cramond, Matthews-Morgan, Bandalos, & Zuo, 2005; Torrance, 1966, 1968, 1969, 1972, 1979, 1980, 1981a, 1981b, 1988, 1998, 2002, 2008). A creativity index that was calculated for the participants from three years of creativity testing in elementary school was compared to a rating of the quantity and quality of their creative achievements 40 years later. The quantity and quality indices were derived from the respondents' answers to a questionnaire and rated by four creativity experts. The predictive validity of the Torrance Tests of Creative Thinking, verbal and figural, is relatively strong (r =.43, p ≤ .01) considering the span of 40 years during which time data were collected .

In addition, a structural equation model was constructed to determine the best fit for the variables collected from the tests in childhood. These included IQ scores as well as the various dimension scores of the TTCT. Although intelligence was a significant predictor of TTCT scores, it explained very little of the variance in these scores ($R^2$ = .085). However, the combination of TTCT and intelligence explained 54% of the variance in creative achievement. When considering the TTCT scores alone, it was concluded that the Creativity Index, a combined TTCT score, was predictive of future creative production, as were the dimension scores when analyzed separately. The fact that TTCT scores could explain 23% of the variance in the creative production is important in view of the length of the study, the decreased number of participants in the last follow-up, and the difficulties of comparing a paper and pencil test from childhood with adult achievements.

A recent follow-up was conducted, 50 years after the initial testing (Runco, Millar, Acar, & Cramond, 2010). Correlations between the scores of fluency, flexibility, originality, and elaboration from the TTCT obtained over 50 years ago showed moderate but significant relationships with measures of personal achievement. The correlations ranged from r = .20 for originality to r = .29 for fluency. Also, a standardized composite score was created from the four test scores, and it was also significantly correlated with personal creative achievements (R = .35, p = .04). Neither the individual scores nor the composite score was significantly correlated with public achievements. Interestingly, the childhood IQ scores were negatively related to both private and public creative achievements, but these relationships were not statistically significant. It is noteworthy that the TTCT proved to be a good predictor of creative achievements after 50 years, but it is unclear why they were related to private and not public creative achievements. It may be due to the participants' stage of life (their average age at the time of data collection was 57) and a resulting emphasis on personal over public creative achievements. However, further investigation would be necessary to determine the cause.

## PRODUCT

Ultimately, what brings a creative person attention and what causes the process to be valued is the product. Whether tangible or not, a piece of art or a new scientific theory, it is the product that is prized and causes the person and process to be labeled innovative. Evaluating creative products is considered the purview of each domain; however, history has shown us that the gatekeepers in a domain are not typically the most forward thinking. It makes sense that they have the most to lose from the shift to a new prototype, whether it be in music, art, economics or physics, people in power don't often welcome the revolution.

So, the problem of evaluating products in a domain becomes one of combining the wisdom of domain knowledge with the sensitivity to and appreciation of innovation. As discussed above, this is usually done by judges of some kind, but there are differences of opinion about whether the judges should be guided by established criteria, as on the Creative Product Semantic Scale (CPSS, O'Quinn & Besemer, 1989; Runco, 2004) or by their inherent standards and implicit understandings of creativity, as in the Consensual Assessment Technique (Amabile, 1982).

In using product evaluation with gifted students, The Student Product Assessment Form (Reis & Renzulli, 1991) should certainly be considered because it was specifically developed for use with that population. The developers provided convincing evidence of content validity, deriving the items from teachers' checklists and further field testing them. They also provided good evidence of inter-rater reliability and stability for the instrument. In addition, the scale is very practical and efficient: (a) it is available in the article for reproduction; (b) it is easily modified through the use of "not applicable" for certain items; (c) it is in a simple single-page format; and, (d) it can be used to create portfolio records of students' achievements over time. If used for identification, the overall numerical rating could be used as a piece of data to make the case for the student's giftedness. It could be used in a system of authentic assessment as addressed earlier to determine what a student can actually do.

### Press

The final P of the system is Press. Though some may feel that Rhodes pushed the alliteration on this one too much because the term is less readily identifiable than the others, the press refers to the environmental factors that affect creativity. Whatever the term, there is certainly agreement among researchers that the environment is an important component of the creative system. Some might refer to the field, such as Florence in the early 15th century with the emphasis on and resulting explosion of art (Csikszentmihalyi, 1988) or the immediate environment of a testing situation which might include a warm-up, psychological safety, and an emphasis on divergent thinking (Torrance, 1988). The press includes time and place as well as the people, culture, physical setting, political climate, resources available, etc.

Although there has been more interest in the environment in business than in education, those aspiring to nurture innovation often wisely consider the environment that would be most conducive to such. Several researchers have sought to determine both the factors in an environment that are conducive to creativity and those that are likely to stymie it. Accordingly, Amabile and her colleagues (1995, 1996) have synthesized such factors from both educational and work environments to develop an instrument for assessing creative climate called the KEYS. KEYS (Amabile, 1995) assesses six practices that support creativity in the work environment (organizational encouragement, supervisory encouragement, work

352

group supports; sufficient resources; challenging work; and, freedom) and two practices that inhibit creativity (organizational impediments and unrealistic workload pressure). Finally, KEYS measures the productivity and creativity of the environment.

A review and comparison of five creative or innovative climate instruments conducted by Mathisen and Einarsen (2004) confirmed that the KEYS was one of the two instruments available that had sufficient information about its validity and reliability to trust it. An extensive report on the psychometric properties of the instrument was published by Amabile et al. in 1996, but it was affirming to see its soundness appraised by two independent researchers unconnected to the Center for Creative Leadership.

Another well-known measure of the innovativeness of the environment was developed by Ekvall (1996) in Sweden. Ekvall's work has been further refined and validated in collaboration with researchers here in the U. S. and in Germany (Isaksen, Lauer, Ekvall, & Britz, 2000-2001). The resulting Situational Outlook Questionnaire (SOQ) measures individuals' perceptions of the nature of an organization in terms of its support of creativity and change. It assesses perceptions on nine dimensions: challenge and involvement, freedom, trust/openness, idea time, playfulness/humor, conflict, idea support, debate, and risk-taking. Although developed to assess the environment of businesses for innovation, it can be applied to other organizations such as schools or even classrooms. Preliminary studies gave evidence for the criterion related validity of the instrument in that companies that were rated as more productive in terms of techni-

cal and market novelty of their products were also ranked higher on the SOQ.

Slightly different in focus, but also designed to assess organizational creativity, Basadur and Hausdorf (1996) developed a questionnaire to measure attitudes within an organization toward creativity and creative problem solving. They were able to ascertain through factor analysis that there were three clusters of factors represented: Valuing New Ideas, Creative Individual Stereotypes, and Too Busy to Try New Ideas. However, they indicated that more extensive work was needed to improve the reliability of the scales.

Of the four Ps, assessment of the Press, or environment, is least related to identification of creatively gifted students. Yet, if the goal is to nurture creativity in all children, then ensuring that schools provide both the climate and opportunities for students to realize their creative potential is important. In such environments, the creatively gifted students will flourish and demonstrate their abilities more readily, allowing for their identification for gifted programs.

## Conclusion

Yes, it is audacious to attempt to measure creativity. Such an ineffable quality that most now believe is dynamic and multifaceted is a challenge to study, measure, or attempt to nurture. However, in the words of novelist Bette Greene, "What is genius, anyway, if it isn't the ability to give an adequate response to a great challenge" (p. 45).

The challenge is a worthy one if we can find and support creativity. The question is how we should assess creativity. The answer certainly depends upon the definition of creativity that is used, the reason for the assessment, the nature of the population being assessed, the efficacy and efficiency of various means, and the psychometric properties desired. Many researchers would advise a battery of tests or assessments in order to more fully measure the various aspects of the construct (Cramond & Kim, 2008; Hocevar, 1979; Hunsaker & Callahan, 1995). However, issues of practicality apply. Williams (1980) created a battery in the Creativity Assessment Packet (CAP) that combine the assessment of creative thinking skills through a divergent production test with a self-report instrument to discover affective factors related to creativity, and a behavior checklist for parents and teachers to complete. Unfortunately, the psychometric properties of the battery are very poor or unreported.

The value of recognizing and nurturing creativity for the good of the individual and society is so great that we should not shirk from the task because it is challenging. Rather, we should use the best means available to identify creative abilities while continuing to refine existing measures and develop new and better ones. Such a task requires audacity, but rather than being daunted, we should remember the words of Disraeli (1833), "Success is the child of audacity" (p. 9).

## REFERENCES

Amabile, T. M. (1982). Social psychology of creativity: A *consensual assessment* technique. *Journal of Personality and Social Psychology, 43,* 997–1013.

Amabile, T. M. (1983). *The social psychology of creativity.* New York: Springer-Verlag.

Amabile, T. M. (1995). *KEYS: Assessing the climate for creativity.* Greensboro, NC: Center for Creative Leadership.

Amabile, T. M., Conti, R., Coon, H., Lazenby, J., & Herron, M. (1996). Assessing the work environment for creativity. *The Academy of Management Journal, 39,* 1154–1184.

Baer, J. (December 1993/January 1994). Why you shouldn't trust creativity tests. *Educational Leadership, 51*(4), 80–83.

Baltzer, S. (1988). A validation study of a measure of musical creativity. *Journal of Research in Music Education, 36,* 232–249.

Barnette, J. J. (2000). Effects of stem and Likert response option reversals on survey internal consistency: If you feel the need, there is a better alternative to using those negatively worded stems. *Educational and Psychological Measurement, 60,* 361–370

Barron, F. (1963). *Creativity and psychological health,* Van Nostrand, Princeton, NY (1963).

Barron, F., Harrington, D.M. (1981). Creativity, intelligence, and personality. *Annual Review of Psychology, 32,* 439–476.

Barron, F., & Welsh, G. S. (1987). *The Barron-Welsh Art Scale.* Menlo, CA: Mind Garden.

Basadur, M., & Hausdorf, P.A. (1996). Measuring divergent thinking attitudes related to

creative problem management. *Creativity Research Journal, 9,* 21–32.

Besemer, S. P., & Treffinger, D. J. (1981). Analysis of creative products: Review and synthesis. *Journal of Creative Behavior, 15,* 158–178.

Besemer, S. P. (1998). Creative product analysis matrix: Testing the model structure and a comparison among products—Three novel chairs. *Creativity Research Journal, 11,* 333–346.

Besemer, S. P., & O'Quin, K. (1999). Confirming the three-factor creative product analysis matrix model in an American sample. *Creativity Research Journal, 12*(4), 287-296.

Binet, A., Simon, T., & Kite, E. S. (1916). *The development of intelligence in children* (The Binet-Simon Scale). Baltimore, MD: Silliams & Silkins Co.

Carson, S. H., Peterson, J. B., & Higgins, D. M. (2003). Decreased latent inhibition is associated with increased creative achievement in high-functioning individuals. *Journal of Personality and Social Psychology, 85,* 499-506.

Cline, V. B., Richards, J. M., & Needham, W. E. (1963). Creativity tests and achievement in high school science. *Journal of Applied Psychology, 47,* 184-189.

Costa, P. T., Jr., & McCrae, R. R (1992). *Revised NEO personality inventory* (NEO PI-RTM) and NEO *five-factor inventory* (NEO-FFI): *Professional manual.* Odessa, FL: Psychological Assessment Resources.

Cox, C. (1926). *The early mental traits of three hundred geniuses.* Stanford: University Press.

Cramond, B. (1994). The Torrance tests of creative thinking: From creation through establishment of predictive validity. In R. F. Subotnik & K. D. Arnold (Eds.), *Beyond Terman: Longitudinal studies in contemporary education* (pp. 229–254). Norwood, NJ: Ablex.

Cramond, B., & Kim, K.H. (2008). The role of creativity tools and measures in assessing potential and growth. In Van Tassel-Baska (Ed.) *Alternative assessments with gifted and talented students* (pp. 203–226) Waco, TX: Prufrock.

Cramond, B., Matthews-Morgan, J., Bandalos, D., & Zuo, L. (2005). The Torrance Tests of Creative Thinking: Alive and well in the new millennium. *Gifted Child Quarterly, 49,* 283–291.

Crocker, l., & Algina, J. (2006) *Introduction to classical & modern test theory.* Belmont, CA: Wadsworth.

Cronbach, L. J. (1970). *Essentials of psychological testing* (3rd ed). New York: Harper.

Cropley, A. J. (2000) Defining and measuring creativity: Are creativity tests worth using? *Roeper Review, 23,* 72–79.

Cropley, A. J., & Cropley, D. (2009). *Fostering creativity: A diagnostic approach for higher education and organizations.* Creskill, NJ: Hampton Press.

Csikszentmihalyi, M. (1988). Society, culture, and person: A systems view of creativity. In R. J. Sternberg (Ed.), *The nature of creativity* (pp. 325–339). New York: Cambridge University Press.

Csikszentmihalyi, M. (1991; 1990). *Flow: The psychology of optimal experience.* New York: Harper Perennial.

Csikszentmihalyi, M. (1996). *Creativity: Flow and the psychology of discovery and invention* (1st ed.). New York: Harper Collins Publishers.

Csikszentmihalyi, M. (1999). Implications of a systems perspective for the study of creativity. In R. J. Sternberg (Ed.), *Handbook of creativity* (pp. 313–335). New York: Cambridge University Press.

Davis, G. A. (1997). Identifying creative students and measuring creativity. In N. Colangelo & G. A. Davis (Eds.), *Handbook of gifted education* (pp. 269–281). Needham Heights, MA: Viacom.

Davis, G. A., & Rimm, S. (1982). Group Inventory for Finding Interests (GIFFI) I and II: Instruments for identifying creative potential in the junior and senior high school. *Journal of Creative Behavior, 16,* 50–57.

Disraeli, B. (1833). *The rise of Iskander.* Retrieved April 1, 2009 from http://www.gutenberg.org/etext/7842

Ekvall, G. (1996). Organizational climate for creativity and innovation. *European Journal of Work and Organizational Psychology (1996)* reprinted by permission of *Psychology Press Ltd., 5,* 105-123.

Eysenck, H. J. (1995). *Genius: The natural history of creativity.* New York: Cambridge University Press.

Feldman, D. H. (1988). Creativity: Dreams, insights, and transformations. In R. J. Sternberg (Ed.), *The nature of creativity,* (pp. 271–297). New York: Cambridge University Press.

Gardner, H. (1993). *Frames of mind: The theory of multiple intelligences* (10th anniversary ed.). New York: BasicBooks.

Gardner, H. (1997). *Extraordinary minds: Portraits of exceptional individuals and an examination of our extraordinariness* (1st ed.). New York: BasicBooks.

Getzels, J. W. & Jackson, P. J. (1962). *Creativity and intelligence: Explorations with gifted students.* New York: John Wiley and Sons, Inc.

Gilliam, J. E., Carpenter, B.O., & Christensen, J. R. (1996). *Gifted and talented evaluation scales* (GATES). Austin, TX: Pro-Ed.

Goleman, D. (1980). 1528 little geniuses and how they grew. *Psychology Today, 13,* 28–43.

Gottfredson, L. (1997). Why g matters: The complexity of everyday life. *Intelligence, 24,* 79–132.

Gough, H. G. (1979). A creative personality scale for the Adjective Check List. *Journal of Personality and Social Psychology, 37,* 1398–1405.

Gough, H. G., & Woodworth, D. G. (1960). Stylistic variations among professional research scientists. *Journal of Psychology; Interdisciplinary and Applied, 49,* 87–98.

Graham, J. R. (1993). *MMPI-2™: Assessing personality and psychopathology.* New York: Oxford University Press.

Graves, M. (1948). *Design judgement test.* San Antonio: Psychological Corporation.

Greene, B. (2003). *Summer of my German soldier.* New York: Dial.

Gruber, H. E., & Davis, S. N. (1988). Inching our way up Mount Olympus: The evolving systems approach to creativity. In R. J. Sternberg (Ed.), *The nature of creativity,* (pp. 243–270). New York: Cambridge University Press.

Guilford, J. P. (1950). Creativity. *American Psychologist, 5,* 444–454.

Guilford, J. P. (1956). The structure of intellect. *Psychological Bulletin, 53*(4), 267–293.

Guilford, J. P. (1962). Potentiality for creativity. *Gifted Child Quarterly, 6,* 87–90.

Guilford, J. P. (1977). *Way beyond the IQ.* Buffalo, N.Y.: Creative Education Foundation

Helson, R. (1971). Women mathematicians and the creative personality. *Journal of Consulting and Clinical Psychology, 36,* 210–220.

Helson, R., & Crutchfield, R. S. (1970). Creative types in mathematics. *Journal of Personality, 38,* 177–197.

Hocevar, D. (1979). *Measurement of creativity: Review and critique.* Paper presented at the Annual Meeting of Rocky Mountain Psychological Association (Denver, CO) ED 175 916 retrieved April 5, 2009 from http://eric.ed.gov/ERICWebPortal/contentdelivery/servlet/ERICServlet?accno=ED175916

Horn, C. A., & Smith, L. F. (1945). The horn art aptitude inventory. *Journal of Applied Psychology, 29*(5), 350–355.

Hunsaker, D. L., & Callahan, C. M. (1995) Creativity and giftedness: Published instrument uses and abuses. *Gifted Child Quarterly, 39,* 110–114

Isaksen, S. G., Lauer, K. J., Ekvall, G., & Britz, A. (2000-2001). Perceptions of the best and worst climates for creativity: Preliminary validation evidence for the situational outlook questionnaire. *Creativity Research Journal, 13,* 171–184.

Kim, K. H. (2005). Can only intelligent people be creative? A meta-analysis. *Journal of Secondary Gifted Education, 16,* 57–66.

Kim, K. H. (2006). Can we trust creativity tests? A review of the Torrance Tests of Creative Thinking (TTCT). *Creativity Research Journal, Special Issue: A Tribute to E. Paul Torrance,18,* 3–14

Kogan, N., & Pankove, E. (1974). Long-term predictive validity of divergent-thinking tests: Some negative evidence. *Journal of Educational Psychology, 66,* 802–810.

Langley, P., & Jones, R. (1988). A computational model of scientific insight. In R.J. Sternberg (Ed.), *The nature of creativity,* (pp. 177–201). New York: Cambridge University Press.

Lee, S., Lee, J., & Kim, N. L. (2004). Creativity of successful business people in Korea. *Korean Journal of Thinking & Problem Solving, 14,* 73–86.

Lissitz, R. W., & Willhoft, J. L. (1985). A methodological study of the Torrance Tests of Creativity. *Journal of Educational Measurement, 22,* 1–111.

Lubow, R. E. (1989). *Latent inhibition and conditioned attention theory.* New York: Cambridge University Press.

MacKinnon, D. W. (1961). Creativity in architects. In D. W. MacKinnon (Ed.), *The creative person* (pp. 291–320). Berkeley: Institute of Personality Assessment Research, University of California.

Maker, C. J. (2009). Discover Projects. Retrieved April 9, 2009 from http://discover.arizona.edu

Maker, C. J. (1992). Intelligence and creativity in multiple intelligences: Identification and development. *Educating Able Learners: Discovering and Nurturing Talent, XVII* (4), 12–19.

Mathisen, G. E., Einarsen, S. (2004). A review of instruments assessing creative and innovative environments within organizations. *Creativity Research Journal, 16,* 119–140.

Mednick, S. A. and Mednick, M. T. (1967). *Examiner's manual: Remote association test.* Boston: Houghton Mifflin.

Messick, S. (1994). The interplay of evidence and consequences in the validation of performance assessments. *Educational Researcher, 23,* 13–23.

Meier, N. C. (1940). *The Meier art tests. I. Art judgment.* Iowa City, IA: Bureau of Educational Research, University of Iowa.

Millar, G. W. (2002). *The Torrance kids at midlife: Selected case studies of creative behavior.* Westport, CT: Ablex.

Okuda S. M., Runco, M. A., & Berger, D. (1991). Creativity and the finding and solving of real-world problems. *Journal of Psychoeducational Assessment, 9,* 45–53.

O'Quin, K., & Besemer, S. P. (1989). The development, reliability, and validity of the revised Creative Product Semantic Scale. *Creativity Research Journal, 2,* 267–278.

Piechowski, M. M. (2003). From William James to Maslow and Dabrowski: Excitability of character and self-actualization. In D. Ambrose, L. Cohen, & A.J. Tannenbaum (Eds.),

*Creative intelligence: Toward theoretic integration* (pp. 283–322). Cresskill, NJ: Hampton Press.

Piirto, J. (2004). *Understanding creativity.* Scottsdale, AZ: Great Potential Press.

Reis, S. M., & Renzulli, J. S. (1991). The assessment of creative products in programs for gifted and talented students. *Gifted Child Quarterly, 35,* 128–134. doi: 10.1177/001698629103500304

Renzulli, J. S., Smith, L. H., White, A. J., Callahan, C. M., Hartman, R. K., Westberg, K.L, Gavin, M. K., Reis, S. M., Siegle, D., & Sytsma, R. E. (2004). *Scales for rating the behavioral characteristics of superior students.* Mansfield Center, CT: Creative Learning Press.

Rhodes, M. (1961). An analysis of creativity. *Phi Delta Kappan, 41,* 305–310.

Richards, R., Kinney, D. K., Benet, M., & Merzel, A. P. (1988). Assessing everyday creativity: Characteristics of the Lifetime Creativity Scales and validation with three large samples. *Journal of Personality and Social Psychology, 54,* 476–485. doi: 10.1037/0022-3514.54.3.476

Rimm, S. B. (1976). *Group inventory for finding talent* (GIFT). Waterton, WI: Educational Assessment Service.

Rimm, S. B., & Davis, G. A. (1983). Identifying creativity. Part II—Self report inventories and the characteristics approach. *G/C/T/, 29,* 19–23.

Runco, M. A. (1994). *Problem finding, problem solving, and creativity.* Norwood, N.J.: Ablex Pub. Corp.

Runco, M. A. (2004). Creativity. *Annual Review of Psychology, 55,* 657–687.

Runco, M. A. (2008). *Creativity: Theories and themes: Research, development, and practice.* Burlington, MA: Elsevier.

Runco, M. A., Millar, G., Acar, S., & Cramond, B. (2009). *Torrance Tests of Creative Thinking as predictors of personal and public achievement: A fifty year follow-up.* Manuscript submitted for publication.

Runco, M. A., Plucker, J. A., & Lin, W. (2000-2001). Development and psychometric integrity of a measure of ideational behavior. *Creativity Research Journal, 13,* 393–400.

Russ, S. W., Robins, A. L., & Christiano, B. A. (1999). Pretend play: Longitudinal prediction of creativity and affect in fantasy in children. *Creativity Research Journal, 12,* 129–139.

Seashore, C. E., Lewis, D., & Saetveit, J. (1939). *The Seashore measures of musical talents* (Revision). New York: The Psychological Corporation.

Simonton, D. K. (1984). *Genius, creativity, and leadership: Historiometric inquiries.* Cambridge, MA: Harvard University Press.

Simonton, D. K. (1988). Creativity, leadership, and chance. In R. J. Sternberg (Ed.), *The nature of creativity* (pp. 386–426). New York: Cambridge University Press.

Sternberg, R. J., Grigorenko, E. L., & Bundy, D. A. (2001). The predictive value of IQ. *Merrill-Palmer Quarterly, 47,* 1–41.

Sternberg, R. J. (1988). A three-facet model of creativity. In R. J. Sternberg (Ed.), *The nature of creativity* (pp. 125–147). New York: Cambridge University Press.

Tardif, T. Z., & Sternberg, R. J. (1988) What do we know about creativity? In R. J. Sternberg (Ed.), *The nature of creativity*, (pp. 429–440). New York: Cambridge University Press.

Torrance, E. P. (1966). *The Torrance tests of creative thinking norms—technical manual figural* (Research ed.*).* Princeton, NJ: Personnel Press.

Torrance, E. P. (1969). Prediction of adult creative achievement among high school seniors. *Gifted Child Quarterly, 13,* 223–229.

Torrance, E. P. (1972). Predictive validity of the Torrance Tests of Creative Thinking. *Journal of Creative Behavior, 6,* 236–252.

Torrance, E. P. (1979). *The search for satori and creativity.* Buffalo, NY: Bearly Limited.

Torrance, E. P. (1980). Growing up creatively gifted: A 22-year longitudinal study. *Creative Child and Adult Quarterly, 5,* 148–158, 170.

Torrance, E. P. (1981a). Empirical validation of criterion-referenced indicators of creative ability through a longitudinal study. *Creative Child and Adult Quarterly, 6,* 136–140.

Torrance, E. P. (1981b). Predicting the creativity of elementary school children (1958–80) and the teachers who "made a difference." *Gifted Child Quarterly, 25,* 55–62.

Torrance, E. P. (1988). The nature of creativity as manifest in its testing. In R. J. Sternberg (Ed.), *The nature of creativity* (pp. 43–73). New York: Cambridge University Press.

Torrance, E. P. (1998). *The Torrance tests of creative thinking norms—technical manual figural (streamlined) forms A & B.* Bensenville, IL: Scholastic Testing Service, Inc.

Torrance, E. P. (2002). *The manifesto: A guide to developing a creative career.* West Westport, CT: Ablex.

Torrance, E. P. (2008). *The Torrance tests of creative thinking norms—technical manual figural (streamlined) forms A & B.* Bensenville, IL: Scholastic Testing Service, Inc.

Wallach, M., & Kogan, N. (1966). *Modes of thinking in young children.* New York: John Wiley.

Wallas, G. (1926). *The Art of thought.* London: Watts.

Wang, C. (1985). *Measures of creativity in sound and music.* Unpublished manuscript. Retrieved April 11, 2009 from http://www.uky.edu/~cecilia/MCSM/mcsm.htm

Williams, F. E. (1980). *Creativity assessment packet.* Austin, TX: Pro-Ed.

## Chapter 13 Study Guide

**Prompt 1** *Knowledge*

Define each of the *Four Ps* and how these may apply to gifted identification.

**Prompt 2** *Opinion*

The authors discuss several dichotomized issues in creativity assessment (i.e., cognitive or personality, eminent or everyday, aptitude or achievement, holistic or specific, subjective or objective, child or adult, divergent or convergent, contextualized or decontextualized, general or specific, self or other). Select one of these issues and prepare a defense for which side of the dichotomy it makes most sense to use in school settings for the identification of gifted students.

**Prompt 3** *Affect*

The authors use the word *audacious* to describe how some might react to the idea of assessing creativity. Does this match your feelings, or would some other word make more sense? If the word *audacious* is a match, explain why. If not, explain what other word you would use and why.

**Prompt 4** *Experience*

Describe any experience you or someone you know has had with any of the assessments described in this chapter. Give reasons for why the experience was helpful or not.

**Prompt 5** *Preconception/Misconception*

Some think that concepts such as validity and reliability are too technical to apply to something as nebulous as creativity. Justify your position on this issue through your agreement or disagreement with points made by the authors about these concepts.

# USING TEACHER RATING SCALES IN THE IDENTIFICATION OF STUDENTS FOR GIFTED SERVICES

KAREN L. WESTBERG, UNIVERSITY OF ST. THOMAS

Toua, a young Hmong boy, was identified for gifted services just six months after being relocated from a refugee camp in Thailand to Minnesota and enrolling in school. Did he score above the 95th percentile on an aptitude or achievement test? No, but his teacher observed his dramatic progress in learning English and his amazing ability in mathematics, spatial learning tasks, and problem solving tasks. When completing a teacher rating form for screening students for gifted education services, she rated him highly on specific traits and behaviors she observed in the classroom and recommended him for services. This true story, along with less dramatic examples, indicates that obtaining teacher input is valuable when considering students for gifted education services.

Experts in the field of gifted education have long recommended using teacher judgment measures among the multiple sources of information for screening and identifying students for gifted education services. According to the most recent *State of the States in Gifted Education* Report (NAGC, 2009), teacher judgment information and test score information are the two most

commonly used sources of information when identifying students for gifted education services. There appears to be universal agreement by experts about the need to include teacher judgment in the identification process. Shore, Cornell, Robinson, and Ward (1991) published a seminal book on 101 recommended practices in gifted education. Among these practices were the need to base identification on multiple criteria (p. 48), and the importance of including teacher nominations in the identification process (p. 65). After reviewing the evidenced-based support for these recommended practices, they concluded, "Nominations forms and questionnaires should address specific characteristics or subject matter, and especially abilities not addressed by formal tests" (p. 65). Lohman and Lakin (2007) also argue for the inclusion of teacher judgment measures when identifying students for gifted services, stating, "Combining evidence of current achievement, reasoning abilities, and teacher ratings can help increase the diversity of gifted programs while also identifying the students in all ethnic groups most likely to benefit from special instruction" (p. 22). The recent *2010*

*Pre-K–Grade 12 Gifted Programming Standards* (NAGC, 2010) underscore this by stating that comprehensive practices and multiple assessments from different sources should be used in the identification process.

## HISTORICAL PERSPECTIVES

Although widely used today, teacher judgment instruments for identification have not always been a recommended practice because of concerns about the validity and reliability of teachers' input. This view could be traced to Terman's (1925) research published in the *Genetic Studies of Genius*. When gathering data for this study, Terman asked teachers to refer the brightest child, the second-brightest child, the third-brightest child, and the youngest child in their classrooms for assessment on the *Stanford-Binet Intelligence Scale*, the instrument he developed. Because he found that the youngest children, more so than the other children, met his criterion of having IQs of 140 and above on the Stanford-Binet, he concluded that teachers were not particularly skilled in predicting which children would score highest on his intelligence scale. This raises the issue of the *criterion* problem, namely, what are we trying to predict with teacher ratings and what should be used as the criterion when validating teacher judgment measures? In Terman's situation, teachers were asked to predict who would score highest on a particular intelligence test (the criterion), which he equated with giftedness.

Pegnato and Birch's (1959) study on the effectiveness and efficiency of using teacher ratings in the identification process, unfortunately, has had a long-lasting impact on views about using teachers' input when identifying students for services. When conducting a study to identify junior high students, they concluded that teacher ratings lacked validity and reliability and, therefore, should not be used. This single, brief study has been cited over the years as a rationale for excluding or providing little weight to teachers' ratings. After years of mistrust about the value of including teacher judgment information in the identification process, a few researchers examined the Pegnato and Birch study more closely. Borland (1978) challenged their findings by stating that if the teachers in the Pegnato and Birch study had rated students on specific behaviors rather than on general ability, the results would have been different. Gagné (1994) conducted a re-analysis of the Pegnato and Birch data, which revealed major methodological flaws in their study. Gagné illustrates how effectiveness (absence of false negatives) and efficiency (absence of false positives) cannot be independent of each other and, therefore, should not have been measured as such. Gagné concluded his investigation by stating, "Educators in the field should stop citing Pegnato and Birch's (1959) study as proof of poor teacher judgment in identifying gifted and talented children; their data do not support such a sweeping judgment" (p. 126). And, finally, Birch (1984) himself, 25 years later, questioned whether there was any value in formal identification at all.

## RATIONALE FOR USING TEACHER JUDGMENT MEASURES

Why use teacher judgment measures when identifying students for gifted education services?

The most common rationale is that they provide additional and different information about the characteristics and behaviors we associate with giftedness, and we should not rely on just one source of information when selecting students for gifted services. Most psychologists and educators no longer believe that a high IQ on an intelligence test, as was Terman's assertion, is equated with giftedness (e.g., see Sternberg and Davidson, 2005). The problem, of course, is that there is limited consensus on what constitutes giftedness. Nonetheless, by using teacher judgment measures, it is anticipated that teachers' observations of traits and behaviors not tapped by traditional ability or achievement tests, such as perseverance, intellectual playfulness, and focused interests, will be illuminated, and students who exhibit capabilities in different ways will be identified for gifted education services.

A variety of teacher judgment measures for screening and identifying gifted learners have been developed over the years. Unfortunately, many have limited or no empirical support. Much too often, we find that consultants or school districts have created their own teacher rating forms or checklists, which have absolutely no support for their reliability and validity. In many cases, these forms have been created in an earnest attempt to find students who demonstrate strengths not addressed on aptitude or achievement measures, but school personnel need to realize that, when using teacher judgment instruments with no empirical support, they are using a highly crude measurement tool, much like using one's arm span to measure the length of a football field. Only published teacher judgment measures with empirical support will be discussed in this chapter, and only instruments

with empirical support should be used in a formal screening and identification process. Other, non-researched instruments (e.g., *Kingore Observation Inventory*, the *Kranz Talent Identification Instrument*) may be helpful for other purposes (e.g., for discussions in professional development sessions, for developing curricular experiences aligned with certain traits), but non-researched instruments should not be used when identifying students for formal gifted education services.

## SCALES FOR RATING THE BEHAVIORAL CHARACTERISTICS OF SUPERIOR STUDENTS

In 1976 Renzulli, Smith, White, Callahan, and Hartman published the *Scales for Rating the Behavioral Characteristics of Superior Students (SR-BCSS),* a series of 10 separate teacher judgment scales designed to obtain information about the manifestations of students' characteristics, which were learning, motivation, creativity, leadership, artistic, musical, dramatics, communication-precision, communication-expressiveness, and planning. The first three or four scales—learning, motivation, creativity, and leadership—are most commonly used. The other scales are used when appropriate for programs that focus on those traits. Readers familiar with Renzulli's (1978) three-ring definition of giftedness will recognize that his conception of giftedness underlies the theory behind these scales (see Chapter 2 of this volume). Two items on the 1976 learning scales include: "Possesses a large storehouse of information about a variety of topics (beyond the usual interests of youngsters his age)," and "Displays a great deal of curiosity about many things; is constantly asking questions about anything and everything." Each characteristic listed on a scale in 1976 was selected because of the empirical support for it; for example, the aforementioned characteristic about curiosity is referenced to work done by several researchers, including Torrance (1962). To respond to the items on the scale, teachers were instructed to rate the frequency with which they observe each characteristic manifested in a student on a 4-point scale (1 = never, 2 = rarely, 3 = occasionally, and 4 = always).

These scales have been arguably the most widely used teacher judgment rating scales for gifted programming in the US and have been translated and researched for use in several countries (e.g., Kalatan,1991; Nazir, 1988; Subhi, 1997; Srour, 1989). The research conducted with the original scales is described in the technical and administration manual for the scales (Renzulli, Smith, White, Callahan, and Hartman, 1976). A few years after *SRBCSS* was originally published, Renzulli and Reis (1985) published teacher-training exercises to accompany the learning, motivation, creativity, and leadership scales. Unfortunately, many users of the scales have not been aware of them nor have they used the teacher-training materials for the first four scales (the most widely used of the 10 scales). The teacher-training exercises were designed to increase teachers' understanding about the key concepts underlying the items and to increase the reliability of teachers' ratings.

The *Scales for Rating the Behavioral Characteristics of Superior Students* were revised and published in 2002 (Renzulli, Smith, White, Callahan, Hartman, & Westberg). When conducting the literature review for the *SRBCSS* revision (examining articles

published between 1976 and 2001), studies were organized into two categories: those examining the construct validity of teacher judgment measures and those in which a teacher judgment measure was used in criterion-related validity studies. Construct validity refers to the extent to which the operationalization of a construct on a test or scale actually supports the construct—that is, does a measure of critical thinking really measure what we mean by critical thinking, and does a scale on motivation really measure motivation (see also Chapter 7 of this volume for a discussion of validity)? Summaries of the limited studies exploring construct validity of all teacher judgment measures are summarized in the *SRBCSS Technical and Administration Manual* (Renzulli, Smith, Callahan, White, Hartman, & Westberg, 2002). Conclusions from these construct validity studies were taken into account when revising the *SRBCSS* scales.

Many of the studies on teacher judgment conducted between 1976 and 2001 involved using the *SRBCSS* scales or other scales as predictors in a criterion-related validity study. Criterion-related validity refers to the degree to which a measure is correlated with another measure presumed to be related to the first measure. Quite often the criterion in investigations of teacher judgment measures has been an intelligence test. Many researchers (e.g., Borland, 2008; Renzulli & Delcourt, 1986) believe that the selection of an intelligence test as a criterion for a teacher judgment measure simply does not support logical inferences. If teachers' ratings are used to predict performance on intelligence tests, what is the rationale for even using the teachers' ratings? In other words, why second guess intelligence tests? This is referred to as the *criterion* problem. Despite this, many studies involving the use of teacher judgment measures have used intelligence tests or achievement tests as the criterion, which the authors of *SRBCSS* believe is inappropriate.

When preparing the revised scales for field tests, a few new items (characteristics) with empirical support were added; scales were modified to include a 6-point response scale (Never, Very Rarely, Rarely, Occasionally, Frequently, Always), as opposed to the original 4-point response scale, which was criticized in the literature as being not on an interval scale; compound items were separated into separate items; and item stems were worded into gender-neutral language (Renzulli, Smith, Callahan, White, Hartman, & Westberg, 2002). Details about the sampling and data-gathering procedures for the field tests of the revised scales with Grade 3–12 teachers are described in the *SRBCSS Technical and Administration Manual* (Renzulli, Smith, Callahan, White, Hartman, & Westberg, 2002). The manual also contains details about the judgmental and empirical procedures used to provide evidence for the content validity (ratings by 60 experts in the field of gifted education), construct validity (principal components analysis), and criterion-related validity of the scales. The procedure for investigating the criterion-related validity warrants some discussion here because it was designed to address the *criterion* problem mentioned earlier. Instead of using an intelligence or achievement test as the criterion, another instrument was developed for this purpose: *Rating Student Performance in a Gifted Program (RSP/GP)* (Renzulli & Westberg, 1991). The *RSP/GP* contains 10 items on a 5-point response scale,

such as "This year, [the student] created quality projects." Classroom teachers completed the *SRBCSS* scales (learning, motivation, creativity, and leadership) in the fall, and a sub-sample of gifted education specialists completed the *RSP/GP* in the spring of that same year on the students who had been receiving gifted education services, resulting in a moderate correlation.

Details about the procedures used to support the alpha and inter-rater reliability of the revised *SRBCSS* are also described in the *SRBCSS Technical and Administration Manual* (Renzulli, Smith, Callahan, White, Hartman, & Westberg, 2002). Strong alpha reliability coefficients (ranging from r = .84 to r = .97) and moderate inter-rater reliability coefficients were obtained (r = .50 to r = .65) on the revised scales. Hence, the above analyses provide technical support for the revised *SRBCSS*.

## Four New *SRBCSS*

Four new *SRBCSS* teacher-rating scales were developed recently for obtaining teacher ratings on Grade 3–8 students in four content areas—reading, mathematics, science, and technology (Renzulli, Siegle, Reis, Gavin, & Sytsma Reed, 2009). These areas were selected for the new scales for two major reasons. The authors realize that variations exist among learners; namely, some students demonstrate strengths in one domain and not another, and the authors wanted to support teachers' attempts to differentiate instruction in specific content areas. To support the content validity of the new scales, experts' ratings (25 experts for each scale) were obtained, and the new scales were field tested in several schools throughout the country. A total of 187 teachers completed ratings on 726 Grade 4–6 students. Confirmatory factor analysis was conducted to examine the construct-related validity support of the new scales. Initially, separate confirmatory factor analyses were conducted for each of the four domains, and the number of items was reduced in each scale to establish the model of best fit. Then, a confirmatory factor analysis was conducted of a model that included all four scales. The fit index of the combined model, $X^2(371) = 1541.22$, was significant ($p<.001$), providing support for the construct validity of the scales, and all alpha reliabilities of the scales exceeded $r = .97$. Additional support for the validity of the scales was established by correlating the ratings on the scales with students' grades in academic subjects, resulting in moderate to strong correlations (e.g., $r = .453$ for technology and $r = .731$ for mathematics.) Additional details about the research procedures and findings can be obtained in the third edition of *Scales for Rating the Behavioral Characteristics of Superior Students Technical and Administration Manual* (Renzulli et al., 2010).

## AUTHORS' RECOMMENDATIONS FOR USING *SRBCSS*

The third edition of the *SRBCSS* manual (Renzulli et al., 2010) includes an explanation of the procedures used to develop the 2002 revised scales, procedures for developing the four content scales in 2009, and recommendations for using the scales. The manual also includes teacher-training exercises for all 14 scales, which were designed to improve teachers' understanding of the behaviors and traits on the scales as well as improve the reliability of their ratings. Before teachers complete the scales, the authors highly

recommend that the teacher-training exercises be used (on different days, not all in one sitting, to address teacher fatigue). Three general guidelines for using the scales are: (1) consider the type of program for which students are being identified when selecting the scales to use (e.g., use the creativity scale if the goals of the program include the development of creativity); (2) examine each scale separately—do not add the scores from the scales together to form a total score (the dimensions on the scales represent relatively different sets of behavioral characteristics, and a composite or total score would overlook unique student strengths); and (3) do not modify or abbreviate the scales by reducing the number of items on each scale (doing so will definitely lower the reliability estimates on the scales).

National norms are not provided in the manual for *SRBCSS* because Renzulli et al. (2010) believe that this information is not meaningful or useful. Instead, the authors believe local norms should be established because *SRBCSS* is purposefully designed to assess students' characteristics within a local reference group. Lohman (2009a) advocates developing local norms when selecting students for gifted education services, stating, "There is a tradeoff between getting a *more precise but less valid* estimate of the student's talent by using an inappropriate national norm group and getting a *less but more valid* estimate by using a more appropriate local or subgroup norm" (p. 238; see also Chapter 10 of this text). The *SRBCSS Technical and Administration Manual* includes information on how to establish local percentile ranks. In order to establish local norms, the teacher ratings need to be completed on a variety of students, including students who do not demonstrate the characteristics to a high degree. Therefore, to establish local norms initially, it is recommended that a subset of teachers in a district complete the scales on all of their students because a large and varied sample is necessary for calculating norms. (It should be noted that the scales are now available online through Creative Learning Press, and when teachers complete the scales online, the system calculates and provides local norms.)

The final recommendation when using *SRBCSS* is this: "As with other test score information, a *SRBCSS* rating should not be used as the single criterion for selecting students for special programs. The information should be used in conjunction with other information" (Renzulli et al., 2010, p. 25). Once again, we are reminded that we should be using multiple sources of information when identifying students for gifted services.

## SCALES FOR IDENTIFYING GIFTED STUDENTS

The *Scales for Identifying Gifted Students (SIGS)* is a series of scales "designed to assist school districts in the identification of students as gifted" (Ryser & McConnell, 2004, p.1). The *SIGS* contains items on seven separate scales (general intellectual ability, language arts, mathematics, science, social studies, creativity, and leadership) to which teachers respond on a 5-point scale (0 = never, 1 = rarely, 2 = some, 3 = somewhat more, 4 = much more). Teachers are asked to respond to items by keeping in mind how each child compares to his or her peers on the characteristic being rated. The authors developed these seven scales because they "recognize these as being seven areas of giftedness,"

and they developed two versions of the scales, the *School Rating Scales (SRS)* form and the *Home Rating Scales (HRS)* form. The items on the scales are identical on both forms. For example, one of the general intellectual ability items states, "Demonstrates a healthy skepticism and curiosity," and one of the language arts items states, "Is able to discuss literature or other issues at an interpretive (explanatory) level." The *SIGS* are designed for ages 5–18 and contain 12 items on each scale. Based on the authors' review of the literature in each of the seven areas, the authors selected characteristics for the scales that indicated strengths within each area. The citations for the literature support are provided in the technical manual accompanying the scales.

When developing the *SIGS*, (Ryser & McConnell (2004) piloted the scales with two groups to establish national norms for "general" and "gifted" students. To obtain the pilot groups, the authors solicited participants who had purchased tests previously from the publisher. Once selected for participation, teachers were asked to complete the scales on students who were already participating in a gifted program and on the general population of their students. The technical manual contains tables for converting raw scores into standard scores and percentile ranks on each scale for the various age groups.

## TECHNICAL SUPPORT FOR *SIGS*

The *SIGS* technical manual (Ryser & McConnell, 2004) includes summary information on the procedures used to support the validity of the scales. Using sub-samples from the pilot group, scales were correlated with students' scores on the *WISC-III, Test of Cognitive Skills, Otis-Lennon School Ability Test, Cognitive Ability Test-2,* and *Torrance Tests of Creative Thinking-Figural* scores to support criterion-related validity. These various analyses resulted in moderate to high correlations on the *School Rating Scale,* with the highest correlations obtained between the seven *SIGS* and the *Test of Cognitive Skills-2.*

The *SIGS* technical manual (Ryser & McConnell, 2004) also includes information on the procedures used to support the reliability of the scales. Internal consistency, test-retest, and inter-rater reliability procedures resulted in moderate to high reliability coefficients. For example, the alpha reliabilities ranged from r = .93 to .96 on the scales from the *School Rating Scale*-gifted subsample. Using a two-week interval on the test-retest procedures, reliabilities ranged from r = .58 to .93 on the scales from the *School Rating Scale*-gifted sample. Inter-rater reliability of the school and home versions was examined, resulting in correlations between the teacher and parent ratings of r = .43 to .53 on the gifted sample.

**AUTHORS' RECOMMENDATIONS FOR USING *SIGS***

Ryser and McConnell (2004) do not suggest summing the scores on the scales. Norms are provided for the seven scales only and not for the composite score. The authors explain that all scale ratings do not necessarily need to be completed on students. For example, if a school has a program for students gifted in mathematics and science, perhaps only the mathematics and science scales should be used.

Ryser and McConnell included a Summary Form along with the scales and technical manual

in the kit (2004). They recommend that a screening/identification committee use this form when selecting the students who will be identified for services. The Summary Form includes an area for recording the *School Rating Scale* and *Home Rating Scale* results as well as areas for recording additional information about a child being considered.

**GIFTED RATING SCALES**

The *Gifted Rating Scales* (GRS) were developed to help teachers to "assess observable student behaviors indicating giftedness" (Pfeiffer & Jarosewich, 2003, p. 1). The *GRS-School Form* contains six scales based on areas mentioned in the 1972 and 1978 federal definition of giftedness: intellectual, academic, creativity, artistic, leadership, and motivation. The authors' rationale for using these areas is based on the assumption that most states or districts use the 1978 federal definition or parts of it. In addition to developing a *GRS-School Form (GRS-S)*, the authors developed a *Preschool/Kindergarten Form (GRS-P)*. The two versions are similar in format, but only 29% of the items overlap, and the leadership scale is not included on the *GRS-P*. Sample items on the *GRS-S* are "Thinks insightfully, intuitively understands problems" (intellectual ability scale); "Completes academic work correctly" (academic ability scale); and "Displays an active imagination, thinks or acts imaginatively" (creative scale). The *GRS-S* is designed for children in Grades 1–8, ages 6.0–13.11. The authors state that the *GRS-P* "identifies giftedness in children between the ages of 4.0–6.11." When rating 6-year-olds, teachers should use the *GRS-P* if the children are in kindergarten and use the *SRS-S* if the children are in Grade 1. The *GRS-P* contains items such as, "Learns difficult concepts easily" (intellectual ability scale), "Completes activities correctly" (academic ability scale), and "Engages in elaborate imaginative play" (creativity scale).

Both the *GRS-S* and *GRS-P* contain 12 items per scale and instruct teachers to rate characteristics along a range of 9 points (Pfeiffer & Jarosewich, 2003). When doing the ratings, teachers are directed to first consider whether the students' characteristics are below average, average, or above average, and then select one of the three points within that category. Ratings of 1, 2, and 3 are in the below average category; ratings of 4, 5, and 6 are categorized as being average; and ratings of 7, 8, and 9 are categorized as being above average. Both Korean and Chinese versions of the GRS have been developed and researched (Lee & Pfeiffer, 2006; Li, Pfeiffer, Petscher, Kumtepe, & Mo, 2008).

## TECHNICAL SUPPORT FOR THE *GRS*

Pfeiffer and Jarosewich (2003) used various procedures to support the validity inferences on the *GRS,* beginning with expert ratings on the items (content validity evidence). Convergent and discriminant validity were examined by correlating responses on all *GRS* scale scores (intellectual ability, academic ability, creativity, artistic talent, motivation, and leadership scales) with measures of intelligence (Wechsler tests), achievement (Wechsler tests), creativity (*Torrance Tests of Creative Thinking*), artistic talent (*SRBCSS* Artistic and Creativity scales, *Expert Art Panel* ratings), motivation (*Academic Competence Evaluation Scales* and *SRBCSS* Motivation scale), and leadership

(*SRBCSS* Leadership scale and number of students' leadership activities). These analyses were conducted with subsets of the standardization sample and resulted in a plethora of correlations presented in 11 tables in the technical manual (Pfeiffer & Jarosewich, 2003). The results of the analyses of the various GRS scales with measures of intelligence generally demonstrated low to moderate correlations. The five *GRS-P* scales were correlated with the *Wechsler Preschool Primary Intelligence Scale-III (WPPSI-III)* subtest and composite scores, resulting in correlations generally in the moderate range (r = .40s). The six *GRS-S* scale scores were correlated with the *Wechsler Intelligence Scale for Children-IV (WISC-IV)* subtest scores, index scores, and full scale score, resulting in correlations in the low to moderate range (r = .30s and .40s).

In addition to looking at the relationship with measures of intelligence, the *GRS* scales were correlated with an achievement measure, the *Wechsler Individual Achievement Test-II (WIAT-II)* subtests and composite scores. The *GRS-P* academic ability and motivation scales correlated most strongly with the *WIAT-II* subtests, with correlations in the low to moderate range (r = .30s and .40s). The *GRS-S* scales correlated more strongly than the *GRS-P* scales with the *WIAT-II* subtests, resulting in correlations in the moderate range (r = .50s), with the strongest correlations between the *GRS-S* intellectual and academic scales and the *WIAT-II* subtests and composite scores.

To examine the predictive validity of *GRS* with creativity, the authors examined the correlations between *GRS* scales with both the *Torrance Test of Creative Thinking (TTCT), Figural Form B* and the *SRBCSS* creativity scale. Interestingly, all five *GRS-P* scales correlated most highly with the *SRBCSS* creativity scale, with r = .76–.88. The same was found for the *GRS-S,* with all six scales correlating more highly with the *SRBCSS* creativity scale, r = .67 on the GRS-S artistic scale and r = .86 on both the *GRS-S* academic and creativity scales. Correlations between the *GRS* with the *TTCT-Figural* were all very low, r = .10s.

To examine the relationship between the *GRS* with measures of artistic talent, correlations were performed between all *GRS* and ratings of students' art samples as well as the *SRBCSS* artistic scale. The results indicated the highest correlations between the five *GRS-P* scales and the *SRBCSS* artistic scale scores, r = .77–.91. Correlations on the six *GRS-S* scales with the *SRBCSS* artistic scale ranged from r = .39 (GRS-S academic scale) to r = .86 (*GRS-S* artistic scale).

The authors also examined the relationship between the *GRS* with measures of motivation, namely, the *Academic Competence Evaluation Scale (ACES)* motivation scale and the *SRBCSS* motivation scale. Similar results were obtained for both the *GRS-P* and *GRS-S* with high correlations (r = .70s and .80s) found on both measures of motivation. The strongest correlations were between the *GRS* motivation scale and the *SRBCSS* motivation scale (r =.90 on both).

The relationship between the *GRS-S* scales and measures of leadership was examined by correlating *GRS* scales with the number of students' leadership activities and teachers' ratings on the *SRBCSS* leadership scale. As with the correlations on creativity and motivation, the strongest correlations were found between the *GRS-S* scales and the *SRBCSS* leadership scale, r = .62–.90.

Pfeiffer and Jarosewich (2003) concluded that these correlation analyses demonstrated convergent and divergent validity evidence for the *GRS* scale scores, illustrating *convergent* validity when, for example, the *GRS-S* creativity scale correlated highly with the *SRBCSS* creativity scale (r = .86) and illustrating *divergent* validity when the *GRS-S* artistic scale correlated somewhat lower with the *SRBCSS* creativity scale (r =.67). This concept would have been better supported if the correlations between the other *GRS* scales and the *SRBCSS* creativity scale had been much lower. The correlations of the five or six *GRS* scales with external measures of intelligence, achievement, motivation, and leadership demonstrated overall evidence for convergent validity and, in some case, for divergent validity, most notably between the *GRS* leadership scale and the intelligence and achievement scores.

In addition to providing support for the validity of the *GRS* scales, Pfeiffer and Jarosewich (2003) conducted procedures to provide evidence for the reliability of the scales. The alpha reliability coefficients on the *GRS-P* scales for the standardization sample were all r = .98 or .99. As with the *GRS-P*, the alpha reliability coefficients on the *GRS-S* scales were also very high, r = .97–.99. Test-retest reliability was also conducted on the *GRS-P and GRS-S* using a subsample of 124 students and 154 students, respectively. Using an average retesting interval of 18 days on the *GRS-P* scales, the test-retest reliability estimates ranged from r = .91 to r = .95 for the entire *GRS-P* subsample. Using a median retesting interval of 7 days on the *GRS-S* scales, the reliability estimates ranged from r = .83 to r = .90 for the entire subsample. Thus, the test-retest reliability estimates were high.

Inter-rater reliability on the *GRS-P* and *GRS-S* scale ratings was also examined by having two teachers/raters complete the *GRS-P* ratings on 56 students and *GRS-S* ratings on 147 students. The intraclass correlation coefficients on the *GRS-P* ranged from r = .62 on the artistic scale to r = .80 on the intellectual ability scale, and on the GRS-S, they ranged from r = .68 on the artistic scale and r = .77 on the academic ability scale. Therefore, these coefficients indicate adequate consistency across different teachers' ratings of the same students.

Pfeiffer and Jarosewich (2003) established national norms using data from the standardization samples. Specific details as to how the standardization samples were recruited and selected are not described in the technical manual, but the authors report that both student samples were stratified to match the US census by ethnicity (White, African American, Hispanic, Asian, and Other) and by parent education level. A total of 90 teachers participated in the *GRS-P* standardization, and a total of 382 teachers participated in the *GRS-S* standardization. The *GRS-S* student sample was stratified within eight 12-month age bands from 6.0 to 13.11 years.

To obtain national norms on the *GRS*, scale raw score totals are converted into a *T* score (which has a mean of 50 and standard deviation of 10) and into cumulative percentages for the *T* scores. The technical manual (Pfeiffer & Jarosewich, 2003) contains conversion tables for determining the *T* scores and cumulative percentages for each age level on the appropriate *GRS* scale. Complete details used to establish the standard scores (*T* scores) are not provided in the technical manual,

but the authors state that norms were based on the performance of the students in the standardization samples (n = 375 on the *GRS-P* sample and n = 600 on the *GRS-S* sample.) The authors classify *T* scores of 70 and above as having a "very high probability" of gifted classification, scores of 60–69 as a "high probability" of gifted classification, scores of 55–59 as a "moderate probability of gifted classification, and below 55 as a "low probability" of gifted classification.

### AUTHORS' RECOMMENDATIONS FOR USING GRS

Pfeiffer and Jarosewich (2003) provide a few guidelines for using the *GRS* in screening students for gifted programs. They recommend that the teacher/rater complete the entire instrument in a single session to ensure consistency when completing the ratings. The authors believe ratings on the 60 items on *GRS-P* can be completed in 10 minutes or less, and ratings on the 72 items on the *GRS-S* can be completed in 15 minutes or less. When asking teachers to complete the ratings, the raters should be instructed to complete their ratings by comparing the child being rated with "typical" students of the same age in a regular classroom setting. When collecting the completed ratings from teachers, the authors suggest the scales be returned to teachers if more than one item is missing from a scale. If a scale is missing two or more ratings, the *T* score and cumulative percentage should not be calculated. If one item is missing, the average of all items on that scale should be inserted for the missing item before totaling the scores on a scale. The authors also note in the technical manual that consumers might want to develop local norms rather than use the national norms provided. They acknowledge that "local norms take into account the unique characteristics of the school district and its community" (p. 20). And, finally, Pfeiffer and Jarosewich want consumers to realize the *GRS* is designed to be an initial screening instrument, and decisions about placement of students in gifted programs should be based on a comprehensive selection process.

## CONCLUSIONS ABOUT USING TEACHER JUDGMENT MEASURES

As described above, the three instruments— *Scales for Rating the Behavioral Characteristics of Superior Students*, *Scales for Identifying Gifted Students*, and *Gifted Rating Scales*—all have empirical support for their use. In addition to reviewing the technical support for instruments, how do school personnel make a decision for which instrument to use? The best advice is to consider, first of all, the needs of their gifted learners and the definition of giftedness being used to develop program services, and then to develop screening and identification procedures and instruments aligned with the definition. If a district is providing advanced classes in language arts and mathematics to its gifted learners, then certain types of teacher rating instruments will be better suited for identifying talent in those areas. In other words, we don't identify students until we know what services we are identifying students for.

When decisions have been made as to the sources and types of information to be considered in the screening procedure, school personnel should be reminded that modifying teacher judgment instruments is not permissible. Removing or adding some items to a teacher rating scale changes the technical support for the instrument. It is analogous to saying that when buying new tires for a car, "Oh, the tires are so expensive, I will just buy three new tires and get along with just three new ones." The vehicle (or program) may suffer greatly because of the change in the support.

Something else that consumers might consider when using teacher judgment measures is the use of local norms. Many scholars and researchers now recommend that contextual assessment and local norms be used when making interpretations from instruments to assist when identifying students for gifted services (e.g., Lohman, 2009b; Lohman & Renzulli, 2007; Peters & Gentry, 2011; Sternberg, 1998). In fact, the National Association for Gifted Children (2010) includes a statement about using local norms in the program standards. Within the standards we find, "Evidenced-based Practice 2.3.1: Educators select and use non-biased and equitable approaches for identifying students with gifts and talents, which may include using locally developed norms or assessment tools in the child's native language or in nonverbal formats." Lohman argues convincingly that "the need for special services depends not so much on a student's standing relative to age or grade mates nationally, but on the student's standing relative to the other students in the class" (2009b, p. 49; see also Chapter 12 of this text). It is the students at the top, regardless of the reference group, whose needs are most likely not to be met in a regular classroom. Lohman and Lankin (2007) explain, "Local score distributions generally provide a better way to determine which students are most likely to be mismatched with the instruction they are receiving than will national norms" (p. 16). Lohman (2009a) also proposes that using local norms is the best way of being more inclusive when selecting students who have had fewer opportunities to learn. It remains to be seen if more developers of teacher judgment measures begin to advocate for greater use of local norms.

In addition to using teacher judgment instruments with a clear purpose, technical support, and local norms, developers of teacher judgment measures all recommend that consumers do not sum scores across scales. The individual scales were developed to assess different traits, characteristics, and domains, and summing the scores across scales in not advised because information about a student's unique strengths would be lost.

Some research suggests that teacher training is very important before asking teachers to complete teacher-rating forms. Hunsaker, Finley, and Frank (1997), in an investigation of teacher nominations and student performance in gifted programs, concluded from their investigation that helping teachers focus on particular manifestations of traits in specific cultural or socioeconomic settings would improve the predictive validity of the ratings. Gear (1978) found that trained teachers, versus untrained teachers, nominate more students. Johnson (2004)

recommends that professional development training on the characteristics of gifted and talented students be employed whenever teachers are involved in the nomination process.

Just as using a single test score is not recommended when identifying students for gifted services, using just a teacher rating scale is not advisable either. Toua, the child described at the beginning of this article, scored at the 82nd percentile using local norms on a standardized test in his school district. Because his score wasn't at the highest levels, the district screening and identification committee spent more time examining other sources of information about him. When examining these other data, the committee members noted the *SRBCSS* ratings provided by Toua's classroom teacher. She rated him very highly on the creativity scale and motivation scale and submitted examples of his classroom work for consideration. After a comprehensive look at several sources of information, including the fact that Toua was just learning English, the committee determined that Toua should be selected for gifted services. This illustrates how important it is to have teachers' input when making decisions about the selection of students for gifted services.

## RESOURCES

### THREE TEACHER RATING INSTRUMENTS DISCUSSED IN THE CHAPTER

Pfeiffer, S. I., & Jarosewich, T. (2003). *GRS: Gifted Rating Scales* [published instrument]. San Antonio, TX: Pearson. Available from http://www.pearsonassessments.com/HAIWEB/Cultures/en-us/Productdetail.htm?Pid=015-8130-502&Mode=summary

Renzulli, J. S., Smith, L. H., White, A. J., Callahan, C. M. Hartman, R. K., & Westberg, K. W., Gavin, M. K., Reis, S. M., Siegle, D., & Systma Reed, R. E. (2010). *Scales for Rating the Behavioral Characteristics of Superior Students* [published instrument]. Mansfield Center, CT: Creative Learning Press, Inc. Available from http://www.creativelearningpress.com/scalesforratingthebehavioralcharacteristicsofsuperiorstudents--50scales.aspx

Ryser, G. R., & McConnell, K. (2004). *SIGS-complete kit: Scales for Identifying Gifted Students* [published instrument]. Waco, TX: Prufrock Press. Available from http://www.prufrock.com/productdetails.cfm?PC=212

## REFERENCES

Birch, J. W. (1984). Is any identification procedure necessary? *Gifted Child Quarterly, 28,* 157–161.

Borland, J. H. (1978). Teacher identification of the gifted: A new look. *Journal for the Education of the Gifted, 2,* 22–32.

Borland, J. H. (2008). Identification. In J. A. Plucker & C. M. Callahan (Eds.), *Critical issues and practices in gifted education* (pp. 261–280). Waco, TX: Prufrock Press.

Gagné, F. (1994). Are teachers really poor talent detectors? Comments on Pegnato and Birch's (1959) study of the effectiveness and efficiency of various identification techniques. *Gifted Child Quarterly, 38,* 124-126.

Gear, G. (1978). Effects of training on teachers' accuracy in identifying gifted students. *Gifted Child Quarterly, 22,* 90–97.

Hunsaker, S. L., Finley, V. S., & Frank, E. L. (1997). An analysis of teacher nominations and student performance in gifted programs. *Gifted Child Quarterly, 41,* 19–23.

Johnson, S. K. (Ed.). (2004). *Identifying gifted students. A practical guide.* Waco, TX: Prufrock Press.

Kalatan, A. R. (1991). *The effects of inservice training on Bahrani teachers' perceptions of giftedness.* Unpublished doctoral dissertation. University of Connecticut.

Lee, D., & Pfeiffer, S. I. (2006). The reliability and validity of a Korean-translated version of the *Gifted Rating Scales. Journal of Psychoeducational Assessment, 24,* 210–224.

Li, H., Pfeiffer, S. I., Petscher, Y., Kumtepe, A. T., & Mo, G. (2008). Validation of the *Gifted Rating Scales—School Form* in China. *Gifted Child Quarterly, 52,* 160–169.

Lohman, D. F. (2009a). The contextual assessment of talent. In MacFarlane, B. & Stambaugh, T. (Eds.). *Leading Change in Gifted Education: The Festschrift of Dr. Joyce Van Tas-*

sel-Baska (pp. 229–242). Waco, TX: Prufrock Press.

Lohman, D. F. (2009b). Identifying academically talented students: Some general principles, two specific procedures. In L. Shavinina (Ed.), *Handbook of giftedness* (pp. 971–998). Amsterdam: Elsevier.

Lohman, D. L., & Lakin, J. (2007). Nonverbal test scores as one component of an identification system: Integrating ability, achievement, and teacher ratings. In J. Van Tassel Baska (Ed.), *Alternative assessments for identifying gifted and talented students* (pp. 41–66). Waco, TX: Prufrock Press.

Lohman, D. F. & Renzulli, J. (2007). *A simple procedure for combining ability test scores, achievement test scores, and teacher ratings to identify academically talented children.* Unpublished paper. Retrieved from http://faculty.education.uiowa.edu/dlohman/

National Association for Gifted Children. (2009). *States of the states in gifted education report: National policy and practice data* [CD Rom]. Washington, DC: Author.

National Association for Gifted Children. (2010). *2010 pre-k–grade 12 gifted programming standards.* Washington, DC: Author. Retrieved August 8, 2011, from http://www.nagc.org/index.aspx?id=6500

Nazar, F. A. (1988). Teachers' and parents' perceptions of the behavioral characteristics of third-grade gifted students in Kuwait. Unpublished doctoral dissertation, University of Miami.

Pegnato, C. W., & Birch, J. W. (1959). Locating gifted children in junior high schools–A comparison of methods. *Exceptional Children, 25,* 300-304.

Peters, S. J., & Gentry, M. (2011, March). *Group-specific norms and teacher rating scales: Implications for underrepresentation.* Paper presented at the American Education Research Association Annual Conference, New Orleans, LA.

Pfeiffer, S. I., & Jarosewich, T. (2003). *GRS: Gifted Rating Scales* manual. San Antonio, TX: Pearson.

Renzulli, J. S. (1978). What makes giftedness. Reexamining a definition. Kappan, *60*(3), 180–184.

Renzulli, J. S., & Delcourt, M. A. B. (1986). The legacy and logic of research on the identification of gifted persons. *Gifted Child Quarterly, 30,* 20–23.

Renzulli, J. S., & Reis, S. M. (1985). *The schoolwide enrichment model: A comprehensive plan for educational excellence.* Mansfield Center, CT: Creative Learning Press.

Renzulli, J. S., Siegle, D., Reis, S. M., Gavin, K. M., & Systma Reed, R. E., 2009). An investigation of the reliability and factor structure of four new *Scales for Rating the Behavioral Characteristics of Superior Students. Journal for Advanced Academics, 21,* 84-108.

Renzulli, J. S., Smith, L. H., White, A. J., Callahan, C. M., & Hartman, R. K. (1976). *Scales for Rating the Behavioral Characteristics of Superior Students.* Mansfield Center, CT: Creative Learning Press.

Renzulli, J. S., Smith, L. H., White, A. J., Callahan, C. M. Hartman, R. K., & Westberg, K. W. (2002). *Scales for Rating the Behavioral*

*Characteristics of Superior Students. Revised edition.* Mansfield Center, CT: Creative Learning Press, Inc.

Renzulli, J. S., Smith, L. H., White, A. J., Callahan, C. M. Hartman, R. K., & Westberg, K. W., Gavin, M. K., Reis, S. M., Siegle, D., & Systma Reed, R. E. (2010). *Scales for Rating the Behavioral Characteristics of Superior Student: Technical and administration manual* (3rd ed.). Mansfield Center, CT: Creative Learning Press, Inc.

Renzulli, J. S., & Westberg, K. L. (1991). *Rating Student Performance in a Gifted Program.* Unpublished instrument. Storrs, CT: The National Research Center on the Gifted and Talented.

Ryser, G. R., & McConnell, K. (2004). *SIGS-complete kit: Scales for Identifying Gifted Students.* Waco, TX: Prufrock Press.

Shore, B. M., Cornell, D. G., Robinson, A., & Ward, V. S. (1991). *Recommended practices in education: A critical analysis.* NY: Teachers College Press.

Subhi, T. (1997). Who is gifted? A computerized identification procedure. *High Ability Students, 8*(2), 189–211.

Srour, N. H. (1989). *An analysis of teacher judgment in the identification of gifted Jordanian students.* Unpublished doctoral dissertation. University of Connecticut.

Sternberg, R. J. (1998). Applying the triarchic theory of human intelligence in the classroom. In R. J. Sternberg & W. M. Williams (Eds.), *Intelligence, instruction and assessment: Theory into practice.* Mahwah, NJ: Erlbaum.

Sternberg, R. J., & Davidson, J. E. *(2005). Conceptions* of giftedness (2nd ed.). NY: Cambridge University Press.

Terman, L. M. (1925). *Mental and physical traits of a thousand gifted children: Genetic studies of genius* (Vol. 1). Stanford, CA: Stanford University Press.

Torrance, E. P. (1962). *Guiding creative behavior.* Englewood Cliffs, NJ: Prentice-Hall.

## CHAPTER 14 STUDY GUIDE

**Prompt 1** *Knowledge*

Prepare a chart on which you summarize the strengths and weaknesses of the three teacher rating scales reviewed in this chapter.

**Prompt 2** *Opinion*

The *criterion problem* suggests that it is not appropriate to evaluate the validity of teacher judgments about student giftedness against an IQ score. What, in your opinion, would be an appropriate criterion?

**Prompt 3** *Affect*

Describe the pressures you feel or would feel if asked to complete a teacher rating scale on students in your class. What could be done to alleviate those pressures?

**Prompt 4** *Experience*

Describe any experience you or a colleague has had in creating a teacher rating scale for gifted identification or in using a locally created scale. Why, according to the author, is this a problem? Were these problems apparent with your local instrument? What should a local educational agency do to verify the validity and reliability of any locally produced scale?

**Prompt 5** *Preconception/Misconception*

Some critics feel that introducing teacher judgment into gifted identification injects additional biases into the system; others believe that teacher judgment is one solution to overcoming the bias inherent in testing. Where do you stand on this issue and why?

# PERFORMANCE ASSESSMENTS: THE ROLE IN THE IDENTIFICATION OF GIFTED STUDENTS

TONYA R. MOON, UNIVERSITY OF VIRGINIA

The issue of identifying students for gifted programs has been one of the most debated areas in the field of gifted education. Discussions have focused on topics such as the identification of minority students (e.g., Lohman, 2005), appropriate identification procedures and practices for young learners (Callahan, Tomlinson, & Piazat, 1993), and types of assessments that should be used in identification systems (Moon, in press). The purpose of this chapter is three-fold. The chapter starts with an introduction to performance assessments and other non-test assessments, including their advantages and disadvantages. This is followed by a rationale for their use in a gifted identification system. Third, issues for consideration when using performance assessments in an identification process will be presented. The chapter ends with a detailed example of a performance assessment to punctuate these points.

## INTRODUCTION TO PERFORMANCE ASSESSMENT AND OTHER NON-TEST ASSESSMENTS

The *Standards for Educational and Psychological Measurement* (hereafter referred to as "the Standards"; American Educational Research Association, American Psychological Association, and National Council on Measurement in Education [AERA, APA, & NCME], 1999) state that performance assessments "attempt to emulate the context or conditions in which the intended knowledge or skills are actually applied" (p. 137). Common formats for performance assessments include open-ended or extended response assessments where students respond to a given prompt. A first, widely used type of extended response assessment is the essay, where students respond in writing for the purpose of demonstrating their reasoning related to a specific topic. With this type of performance assessment, there is a specific amount of time allotted for students to create their responses. A second format for a performance assessment is an extended task where students are actively engaged over a sustained period of time. Typically this type of performance assessment requires students to engage in the research process and demonstrate their understanding of a particular topic through written products, presentations, exhibitions, and/or experiments. The basic four steps for this type of performance assessment include planning and organizing the project, conducting the research, producing the product, and then presenting the product. A third type of performance assessment is the portfolio. Portfolios are collections of works; sometimes the collection is a student's "best work" and other times the collection reflects "works in progress."

Regardless of the format, typical performance assessments ask that students construct an original response (as opposed to selecting from a list of response options that is typical of traditional types of assessments [e.g., multiple-choice items]); assess higher-level thinking, critical thinking, and problem-solving skills; require students to apply their knowledge, skills, and understandings to real-life situations; allow for multiple strategies to solutions as opposed to one right answer; and may include extended periods of time for responding (Baron, 1991; Herman, Aschbacher, & Winters, 1992; Stiggins, 1987). Student responses (the processes used to solve the problem as well as the final product itself) are evaluated through the application of professional judgment guided by an evaluation rubric that reflects criteria developed specifically for the performance assessment.

With the exception of portfolios, performance assessments share some fundamental criteria. One fundamental criterion is that students are presented with situations that reflect or simulate real-life problems. Tasks place students in a contextualized situation, oftentimes mimicking the practice of a disciplinarian where they are required to use critical and higher-order thinking skills (Moon, 2002). In addition, performance assessments are appropriate across all academic and non-academic disciplines. For example in science, scientific inquiry is the backbone of all science content and ranges from developing researchable questions to carrying out an experiment; using tools and procedures to collect, analyze, and report/interpret data; and developing explanations, predictions, and rival hypotheses based on evidence (National Research Council [NRC], 1996). In the area of mathematics, performance assessments are often developed around the key features of mathematics reform—problem solving, reasoning, and effective communication of ideas. Specifically, in mathematics performance assessments are integrated with practical tasks that target students' content and procedural knowledge as well as their ability to use knowledge for reasoning and problem solving (Harmon, Smith, Martin, Kelly, Beaton, Mullis, et al., 1997).

Social studies is defined as "the integrated study of the social sciences and humanities to promote civic competence" (National Council for the Social Studies, n.d.). Furthermore, social studies provide opportunities for multidisciplinary and systematic studies of other disciplines such as economics, geography, history, law, philosophy, political science, psychology, sociology, and anthropology, as well as mathematics, the natural sciences, and humanities. Example topics suitable for a middle school social studies performance assessment include considering the use of tax dollars to restore an historic site or considering specific state government policy. One example might ask students to defend or refute from a variety of diverse stakeholders' perspectives South Dakota's government decision to make Columbus Day a legal holiday, as well as through multiple disciplinary lenses—an economist, a legislator, an historian, or a Native American spiritual leader.

Example 1 (see Appendix 1 at the end of this chapter) provides a specific performance assessment in the area of science for gifted middle school students. In this assessment, students are required to research a particular natural disaster using a variety of complex resources, analyze the causes and effects of the natural disaster, apply their understanding of a chosen natural disaster to make real-world suggestions about how to prevent the disaster or to limit its damaging effects, communicate technical as well as persuasive information, and, in every instance, justify their ideas. In order to accomplish the assessment's purpose, students must have a deep understanding of weather and earth surface patterns and their relationship to one another (i.e., causes and effects of natural disasters), conduct research using a variety of complex resources, and communicate effectively and persuasively through writing in a technical and professional style.

Each performance assessment is linked to a rubric that is aligned with the task's purpose and specific learning goals. The rubric is used to evaluate each student's response to the task and is available to students as they work on the task. The goal of the rubric is to delineate up front to all stakeholders (e.g., parents, students) consistent assessment criteria that reflect specific performance attributes. The criteria are arranged in a hierarchical nature (i.e., levels or gradations of performance) that indicate the degree to which the learning standards

have been met. The rubric associated with Example 1 (also in Appendix 1 at the end of this chapter) is composed of eight domains or dimensions that each have four levels of performance on the continuum from Expert to Novice.

The predetermined explanation of the performance levels provides clear direction to students, and ensures that teachers stay focused on those goals. Because of the subjective nature involved with applying the rubric to student work, it is a fundamental requirement that teachers be trained to appropriately apply the criteria. Teachers should understand the purpose of each domain/dimension as well as the specific criteria associated with each level of performance for each domain. Best practice in the use of rubrics also suggests that teachers as well as students be given exemplars of each domain and level that are annotated so that the subjectivity involved with the application of the rubric can be minimized.

One common misconception regarding rubrics is that they quantify domain areas, such as the number of required elements, rather than the quality of ideas. For example, an inappropriate use of a rubric is to set up the performance levels according to the number of spelling errors that a student has made, as in Table 1. Instead, rubric criteria should reflect the quality of student performance as presented in Example 1. In Example 1, the criteria define levels of quality in student

**Table 1.** Misapplication of Rubric Criteria

|  | **EXEMPLARY** | **INTERMEDIATE** | **NOVICE** |
|---|---|---|---|
| **MECHANICS** | No more than two (2) errors with spelling, grammar or punctuation are included | Three (3) or four (4) errors with spelling, grammar, or punctuation are included | More than four (4) errors with spelling, grammar, or punctuation are included |

work, as opposed to quantity, and are used by the teacher to evaluate student work and for instructional planning; they can also be used by students for self-evaluation and peer evaluation.

## Portfolios: A Specific Type of Performance Assessment

While a type of performance assessment, portfolios differ from other types of performance assessment in that they are a collection of student work samples over time that reflect student learning. In some instances, student work samples represent a student's "best work." The purpose of this type of portfolio is to showcase a student's highest level of achievement. The time period from which pieces are selected by the student can range from one grading period, a semester, a year, or year to year. It is this type of portfolio that is most applicable for use in identifying gifted students.

Another type of portfolio is known as a "work in progress" portfolio and might be considered as one criterion for forming a talent pool in a talent development model. A "work in progress" portfolio houses pieces specifically related to a given topic and is a collection of student work that shows strengths and weaknesses as well as teacher reflection on the student's strengths and weaknesses. In this way, the portfolio, is a collection of pieces that relates to identified learning objectives for a specific content area and documents student progress toward mastery of those objectives.

## Advantages and Disadvantages of Performance Assessments

As with all methods of assessment, there are advantages and disadvantages, and using performance assessments is no different. Using performance assessments requires consideration of both the advantages and disadvantages. Several advantages include the following:

1. They assess complex skills and understandings that are difficult, and oftentimes impossible, to assess with traditional paper-and-pencil, more objective types of methods.

2. They assess content understanding through the creation of some product (e.g., a letter to an editor after a critique of a manuscript based on a science experiment that highlights the strengths and weaknesses of the experiment), and they can also, if developed appropriately, simultaneously assess processes and skills.

3. They highlight the interconnections among the disciplines, allowing a student to demonstrate the application of content across multiple content areas.

While the advantages emphasize areas that are commonly discussed in the field of gifted education surrounding best practices for educating gifted youth (Robinson, Shore, & Enersen, 2007), there are several disadvantages that have to be taken into consideration. In order to use performance assessment in a high-stakes manner (e.g., identification for gifted services), they must be technically sound to support the types of decisions that will be made based on student work. They are also labor intensive for raters (in terms of training and scoring) and for students (in terms of responding). (The intensity can be reduced if a unit of study is specifically built around the performance assessment, and students work over the course of the unit on the assessment.) Users of performance assessments must also consider the procedure that must be put in place to ensure standardization if used for high-stakes decision-making situations like that of determining placement in a gifted program or to receive gifted services. (See later in this chapter for further details).

## RATIONALE FOR USE OF PERFORMANCE ASSESSMENT IN A GIFTED IDENTIFICATION SYSTEM

While there are a multitude of definitions for giftedness, according to the National Association for Gifted Children (NAGC, n.d.), "*Gifted individuals are those who demonstrate outstanding levels of aptitude (defined as an exceptional ability to reason and learn) or s (documented performance or achievement in top 10% or rarer) in one or more domains. Domains include any structured area of activity with its own symbol system (e.g., mathematics, music, language) and/or set of sensorimotor skills (e.g., painting, dance, sports)."*). To identify gifted individuals, there must be a comprehensive and cohesive identification process in place to determine whose individual needs would be more appropriately served through advanced curricular options. As can be seen from Example 1, there exists a relationship between what students produce and the knowledge, understandings, and skills that are of interest. That is to say, performance assessment provides a much more direct way to measure students' depth of content understanding than multiple-choice assessments. Therefore, performance assessments should be one option used to identify advanced level knowledge, skills, and understandings required for gifted services.

Another aspect of performance assessments that makes them promising for use in a gifted identification system is that the assessments can, if developed properly, provide multiple pieces of information (i.e., data) across different content areas. In Example 1, not only is information obtained about a student's current level of understanding regarding particular scientific content but also the student's facility with the use of resources and the ability to communicate effectively to a specific audience, all important and necessary skills to be successful in advanced level content in other disciplines (e.g., science, language arts, history).

Other practical implications of obtaining multiple pieces of information about a student through the use of a performance assessment include a reduction of test administration time. Because performance assessments can be a natural part of the curriculum, there is no separate time required to be set aside for additional testing, something that is often necessary for gifted screening. Furthermore, performance assessments can represent the multi-disciplinary aspects of many content areas, and to be successful on such assessments requires that a student be able to transfer knowledge, skills, and understandings between and among discipline areas, an important criterion for advanced-level curriculum suitable for gifted learners. However, it is important to note that although multiple content areas can be assessed within a performance assessment, it does not preclude the use of multiple criteria for identification for gifted services, something considered as best practice in identification of gifted students (NAGC, n.d.).

## ISSUES FOR CONSIDERATION IN USING PERFORMANCE ASSESSMENTS IN A GIFTED IDENTIFICATION PROCESS

While performance assessments hold much promise as one component that can be used in a gifted identification system, evidence must to be gathered to determine whether these potential benefits are realized in light of possible limitations. While evidence exists on the positive impacts on classroom instruction of using performance assessment as a high-stakes assessment (e.g., Stecher, Barron, Chun, & Ross, 2000; Lang, Parke, & Stone, 2002; Stone & Lane, 2006), less empirical evidence exists regarding gifted program placement decisions. What research has been done (Sarouphim, 2009; Plucker, et al., 1996; Moon, Brighton, Callahan, & Robinson, 2005; VanTassel Baska, Feng, & de Brux (2007a; 2007b) suggests promising results for the use of performance assessment as one component of a gifted identification system.

In the end, there are two important issues that need to be taken into account when considering the adoption of performance assessment as a component in an identification process. These issues are (1) the development of the performance assessments, including prompts and scoring rubrics, and (2) the technical characteristics of performance assessments, including standardization, rater training, the setting of cut scores, and group

performance differences. Each will be discussed in the following section.

## THE DEVELOPMENT OF PERFORMANCE ASSESSMENTS

Developing a performance assessment to use in a gifted identification system is not unlike the process for developing multiple-choice assessments. While it is not the purpose of this chapter to present a step-by-step guide on the development process, it is important to understand the development framework so that one can make informed decisions when opting for the inclusion of performance assessment in an identification process, whether through the use of pre-existing assessments or the actual development of a performance assessment. The development process begins with the delineation of a *conceptual framework* that reflects the construct to be assessed (i.e., giftedness in specific areas), the purpose of the assessment (i.e., gifted program placement), and the inferences that are going to be drawn based upon student performance (i.e., placement or not). From this framework, *test specifications* reflecting the content, the cognitive processes required, the psychometric characteristics of the assessment, and information regarding test administration should be developed. The actual *prompt* and *rubric* are developed iteratively under this framework. Once relevant information has been outlined in the test specifications, each development step in the creation of both the prompt and the rubric is compared to the identified specifications to ensure alignment between the purpose of the assessment and the actual assessment requirements and the components to be evaluated in the rubric. It is important to understand the nature of the development process regardless of whether one is going to actually develop the assessments or opt for already developed assessments to ensure that there is an alignment between the gifted program's definition of giftedness, the services to be delivered, and the purpose of the performance assessment.

## TECHNICAL CHARACTERISTICS OF PERFORMANCE ASSESSMENTS

With the use of performance assessments as one component of a gifted identification system, it is necessary to ensure that the assessments uphold professional measurement standards that have been set (AERA, APA, NCME, 1999). In 1991, Linn, Baker, and Dunn outlined eight criteria that users should have knowledge of when using performance assessments, three of which are directly applicable to the use of performance assessments in a gifted identification process:

1.  *Consequences: Are there positive impacts on educational practice as a result of the performance assessments?*

An important consequence of using performance assessments as one component of an identification system would be that a wider range of diverse students would be identified, particularly those from low income backgrounds, minority groups, or various cultural/language groups. Fuchs, Fuchs, Karns, Hamlett, and Katzaroff (1999) reported that students achieving above grade level, when exposed to mathematics performance assessments, showed stronger problem-solving skills than students who were not exposed to mathematics performance assessments. Fuchs and colleagues

also reported that there was a shift in emphasis away from basic, routine content toward problem solving, with large effect sizes being reported. Others have also reported positive classroom effects as a result of using performance assessments (e.g., Stone & Lane, 2003).

2.  *Fairness: Do the ratings of a student's response reflect the student's true capabilities rather than the bias of the raters evaluating the response?*

Two commonly used methods for training raters for scoring performance assessments are the spiral method and the sequential method (Moon & Hughes, 2002). In many situations involving the use of performance assessments, multiple prompts are used. For gifted identification purposes, these prompts could be across disciplines if data is being sought for placement in a full time magnet gifted classroom, an arrangement often used at the elementary level. Or, for placement in an advanced seminar within a specific content area, as might be done in a high school setting, the multiple prompts may be within that single content area. The main point being made here is the effect different training experiences would have.

In both the spiral method and sequential method of training, trainers provide an initial review of a scoring rubric with illustrative examples drawn from a variety of student responses representing diverse levels of performance. Raters then score anchor papers for various prompts, followed by a discussion of their ratings and the anchor paper ratings. This exercise is repeated until raters meet a predetermined standard of skill in rating. At this point, the training experiences differ for the two methods. Under the spiral method, raters are given a randomized set of prompts to score without further training, though quality controls are built in to indicate if a particular rater may need additional training. Under the sequential method, raters are trained on a given prompt, which they score, and then are retrained on a new prompt, which they score, continuing in this manner with retraining on each prompt (Moon & Hughes, 2002).

In investigating the influence on the way training was conducted (i.e., spiral or sequential), Moon and Hughes (2002) examined the equivalency of scores under the two training procedures and found that raters trained under the spiral method may have to revisit the rubric continually for guidance to avoid the relative comparison of students against one another instead of the rubric, whereas, in the sequential method, raters were better able to keep the standards from the rubric in mind with each retraining.

3. *Cognitive Complexity: Does the assessment require problem solving, critical thinking, comprehension, reasoning, and meta-cognitive processes?*

The Natural Disasters example (in the Appendix at the end of the chapter) includes demonstration of cognitive complexity as well as research skills, analytic skills, and communication skills. Although the tasks are set within a certain content domain (i.e., science), the skills to be successful are from every content domain. Students who perform at the highest levels on this Natural Disasters assessment are those who have the mental capacity to locate information, critically analyze that information, problem solve, and

communicate—all skills that are required for the advanced level learning (Resnick, 1987) central to gifted programming.

4. *Standardizing the Administration Process: Are procedures in place to ensure that all students are assessed against the same criteria?*

Standardization procedures for the performance assessments used in an identification system would need to be established. This would include specified procedures for administering the assessments as well as scoring student responses; specific assessments administered would be the same for all students and would have the same format and set of materials, if applicable. In addition, standardized instructions for administration also needs to be put in place. The purpose of standardized instructions is to avoid any perceived stereotypes associated with testing instruction, a phenomenon that has been reported by Steele and Aronson (1995). By standardizing the administration process and the assessments, biases of individual students or groups of students can be eliminated.

5. *Setting of Cut Scores: Have credible standard-setting procedures been used to categorize individuals?*

The process of setting cut scores on performance assessments used in a gifted identification system, called Standard Setting, is one that has been ignored in the field of gifted education. Although a framework for establishing the process for setting performance standards is provided in the *Standards* (AERA, APA, & NCME, 1999), typical "cut scores" in the field of gifted education have been defined as the top 1–5% of students. (Typical steps for setting performance standards, though beyond the scope of this chapter, have been articulated by Hambleton and Pitoniak [2006].) The purpose of setting cut scores is to identify a single score point to differentiate between two conceivable states (Cizek, 1996) such as eligible/not eligible for gifted programming services. The purpose of setting cut scores for performance assessments used in a gifted identification system is to minimize what is called a Type I error, or false positive, that is, making a claim that someone is eligible for services when in fact they are not eligible for services. Wang, Niemi, & Wang (2007) reported that gifted students are more likely to pass (meet or exceed the cut score) than non-gifted students, a result that supports that use of cut scores with performance assessments in an identification process to ensure that the correct students are identified. Whenever assessments are used in high-stakes decisions like the identification for gifted services, it is important that performance standards on the assessments be established. While the setting of performance assessments has been a controversial one in the field of educational measurement due to the judgmental nature of the process, guidelines have been established in order to produce defensible and valid performance standards (e.g., Hambleton, 2001). It is important to note that the establishment and use of performance standards on educational assessments does not preclude the use of multiple criteria or pieces of evidence for identification.

One consideration that must be taken into account when conducting a standard setting procedure is whether the procedure is to establish cut scores reflecting *current* high accomplishment or cut scores reflecting *potential* for high accomplishment. If one is trying to identify students who are currently highly accomplished then the same high standards (i.e., cut scores) should be employed for all students. If, on the other hand, if one is trying to identify students with potential for high accomplishment, then it is important that the standard setting process take this consideration into account when establishing performance standards, as Linn et al. (1991) noted that learning opportunities and familiarity both impact performance. To not make the distinction between the types of students being identified in an identification process most often results in the underrepresentation of minority students in gifted programs (Lohman, 2005).

6. *Group Differences on Performance Assessments*: Has a fairness investigation been undertaken to ensure that any group differences are bona fide differences?

Linn et al. (1991) cautioned that it would be unreasonable to assume that group differences that are noted on multiple-choice assessments would be alleviated or smaller by using performance assessments. Research investigating gender and ethnic differences on performance assessments has shown mixed results. For example, females tended to outperform males on direct writing assessments (Applebee, Langer, Jenkins, Mullis, & Foertsch, 1990; Willingham, Cole, Lewis, & Leung, 1997) (Willingham & Cole, 1997), and White students tended to score significantly higher than Black students (Englehard, Gordon, Walker, & Gabrielson, 1994). Other research investigating gender differences using data from state writing programs and NAEP math and science performance assessments found that the average gender difference was near zero (Willingham & Cole, 1997). In the area of history, Breland, Dano, Kahn, Kubota, and Bonner (1994) reported that females performed as well as males. Again, it is important to take into consideration the learning opportunities that students have had as this impacts students' performances (Linn et al., 1991). The *Standards* (1999) provide 12 criteria when considering test fairness, of which nine refer to groups or subgroups and three to individuals. (See Chapter 12 of this volume for more discussion on the Standards.)

## RECOMMENDED GUIDELINES

Taking into consideration the issues that should be part of the discussion regarding the use of performance assessments in a gifted identification system, the following three guidelines are offered.

**Guideline 1:** As with any high-stakes situation, students' responses to performance assessments should not be the sole determinant for placement in a gifted program. Rather multiple types of assessments that focus on different types of information should be used in determining eligibility for gifted services.

**Guideline 2:** To be used in making high-stakes decisions, the performance assessments must meet technical adequacy standards such as those established by AERA, APA, and NCME (1999) for the areas of generalizability and validity, including the setting of performance standards and test fairness.

**Guideline 3:** On-going and high-quality staff development opportunities regarding performance assessments must be provided to ensure that all personnel involved in the identification process stay abreast of advances in the areas of gifted education and measurement, including but not limited to developing and scoring the assessments, instructional strategies, content knowledge, classroom management, interdisciplinary instruction, and collaborative learning to name a few.

## CONCLUDING REMARKS

In the field of general education and assessment in particular, the 1980s brought a renewed interest in performance assessments. The majority of the empirical work surrounding performance assessment has been done as a result of this renewed interest, thus these practices are supported by relatively recent empirical evidence. Much of this work, however, has been reported in the literature on educational measurement, with very little reported in the literature regarding gifted education.

To fully realize the potential of performance assessments for use in a gifted identification process, additional research and development is needed. Designing performance assessments that reflect the type of services provided is important to ensure that the services address student need. In turn, additional work is needed in identifying techniques for designing performance assessments and scoring procedures that capture high accomplishment (or potential for high accomplishment) in content domains.

## REFERENCES

American Educational Research Association, American Psychological Association, & National Council on Measurement in Education. (1999). *Standards for educational and psychological testing.* Washington, DC: American Educational Research Association.

Applebee, A. N., Langer, J. A., Jenkins, L. B., Mullis, I., & Foertsch, M. A. (1990). *Learning to write in our nation's schools: Instruction and achievement in 1988 at grade 4, 8, and 12.* Princeton, NJ: Educational Testing Service.

Baron, B. J. (1991). Strategies for the development of effective performance exercises. *Applied Measurement in Education, 4,* 305–318.

Breland, H., Danos, D., Kahn, H., Kubota, M., & Bonner, M. (1994). Performance versus objective testing and gender: An exploratory study of an Advanced Placement History Examination. *Journal of Educational Measurement, 31*(4), 275–293.

Callahan, C. M., Tomlinson, C. A., & Pizzat, P. (Eds.), (1993). *Contexts for promise: Noteworthy practices and innovations in the identification of gifted students.* Charlottesville, VA: University of Virginia, National Research Center on the Gifted and Talented.

Cizek, G. (1996). Setting passing scores. *Educational Measurement: Issues and Practice, 15*(2), 20–31.

Engelhard, Jr., G., Gordon, B., Walker, E. V., & Gabrielson, S. (1994). Writing tasks and gender: Influences on writing quality of black and white students. *Journal of Educational Research, 87,* 197–209.

Fuchs, L. S., Fuchs, D., Karns, K., Hamlett, C., & Katzaroff, M. (1999). Mathematics performance assessment in the classroom: Effects on teacher planning and student problem solving. *American Educational Research Journal, 36*(3), 609–646.

Hambleton, R. K. (2001). Setting performance standards on educational assessments and criteria for evaluating the process. In G. J. Cizek (Ed.), *Setting performance standards: Concepts, methods, and perspectives* (pp. 89–116). Mahwah, NJ: Erlbaum.

Hambleton, R. K., & Pitoniak, M. J. (2006). Setting performance standards. In R. L. Brennan (Ed.), *Educational measurement* (4th ed.), (pp. 433–470). Westport, CT: American Council on Education and Praeger Publishers.

Harmon, M., Smith, T. A., Martin, M. O., Kelly, D. L., Beaton, A. E., Mullis, I. V. S., . . . Orpwood, G. (1997). *Performance assessment in IEA's Third International Mathematics and Science Study.* Chestnut Hill, MA: TIMSS International Study Center, Boston College.

Herman, J. L., Ashbacher, P. R., & Winters, L. (1992). *A practical guide to alternative assessment.* Alexandria, VA: Association for Supervision and Curriculum Development.

Lane, S., Liu, M., Ankenmann, R. D., & Stone, C. A. (1996). Generalizability and validity of a mathematics performance assessment. *Journal of Educational Measurement, 33,* 71–92.

Lane, S., Parke, C. S., & Stone, C. A. (2002). The impact of a state performance-based assessment and accountability program on mathematics instruction and student learning: Evidence from survey data and school performance. *Educational Assessment, 8*(4), 279–315.

Linn, R., Baker, E., & Dunbar, S. (1991). Complex, performance-based assessment: Expectations and validation criteria. *Educational Researcher, 20*(8), 15–21. doi: 10.3102/0013189X020008015.

Lohman, D. (2005). An aptitude perspective on talent: Implications for identification of academically gifted minority students. *Journal for the Education of the Gifted, 28*(3–4), 333–360. doi: 10.4219/jeg-2005-341

Moon, T. R. (2002). Using performance assessment in the social studies classroom. *Gifted Child Today, 25*, 53–59.

Moon, T. R. (2012). Performance assessments and non-test assessments: Considerations for use in an identification process. In C. Callahan & H. Hertberg Davis (Eds.), *Fundamental of Gifted Education*. NY: Routledge.

Moon, T. R., Brighton, C.M., Callahan, C. M., & Robinson, A.E. (2005). Development of authentic assessments for the middle school classroom. *Journal for Secondary Gifted Education, 16*(2/3), 119–133.

Moon, T. R., & Hughes, K. R. (2002). Training and scoring issues involved in large-scale writing performance assessments. *Educational Measurement: Issues and Practice, 21*(2), 15–19.

National Association for Gifted Children. (n.d.). NAGC position statement: *The role of assessments in the identification of gifted students*. Washington, DC: Author. Retrieved from http://www.nagc.org/index.aspx?id=4022

National Association for Gifted Children. (n. d.). Definition of giftedness. Retrieved August 25, 2011, from http://www.nagc.org/index. aspx?id=574&an

National Council for Social Studies. (n.d.). Definition of social studies. Retrieved August 25, 2011, from http://www.socialstudies.org/ standards/introduction

National Research Council. (1996). *National science education standards* Washington, DC: National Academy Press.

Plucker, J. A., Callahan, C. M., & Tomchin, E. M. (1996). Wherefore art thou, multiple intelligences? Alternative assessments for identifying talent in ethnically diverse and low income students. *Gifted Child Quarterly, 40*(2), 81–92.

Resnick, L. B. (1987). The presidential address: Learning in school and out. *Educational Researcher, 16*(9), 13–20, 54.

Robinson, A., Shore, B. M., Enersen, D. L. (2007). *Best practices in gifted education: An evidence-based guide*. Waco, TX: Prufrock Press.

Sarouphim, K.M. (2001). DISCOVER: Concurrent validity, gender differences, and identification of minority students. *Gifted Child Quarterly, 45*(2), 130–138.

Stecher, B., Barron, S., Chun, T., & Ross, K. (2000). *The effects of the Washington state education reform in schools and classrooms* (CSE Technical Report No. 525). Los Angeles: University of California, National Center for Research on Evaluation, Standards, and Student Testing.

Steele, C. M., & Aronson, J. (1995). Stereotype threat and intellectual test performance of

African-Americans. *Journal of Personality and Social Psychology, 69,* 797–811.

Stiggins, R. J. (1987). Design and development of performance assessments. *Educational Measurement: Issues and Practice, 6*(3), 33–42. doi: 10.1111/j.1745-3992.1987.tb00507.x

Stone, C. A., & Lane, S. (2003). Consequences of a state accountability program: Examining relationships between school performance gains and teacher, students, and school variables. *Applied Measurement in Education, 16*(1), 1–26.

VanTassel-Baska, J., Feng, A. X., & de Brux, E. (2007a). A longitudinal study and performance profiles of Project STAR performance-task identified gifted students. *Journal for the Education of the Gifted, 31*(1), 7–34.

VanTassel-Baska, J., Feng, A. X., & de Brux, E. (2007b). Patterns of identification and performance across students identified through performance tasks: A three-year analysis. *Gifted Child Quarterly, 51*(3), 218–231.

Wang, J., Niemi, D., & Wang, H. (2007). *Impact of different performance assessment cut scores on student promotion* (CSE Report No. 719). Los Angeles, CA: University of California, Los Angeles, National Center for Research on Evaluation, Standards, and Student Testing (CRESST).

Willingham, W. W., & Cole, N. S. (1997). Research on gender differences. In W. W. Willingham & N. S. Cole (Eds.), *Gender and fair assessment* (pp. 17–54). Mahwah, NJ: Erlbaum.

Willingham, W. W., Cole, N. S., Lewis, C., & Leung, S. W. (1997). Test performance. In W. W. Willingham & N. S. Cole (Eds.), *Gender and fair assessment* (pp. 55–126). Mahwah, NJ: Erlbarum.

APPENDIX

EXAMPLE 1[1]

NATURAL DISASTERS: SHAKY EARTH, SMOLDERING MOUNTAIN, STORMY WEATHER

You are an earth scientist who specializes in natural disasters. You have been asked to make recommendations concerning a particular city's preparedness for a possible natural disaster. Your recommendations will be part of a full report on natural disaster damage prevention delivered to the Council on Disaster Prevention Board of Directors.

Choose any type of potential natural disaster that you find interesting and engage in a thorough exploratory study of it. Make certain that you understand how and why such a disaster occurs, the historical patterns/trends of the disaster (when and where it typically "hits"), the consequences of the disaster (both positive and negative consequences to people and to the earth), and any other information that you think the Board may need to understand.

Invent a city where your chosen potential disaster could occur. Your city must not be a duplication of a real city. You may, however, base your city on a combination of elements of more than one existing city. Describe the city, its geographical location, its population, and any other information pertinent to the report (major industries, special needs of the population or segments of the population, etc.). Prepare a report on the possibility of this disaster occurring in this city. Your report must follow the following format and contain the following information:

SECTION 1: DESCRIPTION OF CITY

In this section, you should include a brief description of the city of concern, its location and any special features relating to the recommended disaster plan.

SECTION 2: DESCRIPTION OF PROBLEM OR ISSUE

Describe the nature of the disaster in the context of this city and why it is critical for the Board to address the issue of prevention.

SECTION 3: SUPPORTING RESEARCH AND EXPERIMENTATION

In this section, you will need to include important information that you have discovered through various sources about the potential disaster introduced in Section 2. You might include background information you found, predictions about the probable results of the disaster, and/or comparisons to other disasters or to other areas that are threatened by this type of disaster.

---

1 The development of this assessment was done by the National Research Center on the Gifted and Talented at the University of Virginia through the support of the Educational Research and Development Centers Program, PR/Award Number R206R000001-05, as administered by the Institute of Education Sciences, U.S. Department of Education.

## SECTION 4: RECOMMENDATIONS TO THE BOARD

In this section, list your recommendations on how to prepare for the disaster in order to limit damage to the city/region as well as why you believe your recommendations are valid. You may annotate them as you see fit with supporting citations about lessons learned from other disaster sites or brief references to other sections of the report.

## SECTION 5: APPENDIX I

In the story *Volcano: The Eruption and Healing of Mount St. Helen's*, Patricia Lauber states, "Volcanoes destroy some life when they erupt, but they also help make life possible" (p. 51). To what extent is this true about all natural disasters (such as blizzards, plagues, floods, earthquakes, hurricanes, droughts, tornadoes, etc.)? How do natural disasters both destroy and create life?

Explore the life-destroying and life-creating powers of natural disasters. Include your findings in this appendix. What can be done to strike a balance between human needs and the needs of nature? How can we prevent human suffering while allowing nature to take its course? How does striking this balance affect your particular situation and/or your recommendations? Suggest how these considerations could be incorporated into your recommendations to the Board.

## SECTION 6: APPENDIX II: SUPPORTING MATERIALS

You may include additional graphs, tables, or other relevant information in the form of appendices, provided the appendices follow a proper professional formatting style and support the body of the text.

Attach your bibliography to this appendix.

**NATURAL DISASTER SCORING RUBRIC**

| | 4<br>Expert | 3 | 2 | 1<br>Novice |
|---|---|---|---|---|
| **Section 1: Description of City** | You clearly and completely describe your newly invented city. You include important and pertinent information that may impact a disaster preparedness plan. | You describe an original city. You include important information about the city, but leave out minor details that may impact the disaster plan. | You describe your city involved, but you leave out important information that could impact a disaster plan. | You do not describe your city OR your city closely mirrors or is identical to an existing city. |
| **Section 2: Accuracy of Information** | You mention and accurately explain all the elements involved (movement of the earth's crust, weather patterns, etc). Your report shows an accurate understanding of the potential disaster you chose to explore. | You mention major the elements involved in the occurrence of the chosen natural disaster, but leave out minor elements that would increase the Board's understanding of the situation. Your scientific principles and facts are accurate. | You address elements that relate to causing the natural disaster you chose to explore, but important major elements are missing. Scientific principles or facts that you cite are accurate but incomplete. | There are gaps in your report of the elements behind your natural disaster. The scientific principles and facts that you cite are inaccurate. |
| **Section 3: Depth of Research** | You rely mainly on primary sources for your information. The information included in your report illustrates the thoroughness of your research. You point out the complex interactions between the elements that produce the natural disaster. | You use a combination of primary and secondary sources to support your ideas. The body of your report shows a solid understanding of the elements involved. However, you do not address the complex interaction of these elements. | You rely mainly on secondary sources for your research. The body of your report contains only surface details and/or basic information. | Most of the information in your report comes from your textbook. Your ideas are not supported by research. |
| **Section 4: Validity of Conclusions** | You use the ideas that you find in your research, as well as your own analysis of the potential disaster, as the basis for your recommendations. These recommendations are clearly and authoritatively presented. | You attempt to relate your recommendations to your research, but leave out minor details that would more clearly illuminate this relationship. You present your recommendations logically. | Your recommendations seem basically sound, but you make leaps in logic OR fail to consider all the ramifications of your suggestions. | Your recommendations fail to flow logically from your research. You leave out significant details AND fail to consider the ramifications of your suggestions. |

|  | 4<br>Expert | 3 | 2 | 1<br>Novice |
|---|---|---|---|---|
| Section 5:<br>Appendix I | You show an in-depth understanding of the positive and negative effects of natural disasters, clearly showing how natural disasters can create as well as destroy life. You make logical suggestions about ways that humans can live at peace with nature instead of trying to control nature. | You provide information and conclusions about the positive and negative effects of natural disasters. You make general recommendations for ways that we may save human lives but do not specifically consider ways to balance the needs of humans with the "needs" of nature. | You mention the possibility that a natural disaster both creates and destroys life, but you focus mainly on the negative effects of natural disasters. You do not make suggestions for ways that we may save human lives and still allow nature to take its course. | You do not consider how a natural disaster can both create and destroy life. You do not discuss the implications involved in balancing human needs with the "needs" of nature. |
| Section 6:<br>Supporting Materials | You provide extensive and relevant appendices to support the text of your report. Appendices and citations follow a professional format. | You provide appendices that relate to your report. Your appendices and citations contain minor errors but generally follow a professional format. | You include appendices, but they do not have a clear and/or direct relevance to your report. Your appendices and citations contain major errors in formatting. | You fail to include appendices OR your appendices do not support the text of your report. Your appendices and citations do not follow a professional format. |
| Overall Structure | You follow the specified structure of the report. You balance conciseness of expression with appropriate elaboration of ideas. | You follow the specified structure for your report. In general, you present your ideas in a concise manner, but in doing so, you sacrifice minor details that would better clarify your ideas. | You attempt to follow the specified structure for your report. Your ideas are presented in a concise manner, but at the expense of important ideas and/or details, OR your ideas are not presented in a concise manner. | You do not follow the specified report format. Your report contains little or no structure, AND your ideas are not presented in a concise manner. |

## CHAPTER 15 STUDY GUIDE

**Prompt 1 *Knowledge***

Prepare a chart that compares and contrasts the three most common forms of performance assessment: essays, tasks, and portfolios.

**Prompt 2 *Opinion***

Which type of portfolio do you believe would be best to use as part of a gifted identification system: *best work* or *work in progress*. Defend your point of view.

**Prompt 3 *Affect***

Given the technical and practical demands for the legitimate use of performance assessment as suggested by the author, do you believe the use of performance assessment as part of a gifted identification system would be worth the effort? Why or why not?

**Prompt 4 *Experience***

The author contends that, prior to using rubrics, teachers should be trained in their use. Describe any training on the use of rubrics you have received. If you've received none, describe the training you would like to receive.

**Prompt 5 *Preconception/Misconception***

The author says that the professional development needed for the use of performance assessment in gifted identification should be *intensive*. Is this true only for performance assessment, or does this also hold true for all the types of instruments discussed in this book? Which types of instruments, if any, would not require intensive professional development if they were to be effectively used by educators in a gifted identification system? If you've indicated a type of instrument that is exempt, explain why. If you've indicated that there is no exemption for any type of instrument, explain why.

# ABOUT THE AUTHORS

**Dr. Carolyn M. Callahan** is Commonwealth Professor of Education in the Curry School of Education at the University of Virginia. She developed the program in gifted education at the University and is the founder of the Saturday and Summer Enrichment Program. Dr. Callahan has been a principal investigator on projects of the National Research Center on the Gifted and Talented for the past 20 years and has been the principal investigator on four Javits grants. She has published more than 200 refereed articles and 50 book chapters across a broad range of topics including the areas of identification of gifted students, program evaluation, gifted females, the development of performance assessments, and curricular and programming options for highly able students including Advanced Placement and International Baccalaureate programs. She is co-editor of Critical Issues and Practices in Gifted Education: What the Research Says. She received recognition as Outstanding Faculty Member in the Commonwealth of Virginia, Outstanding Professor of the Curry School of Education, Distinguished Higher Education Alumnae of the University of Connecticut and was awarded the Distinguished Scholar Award and the Distinguished Service Award from the National Association for Gifted Children. She is a Past-President of The Association for the Gifted and the National Association for Gifted Children and served as Chair of the American Educational Research Association Special Interest Group, Research on Giftedness and Talent Development. She is currently editor of Gifted Child Quarterly.

**Dr. Bonnie Cramond** is the Director of the Torrance Center for Creativity and Talent Development at the University of Georgia. She is also a professor and the graduate coordinator in the Department of Educational Psychology and Instructional Technology, has been a member of the Board of Directors of the National Association for Gifted Children, editor of the Journal of Secondary Gifted Education, and a schoolteacher. She is on the Advisory Board for the International Future Problem Solving Program and the American Creativity Association, on the review board for several journals, and is a survivor of parenting two gifted and creative people. An international and national speaker, she has published numerous articles, a book on creativity research, and teaches classes on giftedness and creativity. She is particularly interested in the identification and nurturance of creativity, especially among students considered at risk because of their different way of thinking, such as those misdiagnosed with ADHD, those with emotional problems, or those who drop out.

**John Dudley** is currently pursuing a Ph.D. in political science at the University of Mississippi with an emphasis in American politics. He received a Masters Degree in political science at the University of

Southern Mississippi in 2010. He also received a Juris Doctor degree from the University of Chicago in 2006.

**Dr. Megan Foley Nicpon** is an Assistant Professor in the Counseling Psychology Program at The University of Iowa and a licensed psychologist at the Belin-Blank Center for Gifted Education and Talent Development. Dr. Foley Nicpon's research interests include assessment and intervention with twice-exceptional students, particularly gifted students with autism spectrum disorder and ADHD, as well as assessment with gifted and talented students and students from underrepresented groups. Her clinical specialties are in providing clinical services for gifted and twice-exceptional students, including those with autism spectrum disorder, ADHD, emotional difficulties, and/or learning disabilities.

**Dr. Donna Y. Ford** is Professor of Education and Human Development at Vanderbilt University. She teaches in the Department of Special Education. Professor Ford earned her Ph.D. in Urban Education, M. Ed. in counseling, and B. A. in Communications and Spanish from Cleveland State University. Her work focuses on (1) recruiting and retaining culturally different students in gifted education and AP classes, (2) multicultural and urban education; (3) the achievement gap; and (4) family involvement. Dr. Ford has been a board member of the National Association for Gifted Children and serves on numerous editorial boards. She is the author/co-author of Reversing Underachievement Among Gifted Black Students (2010), Multicultural Gifted Education (2011), Gifted and Advanced Black Students in School: An Anthology of Critical Works (2011), In Search of the Dream: Designing Schools and Classrooms that Work for High Potential Students from Diverse Cultural backgrounds (2004), Diverse learners with exceptionalities: Culturally responsive teaching in the inclusive classroom (2008), and Teaching Culturally Diverse Gifted Students (2005). Professor Ford has written over 130 articles and book chapters and made several hundred presentations. Awards include Shannon Center for Advanced Studies; Early Career Award and Career Award from the American Educational Research Association; Senior Scholar Award and Early Scholar Award from the National Association for Gifted Children; Esteemed Scholarship Award from the National Association of Black Psychologists; Outstanding Service Award from the Council for Exceptional Children-The Association for the Gifted, Black Student Alliance Distinguished Faulty Award; and Jimmie Franklin Outstanding Vanderbilt Faculty Award.

**Dr. Scott L. Hunsaker** is an Associate Professor in the School of Teacher Education and Leadership at Utah State University. While at USU he has been recognized as Teacher of the Year and Undergraduate Research Mentor of the Year by the Emma Eccles Jones College of Education and Human Services. An active leader in gifted education at the national and state levels, having served on the Board of Directors of the National Association for Gifted Children and as President of the Utah Association for Gifted Children, Dr. Hunsaker is currently serving as chair of the NAGC Leadership Development Committee. He has received the Early Leader Award from NAGC and the Jewel Bindrup Award from UAGC. Dr. Hunsaker's work has been published in Gifted Child Quarterly, Journal for the Education of the Gifted, Roeper Review, Journal of Creative Behavior, and Exceptional Children.

**Dr. Frances A. Karnes** is a Distinguished University Professor in the Department of Curriculum, Instruction and Special Education at The University of Southern Mississippi. She is founder and director of the Frances A. Karnes Center for Gifted Studies established in 1979. The center conducts programs for gifted children and youth and teachers and parents of the gifted. Her publications include sixty-seven books and over one hundred sixty journals articles and several book chapters. She established and was the first president of the Mississippi Association for the Gifted in 1974. She served on the board of The Association for the Gifted and was president. She also served on the board of the National Association for Gifted Children for six years. Awards received from the University of Southern Mississippi are Distinguished University Professor, Lifetime Achievement Award, Innovation Award, Faculty Basic Research Award, and Faculty Professional Service Award. She received the Distinguished Alumni Award from the University of Illinois. The David Berlin Advocacy Award was received from the National Association for Gifted Children. She has been awarded seven federal grants for research in gifted education over the last seven years.

**Dr. Sally Krisel** is the Director of Innovative and Advanced Programs for Hall County Schools in Gainesville, Georgia. Her responsibilities include coordination of Gifted Education services in grades K—12, as well as the extension of instructional strategies and programming options once associated almost exclusively with Gifted Education to a much larger group of students. Dr. Krisel is also a part-time faculty member in the Gifted and Creative Education Program at the University of Georgia. From 1990 to 1992, Dr. Krisel served as Program Coordinator at the University of Georgia site of the National Research Center on the Gifted and Talented. She was instrumental in designing and conducting training to help teachers recognize and respond to indicators of potential giftedness in economically disadvantaged and limited English proficient students. Dr. Krisel then served for ten years as Georgia's State Director of Gifted Education. She has been recognized for her work in promoting both equity and excellence in Gifted Education by the National Association for Gifted Children, the University of Georgia, the Georgia Association for Gifted Children, the National Research Center on Gifted and Talented, and the Office for Civil Rights.

**Dr. David F. Lohman** is Professor of Educational Psychology at the University of Iowa. He is a fellow of the American Psychological Association, the American Psychological Society, and the American Educational Research Association. He is the recipient of numerous awards, including a Fulbright Fellowship and the Iowa Regents Award for Faculty Excellence. In 2006 and again in 2008, he received the award for Gifted Child Quarterly Research Paper of the year. In 2007, he received the NAGC Distinguished Scholar Award. His research interests include the effectiveness of different curricular adaptations for students who differ in ability or personality, conceptualization and measurement of reasoning abilities, and general issues in the identification and development of talent. Since 1998, he has authored the Cognitive Abilities Test.

**Dr. Tonya R. Moon** is a Professor in the Curry School of Education at the University of Virginia and a Principal Investigator for Project Parallax, a Javits grant focused on problem-based learning, differentiation, and dynamic technology in the area of STEM. She is also a principal investigator for the National Research Center on the Gifted and Talented, a position that she has held for over 15 years. Tonya's expertise is in the areas of research, measurement, and evaluation and she uses that expertise when working with school districts across the country on technical issues associated with educational assessments designed for accountability purposes and on using better classroom assessment techniques for improving classroom instruction and student learning. In addition, she also works with school district administrations in conducting gifted program evaluations and working with them in improving their identification systems. Besides her research and teaching responsibilities at the University of Virginia, she is the Chair of the Institutional Review Board for the Social and Behavioral Sciences, is a member of the Board of Directors of the Virginia Association for Gifted, and is a Past President of the Virginia Educational Research Association. She is also an Associate Editor for Gifted Child Quarterly (GCQ) and the editor for the GCQ Methodological Briefs.

**Rebecca Haslam-Odoardi** is currently an educational consultant in the field of gifted/talented education. She holds a B.S. in Elementary, Secondary and Special Education and a M.Ed. in Education from Utah State University. She recently directed the Utah High-Ability Student Initiative Program, designed to help Utah teachers meet the needs of the high-ability students in their classroom. She retired after eighteen years as Director of Gifted and Talented programs in Davis County, Utah, one of the largest school districts in the state. She has been a regular classroom teacher, a teacher of gifted and talented students, an adjunct professor, and has won awards for her expertise in the field of gifted and talented education. She has been President of the Utah Association for Gifted Children and is currently working with several Utah School Districts in helping them build their gifted/talented program. In addition, she is also working on a biographical chapter for a book titled, "Gifted Education: A Century of Illuminating Lives," with Dr. Nora Cohen and Dr. Kathy Austin.

**Dr. Sally M. Reis** is a Board of Trustees Distinguished Professor at The University of Connecticut and the past Department Head of Educational Psychology Department at the University of Connecticut where she also serves as a Principal Investigator for the National Research Center on the Gifted and Talented. She was a teacher for 15 years, 11 of which were spent working with gifted students on the elementary, junior high, and high school levels. She has authored or co-authored over 250 articles, books, book chapters, monographs and technical reports. Her research interests are related to special populations of gifted and talented students, including students with learning disabilities, gifted females, and diverse groups of talented students. She is also interested in extensions of the Schoolwide Enrichment Model for both gifted and talented students and as a way to expand offerings and provide general enrichment to identify talents and potentials in students who have not been previously identified as gifted. She is Co-Director of Confratute and has been a consultant to numerous schools and ministries of education throughout the U. S. and abroad. Her work has been translated into several languages and is widely used around the world. Sally serves on several editorial boards, including Gifted Child Quarterly, and is a past President of the National Association for Gifted Children. She has been honored with the highest award in her field as the Distinguished Scholar of the National Association for Gifted Children and named a fellow of the American Psychological Association.

**Dr. Joseph S. Renzulli** is a professor of educational psychology at the University of Connecticut, where he also has served as the director of the National Research Center on the Gifted and Talented for the past 20 years. His research has focused on the identification and development of creativity and giftedness in young people and on curricular and organizational models for differentiated learning environments that contribute to total school improvement. A focus of his work has been on applying the pedagogy of gifted education to the improvement of learning for all students. Dr. Renzulli is a UConn Distinguished Professor and holds an Honorary Doctor of Laws Degree from McGill University. The American Psychological Association named Dr. Renzulli among the 25 most influential psychologists in the world and in 2009 Dr. Renzulli received the Harold W. McGraw, Jr. Award for Innovation In Education. He lists as his proudest contribution the annual summer Confratute program at UConn, which began in 1978 and has served over 35,000 educators from around the world. His most recent work is a computer-based assessment of student strengths integrated with an Internet-based search engine that matches highly challenging enrichment activities and resources to individual student profiles.

**Dr. Paul Shepherd** is a retired administrator from Granite School District, a large urban district in Salt Lake County, Utah. He was an educator for 27 years. Paul served as an elementary school teacher, curriculum specialist in elementary mathematics and science education, and as elementary school principal, school services director, and advanced learning programs director. He taught as adjunct faculty for Utah State University in the gifted and talented endorsement program. He has served on various boards including president of the Utah Association for Gifted Children. Paul served in the Utah State Legislature as an elected state representative and served on the education and higher education subcommittees as part of his legislative duties. He has a BS in Elementary Education, a M.Ed. in Foundations of Education, and an Ed.D. in Educational Leadership and Policy.

**Dr. Mary Slade** is a Professor in the Department of Exceptional Education, where she directs the online gifted education program at James Madison University. Mary teaches courses in gifted education, educational foundations, exceptional education, and civic engagement. Dr. Slade served as a member of the Board of Directors of the National Association for Gifted Children and won the Early Leader Award from that organization in 1997. Mary's current scholarship includes professional development, advanced studies, differentiation, consultation and collaboration, and web-based distribution of personnel preparation.

**Ellen Virginia (Ginny) Smith** grew up with seven bright and quirky siblings in Cleveland Heights, OH, an ideal training ground for a budding teacher and an intimate observatory of gifted behavior. She graduated from Brigham Young University with a BS in Elementary Education and taught elementary school in Provo, UT, for twenty-two years before pursuing a Master of Education Degree from Utah State University with an emphasis in gifted education. Ginny's interest in the identification of gifted students led to the development of an identification process for Provo School District as her Masters Project. Subsequently she has served as the gifted coordinator for the district, helping develop gifted magnet programs for both elementary and middle school students and gifted pull-out services for students in neighborhood schools. She finds that fine-tuning their identification process and gifted services are perpetual efforts worthy of conscious care. Her favorite part of the job is working with students K–6 who constantly challenge, amaze, and delight her. Ginny enjoys her ongoing participation in the Central Utah Writing Project (a site of the National Writing Project) as a fellow and recently as a presenter. Ginny lives with her husband, Scott, on a fifty-acre fruit farm in the foothills of the Wasatch Mountains, where they have raised three wonderful children (all grown), a plethora of horses, chickens and dogs, and the tastiest peaches in Utah.

**Dr. Kristen R. Stephens** is an assistant professor of the practice in the Program in Education at Duke University. Prior to this appointment, Dr. Stephens served as the gifted education research specialist for the Duke University Talent Identification Program where she was editor-in-chief of the Duke Gifted Letter. Over the years, she has co-authored numerous books and book chapters. She is also co-editor of the Practical Strategies Series in Gifted Education, a series comprised of over 25 books on issues pertinent to gifted child education. Dr. Stephens serves as governance secretary for the National Association for Gifted Children, is president of the North Carolina Association for Gifted and Talented, and is a member of the board of directors for the American Association for Gifted Children.

**Lu Wang** is currently a doctoral student at the department of Educational Psychology and Instructional Technology, University of Georgia. She received her B.A. in psychology from the University of Pennsylvania, and her master's degree in Human Development and Psychology from the Harvard Graduate School of Education. She is originally from Beijing, China, but is fluent in English, Italian, and also speaks some Spanish. She published her first book in Mandarin Chinese on her travel experience in Europe and Asia at the age of ten. In college, she won the Premio Vittorini—a writing competition award to non-native speakers of Italian. In graduate school, she presented her posters at the National Association for Gifted Children (NAGC) and the American Psychological Association (APA). Her scholarly interests, broadly defined, are giftedness, creativity, and spatial ability. She held memberships in NAGC and APA. Like her research interests, her extra-curricular activities are also wide-ranging: She was a violin player at the Chamber Music Society and the Baroque Ensemble in college, and was a nine-time winner of the international and national Chinese calligraphy competitions in her childhood.

**Dr. Karen L. Westberg** is an associate professor at the University of St. Thomas in Minneapolis, MN, where she teaches graduate courses in gifted education and research methods. From 1990–2000, she was a faculty member at the University of Connecticut where she taught courses in these same areas and conducted research at The National Research Center on the Gifted and Talented. One of the NRC/GT studies for which she served as a principal investigator was The Classroom Practices Study, which has been heavily cited in the literature. She has published chapters and journal articles on several topics in the field of gifted education, including creativity, program development, and identification. She is one of the authors of the revised Scales for Rating the Superior Characteristics of Superior Students, which was originally developed Joseph Renzulli in the mid 1970s. In addition to teaching and conducting research, Karen makes presentations at conferences, conducts workshops in school districts, and conducts program evaluations. In the past year, she has conducted keynotes and workshops in several states about best practices in identification. Before receiving a doctoral degree in gifted and talented education from the University of Connecticut, Karen was a classroom teacher and gifted education specialist in Burnsville, MN.

# Index

## A

## B

## C